ETHICS

Christian Wisdom Series

ETHICS—*A Textbook in Moral Philosophy*
by VERNON J. BOURKE

• •

NATURAL THEOLOGY—*Metaphysics II*
by GERARD SMITH, S.J.

• •

ETHICS

A TEXTBOOK IN
MORAL PHILOSOPHY

VERNON J. BOURKE

Professor of Philosophy
St. Louis University

56980

NEW YORK
The Macmillan Company

NIHIL OBSTAT:

John Kelly, C.S.B.,

CENSOR DEPUTATUS.

IMPRIMATUR:

James C. Cardinal McGuigan,

ARCHBISHOP OF TORONTO.

DATED JUNE 10, 1951.

First Printing

FOREWORD

This textbook in ethics derives much of its content from the moral science of St. Thomas Aquinas. It is well known that this thirteenth-century Dominican theologian occupies a leading position in present-day Catholic philosophy. But there are two good reasons why no original work of St. Thomas' may be used successfully as a textbook in college classes in ethics. First of all, he never wrote an ethics textbook. The *Commentary on Aristotle's Nicomachean Ethics* does not always give us the personal thought of St. Thomas; it is not well arranged for modern teaching; and it is not translated into English. The Questions *De Malo* and the Second Part of the *Summa Theologiae* do express St. Thomas' own mind, but they are treatises in moral theology, not ethics. Secondly, St. Thomas lived under very different circumstances of life from those of the average man in the twentieth century. Moral science must include some practical application of general rules to concrete problems. It is ridiculous to expect to find in the works of St. Thomas a ready-made answer to every moral problem. Consequently, the present book is an adaptation of the thought of St. Thomas to meet the practical needs of the modern student of ethics.

Those who have studied or taught other English textbooks on ethics, by Scholastic writers, will find certain features of the present course quite different from the recent tradition. It is no secret that most ethics texts in use in English and American Catholic colleges today are of mixed thomistic and Suarezian inspiration. The philosophy of Francis Suarez is an important contribution to Catholic thought. It has some affinities with Thomism but it differs radically from the philosophy of St. Thomas on many fundamental speculative and practical issues.[1] One cannot teach the philosophy of nature and the metaphysics of St. Thomas, then suddenly change to the ethics of Suarez, and expect an undergraduate class to understand the matter.

In the present work, a knowledge of the speculative philosophy of St. Thomas is presupposed. An effort has been made to integrate the student's work in moral philosophy with his previous study of the philosophy of man and of being in general. This is particularly true of the content of Part One. There is also an attempt, in this first part, to relate the study of ethics to its sister science, moral theology. This is in keeping with the view, adopted herein, that man's ultimate end in life is a supernatural one. Throughout this book, the student is constantly reminded of the inadequacy of an ethics which formally excludes consideration of the area of grace and the supernatural. An ethics of the purely natural man is possible, as an abstract and highly speculative science; but such a science, excluding the actual supernatural conditions under which man lives, will have little practical value in human living.

Another distinctive feature of the treatment of moral principles, in Part One, is the stress on the psychological analysis of the moral act, on the fundamental importance of the moral order of reason, and on the consequent role of moral conscience as an intellectual act of practical judgment. Associated with this is the emphasis on the process of moral reasoning exemplified in the prudential syllogism. Instead of taking the moral law as something given and beyond investigation, the student should be encouraged to reason for himself to practical conclusions which are universally, or particularly, applicable to his moral life.

Users of this book will find in it little emphasis on the history of ethical theories. This omission results from a conscious and fully intended decision to exclude historical matter which cannot be

[1] Cf. Alejandro, J. M., S.J., *La gnoseologia del Doctor Eximio* (Santander, Miscellanea Comillas, 1948), pp. 54–56; Giacon, C., S.J., *La Seconda Scolastica* (Milano, Bocca, 1946), pp. 203–288; Brouillard, R., "Théologie pratique," in "Suarez, François," *Dict. de Théol. Cathol.* XIV, 2, col. 2691–2728.

treated properly in a first course in ethics. There is little point to the common practice of giving a short, unfavorable, and usually inaccurate, summary of the position of a philosophical "adversary," followed by a declaration that such a position is false. The study of the history of ethics is probably best reserved for graduate courses. One has only to read the two volumes of Cronin's *Science of Ethics* to see how much space may be wasted, in an otherwise good book, on the refutation of inadequately presented views of people, such as Lord Balfour, whom the student will not otherwise encounter in his studies.

What is new in Part Two is the return to St. Thomas' method of treating the problems of special morality under the divisions of the seven virtues. This results in a restoration of the obligations of prudence, temperance and fortitude to their proper place in company with the duties which come under justice. In the necessarily lengthy presentation of the problems of justice, emphasis is placed on the four kinds of justice distinguished by St. Thomas. Many Scholastic writers have treated the obligations under commutative justice as strict duties and have left the impression that equity, common legal justice, and distributive justice are but improper and less binding types of this virtue.

That the solution of our ethical problems requires the guidance of the theological virtues is also a distinctive point of emphasis in Part Two. Charity is usually mentioned with a certain condescension in ethics texts, as if it were a fine thing for those who have it but not really essential to the average good person. The obligations of charity are frequently treated as works of supererogation, ornaments decorating the unusually perfect lives of the saints. Actually, of course, charity and its companion habits in the supernatural life are quite essential to the real attainment of the only happiness which is ultimate and lasting. That is why no apology need be offered for the fact that this book ends with the application of the theological virtues to the problems of the ordinary human being.

The present writer claims no originality in the introduction of any of the foregoing features. It is a lamentable fact that they have not been found previously in English textbooks. Since there is not enough material in English books for background reading, *Appendixes* to each chapter in Part One have been included. These are composed of texts translated for this book from the works of St. Thomas which are not otherwise available in English. They should be carefully studied and supplemented by readings in the *Basic Writings of St. Thomas*, edited by Dr. A. C. Pegis. Moreover, those who can use the works of Sertillanges, Wittmann, Gilson, Lottin, and the other foreign-language items cited throughout, will find that this textbook is greatly in debt to these secondary studies of thomistic moral science.

Designed primarily for a college or university course of two semesters' duration, with about three semester hours for each part, this text may be adapted easily to the special requirements of different schools. In particular, it may be used for a shorter course of one semester by simply taking some of the problems of Part Two in conjunction with the general study of the virtues in Chapter VIII. The important thing to remember is that the general theory of Part One is essential to a scientific knowledge of ethics. Without it, the suggested solutions to typical problems in Part Two could be committed to memory but without adequate understanding of the reasons for these answers.

The content of this textbook, in syllabus form, has been used for several years in teaching the ethics courses at St. Louis University and its Corporate Women's Colleges. Certain revisions have been made in the light of the criticism and suggestions of the instructors who have so used the text. To these colleagues and to those who have assisted in the editing of this book, this is an expression of sincere gratitude.

Vernon J. Bourke

TABLE OF CONTENTS

Part One

MORAL PRINCIPLES

Part Two
ETHICAL PROBLEMS

Part One

MORAL PRINCIPLES

I · THE NATURE OF ETHICS

Man's Moral Problem

All human beings desire to be happy. This basic and natural urge for happiness is deep-rooted in the being of every man. Without it, man would have no good reason for doing anything. It is the original stimulus for all human action. The universal desire for happiness has been known under many other names: the urge for self-perfection, the drive of personal ambition, the desire for success in life. Most people are optimistic in looking forward to the eventual achievement of happiness. But even pessimists feel the attraction of this ideal: they are simply people who have formed such an exalted conception of happiness, or who have been so disappointed in the choice or use of means for this end, that they have become convinced that it is not humanly possible to attain it. They continue to wish for happiness but they despair of fulfilling this wish.

Each man's moral problem, throughout life on this earth, is to select and do the kind of actions which are conducive to true happiness. This is a problem for every individual person who reaches any degree of maturity. Every man must face, and answer for himself, the question: "What should I be doing with my life?" He may be assisted in doing the right things by various external agencies: by advantages of origin, environment and training, by the impact of societal laws and popular opinion, by the advice and example of relatives and associates. Ethical and religious instruction are other extrinsic sources of such help. In the final analysis, however, the living of a good life depends on personal thinking, choosing and acting.

It is essential to grasp this point right at the beginning of this study: *successful human living cannot be predetermined for the individual person by any kind of science or philosophy*. Certainly, it is not the work of ethics to establish a rigid and fixed pattern of individual actions which man must perform mechanically and necessarily, in order to achieve personal happiness. Every human being is a distinct person, living under contingent circumstances peculiar to himself. In ethics, we consider man in relation to his moral problems but always with a view to reaching rational conclusions of some universality. Moral rules must be general and universal; moral actions are individual, concrete events.

Ethics may be defined as the systematic study of human actions from the point of view of their rightness or wrongness as means for the achievement of ultimate happiness. Moral philosophy is merely another name for ethics. The material object (*what* is considered) of ethics is *human action*. (See page 6 for definition.) The formal object (*how*, or *from what point of view* the consideration is made) is the *quality of rightness or wrongness*. The whole subsequent course is an explanation of what this formal object means. For the present, we will take right action to be that which should be done, and wrong action to mean that which should be avoided, in order to achieve happiness.

These names, *ethics* and *moral philosophy*, are derived respectively from Greek and Latin words meaning *custom*. While moral considerations are found in nearly all important literary works, particularly in the religious and folk literature of ancient peoples, the first systematic discussions of morality by known philosophers of the Western world took place in Athens during the period of Socrates, Plato, and Aristotle. This was in the fifth and fourth centuries before Christ. These Greeks saw that what makes a man good or bad is not one isolated human action but the general bent or pattern of all his free actions. They called such customary behavior an *ethos*. Aristotle wrote the first extant treatise on systematic morality, under the title, *Nicomachean Ethics*. In some sense, nearly all subsequent writers on ethics are indebted to this work. If nothing else, it helped to define the field of ethics, to establish its name, and to set it apart as a special section of philosophical study. The *Nicomachean Ethics* is still well worth reading as one of the pioneer classics of moral literature.[1] Latin philosophers, such as Cicero, Seneca, and Marcus Aurelius, used the word *mos* (gen. *moris*) to name customary behavior. From this root have come English words such as morals, morality, and moral philosophy.

While Aristotle's ethics is a very intelligent and sincere body of doctrine, it is limited by the pagan beliefs of its author. Aristotle was not certain of the spirituality and consequent personal immortality of the human soul; he did not see man as a part of temporal creation but as a rational animal in an eternal world; he failed to understand the relation of human freedom to Divine Law, because he viewed God as an impersonal, nonprovidential divinity. Consequently, the ethics of Aristotle cannot be accepted *in toto* by a student of thomistic philosophy. In the thirteenth century, St. Thomas Aquinas wrote a Latin commentary on the *Nicomachean Ethics*.[2] St. Thomas' exposition of the *Ethics* of Aristotle is regarded by many scholars as the best Christian commentary on the work. In several other major works, Aquinas treated moral questions in a more personal manner. Much of the content of the present course in ethics is derived from, or suggested by, the moral reasoning of St. Thomas. That is why there are numerous references to his writings in the following pages. These citations are not given in order to force the student to accept certain views because they have the authority of St. Thomas behind them. An argument based on the personal authority of any man is the weakest possible philosophical argument. Rather, St. Thomas and other writers will be mentioned for two special reasons: (1) to indicate the sources of various teachings embodied in this text, which were not invented by the personal thinking of the present writer; (2) to refer the reader to explanations of detailed points that are given more fully and clearly in these source works than is possible within the limits of a textbook.

---

[1] Students will find Book I of the *Nicomachean Ethics* useful background reading for this chapter; see *Recommended Readings* at the end of this chapter.

[2] This commentary is not translated into English; see *Recommended Readings*, at the end of this chapter.

Actions Suited to the Achievement of Happiness

Not all the actions in which the human agent is involved are ethically significant. It is clear that certain acts connected with man are not controlled by him; these acts are not done by man *knowingly* and *willingly*. Hence, they do not have the quality from which moral responsibility arises. For instance, if a man by chance falls down stairs, he may regret the physical inconvenience of this action in which he is fortuitously involved, but he cannot reasonably blame himself for what has happened and he should feel no moral responsibility for the consequences of this action. This is the kind of action which may be called an *act of man* but not truly a *human* act. Such acts may be excluded from ethical consideration.

A second kind of action performed by man does come under the control of the human agent because he *knows,* at least to some extent, what he is doing and he *wills,* at least to some degree, to do the action. These are the actions for which man should feel some responsibility. If they are good, the agent will feel that he should be rewarded; and if they are evil, he cannot but recognize that he deserves punishment. These acts, of which man knows himself to be the master, are directed by the human intellect and will and are called *human acts*.[3]

Further analysis of the human act and description of the potencies involved in its performance may be left for later consideration.[4]

Ethics as a Practical Science

It will be recalled from the philosophy of man that a *science* is a habitus of the intellect enabling its possessor to reason to true conclusions from first principles, or from previously known and true conclusions which in their turn may serve as principles of further

---

[3] See: Appendix to Chap. I, Text One: *Distinction Between Human Acts and the Acts of Man.*

[4] See: Chap. III, *infra.*

conclusions. The purpose of any science is *to know* something, either for the sake of satisfying a pure intellectual curiosity (and this is the aim of a *speculative* science), or for the sake of understanding how to do something (and this is a *practical* science). Now ethics, or moral philosophy, is a practical science. It is intended to bring to its possessor the knowledge that is necessary in order to do the actions which will culminate in the attainment of happiness.

As a science, ethics should be clearly distinguished from two habitus of the practical intellect of man. It is not the same as *prudence*, for prudence does not find its ultimate conclusion in knowledge. Prudence culminates in right action, in doing things reasonably; whereas every science, even a most practical one, ends in some kind of knowledge and not in action. The classic error of Socratic philosophy, in which it was claimed that virtue is knowledge, rested on a confusion of prudence and science. It is one thing *to know* what is right and good; it is quite another thing *to do* what is right. The knowledge acquired from an intelligent study of ethics *may* be applied by the student to his own particular problems. He *may* translate his moral science into good actions, but not necessarily. If he applies his ethical knowledge to his own life problems, he is more than a skilled ethician; he is a prudent man.[5]

So too, it is necessary to keep the notion of ethics distinct from that of *art*. The habitus of the practical intellect enabling a man *to make things reasonably well* is called an art. Prudence is not an art because it is concerned with doing rather than with making. Art ends with an object, or product, made according to right reason. Its perfection is found, not in the action of the producer, but in the goodness of the objective product. Hence, moral science is not an art, for ethics ends with knowledge. That this knowledge is practical does not mean that it is either a moral action or an art object.

Ethics, or moral philosophy, is a practical science; it is an acquired habit of the human intellect enabling its possessor to reason to true conclusions about the kind of human actions which are calculated to bring man to the attainment of true happiness.

[5] See *infra*, Chap. VII, pp. 235–236.

Ethics and Moral Theology

The question may very properly be asked: Is not moral theology a science which tells man how to live in order to attain true happiness? If this question is answered in the affirmative, as it should be, then one may ask: What is the difference between ethics and moral theology? In order to answer this, let us first notice the broad distinction between philosophy and theology. In general, both are discursive sciences proceeding to conclusions about subject matters which overlap somewhat without being entirely coextensive; but philosophy reasons from principles derived from natural experience, whereas theology reasons from supernaturally revealed principles which are accepted on faith.[6]

In addition to this primary difference of the manner in which their principles are acquired, and to the difference of subject matter (for there are some things which the theologian knows, which the philosopher as such cannot know in his science), there is an important distinction between the *way*, or "*light*," in which the philosopher reasons and the way in which the theologian reasons. The formal object of the two sciences is not the same. The philosopher considers being and its operations, from the point of view of inferior causes. Even eternal verities are seen from below, as it were, by the philosopher. The theologian does not, of course, know things as God does, but he does understand from the point of view of superior, eternal causes. The wisdom of the philosopher moves on a lower level than does the wisdom of the theologian. St. Thomas puts it this way:

There is a twofold wisdom: namely *worldly*, which is called philosophy and which considers inferior causes, that is, caused causes, and it judges according to them; and *divine*, which is called theology, and which considers superior causes, that is divine ones, and it judges according to them. The superior causes are called divine attributes, such as Wisdom, Goodness, Divine Will, and things like that.[7]

It may be wondered, then, whether a purely natural science of ethics, totally divorced from moral theology, is possible. In fact, an

---

[6] See: Appendix to Chap. I, Text Two: *Philosophy and Theology.*
[7] *De Potentia,* I, 5,c.

important group of thomistic philosophers [8] has put forward the claim that a natural ethics cannot treat adequately the actual moral problems which man must face. The force of this view lies in the imperfection of the philosopher's knowledge of man's origin, of the supernatural forces which influence his free actions, and particularly of the true nature of the ultimate happiness of man. The Catholic moral theologian sees man as a creature of God, subject to certain difficulties arising from original sin, assisted by supernatural grace and guided by revealed rules of Divine Law, ordered to the beatific vision of God in Heaven. If man exists and must act under these supernatural conditions, then it would seem that a moral science which blandly ignores them must be but an abstraction. That is to say, ethics is not a really practical study unless it deals with the existential character of human problems.

As a result of this line of argument, Professor Maritain maintains the position that Christian ethics must be considered in "subalternation" to moral theology. [9] The notion of a subalternated science may be illustrated by considering the relation of certain forms of practical mathematics to pure mathematics. It is generally known that a surveyor of land, or a navigator, uses formulae derived from geometry, trigonometry and algebra. In a sense, the arts of engineering and navigation rely on principles established in the less practical types of mathematics. We could say that navigation is a study which is subalternated, or subordinated, to higher mathematics. The suggestion in Maritain's work, then, is that a Christian ethics may, by the same method of subalternation, derive principles from moral theology and so afford more perfect directions for good human action.

This theory of an ethics subalternated to theology has met with strong criticism, however. [10] The chief argument against it is that any science which starts with principles derived from divine revelation,

[8] Jacques Maritain is the able leader of this movement to develop a Christian ethics, subordinated to moral theology; see his *Science and Wisdom*, with the references given in the *Readings* at the end of this chapter.

[9] *Science and Wisdom*, p. 81.

[10] Notably from J.-M. Ramirez, O.P., and more recently from Dom O. Lottin, *Principes de morale*, I, 25-31.

rather than from natural human experience, is a theological science. As a result this subalternated ethics is really a diluted form of moral theology. But ethics is, or should be, a philosophical discipline. That is to say, the principles of ethics, as well as the mode of reasoning used in ethics, should be natural.

A second point of criticism centers in the claim that a purely natural ethics is but a *hypothetical* science. This means that the moral philosopher must consider the moral agent, *as if* he were not subject to the consequences of original sin, to the influence of divine grace, to the supernatural ordering of man to the beatific vision. Such a moral agent, viewed as existing in a *state of pure nature* would, indeed, be but a philosophical abstraction. However, this claim that a natural ethics must be hypothetical rests on an unwarranted assumption. It is not necessary for the moral philosopher to assume that his metaphysical account of the origin, life and destiny of man is a perfect one. In fact, the thomistic ethician is well aware of the possibility of other factors in human life than the purely natural ones. Thomistic ethics should make a valid appraisal of the natural moral obligations of man, without abstracting man from the actual context of human life and actions.

Let us illustrate this second criticism by brief reference to two points which will be more thoroughly discussed later. The moral theologian tells us that, as a result of original sin, each moral agent exists in a precarious condition, his sense appetites tend to disrupt the processes of reasoning rightly and of choosing rightly. Now, of course, if the ethician were to deny this and claim that man is, in his present existential condition, inclined to reason and choose perfectly, then this ethician would be dealing with a hypothetical agent, that is the wholly rational, natural man. But a good ethician recognizes the omnipresent ethical fact of the disturbance of the life of reason by the passions. The moral philosopher and the moral theologian do not differ widely on the actual facts of human existence. They differ in this: the moral theologian has an ultimate explanation (in the Fall of man and consequent original sin) of a group of observable data, whereas the moral philosopher has but a proximate and imperfect explanation of the same data. Similarly, the moral theologian can give a better account of the nature of ultimate human happiness than can the ethician. This is quite different from the statement that the philosopher can know nothing about man's ultimate destiny—which is an untrue proposition.

To sum up this criticism, let us consider two conclusions. First, our philosophical knowledge of morality is less perfect than that of the moral theologian.[11] Second, though imperfect the science of ethics is not false. It does not ask us to think of that purely hypothetical agent (the "natural" man, in the sense of a rational animal entirely removed from the real difficulties of human life) but only of man as we find him in actual existence.

Thomistic ethics is a natural science forming part of the broader science which is thomistic philosophy. The student of ethics should recognize the limitations of his subject. He may be well aware, for instance, that ordinary experience of human life does not give him as accurate a knowledge of some forms of human conduct as do the specialized sciences of psychology and psychiatry. Similarly, the ethician may be fully aware of the possibility of more perfect knowledge being acquired from supernatural revelation. He can grant the possibility that some things which remain inexplicable to the philosopher may be quite well reasoned out, and explained, by the moral theologian.

Such a Christian ethics might be called an "open" science. This means that a thomistic ethician will be ready to note other than philosophical answers to some of his moral problems. Many sciences overlap in their subject matters. They differ always in their formal objects, or rational methods of procedure. A purely natural account of what is right and wrong in human conduct may be right and valid within the limits of this formal object. Yet it may recognize other, and even superior, methods of treating somewhat the same subject matter. Ethics only becomes invalid and false, if it claims that its account of human morality is perfect and exclusive of all other attempts to reason about human obligations.

Of course a philosopher needs faith—not only a *natural* faith in

---

[11] See: Appendix to Chap. I, Text Three: *How Philosophy Is Related to Theology*. Read also: Maritain, *Science and Wisdom*, pp. 174–209.

the trustworthiness of creditable witnesses to experiences other than
his own, and in the authority of teachers and specialized scientists,
but also *supernatural* faith. But the reasons for this need of supernatural faith lie in the fact that the philosopher is a human being who
must live and act rightly in his own life, before and while he is
achieving that partial understanding which comes from years of
philosophical study.[12] However, the knowledge which is achieved by
reasoning from the principles of religious faith is not philosophical
but theological science.

In the development of this course in ethics, we shall notice at certain points the teachings of thomistic moral theology, in order more
fully to explain the moral obligations of man. This will be done to
emphasize the tentative and imperfect character of purely natural
ethics. Such brief mention of theological teachings is not to be understood as an attempt to incorporate moral theology into ethics;
actually, in any such combination, ethics would have to be the sub-
sidiary, and theology the principal, science. For the student who
shares the same religious faith as St. Thomas (that is, for the Catholic
student), this procedure will help to integrate the two great sources
of moral knowledge, reason and faith. For the student who is not of
the Catholic faith, three things should be stated frankly. First, the
fact that he does not have the same religious beliefs as Catholics
should in no way prevent him from understanding the purely philosophical teaching of ethics. Second, whether he is a formal adherent
of some Protestant or Jewish church or not, he will find that much of
the teaching of thomistic moral theology is familiar to him from the
reading of history and the great classics of literature, because many
of the great world figures and many of the great writers of the past
shared this tradition of morality. The Ten Commandments are at
the core of our civilization and culture. Finally, the non-Catholic
student need not feel that personal acceptance of the teachings of
Catholic faith is necessary to academic success in this course. Catholics believe that religious faith is a gift which cannot be imposed
forcibly on those who do not have it. Under such conditions, the
non-Catholic student may regard any statements of Catholic the-

[12] See: Appendix to Chap. I, Text Four: *Why Man Needs Faith.*

ology as matters of general information—just as he might study something about the teachings of Mohammedanism in order to understand the invasion of Spain by the Moors.

Ethics and Metaphysics

There are today, many special sciences which treat human conduct from diverse points of view. With the growth of positivism in mid-nineteenth-century France, under the leadership of Auguste Comte, sociology and various social sciences were developed. These studies are descriptive in character and make some use of statistical procedures. When they treat moral right and wrong, they do so in terms of the actual fluctuation of social customs and opinions from one age to another, and among peoples of various levels of culture and civilization. The general evolutionary hypothesis has been taken quite seriously in these embryonic social studies, with the frequent result that absolute moral standards are not recognized. This emphasis on the relativism of moral standards has also been prominent in recent British ethics (under the influence of Herbert Spencer) and in American moral philosophy, in which John Dewey's instrumentalism, or modified pragmatism, has still a leading role.

Ethics, however, is not a descriptive social science. Its purpose is not to tell us about variations of popular opinion on moral questions. Moral philosophy is a *normative* science; that is, it should offer an opportunity for the study of the absolute difference between right and wrong in human conduct. It should aim at the establishing of definite *norms*, or rules, of behavior for men. Without this, the basic ethical concepts of duty, of obligation, of moral responsibility, of a pattern of human action which is universally good for all men under all circumstances, lose their meaning. The validity of such norms cannot be established by statistical procedure, by popular surveys, any more than the propositions of geometry can be demonstrated by popular vote.[13]

[13] For a useful treatment of the relation of sociology to thomistic ethics, see: Deploige, S., *The Conflict Between Ethics and Sociology*, translated by C. C. Miltner (St. Louis, 1938), in particular pp. 261–280.

It is not possible to develop a science of ethics, with definite teachings on the nature of right and wrong, and with the reasons for such teachings, without the assistance of metaphysics. The classic Greek philosophers were convinced that we live in a rational world and that man is a reasonable being equipped to direct his life in a reasonable way, if he so desires. St. Thomas Aquinas continued, in his metaphysics, this tradition of sober rationalism. His philosophy of being offers an interpretation of reality which preserves the Greek respect for reason in all things, and which opens up an area of vision new and unknown to the Greeks, the supernatural. The present course in ethical theory presupposes on the part of the student a general understanding of the thomistic philosophy of being.[14]

Moreover, to understand thomistic ethics, one should know in some detail the interpretation of *human nature* which was developed by St. Thomas. The philosophy of man is not psychology in the modern sense, but a metaphysical analysis of the being, potencies, habits and destiny of man.[15]

Since the time of Immanuel Kant,[16] whose views have had a tremendous influence on modern ethicians, it has been customary, even among Catholic moralists, to speak of certain "postulates" of moral philosophy. In his theoretical philosophy, Kant came to the conclusion that it was not possible to give wholly convincing philosophical demonstrations of such truths as the existence of God, the immortality of the human soul, and the freedom of man. However, Kant understood that a real ethics cannot do without these truths. Hence, he decided to use them as *postulates* in his course in ethics. He had *to suppose* that they are true in order to explain and justify the notion of moral duty. For some odd reason, many books in the field of Scholastic, or thomistic, ethics continue to speak of these truths as "postulates."

[14] The student should be familiar with the content of a work such as Renard, H., S.J., *Philosophy of Being* (Milwaukee, 1943).

[15] Klubertanz, G. P., S.J., *The Philosophy of Human Nature* (St. Louis, 1949), or Brennan, R. E., O.P., *Thomistic Psychology* (New York, 1941), give an exposition of this philosophy of man. Students who have used these works would profit by a reading of the First Part of the *Summa Theologica* of St. Thomas; this portion of the work is printed in English, in the first volume of Pegis, A. C., *Basic Writings of Saint Thomas Aquinas* (New York, 1945).

[16] The *Critique of Practical Reason* was first published in 1788.

We may immediately agree with Kant that these three truths must be accepted in order to give meaning to moral science. If man is not *free* to regulate some of his actions, then there is no point in trying to teach him how to do it. If man is not *immortal*, then he should look neither for reward nor punishment in a future life, for there would be none. If there were no *God*, then it would be quite intelligent to practice the doctrine that might is right. However, these truths are not *postulates* in thomistic ethics. They are demonstrable conclusions of thomistic metaphysics. They are an important part of the metaphysical basis which forms the groundwork for the moral philosophy of St. Thomas. The famous five ways of proving the existence of God are to be found at the beginning of the *Summa Theologica*, and in more extended form in the *Summa contra Gentiles*.[17] In the treatise on man,[18] we may read St. Thomas' arguments for immortality and freedom. It is not easy to understand these demonstrations, particularly if they are taken out of the complete context of thomistic metaphysics. To understand an isolated proposition in geometry, taken out of its context, is not easy, either. However, it is sheer nonsense to speak of them as if they were merely *supposed* to be true in thomistic ethics. Kant had very little metaphysical basis for his moral philosophy. He needed postulates. There is a well-developed metaphysics in thomism and these three propositions are parts of that metaphysics. Hence, the existence of God, the immortality of the soul, and the freedom of man are to be used in thomistic ethics. The ethician need not try to prove them; he takes them over from metaphysics.[19]

The Divisions of Ethics

If, as we have seen, the purpose of ethics is to consider how best to order man's free acts so that they will lead him to happiness, then

[17] *S.T.*, I, q. 2, a. 1–3; in Pegis, *Basic Writings of St. Thomas*, I, 18–24; *C.G.*, I, cap. 13.

[18] *Summa Theologica*, I, questions 75 and 83.

[19] On the relation of St. Thomas' ethics to the other parts of his philosophy, read: Gilson, E., *Moral Values and the Moral Life*, translated by L. R. Ward, C.S.C. (St. Louis, 1941); "Introduction," pp. 1–12; and "Morals and Metaphysics," pp. 15–19.

there will be as many parts of ethics as there are kinds of order in which human acts may be involved. Order issues from reason and in practical matters must be determined in relation to a final cause, to an end.

Certain human actions can be directed to the end of man as an individual person having his own problems. The rational ordering of these actions is the concern of that part of moral philosophy which St. Thomas called *monastics*. This name, which was well chosen for it suggests the consideration of man as an individual unit, a *monas*, is no longer so used in English terminology. Since its use might cause some confusion, because of its etymological similarity to monasticism which reminds us of community life, we may simply call this division of moral philosophy, *individual ethics*.

Another type of human action is characteristic of man as a member of a domestic group. These actions are rationally ordered in the light of the purpose, or end, of family life. *Economics* is the name which St. Thomas used for this part of moral philosophy. Here again, because it is at variance with accepted modern terminology, in which economics is a science concerned almost exclusively with problems associated with wealth, we may reasonably substitute the term *family ethics*.

Finally, there are human actions proper to man as a citizen, as a member of the largest organized social group, the state. The end of the state is not identical with the end of the individual person. The scientific consideration of actions as directed to this end is called *politics*, in thomistic nomenclature. Though this name has acquired a pejorative meaning in our day, it is still used by philosophers to designate the study of statecraft. We may, then, call this third division of ethics, politics or the *ethics of the state*.[20]

From the point of view of the presentation of the subject matter, a different sort of division should be noted. It is advisable, in a science of this sort, to deal first with the most general principles and their conclusions. Hence, the first section of our work in moral philosophy may be called *ethical theory*, or *general ethics*. The conclusions of this section of ethics, which is treated in the present Part, are in-

[20] Read: Appendix to Chap. I, Text Five: *Ethics and Its Parts*.

tended to be practical, but in a universal way. They constitute the preliminary basis for a more specific type of reasoning about human actions.

A second part of moral philosophy (*infra*, Part Two) aims at getting as close to the solution of man's particular moral problems as a science can. It will be realized that no science can deal with concrete, individual, contingent actions in all their particularity. Science terminates in universal conclusions. But that section of ethics which most nearly approaches the rational regulation of the individual human action is sometimes called *special ethics*.[21]

The Degree of Accuracy Possible in Ethics

Sciences differ not only in their formal objects, which are the specific approaches to, and the rational methods used in, the interpretation of their subjects; they also are distinguished by the character of their material objects, or subject matters. Speculative sciences, such as metaphysics and pure mathematics, may attain to a high degree of accuracy because their subject matters are unchangeable. No reasonable person could expect a practical science to be as precise, for the order of practice is laid in the contingent world of actual existence. Human actions in the concrete are ever new and changing in character. The more detailed our study of these actions, the less may we aim at metaphysical certitude. General ethics can be more accurate in its conclusions than special ethics. They are necessarily somewhat provisional and tentative, yet they remain sciences as long as they lead to understandable conclusions with some universality of scope. When a man reasons about his own concrete and particular problems, he is going beyond even practical science; he is then in the area of prudence, which will be discussed in chapter seven.[22]

[21] These two sections, general and special, correspond roughly to the division of the *Prima Secundae* and *Secunda Secundae*, in the *Summa Theologica* of St. Thomas.

[22] Read: Appendix to Chap. I, Text Six: *The Certitude Proper to Moral Philosophy*.

Summary of Chapter I

This introductory chapter is intended to show that the moral problem centers in man's effort to regulate certain of his actions, issuing from reason and freely performed, so that he may achieve ultimate happiness. The intellectual habitus by which man may reason philosophically about these actions is the practical science called ethics or moral philosophy. While ethics cannot provide a perfect guide for man's moral life, for it is a less perfect kind of moral science than moral theology, the present course will endeavor to remedy this inadequacy by indicating some of the relevant teachings of moral theology. The need of a metaphysical foundation for ethical reasoning is next emphasized. It is not possible to distinguish right from wrong in human acts unless we possess a speculative philosophy on which these distinctions may rest. The so-called "postulates" of ethics are part of this metaphysical basis and are not really postulates at all. Individual, family, and state ethics are the three parts of thomistic moral philosophy. The order of presentation requires us to study, first, general moral theory; second, special conclusions about moral problems. Finally, the contingent nature of human actions is indicated as the reason why one should not look for as much certitude in moral science as is possible in speculative science.

Appendix to Chapter I

¶ TEXT ONE: *Distinction Between Human Acts and the Acts of Man.* Of the acts done by man, those alone are properly called human which are proper to man insofar as he is man. For man differs from other, irrational creatures in the fact that he is the master of his own actions. Hence, only those actions, of which man is the master, are properly called human. Now man is the master of his acts through reason and will, and as a result free choice is said to be "the faculty of will and reason." Therefore, those actions are properly called human which proceed from a deliberated will-act. But if some other actions pertain to man, they can indeed be called actions of man (*hominis actiones*), but not properly human, since they do not pertain to man insofar as he is man. (*S.T.*, I–II, 1, 1,c.)

¶ TEXT TWO: *Philosophy and Theology.* Since the intelligible essence (*ratio*) of a science consists in the fact that some things which are not known may come to be known through other things which are known, and this does occur in regard to divine things, it follows that there can be a science of divine things. But the knowledge of divine things can be arrived at in two ways: in one way, from our viewpoint, and in this way they are only knowable to us in terms of creatures, the knowledge of which we receive from the senses; in another way, in terms of their own [divine] nature, and in this way they are of themselves most knowable, though they are not so known by us but by God, and by the Blessed according to His way.

Thus, there is a twofold science of divine things. One is according to our way, in which we take the principles of sensible things in order to know the divine, and it is in this way that the philosophers have treated the science of divine things, speaking of first philosophy as a divine science. The other [science] is according to the way of divine things themselves, so that these divine things are grasped in themselves. Now this, in its perfect form, is not possible to us in our earthly lives. However, a certain participation in this knowledge, and an assimilation to divine knowledge, do come to us in this life, inasmuch as we may adhere to the very first Truth because of Itself, through the faith which is infused into us. And, just as God from the fact that He knows Himself, also knows other things in His own way, that is, by a simple intuition and not by discursive reasoning, so also do we come, from those things which we take on faith and by adhering to the first Truth, to the knowledge of other things according to our own way, namely, by discursive reasoning from principles to conclusions. Hence, first of all, those things which we hold by faith are like first principles for us in this science [*i.e.*, theology] and other things are like conclusions. And it is clear from this that this science is higher than the other divine science, handed down by the philosophers, since it proceeds from higher principles. (*In Boetium De Trinitate*, II, 2,c; ed. Mandonnet, III, 46–47.)

¶ TEXT THREE: *How Philosophy Is Related to Theology*. To clear this up, one should understand that all men who have thought rightly have considered that the end of human life is the contemplation of God. Now the contemplation of God is twofold: one is through creatures, and it is imperfect, for the reason already given; and in this contemplation, Aristotle (*Ethic. Nic.* X, c.9) placed contemplative happiness, which is of course the happiness of this life; and the entirety of philosophical knowledge is directed to this, which proceeds from the rational principles of creatures.

There is another contemplation of God, in which He is seen immediately through His Essence; and this is the perfect one, which will be in Heaven and it is possible for man on the basis of faith. Hence it is necessary, because those things which are means to an end should be proportionate to the end, that insofar as man is brought to this contemplation during his earthly life, [it is] through a knowledge which is not received from creatures but which is inspired immediately from the Divine Light; and this is the teaching of theology.

From this we can have two conclusions. One is, that this science [theology] commands all others as a principal; the other is, that it uses for its service all other sciences, as if they were vassals; just as is evident in all arts so ordered that the end of one is below the end of another; as the end of the pharmaceutical art, which is the making of medicines, is directed to the end of the medical art, which is health, hence the medical doctor commands the pharmacist and uses the drugs prepared by him, for his own end. Thus, since the end of the whole of philosophy is below the end of theology, and is ordered to it, theology should command all the other sciences and use those things which are handed down in them. (*In I Sent.*, Prolog.; ed. Mandonnet, I, 7–8.)

¶ TEXT FOUR: *Why Man Needs Faith*. In the beginning, man is imperfect in knowledge and, in order that he may seek perfection in science, he needs some instructor who will lead him to perfection in science. And he [the instructor] cannot do this unless he possesses the science perfectly; that is, he must understand the reasons for the things which come under his science. Now, he does not immediately hand over to him who is being instructed, right at the beginning of his teaching, the subtle reasons for the things which he intends to teach, for then the student would possess the science perfectly, all at once and at the beginning. Rather, he imparts to him certain things, the reasons for which the student does not know when he is first being taught, but he will know them later, when he is perfect in his science.

And so it is said that the learner must believe. He cannot otherwise attain perfect science, unless he accepts those things which are imparted to him at the beginning, the reasons for which he cannot then grasp.

Now, the ultimate perfection to which man is ordained consists in the perfect knowledge of God, which he cannot arrive at unless by the working and instruction of God, Who is His own perfect Knower. Man is not capable of perfect knowledge all at once and at the beginning. So, he ought to take something on the basis of belief, through which he may be led to the attainment of perfect knowledge. And some such things, of which he cannot have perfect knowledge in this life, are such that they completely exceed the power of human reason. These we should believe as long as we are in this life, for we shall see them perfectly in Heaven.

There are other things which we can get to know perfectly, even in this life, such as the things which can be proved demonstratively of God. Nevertheless, at the beginning, these must be believed, because of five reasons which Rabbi Moses [Maimonides] gives.[23] The first of these is the profundity and subtlety of those objects of knowledge which are very remote from the senses; hence, man is not fitted to know them perfectly at the beginning. The second reason is the weakness of the human intellect at the beginning. The third is the great number of those things which are prerequisite to the demon-

---

[23] These reasons are given by the twelfth-century Jewish scholar, in his *Guide for the Perplexed*, Book I, Chap. 34.

stration of such matters, and these man cannot learn unless after a
very long time. The fourth is the indisposition to scientific thinking,
which [indisposition] is found in some people because of unsuitable
temperament. The fifth is the need of keeping busy in providing the
necessities of life.

From all of these, it is clear that, if it were necessary to accept
only those things needed for the knowledge of God, which can be
demonstrated, very few people could reach this knowledge, and
even these only after a long time. Hence, it is evident that the way of
faith is provided for man in a beneficial way, and through it an easy
approach to salvation is manifested to all men in every time. (*De
Veritate*, q. XIV, a. 10,c.)

¶ TEXT FIVE: *Ethics and Its Parts*. As Aristotle says, at the beginning of his *Metaphysics*, "to order is the function of the sage"
(*sapientis est ordinare*). The reason for this is that wisdom is above
all else the perfection of reason and the proper function of the latter
is to know order. For, though the sense powers do know some
things, considered as individuals without relation to other things
(*absolute*), nevertheless the knowing of the orderly relation of one
thing to another is exclusively the work of intellect or reason.

Now, there are two kinds of order in things. One kind is that of
parts in relation to each other within a given whole or group (*multi-
tudo*); thus the parts of a house are ordered among themselves.
Another kind is the order of things in regard to an end. This order
is more important and original than the first. For, as Aristotle says in
the *Metaphysics* (XII, ch. 10, 1075a20), the order of the parts of an
army among themselves exists by virtue of the order of the whole
army in relation to its leader.

Order may be related to reason in four ways. [i] There is one kind
of order which reason does not make but simply beholds, such as
the order of things in nature. [ii] Then, there is a second kind of
order which reason makes by its own act of consideration; for instance, the ordering of its own concepts among themselves, and of
the signs of its concepts, for they are words expressing the meanings
of the concepts (*voces significativae*). [iii] Again, there is a third

kind of order, which reason makes when giving consideration to operations of the will. [iv] And, there is a fourth kind of order which reason makes, by its act of consideration, in external things of which it is the cause, as in the production of an arch or of a house.

And, since the act of reason in considering something is perfected by a habitus, there are various sciences depending on the various orders whereby reason performs its acts of consideration. For, [i] it pertains to *natural philosophy* to consider the order of things, which the human reason beholds but does not make; thus understood, even metaphysics is included within natural philosophy. But, [ii] the order which reason makes by its own act of consideration pertains to *rational philosophy*, whose function is the consideration of the order of the parts of speech among themselves, and the order of principles to each other and to their conclusions. Again, [iii] the order of voluntary actions pertains to the consideration of *moral philosophy*. Finally, [iv] the order which reason, in its act of consideration, makes in external things produced by the use of human reason, pertains to the *mechanical arts*. And so, the proper function of moral philosophy, which is our present concern, is to consider human operations insofar as they are ordered among themselves and in relation to an end.

Now, I am talking about *human operations*, those which proceed from the will of man according to a rational order. For, if some operations are found to take place in man which are not subject to will and reason, they are not properly called *human;* rather, they are *natural*. This is clearly the case with operations of the vegetative soul. These in no way fall under the consideration of moral philosophy. For, just as the subject of natural philosophy is motion, or things capable of motion, so the subject of moral philosophy is *a human operation ordered to an end*, or even *man insofar as he is voluntarily acting for an end*.

It should be understood that, since man is naturally a social animal, and inasmuch as he needs many things for his own life which he cannot obtain by his own solitary effort, it follows that man is naturally a part of some group, through which he may be provided with the assistance needed for a good life. And there is a twofold need of such assistance. Firstly, from the point of view of those things which are necessary for life and without which he could not go through this present life, the domestic group, of which he is a part, provides assistance of this kind. For, every man is indebted to his parents for his coming into being, for his sustenance, and for his training. And in the same way, individuals who are parts of a domestic family help each other in regard to the necessities of life. Man is helped, in a second way, by a group of which he is a part, in regard to the perfect fullness (*sufficientiam*) of life; that is, so that man may not only live, but *live well*, having all things that suffice for his life. And in this way, the civic group, of which he is a part, helps man not only in regard to bodily things (thus, for instance, there are many manufactured objects in a city which could not be provided within one household), but also in regard to moral matters; that is, insofar as delinquent young people, whom paternal punishment is too weak to correct, may, by public force, be controlled by the fear of punishment.

It should also be understood that this whole, which is the civic group or the domestic family, has solely the unity of order; for, it is not a thing which is absolutely one. Therefore, a part of this whole may have an operation which is not that of the whole. Nevertheless, the whole does itself have a certain operation which is not proper to any part, but to the whole, as is the case when there is a concerted assault made by a whole army. So too, the rowing of a boat is the operation of the group of oarsmen.

There is, however, a kind of whole which possesses not only the unity of order, but of composition, or colligation, or even of continuity, and according to this unity, a thing is one in an absolute way. Here, there is no operation of a part which is not an operation of the whole. Thus, in things that are all of one piece (*continuis*), the motion of the whole is the same as that of the part; so too, in composites, or in things bound together, the operation of a part is mainly that of the whole. Hence, it is necessary for the consideration of such a whole and its part to belong to the same science. But, it does not pertain to the same science to consider the whole which has solely the unity of order, and [to consider] its part.

This is why moral philosophy is divided into three parts. The first of these considers the operations of one man, as ordered to an end; and this part is called *monastics*. The second considers the operations of the domestic group; and this is called *economics*. The third considers the civic group; and this is called *politics*. (*In I Ethic.*, lect. 1; ed. Pirotta, pp. 1–2, nn. 1–6.)

¶ TEXT SIX: *The Certitude Proper to Moral Philosophy*. It pertains to the disciplined man, that is to the man who is well trained, to seek in each and every matter only that certitude which the nature of the thing permits. For, there cannot be as much certitude in variable and contingent matter as there is in necessary matter which is always the same. And so, the well-trained student should not demand any greater certitude, nor be content with any less, than is suitable to the thing which is being studied.

It would seem to be almost a sin, if a person were to accept a mathematician who used the merely persuasive arguments of rhetoric, and if he were to expect absolutely certain demonstrations, such as the mathematician offers, from a rhetorician. Both mistakes would depend on this fact: that the method (*modus*) which fits the matter is not taken into consideration. For, mathematics deals with matter in which complete certitude is found. But rhetoric treats popular matters, in which a great variety of changes occur. (*In I Ethic.*, lect. 3; ed. Pirotta, pp. 12–13, n. 36.)

Recommended Readings [24]

Aristotle, *Nicomachean Ethics*, Book I (in *The Basic Works of Aristotle*, ed. McKeon, pp. 935–952).

Cronin, *The Science of Ethics*, I, 1–27.

Deploige, *The Conflict Between Ethics and Sociology*, pp. 261–280.

Gilson, *Moral Values and the Moral Life*, pp. 1–19.

Maritain, *Education at the Crossroads*, pp. 71–75; *Science and Wisdom*, pp. 70–133, 198–209.

Phelan, "*Theology in the Curriculum of Catholic Colleges and Universities*," *Man and Secularism*, pp. 128–240.

[24] See the *General Bibliography* for a complete description of the books and articles mentioned in this, and following, chapter reading lists.

ADVANCED READINGS

De Bruyne, "Réflexions sur les méthodes en morale," *Revue néoscolasti-que de Philos*, 38 (1935) 194–212.

Deman, "Sur l'organisation du savoir moral," *Revue des sciences philos. et théol.* 23 (1934) 270–280.

Lottin, *Principes de morale*, I, 13–52.

Pegis, "Matter, Beatitude and Liberty," *Maritain Volume of the Thomist*, pp. 265–280.

Ramirez, "De philosophia morali Christiana," *Divus Thomas* (Fribourg) 14 (1936) 87–122, 181–204.

Sertillanges, *La philosophie morale de s. Thomas*, pp. 1–10.

Simon, *Critique de la connaissance morale*, 166 pp.

Thomae Aquinatis, S. *In X Libros Ethicorum Aristotelis Expositio*, lib. I, lect. 1–12.

Wittmann, *Die Ethik des hl. Thomas von Aquin*, pp. 1–72.

Histories of Ethics

Dittrich, *Geschichte der Ethik. Die Systeme der Moral Altertum bis zur Gegenwart* (Leipzig, Meiner, 1926) 4 Bde.

Le Senne, *Traité de morale générale* (Paris, Presses Universitaires, 1942) pp. 375–515.

Sidgwick, *History of Ethics* (London, Macmillan, 1931).

Topics for Assignment

1. Does the Pessimist Lack the Desire for Happiness?
2. The Difference Between a Speculative and a Practical Science
3. Maritain's Theory of Ethics as a Subalternated Science
4. The Importance of the Immortality of the Soul in Ethics
5. Why Ethics Is Not as Accurate as Mathematics

The Necessity of a Teleological Approach in Ethics

We began our study of ethics by noting the natural desire which all men have for happiness. This desire must now be examined, in order to see just what it implies. Two things should be understood at the start of this investigation. First of all, it cannot reasonably be maintained that all men are in agreement as to what precisely constitutes happiness. What is desired is felicity in general. All human beings would like to have their wishes fully satisfied, but they do not all actually wish the same things. Hence, we cannot pursue our investigation by taking a vote as to the nature of happiness; that would merely lead to an amazing variety of popular opinions. And opinion is not science. Nor are we going to attempt a psychological analysis of this desire, for such a study would lead only to the conclusion that most men's notions of happiness are very vague. Secondly, this desire is not an act, in the metaphysical sense, but rather a sort of inclination, a strong disposition, of man's will toward the good. Because it is an innate tendency, the natural desire for happiness is not free; it is an inclination of the will, *considered as a nature*, that is, in its essence. This tendency is a necessary one; it is not elective. Freedom lies in the actuation of this tendency by series of particular human actions. St. Thomas explains this very clearly:

The will naturally tends toward its ultimate end; for every man naturally desires happiness. And all other volitions are caused from this natural volition, since whatever a man desires is wished on account of an end. Therefore, the love of the good, which man naturally desires as an end, is a natural love; but the love derived from this, of a good loved for the sake of the end [in other words, the love of a means to the end], is an elective [*i.e.*, free] love.[1]

Human happiness, then, can only be understood by giving some thought to the end, or purpose, of man. To do this, let us first recall, from the philosophy of being, what a final cause is. In giving the reasons for anything, the metaphysician looks for four kinds of causes: material, formal, efficient, and final. Of these, the final cause is that for the sake of which something exists or is done. Finality is by no means the least important kind of causality. Unless we know the purpose of a thing, we do not really understand it.

When a final cause is thought of as the object of desire, it is called *a good*. When it is considered as the terminus of an act, it is called *an end*. Thus, though minor formal differences of meaning distinguish the terms, the same thing, in the same relationship, is a good, an end, and a final cause. The study of things from the point of view of final cause is named *teleology*, because *telos* is the Greek word for end. To say that ethics is necessarily a teleological science, means that we cannot get along in moral philosophy without giving some thought to the final cause, or end, of human actions.

In fact, we know without technical study that a life which is actually purposeless is not a reasonable life. No man can be good unless he work for some purpose which is proper to his kind of being. One of the worst aspects of despair, one of the truest indications of human failure, is the abandonment of all purpose in life. As long as a man aims at something, he retains a modicum of ambition and human dignity. As soon as he becomes an aimless wanderer in the byways of life, not knowing why he is alive, he loses his only guidepost to happiness. Such a person is a failure because he can no longer, in such a condition, order his actions in any reasonable way.

To avoid any possible misunderstanding, occasioned by the use of the familiar but ambiguous word *purpose*, let us notice next that there is quite a difference between an end which an agent, possibly quite arbitrarily, sets up for himself as the culmination of his actual ambitions, and the end to which his nature is metaphysically directed

[1] *S.T.*, I, 60, 2,c.

from the first moment of his existence. In the first sense, the actually intended end of the human agent is his private purpose in living; it is something like the *end of the agent* (*finis operantis*), by which term we designate the personal purpose which the individual may have, in undertaking any kind of work. Thus, a man may build a house *in order to sell it at a profit;* the italicized phrase describes his end as an agent. This sort of individual purpose should be distinguished from what is called the *end of the work* (*finis operis*). The latter is the goal toward which some definite species of activity is directed by its specific nature. Thus, the end of the work of building houses is *a house*.[2] The present consideration of the purpose of human life is not concerned with the individually intended end of a given man but with the specific end for which all men are fitted by their essence, as rational animals. It is as if we were thinking of the end of the work of man as man, understanding this work to be the whole series of human actions which make up a human life. Our question then becomes: Is there a specific end, or purpose, of human life?

Now, it has already been established in thomistic metaphysics that all things are for an end. There is a reason why every being exists or can exist. This is precisely to say that there is a final cause for every finite being. It is particularly evident that every agent acts for an end. Here, there are only two possibilities. An agent may be of the kind which is not capable in its nature of knowing its end, and in this case it must be directed toward its end by some intellect which does not form part of the agent but which oversees its work, or which makes it in such a way that it, unknowingly, achieves its purpose. Such an agent, lacking in cognition of its end, will obviously possess no freedom; it necessarily tends towards its primary purpose, when it is in operation. All the world of beings below man is something like this; not precisely mechanical but naturally determined by God, its Maker, to certain predetermined purposes which are part of the formal nature of these subhuman things. If we do not agree to this teleological interpretation of natural operations,

[2] For this distinction of the end of the agent, and of the work, see: *S.T.*, II–II, 141, 6, *ad primum.*

then we must think that the events of the natural world are all purposeless events. This would mean that the world is disorderly and entirely irrational in its activities. In turn, this would lead to the conclusion that neither science nor philosophy is possible, for a world of purposeless events cannot be understood, by either the scientist or the philosopher.

The other possibility, besides that of agents naturally and necessarily ordered to their ends, is that of an agent so made that he can know his own specific end and freely order his actions so as to attain this end. This is the case with men. They have certain operations which are necessitated, or determined by their nature, to set ends. Nutrition and the operations associated with biological functioning are like this. Men can perform other operations, which are distinctively human in contrast to the biological operations which are of the genus of animal functions, and these human actions can be regulated by human reason in view of a known end.[3]

If we remember that the only kind of actions that are studied in ethics are the free acts of man, that is, actions taking their origin in a rationally controlled will, then we may sum up the thought of this section, in these words of St. Thomas: "It is evident that all actions proceeding from any potency are caused by it according to the formal nature (*ratio*) of its object. Now the object of the will is the end and the good. Hence, all human actions must be for the sake of an end."[4]

Is There a "Natural" Ultimate End for Man?

Each and every job, or line of work, in which men engage, has its own special end. The end of the medical profession is to restore and maintain health. The end of the military art is victory, and one of the important means to this end is the taking away of the lives of certain men, of the enemy. It may be seen that the special ends of

[3] Read: Appendix to Chap. II, Text One: *All Actions, Necessary or Free, Are for an End*. Also read: *Summa contra Gentiles*, II, c. 1–3; in Pegis, *Basic Writings*, II, 3–9.

[4] *S.T.*, I–II, 1, 1,c.

different species of work may be quite different; sometimes they are almost diametrically opposed. The professional actions of a medical doctor are good, judged by the standards of his profession, if they are reasonably calculated to attain the end of his work. The same teaching applies to the soldier. It is good for the soldier, under certain circumstances, to kill his enemy. On the other hand, it is good for the medical man to save the life of his patient. However, when we speak of a "good" action in this way, we speak relatively. That is, we are thinking of special kinds of limited goodness, of "medical" goodness, or of "military" goodness.

But before a human being is a doctor, or a soldier, or a worker of any other specific kind, he is a *man*. There will be, then, a broad end of man considered simply as a rational animal, without limiting him to the special end of this or that line of work. This broad end of every human agent is not relative but absolute. No matter what kind of work we do, we must live a reasonably *human* life in order to attain happiness. Our special ends, depending on the kind of career we follow, will have to be subordinated to this absolute, human end. One may choose to follow the career of a thief; his actions will be "good," within the limits of this line of work, if they are such as to achieve the end of this possible "career." But acts of thievery are not *morally* good. The reason for this is that the end of the thief (which we may take to be the illegal appropriation of other people's property) is not in keeping with the end of human life as a whole. Hence, it is necessary for the ethician to think in terms of the broad, absolute end of human life. This is called the *ultimate end of man.* It is defined by St. Thomas as that end, "for the sake of which, all other things are desired, and which is not itself desired for the sake of anything else." [5] Of course, we may say, with admitted vagueness, that the ultimate end of man is happiness.[6]

We may now ask: Is there an end which is ultimate, and which man may attain without any supernatural aid, solely by the use of his natural powers and the natural objects of these powers? By

[5] *In I Ethic.*, lect.1; ed. Pirotta, p. 8, n. 22.
[6] Read: Appendix to Chap. II, Text Two: *The Ultimate End of Man.*

natural powers we mean all those potencies which are proper to the specific essence of a rational animal, which have been studied in the philosophy of man.

Many great philosophers have tried to answer this question. To appreciate their efforts, we must first note the difference between the ultimate end considered *objectively*, and the ultimate end considered *subjectively*. In the objective sense, this end must be a *thing;* subjectively, this end is the *use, possession,* or *attainment* of that thing. For instance, the objective end of a miser (relative to his career as a miser) is wealth. But his subjective end is simply what he wants to do with the wealth:—to own it, count it, gloat over it. These are not two metaphysically distinct ends; there is but one ultimate end. From one formal point of view, it is a thing, an object of desire; from another formal point of view, it is the actual use, by the moral agent, of that thing. St. Thomas explains this briefly:

The end is spoken of in two ways. In one way, it is the thing itself (*ipsa res*); in another way, it is the attainment of the thing (*adeptio rei*). Now these are not two ends, but one end, considered in itself, or as applied to another being.[7]

What objective ultimate end, what thing, is such that its attainment will constitute the true and perfect happiness of man? In his attempt to answer this question, Aristotle reviews many goods which various people have regarded as the object of perfect happiness. Pleasure, honor, wealth, natural virtue, practical wisdom—these and other things are considered and eventually rejected. He selects the life of speculative wisdom as that which is most fitting to man's highest capacities. In this case, the objective end would seem to be *perfect truth*. But Aristotle could not find any *thing*, which is perfectly true, and which could be contemplated by man. He was a very reasonable man and he could see that there is no such perfect thing available to man in this world. Of course, he had so defined the human soul that it did not seem reasonably possible for it to live in a future life without its body. And he had made "God" into a perfect being, so transcendent that man could never know this

[7] *S.T.,* I–II, 11, 3, ad 3m. For the same teaching, plus the example of the miser, see: *S.T.,* I–II, 1, 8,c.

"God" in any essential way. Hence, Aristotle with great reluctance admitted that the life of contemplation is too high an ideal for man. He concluded that, in practice, man's highest happiness must be sought on this earth in a life of practical wisdom accompanied by reasonable pleasure. Let us remember in reading this classic passage, that we have here one of the greatest intellects of all time, seriously and sincerely, trying to find in nature an object which could guarantee perfect happiness to the good man. And let us emphasize that he did not find such a natural object.[8]

In a work which may have been written by Aristotle, or possibly compiled by a follower from parts of his other ethical writings, it is suggested that the greatest happiness may consist in "the worship and contemplation of God." [9] It is this suggestion which is emphasized and further developed by two early Christian thinkers in their discussions of the same point. Both St. Augustine of Hippo and Boethius review the various goods available to man in this earthly life, decide that none of them is adequate to satisfy the desires of man, and point to the vision of God in Heaven as the ultimate end of man. In the view of these men, this is, of course, a supernatural end.[10]

These classic considerations are an important part of the background of St. Thomas' discussion of the problem. In a very logical way, he classifies the many natural goods under three categories: (1) goods of fortune; (2) goods of the body; and (3) goods of the soul.[11]

Goods of fortune include: wealth, honors, fame or human glory, and power. All of these are unsatisfactory as ultimate objective ends, for four reasons. Firstly, the ultimate end really means the supreme good; it must be of such a nature that it is completely dissociated from evil. None of the goods of fortune satisfies this requirement.

[8] Read: Aristotle, *Nicomachean Ethics*, I, 1095b14–1101a20 and 1177a12–1179a33; in McKeon, *Basic Works of Aristotle*, pp. 938–948 and 1104–1108.

[9] *Eudemian Ethics*, 1249b20.

[10] Read: St. Augustine, *The City of God*, transl. by J. Healey (London, 1940), pp. 123–129; this is Book XIX, c. 4, of the original work. Read also: Boethius, *Consolations of Philosophy*, transl. by H. F. Stewart and E. K. Rand (New York, Loeb Series 1926), Book III *in toto*, pp. 224–297.

[11] *S.T.*, I–II, 2, articles 1–8.

Secondly, the objective ultimate end must be sufficient of itself to satisfy all man's desires; this is true of none of the foregoing. Thirdly, a perfectly satisfactory good must be such that no evil can come from it; but evil may arise from any of the goods of fortune. Lastly, human happiness is that to which man is directed by an internal urge, its satisfaction cannot lie wholly in external things. But all the goods of fortune are external goods. So happiness cannot consist in the attainment of any of these things.[12]

Goods of the body include such things as long life of the body, strength, health, and physical beauty. These cannot be the objective ultimate end of man, because they are only perfections of a part of man's being and that is a minor part. The soul does not exist for the sake of the body; its best operations are those which are capable of being performed independently of the body. Bodily pleasures are a special problem. St. Thomas is far from denying that these have a strong attraction for man in this life. Still, they cannot be the good in which man's true happiness lies. These pleasures of sense, and this is true of all pleasure, are but by-products of the essential act whereby man attains the good. Pleasure follows perfection of action; it is not itself perfect action. Moreover, the pleasures of the body are inferior in quality to those of the soul.[13]

The *goods of the soul* are the soul itself, and any of its potencies, habitus, or acts. Specifically, some people have thought that perfect knowledge, or wisdom, or art, or moral virtue, or the acts of these habitus, may constitute the ultimate end of man. Here we are dealing with important goods and it is necessary to be very clear about them. St. Thomas reminds us of the difference between the *thing* whose attainment is happiness, and the *attainment or use* of that thing. This is, again, the distinction between the end viewed objectively and subjectively. Now it is apparent that none of the goods of the soul is a thing. The soul itself might seem to qualify on this basis, but the fact is that the soul is in potency to many perfections; hence it cannot be the perfect good. The *subjective* end is an act of the soul. What this act is, we shall inquire presently. But the *objective* ultimate end is not anything which belongs to the nature of the hu-

[12] *S.T.*, I–II, 2, 4,c.   [13] *S.T.*, I–II, 5 and 6,c.

man soul. If it were, there would be no point in struggling to possess it; we would already have it from birth.[14]

By this process of elimination, we have discarded any and all created goods as possible candidates for the position of objective ultimate end of man. This is to say that such an end is not to be found anywhere in created nature. After all, a desire for the perfect good cannot be fully satisfied with anything of limited perfection; and all natural things are so limited. The only thing left is God. He must be the object in Whom man's natural desire for happiness will find its ultimate satisfaction. *God is the ultimate objective end of man.*

This is a very important conclusion. It may already be seen that it means that there is no *natural* ultimate end for man. If anything is supernatural, God is. It remains for us to examine whether the manner in which the perfect good, God, is to be attained by man, is natural.[15]

The Attainment of the Ultimate End

So far, we have been talking in a most general way about the "attainment," or "achievement," of the ultimate objective end. Perfect happiness for man has been said to consist in this attainment. What this is must now be made clear. The first thing to notice is that this attainment is *an act* and not merely a state. Possibly the English word, happiness, is somewhat misleading here. If it suggests merely a sort of habitual condition of enjoyment or pleasure, then we shall have to discard this connotation. What we are talking about now, is the end of man viewed subjectively. This will be that which is most perfect within the individual human agent. Every state (whether a potency, a disposition, or a habitus) is metaphysically

[14] *S.T.*, I–II, 7,c.
[15] Read: *Summa contra Gentiles*, III, Chaps. 25–37; in Pegis, *Basic Writings*, II, 43–60. Read also: Gilson, E., *Moral Values and the Moral Life*, pp. 26–36, "In Quest of the Master Value." It should be noted that the translator of this book uses the term "value" when he means "good." Advanced students may consult with profit: O'Connor, W. R., "The Natural Desire for God in St. Thomas," *New Scholasticism*, XIV (July, 1940) 213–265.

imperfect in comparison with the act of which that state may be a principle. In more simple language, this means that it is far better *to do something well*, rather than just *to be able to do something well*. St. Thomas illustrates this point with an interesting example:

Up in Macedonia, there is a very high mountain which is called Olympus. It was customary to hold games and contests there, and they were called the Olympics. Now in these games, they didn't give the prizes to whose who were the strongest or best fighters, but to those who actually struggled and won victories. The man who did not fight could not win a victory. Now the same thing applies to those people who are good and best in the way of moral virtue; only those *who do things rightly* are illustrious and happy. So, it is better to say that happiness is action in accordance with virtue, than that it is virtue itself.[16]

The ethical theory which maintains that the end of man lies in some vague state of happiness is called *eudaimonism*, from the Greek, *eudaimonia*, meaning happiness, or more literally, good spirits. A closely related theory is *hedonism*, in which it is claimed that the ultimate end is pleasure of some sort (Greek: *hēdonē*, pleasure). Now, the ethics of St. Thomas, and this is true of Aristotle too [17] is neither precisely eudaimonistic nor hedonistic. It is an ethics in which the true happiness of man is held to consist in the continued action of man's highest potency, used in the most perfect way.

Our question may now be restated: What is the highest potency of man, and what is its most perfect act? The soul of man is the principle of his vital acts, and the proximate, specific principles of the different kinds of human acts are the various operational potencies which have been studied in the philosophy of man. Man's characteristic perfection of action cannot be found in the acts of the vegetative order, for these lowest vital functions are shared in common with all plants and animals. To say that man's happiness lies in growing up, or in assimilating food, or in producing offspring, would be to reduce man to the level of a vegetable. Moreover, these vegetative functions are not, in themselves, free human actions. Nor can acts of the sensitive powers, cognitive or appetitive, be of the essence of human perfection. The senses are concerned with bodily

---

[16] *In I Ethic.*, lect. 12; ed. Pirotta, p. 50, n. 153.
[17] Cf. Ross, W. D., *Aristotle* (London, 1923), p. 190.

objects and we have seen that such things cannot give man true happiness.[18]

We are left with the conclusion that man's perfect happiness must consist in some operation of the rational potencies; these are intellect and will. Intellectual appetite is that capacity whereby man *desires* happiness as a perfect good. Will also *enjoys* this good, after it has been attained. The desire is antecedent to the act of attainment; the joy is consequent upon it. No act of the will is precisely the act of attainment. This is the way St. Thomas puts it:

> It is evident from our previous discussion that happiness is attainment (*consecutio*) of the ultimate end. Now the attainment of the end does not consist in the very act of the will. The will is impelled toward an end which is absent, when it desires it; and when it [the end] is present, it rests and enjoys it. Now, it is clear that the desire of the end is not the attainment of the end, but is a movement toward the end. And joy comes to the will from the fact that the end is already present; but the contrary is not true: nothing is present by reason of the fact that the will is enjoying it. Therefore, there must be something else besides the act of the will, whereby the end itself becomes present to the will.[19]

The only other rational potency in man is his intellect. It must be by an act of the intellect that man actually grasps the ultimate objective end. The intellectual operation of contemplation is the best kind of human act; when performed in regard to a perfect object, it constitutes man's highest perfection. This is an act of the speculative intellect, not of the practical intellect. It is for the sake of other actions that the practical intellect works, but the act of speculation is for its own sake alone. Hence, *the essence of happiness is found in the speculative contemplation, by the intellect, of divine things.* There is no question as to the agreement of this conclusion with the whole metaphysical and moral outlook of St. Thomas:

> The best potency is the intellect. Its best object is the divine Good, and this is not the object of the practical intellect, but of the speculative. Hence, happiness chiefly consists in such an operation, namely, in the contemplation of divine things.[20]

[18] *S.T.*, I–II, 3, 3,c.
[19] *S.T.*, I–II, 3, 4,c.
[20] *S.T.*, I–II, 3, 5,c.

Of course, the will's operation is a necessary adjunct to intellectual contemplation. As we have seen, the act of desire precedes that of speculative contemplation and finds its rest in connection with the contemplation of the highest Being. Also, the will takes pleasure in the act of contemplation, and this delight or joy necessarily follows and completes man's intellectual act. The very substance of happiness is in the intellectual operation; the acts of the will are peripheral, like proper accidents.[21]

The next problem is concerned with *how* this act of contemplating God is to be performed. There is a kind of *imperfect* contemplation which is achieved by the philosopher in this life. Apparently, this was the ideal end which Aristotle tried to set up but found practically impossible. Philosophic speculation on earth is but a faint participation in the eventual happiness of the man who has reached final perfection. It is not perfect, for it cannot last; it is not undisturbed by practical cares and even evils; it is not even certain just what its object is. The speculative sciences depend necessarily on knowledge abstracted from phantasms. The intellect of the philosopher is indebted to sensation for the beginnings of all his natural knowledge. He can wish for a better kind of knowledge but he cannot attain it by natural means. Nor is it of any help to suggest that man may find happiness in the contemplation of immaterial substances, of angels. These angels are not perfect beings, albeit they are more perfect than men. It is possible to desire to know something better than angels. Besides, we know very little about angels in this life. What we do know, by natural means, is laboriously reasoned to, on the basis of their remote analogical resemblances to earthly things. The same is true of the human soul; neither it, nor angels, are immediately contemplated in their essences by any of man's natural powers, in this life. In a future life, even if directly known, finite spirits would be found to have only participated being. They are not pure acts; they are imperfect beings and imperfect goods.[22]

---

[21] Read: Appendix to Chap. II, Text Three: *The Essential Act of Perfect Happiness.* Read also: Gilson, E., *Moral Values and the Moral Life,* pp. 37–51, "Happiness and Morals."

[22] *S.T.,* I–II, 3, 6 and 7,c.

What is needed is an immediate intellectual vision of the Essence of God. Intellectual knowledge is incomplete and imperfect until it reaches the essence of its object. We can know many things *about* a being, but, until we know *what it is*, we cannot be fully satisfied with our knowledge. No man can know God's Essence, in and through Itself, in this life. We are talking about man's *natural* mode of intellectual knowledge, now. There were some men in the nineteenth century, who thought it possible for the philosopher first to know God's Being and then to know finite beings through God. This theory is called *Ontologism*, and it was advocated by Gioberti, Gerdil, and possibly Rosmini.[23] It is not in keeping with our natural experience, with philosophic truth, or with the teachings of Christianity. It has been gathered from the study of the philosophy of man that all human knowledge, on this earth, comes originally through the senses. God is not an object of sensation. Moreover, if we could know God directly and in His Essence, in our present condition, we would already be in Heaven. The essential operation of the blessed people in Heaven is the immediate contemplation of the Divine Essence. This is what the theologian calls the *Beatific Vision*.[24]

Whenever we know any being essentially, our possible intellect must be informed by the intelligible species of that thing and brought into act by the agency of the agent intellect. This has been explained in the philosophy of man. To know God's Essence directly, the theology of St. Thomas tells us, man would need to be informed with the Divine Species, which is already intelligible in an actual way by Its Nature. But the agent intellect only works in regard to species that may be abstracted from phantasms. It cannot abstract the Divine Species from sense cognition. However, these (agent and possible intellect) are our highest cognitive potencies. Hence, if man is to be equipped to see God intellectually in His Essence, then man must be aided by some higher power than that of the agent intellect. It is common to speak of the power of the agent

[23] Students will find a brief account of Ontologism and its condemnation by Catholic authorities (in 1861) in: Glenn, *History of Philosophy*, pp. 356-358.

[24] Read: *In Boetium De Trinitate*, q. VI, art. 3 and 4, as translated by Sister Rose Emmanuella Brennan, *The Trinity* (St. Louis, 1946), pp. 187-197, "That We Cannot See God's Essence in This Life."

intellect as a "light," because this power makes potentially intelligible things to be actually intelligible, in somewhat the same way that bodily light makes potentially visible things to be actually visible. We may, then, try to use this analogy in suggesting the sort of help which is required in order that man may be raised to the level of operation, on which he may contemplate the Divine Essence.

Just as the agent intellect provides by its act the species whereby the essence of a bodily thing may be conceived, and further furnishes the light needed by the possible intellect to see the thing intellectually, so also some agent must provide man with the Divine Species and must offer a *light* which will perfect the human intellect so that it may see this supernatural Object. Only God can give this Species and this Light. Whether we understand all this or not (and one should not be disappointed if it is not thoroughly understood, it is but an analogy and analogous knowledge is never wholly clear) we can see that this is no ordinary, natural process. The knowing of the Essence of God, in the Beatific Vision, is a distinctly supernatural event. And yet, this is the only wholly satisfying kind of knowledge for man. His natural desire does not urge him toward this specific Vision, because few people on earth ever know, even with this amount of precision, what the Beatific Vision means. But man can desire more than he knows in detail. Browning has expressed the thought beautifully: "a man's reach must exceed his grasp. Or what's a heaven for?" [25] Hence, we can say that the human desire for happiness, which is quite natural, only finds its rest in a supernaturally performed act, which is far more than natural.[26]

Man could obtain *imperfect* happiness with natural means alone; aided by God's grace, man can achieve subjectively *perfect* happiness which does not destroy, but perfects, natural happiness in a supernatural way.

[25] *Andrea del Sarto*, lines 96-97.
[26] Read: Appendix to Chap. II, Text Four: *The Contemplation of God's Essence and Man's Natural Desire of His End*. For a short explanation of what is meant by the Divine Light, mentioned above, read: Appendix to Chap. II, Text Five: *What Is the Light of Glory?* For a more thorough explanation of the whole teaching, read: *Summa contra Gentiles*, III, chap. 38-63; in Pegis, *Basic Writings*, II, 61-96. Consult also the articles by G. Smith, S.J., and A. C. Pegis, in *Proc. of Amer. Cath. Philos. Assoc.*, as cited at the end of this chapter.

Ethics and Theology on the End of Man

The relation of ethics to moral theology, which was mentioned in general in the first chapter, may now be understood better. It is necessary in moral science to know what the ultimate end of man is. However, the philosopher left to his own devices cannot find in the natural order of things any end which can fully satisfy man's aspirations. This is well illustrated by Aristotle's failure to come to any precise conclusion on this point. The moral theologian, on the other hand, believes that perfect happiness lies in the Beatific Vision of God's Essence throughout an indefinitely long future life. There is no contention to be made here that the philosopher can fully understand this ultimate end, by the use of unaided reason. Rather, it must be admitted frankly that the establishment of the supernatural character of this end is beyond the limits of any kind of natural philosophy.

What the Christian moral philosopher may do is to consider this suggestion from theology and see whether it provides a principle whereby man's moral actions and problems may be rationally ordered. That this concept of a supernatural end does bring reason and order into the lives of men who think and act in terms of it, is something which is demonstrable from history. Just a few years ago, one of the greatest contemporary philosophers, Henri Bergson, wrote a book about ethics and religion.[27] He was a man trained in the biological sciences, and he brought a new and profound understanding to contemporary philosophy. It should also be remembered that he was not a Christian; he was of Jewish origin. In his book, he tried to describe the men who had lived the best human lives. These would actually be the most successful men that the world has known. He finally decided that the only good examples of such men, that he knew, were the great Christian saints. Among the names which he gives, are those of some of the most noted contemplatives: St. Paul, St. Francis, St. Teresa, and St. Catherine of Sienna. He also points out that they were among the most active in

[27] Les Deux Sources de la Morale et de la Religion (Paris, 1932).

the spreading of Christianity. Theirs is the real success story, if we are to accept the evidence of moral theology as to the real purpose of human life.

The end is a primary principle in a practical science, such as ethics. From it we take our start in reasoning about all our moral problems. We shall see how this works, in the next section of this chapter. Natural ethics glimpses but dimly and imperfectly the character of man's ultimate end. Moral theology provides a more perfect knowledge of this, as well as other moral factors. Those who believe the account, given in the Book of Genesis, of the origin and life of Adam and Eve, accept the fact that all descendants of the first man and woman are subject to a sort of distortion of personality, which is one element in the constitution of what is called original sin. This distortion consists in a lack of obedience of the sense appetites to reason. Human emotions, or passions, tend to get out of hand and to make it hard to be reasonable in thought and action. It is not too much to say that this distortion is an observable, empirical fact. The struggle of "the flesh and the spirit" has been noticed by many natural philosophers. But it is not possible fully to understand this, from the natural point of view.

The moral theologian will tell us, and we shall examine this teaching in Chapter III, pp. 87–88, that there is more to original sin than just this deformity, or disorder, of human personality. He will tell us that man before the Fall was in a better than natural condition, that he enjoyed certain gifts and graces of which he was deprived after the Fall. The lack of these preternatural graces has left its mark on men as they actually exist now. If we may use a very far-fetched analogy, it is as if we were considering the son of a once-rich father. This son is now in moderate circumstances, but he misses the things which his family once enjoyed in abundance. He experiences a certain *privation* of the things that he might have had. Now, the descendants of Adam also experience a feeling of loss. They long for things which are unobtainable with their natural powers. Divine grace, theology teaches, will help man to acquire these things.

It was the consideration of the inability of man's natural processes of reasoning to achieve a perfect understanding of the essential nature of the ultimate end and of such factors as original sin that led Jacques Maritain to conclude that an adequate science of ethics must be subordinated to moral theology.[28] We have pointed out, in the first chapter (p. 11) that ethics should be open to the consideration of any valid information about man's moral life, including an examination of the teachings of moral theology. With particular reference to the problem of the ultimate end of man, these things should be kept in mind: (1) The ethician can demonstrate by philosophical means that no finite being is the objective end and that, by elimination, this end must be an infinite Being, God.[29] (2) It is when we come to examine the nature of the final intellectual contemplation of God, by the man who has lived a good life and has achieved his ultimate end, that we realize the inadequacy and imperfection of strictly natural ethics. The philosopher does not understand the Beatific Vision, though he may see that no other form of contemplation is perfectly satisfactory. The moral theologian does not fully understand the nature of the Beatific Vision either, but he has a much better grasp of what this ultimate act of happiness means.[30]

The End and the Specification of Moral Good and Evil

It is now possible to make a first, general conclusion about right or wrong, goodness or badness, in human actions. ⌐Man's free acts are good when they are of such a nature as to advance him toward the attainment of his ultimate end; they are bad when they draw him away from this goal.⌐

⌐The reason for this conclusion lies in the fact that the end is a formal principle in regard to the will. This means that, from the

[28] See not only the pages of *Science and Wisdom*, mentioned above (Chap. I, p. 25) but also the earlier formulations of this notion of subalternation, or subordination, in: J. Maritain, *Les degrés du savoir* (Paris, Desclée, 1932) pp. 618–627, 879–895; and *De la philosophie chrétienne* (Paris, Desclée, 1933) pp. 69–77, 101–166, 248.

[29] This is the reasoning used by St. Thomas in the *Summa contra Gentiles*, III, cap. 26–52.

[30] Read the excellent article by G. P. Klubertanz, "Ethics and Theology," *The Modern Schoolman*, XXVII (1949) 29–39.

point of view of the will-act, differences of kind, of species, are due to differences of ends. Any good may be fastened upon as an end by the will. Such goods are many, imperfect, and proximate, in contrast to the one, perfect, ultimate Good. Anything that is desired is either a real good or an apparent good. When an object of desire is such that it is unsuitable to the rational nature of man in relation to his ultimate end, then it is wished because it *appears* to the agent to be good in some sense, but it is morally bad because it lacks something of the full nature of a real good in conformity with man's reasoned ordination to his ultimate end.

Let us take the example of a man who chooses to spend nearly all his time gambling, instead of working to support himself and his family. Let us further agree, for the sake of the example, that he has made a bad choice. This man has not chosen evil, as such, however. His will is attracted by some aspect of gambling which appears to him to be good. The will is never drawn to sheer evil. We know from metaphysics that no being can be wholly bad, because metaphysical evil is a privation of goodness. It is of the nature of the will to be drawn toward the good. So, this gambler thinks that there is something good about what he is doing; otherwise, he would not choose to do it. However, it is his duty as a moral agent to choose proximate ends of his actions, which ends will not be out of keeping with his one, ultimate end.

The ultimate end is not something which man is free to choose or to reject. He is naturally, and that means necessarily, directed to this ultimate end by the demands of his specific nature. No human agent is free to change his species and thus try to be, for instance, a stone, or a horse. He *must* exist, live, and act, as is becoming to the species, as a rational animal. Hence, the ultimate end is a fixed principle, but the various *means* to be used in reaching this end are not fixed. Freedom of choice applies to these means. Man is so free that he may select means that are either good or bad from the point of view of his ultimate end. This marks the primary division of human actions into two major classes, or species, according to the method of consideration which is proper to ethics. One species includes all those human acts which are suitable to the attainment of the ultimate end;

these are *morally good acts*. The second species includes all human actions which are unsuitable to the attainment of the ultimate end; and these are *morally bad acts*. To show how this naturally desired end is a first principle of moral specification, St. Thomas compares it to the first principles of knowledge, from which all true, cognitive conclusions are derived:

In those things which pertain to the intellect and will, what is first is what is according to nature, and all other things are derived from it. Thus, the knowledge of conclusions is derived from the knowledge of the first principles which are naturally known. So too, the election of all means to the end, is derived from the willing of the end which is naturally desired.[31]

The foregoing is meant to indicate only a preliminary and most general distinction between moral good and evil. In practice it is not enough for a man simply to know his ultimate end and then choose acts which seem to be suited to this end. Moral decisions are more difficult and complex than this. Besides intending proximate ends that are morally good, the virtuous man must think carefully about the circumstances and the kind of action which he proposes to use as a means to these ends. These things will be studied later.[32]

As a final point, we should notice that this chapter has treated the relation of man to his ultimate happiness *analytically*. That is, we have separated out those potencies which are most directly involved and which are dominant in the final and most perfect act possible to man. These powers are: the *intellect*, essentially; the *will*, accidentally. Still, this analysis must not be carried to an extreme; we must not think that man eventually is to become an *intellect*, associated with a will. It has been learned in metaphysics, that actions belong to the whole and complete substance of the agent (*actiones sunt suppositorum*). Man, in his final perfection, should be a complete member of his species, a supposit. While there is no philosophical

---

[31] *S.T.*, I–II, 17, 9, ad 2m. Read: Appendix to Chap. II, Text Six: *The End and the Distinction of Moral Good and Evil;* Text Seven: *Free Choice and the Difference Between Good and Bad Acts.* Read also: *S.T.*, I, 48, 1, ad 2m; in Pegis, *Basic Writings*, I, 465.

[32] For a good, brief survey of the teaching of St. Thomas on the subject matter of this chapter, see: Gilson, E., *The Philosophy of St. Thomas*, Chap. 16, "The Last End."

demonstration of the Christian teaching that the human soul will
be rejoined by its glorified body after the Last Judgment, it does
seem quite reasonable that man's whole being should be engaged
in the ultimate and everlasting act of perfect happiness. The soul
separated from its body may perform the essential act of intellectual
vision of God, but for the most complete perfection of human happiness, the *whole, integral man,* body and soul, would seem to be
required. And that is the conclusion of St. Thomas:

> Since it is natural to the soul that it be united to the body, it cannot be
> that the perfection of the soul would exclude its natural perfection. And
> so, we have to say that the perfect disposition of the body is required for
> the happiness which is perfect in all ways.[33]

Summary of Chapter II

Since all actions in nature are for some end, the free acts of man
must be for the sake of an end. This end of all human acts, considered from the point of view of the unity of the human species,
must be one ultimate end for all men. As a thing, in the attainment
of which all man's natural desires can be satisfied, the objective ultimate end must be a Perfect Being, God. This Being is transcendent
and there is nothing in the world of nature that can be a satisfactory
ultimate end for man. The attainment of the end is subjective, and
it consists essentially in the most perfect act of man's best power, the
intellect. The will brings an accidental but necessary complement to
the intellectual vision of God, by adding appetitive enjoyment. The
Beatific Vision is the perfect end for man; it is a supernatural act,
to be performed in a future life. A special Divine Light, or help, is
needed for the actuation of this Vision. All of this teaching goes
beyond the unaided reason of the philosopher; it may be seen to be
quite a reasonable climax, however, to the thomistic metaphysics of
man. This explanation of the supernatural end of man is a definite
example of the value of a Christian ethics. It is necessary to know
the ultimate end of man in order to understand the primary division

[33] *S.T.,* I–II, 4, 6,c.

of human acts into two great species: moral good and moral evil. The final perfection of man is an integral happiness of his whole being, body and soul, viewed as the being of a complete member of the human species.

Appendix to Chapter II

¶ TEXT ONE: *All Actions, Necessary or Free, Are for an End.* Every agent acts on account of an end, for all things desire the good. Now, the action of an agent, in order that it be in agreement with an end, should be adapted and proportioned to it; and this cannot be done except by some intellect which knows the end, and the formal nature (*ratio*) of the end, and the proportion of the end to that which is for the end [i.e., the means]. Otherwise, the agreement of the action with the end will be a matter of chance.

But, the intellect which preordains to the end is sometimes conjoined to the agent or mover, as is the case of an arrow which tends toward an end determined, not by an intellect conjoined to it, but by the intellect of the man who aims it.

Now, it is not possible for that which acts from the necessity of nature to determine its own end for itself. A thing which acts in this way is an agent of itself (*ex se*); and a thing which acts or moves of its very self, possesses within itself the power to do or not to do, to be moved or not, as is said in Book VIII of *Physics* [of Aristotle]. This cannot be true of that which is moved from the necessity of nature, since it is determined to one way of acting.

Hence, it is necessary that the end be determined by some intelligent being, in the case of everything which acts from the necessity of nature. For this reason, it is said by the philosophers that the work of nature is the work of intelligence. And so, if at any time a natural body is joined to an intellect, as is the case in man, then, in regard to those actions whereby its intellect determines the end, nature obeys the will, as is evident in the motion of a man from one place to another. But, in regard to those actions in which it does not determine the end, there is no obedience [to will], for instance, in the act of nutrition and growth. (*De Potentia*, I, 5,c.)

❡ TEXT TWO: *The Ultimate End of Man.* We must return to the good with which our inquiry is concerned, namely to happiness, so that we may investigate what it is. And the first thing to be considered about it is that there seem to be different goods intended in different works and arts. For instance, health is the good intended in the medical art, and victory is the good intended in the military art, and in other arts there are other goods.

And, if it be asked, what is the good intended in any art, or in any kind of undertaking, it should be understood that it [the good] is that for the sake of which all other things are done. For, in medicine, all things are done for the sake of health. In the military art, all things are done for the sake of victory. And, in building, all things are done for the sake of constructing the house. Similarly, in any business, whatever, there is some other intended good, for the sake of which all things else are done. Now, this intended good in each and every work, or act of choice, is called the end. For, the end is simply *that for the sake of which other things are done*.

Therefore, if some end is immediately encountered, to which all the things done in all human arts and works are ordered, then such an end will be the good which is worked for, absolutely (*simpliciter*); that is, what is intended in all human works. However, if, in this connection, several goods (to which the various ends of the various arts are ordered) are encountered, it will be necessary to our rational enquiry to transcend this plurality, until it arrives at the thing itself; that is some *one* thing. For, the ultimate end of man, insofar as he is man, must be *one*, because of the unity of human nature; just as there is one end for the medical doctor, insofar as he is a medical doctor, because of the unity of the medical art.

And this ultimate end of man is called the *human good;* which is happiness. (*In I Ethic.*, lect. 9; ed. Pirotta, p. 36, nn. 104–106.)

❡ TEXT THREE: *The Essential Act of Perfect Happiness.* Felicity, or happiness, consists in an operation, and not in a habitus, as the Philosopher proves in the *Ethics* (I, 8; 1098b30–1099a6). Hence, the happiness of man can be related to any potency of the soul, in two ways. In one way, as the object of the potency; and, in this way, happiness is chiefly related to the will. For, happiness names the ultimate end of man, and his highest good. Now, the end and the good are the object of the will. In another way, as act is to potency; and, in this way, happiness *originally and substantially* consists in an act of the intellect. *Formally* and from the point of view of *fulfillment*, it consists in an act of the will, for it is impossible for the act itself of the will to be the ultimate end of the will.

The ultimate end of man is that which is primarily desired. Now, it cannot be that what is primarily desired is an act of the will. For, first of all, a potency must be directed to some *object*, before it may be directed upon its own act. The act of any potency is understood prior to its reflection upon that act, for the act terminates in the object; and so, any potency is directed to its object, before it is to its act. Sight, for instance, first sees color, rather than itself as seeing the color. So too, the will wishes some good before it wishes its act of wishing. Thus, the act of will cannot be primarily the object of will, and consequently it cannot be the ultimate end.

But, every time some external good is desired as an end, that act of ours is for us a sort of interior end, in that we first attain it perfectly. We say, for instance, that eating is an end, and the happiness of him who regards food as his end; likewise, possession is the end of him who takes money as his [objective] end.

Now, the end of our desire is God. Hence, the act whereby we are primarily conjoined to Him is originally and substantially our beatitude. But we are primarily conjoined to Him through the act of the intellect; and therefore, the vision of God, which is an act of the intellect, is substantially and originally our beatitude.

But, since this operation is most perfect and the object is most fitting, it is, therefore, followed by the greatest enjoyment, which adorns this operation and perfects it as beauty does youth, as is said in the *Ethics* (X, 4). Hence, this enjoyment which belongs to the will is that which completes happiness formally. Thus, the ultimate source (*origo*) of happiness is in vision, but its complement is in fruition. (*Quaest. Quodl.*, VIII, q. 9, a. 19,c.)

¶ TEXT FOUR: *The Contemplation of God's Essence and Man's Natural Desire of His End.* Now, a thing is in potency in two ways. In one way, *naturally;* that is, in regard to those things which can be reduced to act by a natural agent. In another way, in regard to those things which cannot be reduced to act by a natural agent but by some other agent; and this is evident in the sphere of bodily things. For, it is a matter of natural potency that a man be made from a boy, or that an animal be made from semen. But, it is not a matter of natural potency, that a bench be made from wood, or that a seeing agent be made from a blind one; and so too, does it happen in connection with our intellect.

For, our intellect is in natural potency in regard to some intelligible objects; namely, those which can be reduced to act by the agent intellect, which is the inborn principle in us whereby we are rendered *actually* intelligent. Now, it is not possible for us to seek the ultimate end through the fact that our intellect is reduced to act in this way. For, it is the perfection of the agent intellect to make actually intelligible the phantasms which are *potentially* intelligible, as is clear from the things above. But, phantasms are received through the senses. Therefore, our intellect is reduced to act by the agent intellect, only in respect to those intelligible objects which we can get to know through sensible things. Now, it is impossible for the ultimate end of man to consist in this kind of knowledge; for, when the ultimate end is attained, natural desire rests. But, no matter how proficient in understanding one may be, according to the aforesaid manner of knowing, whereby we receive knowledge from the senses, there still remains the natural desire to know other things.

For, there are many things which the senses do not reach, concerning which we can get only some slight knowledge through sensible things. Thus, perhaps, we may know that these things exist but not what they are, because the essences of immaterial substances are of a different genus from the essences of sensible things, and they transcend them almost as if they were entirely out of proportion. Even in regard to those things which do fall within the range of sensation, there are many things whose intelligible essence (*ratio*) we cannot know with certitude; some of them, indeed, we cannot know at all, and others only faintly. One thing always remains: *the natural desire for a more perfect knowledge.*

Now, it is impossible for a natural desire to be in vain. Therefore, we pursue the ultimate end in this way: our intellect is actuated by some more sublime agent than the agent which is connatural to us [*i.e.*, than the agent intellect]. And this [more sublime agent] may give rest to the desire to know, which is naturally present in us. Now, the desire within us to know is such that, in knowing effects, we wish to know their cause. In regard to any sort of thing, when we know any of its surrounding conditions, our desire does not rest until we know its essence. Therefore, the natural desire for knowledge cannot be satisfied in us, until we know the first cause, not just in any way but *in its essence*. Now, the first cause is God, as is clear from what has been said above. Therefore, it is the ultimate end of the intellectual creature *to see God through His Essence*.

(CHAPTER 105)

How this may be, should be considered. It is evident that, since our intellect does not know anything except through some species of it, it is not possible for it to know the essence of one thing through the species of another. And, the more distant is the species, through which the intellect knows, from the thing known, the less perfect is the knowledge which our intellect possesses of the essence of that thing. For example, if it were to know an ox through the species of an ass, it would know its essence imperfectly; that is, only in terms of its genus; and even more imperfectly, if it were to know it through a stone, for it would know it through a more remote genus. And, if it were to know it through the species of some thing which has nothing generically common with an ox, it would not know the essence of the ox at all.

Now, it is manifest from above that no creature has anything in common with God, generically. God cannot be known in His Essence through any created species whatsoever then; not only not through a sensible species, but also not through an intelligible one. Therefore, in order that God Himself be known in His Essence, it is necessary that God Himself become the Form of the intellect knowing Him, and that He be conjoined to it, not in such a way as to constitute one nature, but as an intelligible species is to the knower. For, just as He is His own existing Being, so also is He His own Truth, which is the Form of the intellect.

Moreover, it is necessary that everything which goes along with any form should go along with any disposition toward that form. Our intellect is not, of its own nature, in ultimate disposition to that Form which is Truth, for then it would seek it from the beginning. Therefore, it is necessary that, when it does seek it, it should be elevated by some newly added disposition which we call the *Light of Glory*. By it, our intellect is perfected by God, Who alone in His proper Nature possesses this Form; just as the disposition of heat to the form of fire can only come from fire; and it is concerning this Light that *Psalm* 35 says: "In Thy Light, we shall see the light."

(CHAPTER 106)

Now, if this be attained, the natural desire must come to rest; for, the divine Essence, which may be conjoined in the aforesaid manner to the intellect of the one who sees God, is the sufficient principle for the knowing of all things, and is the source of all goodness, so that nothing could remain to be desired. And here also, is the most perfect manner of seeking after the divine Similitude; namely, that we know Him in the same way that He knows Himself; that is, through His Essence. Of course, we may not comprehend Him exactly as He comprehends Himself; not that we would be ignorant of any part of Him, since He has no part, but because we may not know Him as perfectly as He is objectively knowable; for, the power of our intellect cannot, in its act of understanding, be adequated to His Truth, in accordance with which He is knowable, since His clarity or truth is Infinite, whereas our intellect is finite; and His Intellect is Infinite, just as His Truth is. And so, He knows Himself to the full extent of His cognoscibility, in the same way that a man, who knows demonstratively, comprehends a demonstrable conclusion, but not he who knows it in a more imperfect way, for instance, through probable reasoning.

And since we say that happiness is the ultimate end of man, then man's felicity, or happiness, consists in this: that he see God through His Essence, even though he may be quite far from God, in the perfection of his happiness; for God possesses this happiness through His own Nature, but man attains it by a participation in the divine Light, as was said above. (*Compendium Theologiae*, Pars Prima, cap. 104–106; ed. Mandonnet, vol. II, 69–71.)

¶ TEXT FIVE: *What Is the Light of Glory?* [St. Thomas first describes three different media which may be involved in intellectual cognition: (1) that *under which* (*sub quo*) the intellect sees its object; it disposes the intellect to its act of cognition (for natural objects, this medium is the light of the agent intellect, which is related to the possible intellect as the sun is to the eyes of the body); (2) that *by which* (*quo*) the intellect sees (*i.e.*, the intelligible species, which is to the possible intellect as the species of a stone is to our eyes); and (3) that *in which* something is seen (*i.e.*, a thing through which we proceed to the knowledge of another thing). Then, St. Thomas continues:] . . . It remains, therefore, that the first kind of medium, only, will be found in this vision [of God in His Essence]; and this [medium] is the Light of Glory, whereby the intellect will be perfected in order to see the divine Essence. Concerning this, it is said in Psalm 35:19, "In Thy Light, we shall see the light."

Now, this Light is not needed to make the potentially intelligible to be actually intelligible (for which reason the agent intellect is needed by us), for the divine Essence, since separated from matter, is of Itself actually intelligible. But, it will be needed only to perfect the intellect, so that for the present the light of the agent intellect may be sufficiently strong. But, the aforesaid Light of Glory will sufficiently perfect the intellect to see the divine Essence, inasmuch as the divine Essence is intelligible Light in all its completeness. Hence, the Light of Glory, coming down from It into the intellect, does the same thing in regard to the divine Essence that it does in regard to other intelligible things, which are not simply Light but the species of the thing understood, together with the Light. It is just as if sensible light were to exist *of itself;* then, it would be enough for the vision of it, to have the light perfecting the eye without any [added] similitude. (*Quaest. Quodl.,* VII, q. 1, a. 1,c.)

❡ TEXT SIX: *The End and the Distinction of Moral Good and Evil.* Actions differ in species according to a diversity of forms, which are the principles of actions, even though the agents may not be of different species. So, to heat and to cool, are specifically different actions, because heat and cold are [different forms]. Now, the form of the will is the end and the good, which is its object and the thing desired. Therefore, it is necessary that the specific difference in acts of the will be discovered from the essential nature of the end (*secundum rationem finis*). And, since acts belong in the genus, moral, because they are voluntary, so the specific difference in the genus of moral acts is based on a diversity of the end. (*In II Sent.,* d. 40, q. unica, a. 1,c; ed. Mandonnet, II, 1011.)

❡ TEXT SEVEN: *Free Choice and the Difference Between Good and Bad Acts.* Virtue and vice indicate some difference of movement and of act, according to good and bad. For, a virtue is that whereby anyone is related, in a good way, to doing things and undergoing things; a vice, in a bad way. And the same is true for the other habitus, either intellectual, as science, or bodily, as health.

Nevertheless, well and badly (*bene vel male*) chiefly pertain to quality in living things; and principally in things having *proairesis,* that is, choice. And this [is] because the good has the formal nature (*ratio*) of an end. Indeed, those things which act through choice, act because of an end. But, to act because of an end belongs chiefly to animate things. For, inanimate things act, or are moved, because of an end, not so much as knowers of the end, nor as themselves acting for the end, but rather they are directed by another being who gives them a natural inclination; as the arrow is directed to the end by the archer.

Of course, irrational animate things know the end and desire it with animal appetite; and they move themselves locally to the end, as possessors of a judgment of the end. But, the appetite for the end, and of those things which are for the sake of the end, is determined for them by a natural inclination. For this reason, they are things acted upon, rather than agents. So, there is not free judgment in them.

But, rational beings, in whom alone choice is found, know the end, and the proper relationship (*proportionem*) of those things which are for the sake of the end itself. And therefore, just as they move themselves toward the end, so also [do they] to the desiring of the end, or of those things which are for the sake of the end; and because of this, free choice is found in them. (*In V Metaph.*, lect. 16; ed. Cathala, p. 315, nn. 999–1000.)

Recommended Readings

Aristotle, *Nicomachean Ethics*, Book X (in *The Basic Works of Aristotle*, ed. McKeon, pp. 1093–1112).

Cronin, *Science of Ethics*, I, 46–88.

Farrell, *Companion to the Summa*, II, 1–20.

Gilson, *Moral Values and the Moral Life*, pp. 26–36, 37–51.

Klubertanz, "Ethics and Theology," *The Modern Schoolman* XXVII (1949) 29–39.

O'Connor, "The Natural Desire for God in St. Thomas," *New Scholasticism* XIV (1940) 213–265.

O'Connor, *The Eternal Quest*, (New York, Longmans, Green, 1947).

O'Connor, "Some Historical Factors in the Development of the Concept of Human Finality," *Proc. Amer. Cath. Philos. Assoc.* XXIII (1949) 15–35.

Pegis, "Nature and Spirit: Some Reflections on the Problem of the End of Man," *Proc. Amer. Cath. Philos. Assoc.* XXIII (1949) 62–79.

Rickaby, *Aquinas Ethicus*, I, 1–38.

Smith, "The Natural End of Man," *Proc. Amer. Cath. Philos. Assoc.* XXIII (1949) 47–61.

Thomas Aquinas, St., *The Trinity*, trans. Sister Rose Emmanuella Brennan, pp. 187–197.

Thomae Aq., S., *Summa contra Gentiles*, III, 1–63 (in *Basic Writings*, ed. Pegis, II, 3–113).

Thomae Aq., S., *Summa Theologiae*, I–II, qq. 1–5.
Wittmann, *Die Ethik des hl. Thomas von Aquin,* pp. 20–72.

Topics for Assignment

1. Why All Human Beings Have the Same Objective Ultimate End
2. A Criticism of Hedonistic Ethics
3. Intellectual Contemplation as the Perfection of Human Action
4. The Inadequacy of Goods of Fortune as Goals for Human Life
5. The Role of the Will in the Attainment of the Ultimate End

ACT - IMPUTABLE TO AGENT
AGENT - RESPONSIBILITY

Analysis of the Moral Act in the Will and Intellect

Morality is the general name for a definite property which is found in connection with every human act. By this property, the agent is responsible for his act; that is to say, he performs the action *himself*, and *freely*, and so he is entitled to credit if his action is good, discredit if it is bad. From the side of the act, we speak of such an action being *imputable* to the agent. Imputability, then, is that property of the human act which indicates that the act, whether good or bad, belongs to a definite moral agent. These are correlative terms: *responsibility* in the agent, *imputability* in his moral action. (Note that, as far as this life is concerned, *human actions* are identical with *free acts of man*, and also with *moral actions of man*.)

One pioneer ethician, Peter Abelard (A.D. 1079–1142), took the position that the morality of the human act depends exclusively on the goodness or evil of the *intention* of the agent performing it.[1] We shall see that this is an oversimplified view, but it stresses a partial truth: what goes on *within* the agent is far more important morally, than the externally observable portion of his moral act. Fully to understand morality, we must examine in detail the internal structure (including the intention and other psychological factors) of the human act. (This is the purpose of this section.) We must also study the ways and degree in which various internal dispositions and external factors influence the moral quality of the human act. (This is to be done later in the present chapter.)

[1] Cf. E. Gilson, *La philosophie au moyen âge* (Paris, 1947), pp. 289–291.

57

Let us now consider the different parts, or steps, in the progressive completion of a moral act within the essentially rational powers of the agent. These are will and intellect. This analysis requires us to keep in mind the explanation of human nature, already studied in the philosophy of man, or rational psychology.[2] This part-by-part consideration of the moral act is not the result of psychological introspection (though some of these stages may be noticed by the agent as his total act progresses); rather, it is a metaphysical analysis of the successive moments of efficient causality in the activity of the will, and of formal causality on the part of the human intellect and its objects. There is no suggestion that each moral agent must advert to all these analytical steps at the time of performing the act. Just as a person may walk, without thinking of the complicated physiological analysis of such an action, so may a moral agent perform a moral act without introspecting on the parts of his action.

Since all moral action is purposive, we shall first take the steps concerned with the *end*, then those dealing with the *means* to the end, and finally those connected with the *execution* of the moral act.[3]

STEPS CONCERNED WITH THE END

¶ *Intellectual Apprehension of the End.* It is not by means of the will that man knows any object. The will must be supplied a known object, by the intellect. The first step, then, is the intellectual understanding of something as desirable for its own sake; this end may be either the ultimate end, or some proximate end which is viewed as desirable in itself. This is an act in which the end is apprehended as a good, and is consequently presented, or proposed, as a known good to the will. It is thus described by St. Thomas: "The intellect moves the will in the way in which an end is said to move; that is, it pre-

---

[2] The necessary points are covered by St. Thomas, in his treatise on man, *S.T.*, I, qq. 75–83; in Pegis, *Basic Writings*, I, 682–792.

[3] Cf. *S.T.*, I–II, 15, 3,c: "Now, in the orderly sequence of actions, it is necessary to take up firstly the apprehension of the end, then the appetitive inclination to the end, then the deliberation concerning the means to the end, and then the appetitive action in regard to these means to the end."

conceives the knowable essence (*rationem*) of the end, and proposes it to the will." [4]

¶ *Wishing the End, with the Will.* It is the nature of the will to incline favorably toward any object that is presented to it as a known good. This initial tendency of the will is not free; it is a natural (and so, *necessary*) inclination, so closely connected with the essential character of the will that, in Latin, this step is called by the same name as the power of will (*voluntas*) or the act of willing (*velle*). This will-act is not concerned with doing anything to attain the end, for the question of the possibility of achieving the end has not yet been considered by the intellect. Thus, it is quite conceivable that one might think of living forever on this earth, as a good thing (intellectual apprehension), and then one might wish to do so, without stopping to consider whether it is possible or not. The simplicity of the wish, in regard to the unqualified good, is like the simplicity of the intellectual intuition of very first principles of knowledge. The intellect sees these principles as true, without any rational discourse; so too, the will, in wishing, just embraces the end as a good, without any "discursive" action in regard to possible means.[5] This tendency is natural, and so, a *right* inclination. It does not guarantee the eventual rightness of the completed moral act, but it starts the agent on the path of moral rectitude. As St. Thomas points out, it is not to be confused with the *intending* of an end: "For, the movement of the will toward the end is not, in its unqualified sense, called intention, but simply wishing. . . . He who wishes health, is said to wish it without qualification (*simpliciter*); but he is only said to intend it, when he desires something on account of health." [6]

¶ *Intellectual Judgment of the End as Attainable.* This is not a simple apprehension but a judgment (*judicium*) that the end may be achieved by some means.[7] Of course, it may be that the end will be judged to be really impossible of attainment, in which case the agent cannot proceed to do anything more about it. But if judged possible to the agent, then the end so known stimulates the next movement of

[4] *De Veritate*, q. 22, 12,c; cf. *S.T.*, I–II, 13, 5, *ad primum*.
[5] *S.T.*, I–II, 8, 2,c.
[6] *De Veritate*, q. 22, 14,c.
[7] *S.T.*, I–II, 12, 3 and 4,c.

will, which is intention. "When [reason] proposes something to itself under the formal nature of a good, to which other things may be
ordered, as to an end, then it tends to that [end] with an orderly
relation. . . ." [8]

¶ *Intention of the End.* With this step, the will is roused from the
complaisant approval of the second step, wishing the end with the
will, and it now tends toward personal action. Thus, if one first
wishes for good health, the next volitional step is to desire it actively
for oneself. This intention is not yet a *free* act, for it is a natural and
necessary thing to be attracted to what is good for oneself, provided
it is thought possible of attainment. Strictly speaking, there is as yet
no complete moral act. Intention can only be said to be good or bad,
if the end is good or bad. The moral character of the end is the sole
determinant of the incipient morality of the volitional movements of
wishing and intending.[9] To wish and intend the ultimate end, and
those things which are immediately recognized as essential to its
achievement (such as being, life, knowledge of truth, freedom of
action)—such will-acts are always right and good. But the wishing
and intending of proximate ends may be good or bad, depending on
the relation of these proximate ends to the ultimate end.

Intention looks to the end as the terminus of the movement of the will.
Now, in a movement, the terminus can be understood in two ways: first,
as the ultimate end at which there is rest, and this is the terminus of the
whole movement; second, as an intermediate position (*medium*) which
is the beginning of one part of the movement and the end or terminus of
another. Thus, in a movement from A to C through B, C is the ultimate
terminus, but B is a terminus, though not ultimate. Intention may occur
in regard to both. Hence, though always in regard to the end, it does
not always need to be to the ultimate end.[10]

STEPS CONCERNED WITH THE MEANS

¶ *Intellectual Deliberation on the Means.* In the fifth step, which
is also called counsel (*consilium*), the intellect goes through a discursive process of reasoning. The agent discovers and proceeds to

[8] *De Veritate,* q. 22, 13,c.   [9] *De Malo,* q. 7, 4,c.
[10] *S.T.,* I–II, 12, 2,c; cf. *De Veritate,* q. 22, 13,c.

evaluate the various means which seem suitable to the attainment of the end, under the actual circumstances which can be known to apply to the problem. Usually a plurality of means can be discovered as generally suitable to the end in view. Thus, if one's end is good health, the possible means may include consultation of various physicians, taking a vacation in various places and at different times, modifying one's diet, and so on. Such a process should terminate in a judgment, a definite decision as to what means should be used. This decision (*sententia*) may be somewhat theoretical and impersonal, at this point. One might decide, for instance: "Under these circumstances, the best thing to do is to go to a hospital for a thorough medical examination." Such a decision does not necessarily mean that the agent will choose to do so; it is simply his best judgment on the problem, viewed rather objectively and impersonally. A decision of this type is applicable to another man's problem, and we call such application the giving of counsel, or advice.

In proposed actions, many things are uncertain, because actions are concerned with contingent singulars, which are uncertain because of their changeableness. Now, reason does not offer a judgment on doubtful and uncertain things without some preliminary investigation. And so, a rational investigation (*inquisitio*) is needed before a judgment on matters of choice, and this investigation is called counsel.[11]

¶ *Volitional Consent to the Deliberation of Means.* If the agent is to make personal use of the previous deliberation, he must now be attracted in his will to the results of his process of counselling. He must will to apply this reasoning to himself. This is the step called consent (*consensus*). We are approaching the decisive moment of actual choice. So, there is something like freedom in the will-act of consent. St. Thomas defines consent as "the application of the appetitive movement to the determination of counsel." [12] Such personal favoring of the results of deliberation may be an inclination of will which is called forth by higher reasoning (the *ratio superior* deliberates on the basis of eternal truths, *e.g.*, the Law of God); or, consent may be given from the point of view of lower reasoning (the *ratio inferior* considers the means from the point of view of

[11] *S.T.*, I–II, 14, 1,c.   [12] *S.T.*, I–II, 15, 3,c.

natural principles, *e.g.*, the natural moral law). It is the work of superior reason to relate the moral act to the ultimate end.[13]

¶ *Practical Judgment of Choice.* Deliberation ends in a final judgment determining the choice which the agent completes by a will-act of acceptance of, or adherence to, this judgment. We shall see that the process of deliberation entails the use of a practical syllogism, or syllogisms.[14] At the will of the agent, deliberation may stop at any practical judgment which the agent favors; but, when the will makes the act of choice, it must be guided by the immediately preceding practical judgment. "Election follows the decision or judgment, which is like the conclusion of the operative syllogism."[15] We are, here, at the decisive moment of freedom in the moral act. Free choice is not an exclusive act of either intellect or will; it is the special function of intellect and will, acting in closest conjunction. In this combined function, the role of the intellect (*i.e.*, this step) is to make the final decision which formally determines the choice.[16]

¶ *Will-Act of Choice.* Concomitant with the intellectual judgment of choice (the *arbitrium*) the will performs the volitional act of adherence to this decision. This will-act is called election (*electio*), or choice. As far as the will is concerned, this election is a movement in the order of efficient causality, by which the agent actively commits himself to follow the last practical judgment.[17] With this step and the step just preceding, the moral act reaches its climax. The earlier steps are but a preparation for the practical judgment and the choice; the later steps continue the use of freedom of action but are not really needed to constitute a complete moral act. Moreover, we should note that an end, as such, is never an object of choice; only means are chosen. "Since choice does not have to do with the end, but with the means to the end, as has been said, it is not concerned with the Perfect Good which is happiness, but with other particular goods. And so, man does not choose of necessity, but freely."[18]

[13] *De Veritate*, q. 15, 3,c.   [14] To be treated later in Chaps. VI and VII.
[15] *S.T.*, I–II, 13, 3,c.   [16] *De Veritate*, q. 24, 2,c.
[17] *S.T.*, I–II, 13, 1,c; *In II Sent.*, d. 24, 1, 2,c; *De Veritate*, q. 22, 15,c.
[18] *S.T.*, I–II, 14, 6,c.

STEPS CONCERNED WITH THE EXECUTION OF THE ACT

¶ *Intellectual Commanding of Action.* With the ninth step, we enter the order of execution. In this order, the intellect and will are directed to the actual carrying out of the proposed work, which execution usually requires the use of other powers of man (sense appetites, internal and external cognitive powers of sensation, motor capacities of the living body) under the command of reason. While the series of will-acts described in this analysis are called *elicited acts* (*actus eliciti*), the acts of any power of man working under the control of intellect and will are called *commanded acts* (*actus imperati*). A moral command (*imperium*) must, first of all, be reasonable; it must issue from the intellect, supported by the active power of the will.

To command is essentially an act of reason; for the commander orders the one, to whom the command is given, *to do something*, and this order is conveyed by way of declaration or announcement. Now, to order in this way, by means of some sort of declaration (*intimationis*) is the work of reason. But reason can declare or announce something in two ways. First, *absolutely*, and this sort of declaration is expressed by a verb in the indicative mood, as when one man says to another: "This is something you should do." At other times, however, reason declares something to a man, *by moving him to it*, and such a declaration is expressed by a verb in the imperative mood, as when one would say to another: "Do this.". . . Hence, the conclusion is that to command is an act of reason, founded on a previous act of will, in virtue of which reason moves by command, to the exercise of the act.[19]

¶ *Will-Act of Use.* This act of will is the principal, efficient cause of the commanded act; the other commanded potencies are instrumental causes, used by the will. So, this act is called use (*usus*). "An action is not properly attributed to the instrument but to the principal agent, as building is the act of the builder, not of his tools. Hence, it is evident that *to use* is properly an act of will."[20]

¶ *Intellectual Attainment of the End.* When the commanded potencies (*potentiae executivae*)[21] carry out the work commanded, the

[19] *S.T.*, I–II, 17, 1,c; cf. *De Veritate*, q. 22, 12, ad 4m.
[20] *S.T.*, I–II, 16, 1,c.   [21] *S.T.*, I–II, 17, 3,c.

intellect contemplates the finished, or continuing, act. It judges that it is good (if it be fitting) in relation to the end originally intended.[22] If the act of attainment be essentially intellectual (as in the contemplation of the ultimate End) then this step is simply the apprehension of the suitability of the act to the end.[23]

¶ *Fruition in the Will.* This final step is the appetitive enjoyment (*fruitio*) associated with the fulfillment of the act in relation to the end. Just as a tree reaches its perfection and gives pleasure, when it bears fruit, so the moral act reaches its fruition in its final stage. This is normally the last step and it brings us back to the end originally intended, now not merely desired but attained. "Sensible fruit is what is looked for in the final stage of the tree, and it is perceived with some sweetness. Hence, fruition seems to pertain to the love or the delight which one possesses concerning the final result that is looked for, which is the end." [24]

The twelve steps of the foregoing analysis may be reviewed conveniently in the accompanying *Table of Steps in the Moral Act*. It

Table of Steps in the Moral Act

	INTELLECT	WILL
IN REGARD TO END	I. *Apprehension* of end (intellectus) III. *Judgment* of attainability (judicium de fine)	II. *Wishing* the end (voluntas, velle) IV. *Intention* of end (intentio)
IN REGARD TO MEANS	V. *Deliberation* on means (consilium, deliberatio) VII. *Judgment of Choice* (judicium electionis)	VI. *Consent* to means (consensus) VIII. *Choice* (electio)
IN REGARD TO EXECUTION	IX. *Command* (imperium) XI. *Apprehension* of suitability (perceptio convenientiae)	X. *Use* (usus) XII. *Fruition* (fruitio)

is not necessary that each moral act should follow exactly the pattern of this analysis. The process may be stopped at any point. Cessation may result from the distraction of attention, due to the occur-

[22] *S.T.*, I–II, 11, 2, c.   [23] *S.T.*, I–II, 11, 1, ad 3m.   [24] *S.T.*, I–II, 11, 1, c.

rence of some external event, or because of a will-act resulting from some motivation within the agent. We shall study later the influence of passions, ignorance, moral experience and habits, on such an act. Certain steps may occur at several points in the analysis. Intention, for instance, continues more or less firmly until the final fruition. In this connection, it should be noted that an *actual intention* of the *ultimate end* is not required in every morally good act. It is enough that the agent has thought of God, and so desired Him, as the Ultimate End. Such an intention must be explicitly formed and then remain, at least in the form of a habit, throughout one's moral life. "Just as in the demonstrative sciences the conclusion is not taken rightly, except through a resolution to the first principles, so too, the appetite of a rational creature is not right, except through an explicit appetition of God Himself, either actual or habitual." [25] Of course, we shall see that the virtue of *religion* requires each man to perform some definite acts of intellect and will, in order to satisfy his debt to God.

It should also be noticed, in connection with the fifth and seventh steps (see pp. 60 and 62), that the *Table* offers a simplification of what may be in many moral acts a rather complex process of practical reasoning, terminating in several quite distinct judgments. This process will be studied more thoroughly in Chapters VI and VII; but, to avoid misunderstanding at this point, we may distinguish the following five practical judgments. Prior to deliberation about a given moral problem, the agent with any moral experience knows (1) certain primary and most general principles of morality. These most universal judgments are formed naturally by the human intellect, endowed with the habit of synderesis. [26] The general formula of such a judgment is: "Good should be done; evil avoided." The agent is also possessed of (2) certain universal practical judgments which are the conclusions of moral science and the enactments of positive law. Such a judgment would be: "Stealing is an evil to be avoided." Moral deliberation makes use of both such universal practical judgments, as well as more particular knowledge, in working to a definite decision on a concrete moral problem. In such counselling,

[25] *De Veritate*, q. 22, 2,c.   [26] See Chap. V, pp. 172–177.

the agent may elicit (3) a particular practical judgment which does not yet involve himself, personally. Such a judgment will take the form: "This act of stealing should not be done under these circumstances." This may be called moral conscience (for, in thomistic ethics, conscience may be *objective* and *impersonal*). Next, the agent may make (4) a personal judgment concerning this proposed act. It will take the form: "I should not do this act of stealing under these circumstances." This is the judgment of moral conscience, in the *subjective* and *personal* sense. Such a judgment does not determine the will to choose in accord with it; the agent is free to reject it. We shall discuss later to what extent it is morally obligatory to follow this subjective decision of conscience. Finally, the agent freely makes (5) the judgment of choice (which is the last practical judgment) and it takes the form: "The best choice for me, here and now, under these circumstances, is to omit this proposed act of stealing." (Of course, he may decide, contrary to judgment four: "The best choice for me, under these circumstances, is to do this act of stealing." In this case, he must choose in accord with this judgment, and, since it is contrary to his conscience, it elicits a bad choice and a bad moral act.) The judgment of choice is made by the intellect, under the direct influence of the will; so, this last practical judgment is inseparable from the elective act itself. Free choice is an act of intellect-and-will (studied in the philosophy of man); intellectually, it is this final judgment of preference; volitionally, it is the final and personal adherence of the will to the choice.

Consent (the sixth step) is formally placed after the preliminary process of deliberating on the means, but there is something like a function of consent, in association with the acts of choice and of use. The same thing may be said about fruition; the will may take a delight in the accomplishment of any part of the moral act, even before the whole act is completed.

Since there are few English studies of the details of this analysis, special mention should be made of a recent article: M. Childress, "Efficient Causality in Human Actions," *The Modern Schoolman*, XXVIII (1951) 191–222. It stresses the efficient causality of the will in the moral act.

Voluntariness and the Moral Act

In order to understand the concept of moral imputability, we must now consider two properties of the human act, *voluntariness* and *freedom*, which have a bearing on the degree to which an agent is responsible for his act. We shall first discuss voluntariness, and then freedom.

While all things act, or are moved, for the sake of some end, it is not true that they all move toward or away from their end for the same reason. Some things are of such a nature, as we have seen, that they cannot know what their end is. This is the case with all things below the level of man. Brute animals, plants and inanimate things do not know what they are living for, or working for; hence, they must be directed toward their natural ends by some intelligence which is external to them. Their acts never spring from a source which is wholly interior to them. They cannot be held to account, morally, for what they do; and so, they are not moral agents.

Men, on the other hand, can know the purpose or end of their activity. This makes them the sole, immediate source of some of their actions, and even of certain failures or omissions of actions. This last point should be noticed: "Omission is voluntary, not from an act of the will passing into it, but because it is within the power of the will not to do the act, and also to do it. And therefore, just as an act is called voluntary because it is within the power of the will, so too is the omission of the act." [27] The voluntary situation, then, is found where an agent acts, or omits an action which, in view of the circumstances, should be performed. Voluntariness exists by virtue of an interior appetitive inclination which is exercised according to rational knowledge of an end. Two possibilities in regard to voluntary omission may be noted. First, the moral agent may omit to perform an external act, because he *wants to* omit it. For instance, a man might stand and watch his enemy drown, without making any physical effort to save him. In this case, the agent would omit the bodily act of life-saving, which is called for, by the circumstances; but he

[27] *In II Sent.*, d. 35, art. 3; ed. Mandonnet, II, 907.

would perform the interior will-act of wishing his enemy to die. Here, the agent is voluntary in regard to both the interior and the exterior act. Second, a man might make no effort to save a drowning person, and might *fail to make any will-act* in such a situation. But he should act in such a case, and his failure to act, with his will and with his body, constitutes a voluntary lapse from reason, for which he is morally responsible.[28]

We may then define ⌈voluntariness as: *that property of a moral situation* (either an act or an omission) *whereby action or omission results from a source within the agent and from some knowledge which the agent possesses of the end.*[29]⌋

For a better understanding of this matter, let us consider, now, what *violence* is. ⌈The act of an agent which is caused by a principle external to that agent, is called *coaction*. Such a situation is one of violence. If a man is physically forced to bow before some person, his external, bodily action is caused by violence. But the human will cannot be violated by any type of force. The will is not directly subject to any kind of finite force, either physical or spiritual; it is itself a first, efficient cause; there is no finite efficient cause which can be brought to bear immediately upon the human will. Only final causes work upon the will, and in the world of nature there is no good, or final cause, which compels the will to embrace it. Violence has no direct effect upon the inner act of man's will.[30]⌋ This is an evident conclusion, if we understand what the will is, in thomistic philosophy.

Since the will, itself, is an inclination, from the fact that it is an appetite, it cannot happen that the will wish something and that this be other than *its own* inclination. So, it is impossible for the will to wish something as a result of coaction or violence. . . .[31]

It is precisely at this point that a difficulty might appear, in regard to the teaching of Christian theology, that God is the First Mover of all things. If God moves the human will, and He does, how can we say that the will is not subject to violence? The truth of the matter is that God is more powerful than the will, and can move it. But

[28] Cf. *S.T.*, I–II, 6, 3,c, and ad 2m.
[29] Read: Appendix to Chap. III, Text One: *The Meaning of Voluntariness.*
[30] *S.T.*, I–II, 6, 4,c.   [31] *De Veritate*, q. 22, a. 5,c.

He does not move it from without, by violence, because such an action would not be an action of the will. It would be an action *against the will*. When God moves the will, it is by an impulsion which is in keeping with its nature and therefore from within the will. Just as the natural motions of physical forces are ultimately attributable to God, because He made these things naturally capable of acting in certain ways, so the natural inclination of the human will to the good stems ultimately from God, Who gave it this inclination. Even if God supernaturally inclines the will towards a supernatural good, this will be an inclination added to its nature as will, and not an impulsion destructive of will. For, if God were to destroy the will, He would not force the will to act by violence, since there would be no will, in this case.[32]

With regard to the inner elicited act of the will, violence has no effect upon voluntariness. However, there are human actions which are performed at the command, or under the orders, as it were, of man's reason. It is the work of the intellect to see that such a command is issued in a reasonable way; but it is the work of the will to make this reasonable command effective. Acts so commanded may be done by almost any of the operative potencies of man (with the exception of the vegetative powers); thus, a *commanded act* may be performed by the will, by the intellect, by the sense potencies, and by the motor capacities of the body. In most cases, commanded acts consist of the willing use of man's physical powers. Of course, such acts are voluntary, because they come under the control of the will. So, St. Thomas sums up the point, with sufficient precision for the present, by saying: "An action may be said to be voluntary, in two ways: first, because it is *commanded* by the will, for example, walking or talking; second, because it is *elicited* by the will, for example, the very act of wishing.[33]

Now, these exterior, commanded acts can be directly influenced by force which is external to the moral agent. If I wish to go for a walk, and a bigger man holds me down, I cannot perform the external act of walking because of his use of violence. Yet, I may con-

[32] Cf. *S.T.*, I–II, 6, 4, *ad primum;* and the more thorough discussion in: *De Veritate*, q. 22, a. 8,c.

[33] *S.T.*, I–II, 1, 1, ad 2m.

tinue *to wish* to go for the walk, and nothing can be done by the big fellow to force me to stop wishing it. In such a case, my inner will-act of wishing remains voluntary; but my external act (here, it is a forced omission of the external act of walking) is *against my will;* that is, the external act is rendered *involuntary*, as a result of the big man's violence. Hence, one of the things which makes a human act involuntary, or unwilling, is violence; but this only applies to the commanded act, not to the elicited act.[34]

The foregoing example may be used, also, to illustrate the manner in which another factor, namely *fear*, may modify voluntariness. When it was said above that the big man can do nothing to force my inner act of wishing, one may have thought that he could scare me so much that I would never want to go walking again! Let us now think over the effect of fear on voluntariness.

We should notice two points at the beginning. The first is that fear is a passion, or emotion, taking place in the irascible appetite of the moral agent. This may be recalled from the philosophy of man; it will also be more fully treated, toward the end of this chapter. So, fear is not the same as the violence which may induce it. Fear is an event internal to the moral agent; violence comes from outside the agent. The second point to be remembered is that moral acts are performed in the concrete circumstances of life. They are not universal abstractions, but singular and particular actions.

Now, if we think of this case in an abstract and universal way, we could say that no one, in this life, would *voluntarily* be deprived of the power to walk. But this would mean that such a privation would be involuntary, from the point of view of a general intellectual consideration. However, when we think of the problem, in the concrete conditions which here and now apply to it, the conclusion is different. If the big man threatens to beat me, every time he sees me out walking, I can think the matter over and decide, *willingly* in view of the circumstances, that there is little or no good to attract me in the action of walking under such conditions. So, I may will to stay at home. Here, my will-act is absolutely (*simpliciter*) voluntary. If conditions were otherwise, I would stay at home all the time, only

[34] Read: Appendix to Chap. III, Text Two: *Violence and Voluntariness.*

against my will, *i.e.*, involuntarily. But the conditions are not otherwise. To be practical, I must view things as they are; and, in this
concrete case, my will chooses the greater good, to stay at home and
remain whole. It must be admitted, of course, that I could wish that
things were otherwise. Hence, I am *involuntary* and *voluntary* at the
same time. It is a mixed case, as Aristotle and St. Thomas realized.
But, let us give a simple answer to the question: Do I stay at home
because I want to? The reply must be: I do. This fellow has made
things so difficult, that I now wish to stay at home. This "wish" and
the consequent commanded act of staying at home, both come under
the control of my will and thus my fear of the big fellow does not
make me wholly involuntary.[35]

If we think, briefly, of the more positive case which is traditionally used to illustrate this point, we may understand it better. Consider a merchant on a boat in a bad storm. He decides to throw his
valuable cargo overboard to save his own life. Does he do it voluntarily? Yes, because he values his life more than his goods. Of course,
he does it with some reluctance. He wishes that things were otherwise. But, under these circumstances, he *voluntarily* gives up his
cargo to save his own life. His decision is a moral act; he is simply
voluntary, because he can still control his action; relatively involuntary, because one of the conditions of his action is against his will.[36]

Obviously, if the moral agent is so appalled by threatening circumstances that he loses entirely his ability to reason, and to make a
rational choice, then his action will not be voluntary. If he acts, in
such a condition, his action is much like the instinctive action of a
brute animal. There is, then, no moral problem, provided the agent
did not previously will to be in this condition and provided he does
not later approve his action, if it were objectively bad, or disapprove
it, if it were objectively good. Such cases are very rare; they are
really examples of temporary insanity. We do not call such actions
involuntary; they are simply *not voluntary*. Thus, St. Thomas says:

If the restrictive binding (*ligatio*) of reason by a passion were to proceed
to such an extent that it would no longer remain within the power of the
will to remove this bond (for instance, if one were to become insane as a

---

[35] *S.T.*, I–II, 6, 6,c, and *ad primum*.
[36] Read: Appendix to Chap. III, Text Three: *Fear and Voluntariness*.

result of some passion of the soul), then whatever one would do would not be imputed to him as a moral fault, just as in the case of any other insane person, unless he were voluntary in regard to the beginning of such a passion. For, perhaps the will was able in the beginning to prevent the development of the passion to this extent; just as a homicide done in a state of intoxication is imputable as a fault to the human agent, because the beginning of the state of intoxication was voluntary.[37]

Concupiscence is another kind of passion which must be examined, in this connection. It is a passion of the other sense appetite, the concupiscible. This appetite inclines toward objects known through sensation as goods which are easy to deal with. We know from the philosophy of man that the concupiscible appetite has six chief passions, but the name, concupiscence, may be used to speak of the general tendencies of this potency. It may be noted immediately that concupiscence *may*, in extreme cases, be so sudden and strong that it takes away the use of reason and will. Such acts are *not voluntary*. This does not mean that they are involuntary, that is, against one's will; they are simply unrelated to will.

If concupiscence were to take knowledge away totally, as in the case of people who lost their minds as a result of concupiscence, then it would follow that concupiscence would take away voluntariness. In this case, there would not be involuntariness, for in those who lack the use of reason, there is neither voluntariness nor involuntariness.[38]

In practically all instances, concupiscence does not render the agent involuntary; rather it tends to make the agent voluntary. The reason for this conclusion lies in the very nature of sensual desire, which is what we are talking about. Fear is a passion whose object is an evil, real or apparent. But the object of concupiscence is a good in the sensory order, either real or apparent. The object of the will is an intellectual good. Now, when the will is accompanied by fear, it is, in a way, slowed down in its desire for its good. However, when a concupiscent passion arises, the effect is just the opposite. To the good of reason is added the good of sense. The will is more strongly moved to act, when its object is accompanied by sense desire. Even if the object of sense desire is not in keeping with reason, the will must embrace it voluntarily, provided the agent does not

[37] *De Malo*, q. 3, a. 10,c.   [38] *S.T.*, I–II, 6, 7, ad 3m.

reject it. If he rejects it, he is voluntary; if he embraces it, he is also voluntary.[39] In the conclusion of St. Thomas: "what is done through fear, is, in a way, involuntary; but what is done through concupiscence, is not, in any way." [40]

For the sake of clarity, we may anticipate a point on the general relation of the passions to the rational potencies of man. *Perfect voluntariness* is the name of that subjective condition of the moral agent in which the will gives rise to an act, with full rational knowledge of the end, and of the means to be used in attaining this end. The perfection of the voluntary act is directly dependent on the perfection of the agent's rational knowledge of the end and of the things conducive to the end. Where such knowledge is more or less lacking, the agent is more or less imperfect in his voluntariness. Since brute animals have a certain capacity to adapt their actions to their ends, without precisely knowing what their end is, or what are the proper means, they perform actions which are, in a sense, imperfectly voluntary.[41]

Now, human passions do influence the *perfection* of the voluntariness of the agent. When a passion *precedes* the act of rational deliberation, it tends to becloud and impede the use of reason. Hence, an antecedent passion can diminish the voluntariness of any given act of the moral agent. An act performed, even partly, as a result of passion, is less than perfectly human; it is a partly animal act. If such an act is morally good, it is less meritorious, when it springs from passion, than it would be if resulting from pure reason and will. Conversely, if the act be bad, it will be less blameworthy because of its origin in a passion.

Should the passion follow the act of will, then it cannot diminish the voluntariness of the action. A consequent passion is, in fact, an indication of the strength of the will-act, and so, of its voluntariness. The total goodness or badness of a moral act is increased by a consequent passion.[42]

What is needed for perfect voluntariness, is rational knowledge as

[39] *S.T.*, I–II, 6, 7,c, and *ad primum*.   [40] *Ibid*.   [41] *S.T.*, I–II, 6, 2,c.
[42] *De Malo*, q. 3, a. 11,c; *De Veritate*, q. 26, a. 7,c, and *ad primum*; *S.T.*, I–II, 77, 6 and 7,c. For a more thorough treatment of the influence of passion, see pp. 85–94, of the present chapter.

well as the power to will. It is pretty clear, then, that *ignorance* modifies voluntariness, at least in some cases.

Let us think of the plainest cases first. There is a kind of ignorance *which cannot be avoided* by the moral agent. Such a privation of knowledge may be such that it cannot be known with certitude. Thus, no man can know just how many people are alive on this earth, at any one time; by the time he would have them counted, there would be a change in the actual number. Or, the human agent, through no fault of his own, may not have sufficient education or experience to understand some difficult point of law or of fact. Or, it may be that the knowledge of which the agent is ignorant could be attained but only by an unusual and unreasonably great effort on the part of the agent. Such ignorance is called *invincible*, because it cannot be overcome by the average man. Now, this kind of ignorance is involuntary, and the moral act resulting from it is involuntary, and not subject to blame or praise. St. Thomas usually calls that ignorance invincible, which cannot be overcome by any effort, however great it may be; and he speaks of *morally invincible* ignorance (a term much used by later writers) as ignorance of that which a man is not obliged to know. "But, if ignorance be such that it is altogether involuntary, either because it is invincible, or because it pertains to that which a man is not obliged to know, then such ignorance completely excuses one from wrong-doing." [43]

All other ignorance is *vincible*, that is, a privation of knowledge which the agent can acquire. When ignorance accompanies the performance of a moral action, but is not the cause of the action, it is called *concomitant* ignorance. Of course, ignorance is the *cause* of an action in any case where the act would not be done, if the knowledge (of which the agent is ignorant) were possessed. Consider this example: a man likes another man's topcoat; without knowing his mistake, he takes this coat instead of his own on leaving a restaurant. When he discovers his error, he keeps the coat. It is true that he did not know what he was doing *at the time* of taking the other man's coat. It is equally obvious, however, that his action is voluntary and

[43] *S.T.*, I–II, 76, 3,c.

that he has done something wrong. The mark of his wrongdoing is his failure to return the coat, where that is possible. The whole situation, though not planned by the agent, was not contrary to his will. Hence, we cannot say that he is involuntary in the matter. He is morally responsible for a bad action. Concomitant ignorance does not necessarily take away voluntariness.

A second sort of ignorance is that which is called *consequent*. This kind is *willed by the agent;* so, it follows his will-act. There are two possibilities here. First, the agent may directly wish to remain in ignorance, so that he may plead ignorance as an excuse for what he wants to do. Thus, a man may have heard rumors that there are laws governing the number of ducks which may be shot in certain seasons, but he takes good care not to learn anything about these laws. If he shoots more than the legal number of ducks, he is voluntary in this action. This is what is called *affected* ignorance. Second, the human agent may not directly wish to remain in ignorance, but he may, through his own *negligence*, fail to make the effort to acquire knowledge which he should have. Possibly, at the time of his action, he is so eager to act (because of a passionate, or habitual, inclination) that he does not take care to stop and think whether his proposed act is right or wrong. Or again, he may fail to keep himself informed, beforehand, on the rules and the facts applying to his proposed action. (Thus, a student who knows that the time for examinations is customarily announced on bulletin boards, may simply neglect to read these notices.) Or, the agent may voluntarily do something from which ignorance results, directly or indirectly. (For example, a student who knows that assignments are usually given in class on Fridays, may absent himself from class on this day and so be ignorant of the nature of the assignment.) These various kinds of consequent ignorance do not make the moral action involuntary. The agent is responsible for his ignorance, and the act resulting from such ignorance is voluntary.

This is not to be interpreted to mean that these various kinds of consequent ignorance have the same degree of moral responsibility attaching to them. Direct, affected ignorance increases the voluntariness of the action; hence, it increases the guilt connected with an otherwise bad act. Ignorance associated with ordinary negligence to reason carefully at the time of the performance of an action does not increase the voluntariness, but the act does remain voluntary. Ignorance arising somewhat accidentally, from the fact that an agent was doing something else when he should have been acquiring morally necessary knowledge, may decrease the voluntariness of the action, without removing it entirely. Legal writers distinguish ignorance of law from ignorance of fact, but in the case of consequent ignorance both these types are presumed to be capable of being overcome by the agent and he continues to be, at least partially, responsible for his action.[44]

A third kind of ignorance, considered in relation to the moral act (as are concomitant and consequent ignorance) is called *antecedent* ignorance. This privation of knowledge precedes the moral act. Such ignorance is the cause of the act, in the sense that the agent would not so act if he knew all the circumstances of his action. For instance, an electrician working on a circuit turns on the current and electrocutes a fellow worker, who is not supposed to be working on this circuit. If the electrician has taken all due precautions, and if he is duly sorry for the accidental result of his action, he is not morally guilty of any wrong. His act is not voluntary, because it is not within the power of his will. This is really a case of morally *invincible* ignorance.

We may sum this matter up, by adding that it is not necessary for the average moral agent to know the foregoing analyses in detail. The student of ethics should, for he is studying to be an expert in these matters. But the ordinary person is only required to do what is morally possible. Now, the average agent realizes when he is responsible for an act done through ignorance. He may try to plead ignorance as an excuse for wrongdoing, even when he knows that this is not reasonable. But, within his own mind, the moral agent knows when his ignorance is invincible (this he will discover later, if

[44] The advanced student may consult the very thorough treatment of these types of ignorance, in: *De Malo*, q. 3, a. 8,c.

he is ever worried about his action); and in the case of vincible ignorance, he knows that it does not wholly excuse his bad action. If he
does not, he is subnormal and cannot be held to account for his moral
actions.[45]

In the foregoing, emphasis has been placed on the effects of ignorance on the badness of a moral act. Of course, invincible ignorance
as the source of an objectively good act removes the act from moral
consideration. One is not entitled to moral credit for helping another man, let us say, when he does not, and cannot, know even in a
general way that he is helping him. Such an act is not voluntary. On
the other hand, an objectively good act resulting from concomitant,
vincible ignorance is an act of chance. Thus, I might, through ignorance, leave the water running in my apartment and, unknowingly,
put out a fire in the apartment below me. This benefits the other
tenant and is good for him, but I am not voluntary in regard to this
unknown good result. Consequent ignorance is rather difficult to
conceive in relation to an objectively good act. However, a man
might be ignorant of a law or a fact, because he wants to be or because he does not take the proper measures to keep informed, and if
he acts in accordance with the unknown law or fact, then he does
so by chance and is not voluntary in the matter.

The case of an *habitual intention* is not the same. A trapper may
always leave some food in his cabin, with the intention of helping
any lost person who comes by and needs the food to save his life.
If someone is so saved from death, unknown to the trapper, then the
trapper has done a good act because he had the general, antecedent
intention to help anyone in such a predicament. Even though he
never knows the detailed result of his action of leaving the food, the
trapper has done a voluntarily good action. In general, we may say
that the agent must know something (at least in a broad way) of the
end of his action, before he is entitled to moral praise, or credit, for
the objectively good act.

[45] Read: Appendix to Chap. III, Text Four: *Types of Ignorance;* and Text
Five: *Ignorance and Voluntariness.* Read also: Gilson, E., *Moral Values and
the Moral Life*, pp. 52–60.

Freedom of Choice and the Moral Act

It might be thought that it would be simpler just to say that ethics deals with the *free* acts of man, and thus dispense with the long consideration of voluntariness. Then we could define ethics as the study of the proper use of human liberty and everything would be very clear. However, voluntariness is not identical with freedom.

The voluntary is a genus embracing two species: the *necessary* and the *free*. Man's desire, or wish, for his ultimate happiness is voluntary but not a matter of free choice. The basic and natural inclination of the will toward the absolute good is actualized in the initial will-act, called wishing (*velle*). Strictly speaking, then, man wishes for somethings *as an end*. The act of choice, or election (*electio*), has to do solely with *means* to the attainment of an end. Both are acts of will, and so voluntary; but only choice is free.[46]

Man may *wish* for the impossible; he cannot *choose* the impossible. Thus, many men have wished that they would never die. They have known their wish was impossible of fulfillment. When we choose, we select a certain means or group of means, which are calculated to advance us toward some end. Underlying this choice is the understanding that these are possible means.[47] Freedom for man lies in his ability to reach a decision about the goodness of certain means, in relation to an end, and in his ability to act upon this decision. Part of this process pertains to an intellectual operation, which is called deliberation. Another part belongs to the rational appetite, or will. It is because both intellect and will are involved in human freedom that St. Thomas does not speak, as a rule, of *free will*, but only of free decision, or free choice (*liberum arbitrium*). The following passage explains clearly the difference between a simple act of will, and the more complex act of free choice.

Reason and will are operative potencies which are mutually related according to a certain order. Considered without qualification, reason is prior; though, by reflection, will may become prior and superior, inasmuch as it moves reason. Hence, will can have two acts: one which belongs to it according to its nature, insofar as it inclines toward its own

[46] *De Veritate*, q. 22, a. 13, ad 9m.   [47] *Ibid.*, ad 12m.

WISHING

object, without qualification; and this act is attributed to the will, *simply;* for instance, to wish and to love, although an act of reason is presupposed in regard to this act; and it has another act which pertains to it because of something left in the will from the imprint of reason. For, since it belongs to reason to order and compare, and sometimes comparing and ordering appear in the act of the will, such an act will not belong to the will simply, but in relation to reason. This is the way that intention is an act of the will; since to intend may be seen to be nothing other than, from the fact that one wishes, one tends toward a thing as to an end. And so, to intend is different from to wish, in that the act of wishing tends to the end without qualification, but the act of intending indicates an or- dered relation to the end, because the end is that toward which the means are ordered. For, since the will is moved toward its object as presented by reason, it is moved in different ways, depending on the various ways in which the object is presented to it. Hence, when reason presents something to it, as an absolute good, the will is moved toward it, without qualification (*absolute*); and this is the act of wishing (*velle*). . . . But choice is the act of the will in an ordered relation to reason which makes a comparison of the means as they are interrelated.[48]

Thus, we can say that, if to the original voluntary inclination of the will *deliberation* be added as a prerequisite, then freedom of choice results. This situation does not arise in regard to the initial movement of the will toward the good-in-general, but in the con- sequent moment, when there is something to be done about the end. At this point in the sequence of voluntary acts, choice freely occurs as a result of "intellective appetite." [49]

The truth of the matter is that there is a constant interplay of the intellect and will during the concrete development of the complete moral act in man. Man is not a moral agent simply because of his will, nor simply because of his intellect. The intellect keeps con- sidering the good, more and more definitely, working from the uni- versal to the particular. The will keeps thrusting toward these more and more definite goods, as they are more definitely proposed by reason. The agent comes to the point where he can make a choice of things which are good as means to an already desired end. It is at this point that freedom is greatest, though at any point in the in- tellective-volitive process the agent may freely decide to stop it, or

---

[48] *De Veritate*, q. 22, a. 13,c, et ad 16m.
[49] *S.T.*, I, 83, 3,c; I–II, 14, 6,c; *In VI Ethic.*, lect. 2, ed. Pirotta, p. 378, n. 1137.

to continue it further. Something of the nature of this process should be understood from the consideration of free choice, in the study of the philosophy of man. But ethical theory requires a very precise understanding of the matter, and it is to this analysis that the following section is devoted.[50]

The moral act of man is proximately produced by the will, acting as an efficient cause. Ultimately in the finite order of causes, the whole man is the agent who performs his own actions. However, within man, the potency which is the immediate and active source of moral operations is the will. Now the will acts because it is attracted by the goodness of some end. Thus, the final cause of the will-act moves the will, not efficiently but by attraction. Since such goodness is not perfect, other than in the case of the ultimate end, the will may embrace or reject any given end which is presented to it in knowledge. Here, we find a sort of liberty, or freedom, which does not involve the choice of various means. It is simply that the will may *act*, or *not act*. There are, at this point, but two alternatives, and they are contradictory. To do, or not to do: this is a question for the will. The technical name for this sort of freedom is: *liberty of exercise*.

This may be illustrated by the case of a young person who is just finishing high school. He may decide to go to college, or not to go to college. This contradiction must be viewed as one of ends. That is, going to college must not, at this moment, be considered as a means to some further end—if it were such a means, then the student would have to consider whether or not to seek this end. So, liberty of exercise is a kind of freedom which arises from the moral agent's own power to determine himself to act, or not to act.

Since every moral action must be performed in the concrete, it is necessary that the act be specific. One must not only act; he must do

[50] Read: Appendix to Chap. III, Text Six: *Free Choice and the Voluntary;* Text Seven: *On Human Election, or Free Choice;* and Text Eight: *Freedom and Necessity in Will-Acts.* A very good exposition of the thomistic teaching will be found in: Gerard Smith, S.J., "Intelligence and Liberty," *New Scholasticism,* XV (January, 1941) 1–17; the same article may be read in: *Proceedings of the Amer. Cath. Philos. Assoc.,* XVI, 69–85. Advanced students should read: A. C. Pegis, "Necessity and Liberty," *New Scholasticism,* XV (January, 1941) 18–45; also in *Proc. A.C.P.A.,* XVI, 1–26; and G. B. Phelan, "Person and Liberty," *op. cit.,* 53–68.

a definite kind of act. This determination of the moral act to a definite species, is the work of the intellect as impressed by some specific form, which form comes from the object of the intellect. This is a question of formal causality. The intellect specifies the moral act, so that the act comes to be of a certain definite kind. There is freedom here too, in the choice of the kind of act which will be performed. This is called: *liberty of specification*.

In the example used above, let us say that the student decides to go to college. This is liberty of exercise. But his act cannot be brought to completion, that is, he cannot actually go to college, until he picks out one college and acts on this choice. Thus, if he considers colleges A, B, and C, and decides that B is the best for his purposes, then he may choose B. He is also free to reconsider. But he must reach a specific conclusion to this consideration before he can make full use of his liberty. If he chooses B, then he can go ahead and perform the commanded act of attending this college. It is clear that he cannot attend just "college-in-general." He must go to some school which he picks out from his knowledge of various colleges. Of course, if the college is selected for him by another, he is not free in this act of selection, because it is not his act. But he remains free to accept or reject the proposed selection, if he is a moral agent. In liberty of exercise, there can be but two possibilities; in liberty of specification, there may be any number of plural choices.[51]

Let us think, finally, of the unusual situation of a person who has no more choices to make. Can he be said to be free? Such a person would have to be in the enviable condition of one who is face to face with the Perfect Good. This is the situation in the Beatific Vision. In such a case, there would obviously be no freedom of exercise or of specification, in the limited sense in which these terms are used of an earthly agent. The Perfect Good is a compelling final cause, and there is here no question of means because the ultimate end has been attained. The agent would want no choice, because to choose anything less than God would be irrational. And, in this situation, human rationality is at its peak of perfection.

[51] Read: Appendix to Chap. III, Text Nine: *Liberty of Exercise and Liberty of Specification.*

This then, is a special situation. Ordinary freedom does not apply. Now, earthly freedom has two aspects; it includes the absence of external restraint, and the positive presence of the power of self-determination, in the agent. For the use of this capacity of self-determination, there must be plural possibilities of action. In the Beatific Vision, there is no point in considering plural possibilities, hence the second aspect of human freedom drops out. What remains is the absence of restraint. The agent can and does know the Perfect Good. He desires nothing else. He has reached the apex of freedom; he can now do what he has always wanted most to do. If we put it in terms of happiness, we may understand it better. The agent contemplating God has already attained complete happiness. If we say: "Poor man, he has to do this, he is not free," what we mean is that he is not free, now, to choose unhappiness. Still, he is quite voluntary. The point is that he would not want to choose unhappiness. He is still free, in the sense that he is fully willing to enjoy the greatest Good. It is at this point that voluntariness and freedom coalesce and become concretely identical. The human agent, in the Beatific Vision, is most free and most voluntary. This freedom may be called *eminent liberty*, or perfect *spontaneity*. It is the climax of the perfection of the human person. The blessed, who enjoy the Beatific Vision are eminently free. As St. Thomas explains, in reference to the freedom of one who has taken a vow: "Just as the inability to sin does not diminish freedom, so too, the necessity of a will firmly established upon the good does not diminish freedom, as is clear in the case of God, *and of the blessed*." [52]

The degree of freedom in the agent may vary, from time to time, and from one act to another. As a consequence of this variation in freedom, the degree of imputability of his moral acts will vary. The factors which modify freedom of choice are those which work from within the agent, so as to increase or decrease the autonomy and independence of the judgment of choice. Three such factors may be distinguished: (1) theoretical moral convictions; (2) operative habits; and (3) passions.

[52] *S.T.*, II–II, 88, 4, *ad primum;* see the same point made, in regard to the good angels' inability to sin: *S.T.*, I, 62, 8, ad 3m.

Theoretical moral convictions are those universal judgments about reality, life, the nature of man, the end of man, ethical obligations, and so on, which are formed by the personal reflection of the agent. They make up the content of what is called, "one's philosophy of life." They are to be distinguished from another vast group of opinions (right and wrong) which are acquired rather passively, from instruction in home, school, and Church, from the advice and example of associates, from various organs of popular opinion, such as books, magazines, plays, movies and radio. These latter opinions form part of man's moral knowledge, but on the nonreflective level.

Now, the effect of passively accepted and nonreflected moral views is to reduce the agent to the level of an imitative animal, or even of an automaton. The man who is guided in his moral decisions by the sole norm of popular custom, of what is "fashionable" in society, of what is done by most people, is not really the boss of his own actions. Slavish adherence to moral opinions which have not been critically examined reduces the moral freedom of the agent; it also decreases the imputability of actions which are good or evil, in the objective sense. On the other hand, at least some people (and certainly most of those who study ethics) devote some time to personal reflection on the meaning of life and its consequent obligations. From such thinking, judgments are developed which are not immediately practical but which are easily transformed into personal rules of action. Thus, if one has thought hypothetically about the right to kill an unjust aggressor under certain circumstances and has decided that it is sometimes permitted to take life in this way, then, when actually attacked under these circumstances, one's freedom to deal with the situation is increased. The general effect of reflectively formed moral convictions is to heighten the freedom and autonomy of the moral agent. By such thinking, he lifts himself above the level of an automaton and adds to his natural ability to control his life reasonably.

Operative habits also influence the freedom of the agent. A habit is a rather permanent quality of some operative potency (will, intellect, sense powers) inclining the agent to act in a manner which is more prompt, more accurate, and easier than is possible without such a habit. Now, a habit is an *internal* principle of action and it increases the spontaneity, or voluntariness, of human acts. Both virtues and vices, for instance, add to the natural volitional tendencies of the agent.

But, as far as freedom is concerned, habits are of two kinds: those freely acquired, and those developed under the impact of some external agency, thus, not freely acquired. It is clear that freely acquired habits do not diminish the total freedom of the agent. An act done out of habit (and so, not wholly free at the time of occurrence) is fully imputable to the agent, because he was quite free in developing the habit. There is an exception in the case of the agent who formally repudiates a bad habit and who forms a good intention of never acting in accord with the bad habit. If he does a materially bad act, inadvertently resulting from his vice, his action is not morally imputable. In other words, man always retains freedom of moral choice and action; he never becomes so habituated to vice that he is unable to reform his life.

In the second place, habits acquired involuntarily, not freely, do take away some freedom from the agent, in regard to the acts which they prompt. Thus, habits acquired in early childhood, or as a result of factors over which the agent has had no control, may give rise to some acts which are not free, and not morally imputable. Obviously, if the agent cannot prevent some of these acts from happening, they are not human acts. If he is partially able to control such acts, then they are partially imputable to him. The habit of using blasphemous language is a case in point. Some men may learn such expressions in earliest childhood. It may have become a second nature to them, to speak in such terms. Provided they do their best as adults to avoid such language, their occasional involuntary lapses are not morally imputable because they are not free, human acts.

Finally, *passions* may modify the freedom of the human act. We shall discuss the imputability of passions, in the next section. At this point, we should observe that involuntary passions may occur, before the judgment of choice (these are called *antecedent passions*) and thus influence the making of this judgment. If antecedent passions are so strong that they take away the use of reason, then the result is a complete loss of moral freedom in the consequent act. If antecedent passion simply reduces the use of reason to something less than normal clarity, then the judgment of choice is made with decreased freedom. Most actions arising out of antecedent passion are partly imputable to the agent but not wholly so. Passions which follow the judgment of choice and which are stimulated by this judgment (*i.e., consequent* passions) do not affect the freedom of this choice, but they do indicate an increased voluntariness in the total act.

In retrospect, we should notice that human freedom is far from being perfect. Most moral acts, perhaps, include a choice which is not perfectly free. But an act does not need to be fully free, in order to possess some moral imputability. If we had to judge the degree of praise or blame to be given to any concrete moral act, we would have to examine carefully the amount of freedom exercised by the agent on that occasion. Fortunately, the purpose of ethics is not to enable us to judge the moral acts of other people.

Passions and the Moral Act

Man is a very queer kind of being. He is partly like a brute animal and partly like an angel, but it is a mistake to try to identify him wholly with either animals or angels. So far, our analysis of the moral act has had to do with the central operations which are elicited by intellect and will. Were we to stop with this, our study would fail because it would have neglected one whole metaphysical part of man: his material nature. Just as the operations of sense cognition must be studied, as well as those of intellection, in order to achieve an adequate explanation of man's cognitive functions, so too, the operations of the sense appetites must be considered, as well as those of the intellectual appetite, in order to get a good understanding of the moral functions of the human agent.

In modern language, what we are to examine in this section is the part played by the emotions and feelings of man, in his human actions. In Greek philosophy and in the language of St. Thomas,

these emotions are called *passions*. We will use this name, passion, because it serves to connect this topic with the important metaphysical
theory of potency and act; but there can be no objection to the
modern term *emotion*. It means literally an outgoing movement, and
it even suggests that this is a passive motion. Thus, in the physical
application, we might say that a householder who is put out of his
home for not paying his rent, has suffered an *e-motion;* he has been
moved out. Other names used in the classical tradition of philosophy
(*motus animi*, in St. Augustine, *perturbationes*, *affectiones*, in Cicero) suggest the same notion of an affective movement of human
consciousness.[53]

We know from the philosophy of man that the human agent undergoes a passion of his soul, when he is consciously attracted to, or
repelled by, some object which he knows through his cognitive
senses. These passions, then, are movements of the sensory appetites.
All animals suffer them, whether they be rational or irrational. The
fact that passions also occur in brute animals, is one reason why they
were not included in the previous analysis of the human act. They
are not specific to man; they belong to the human agent by virtue
of his genus (animal), rather than by virtue of his species (rational
animal). This is also, in part, the reason why an important group of
ethicians came to the conclusion that all passions are bad for man.
The Cynics and Stoics in Greek thought, and Spinoza and Kant in
modern philosophy, regarded almost all passions, particularly the
violent ones, as incompatible with the rational nature of man. The
term *apathy* had the meaning, originally, of a highly developed moral
condition, in which the virtuous man had stilled the urgings and disturbances of his animal nature, of his passions. Apart from philosophical theories, we know from experience that a man who acts in
anger, or as impelled by love, is not always reasonable in his action.
It is well for us, at the beginning, to recognize the partial truth of
this Stoic position. There is no doubt that many of man's moral
difficulties arise out of passions. The question that must be faced,
however, is whether it is better for the human agent to try to
eradicate all strong movements of his sense appetites (and thus force

[53] Cf. *S.T.*, I–II, 22, 2, *sed contra*.

one whole part of his human nature to become atrophied, as it were), or to endeavor to assert rational control over his passions (and thus use them in his search for happiness).

Thomistic philosophy is wholly in favor of the latter alternative. From the natural point of view, man's animal nature is not a bad thing. It is metaphysically good, and capable of morally good use. From the supernatural point of view, it is also essentially good; but in man's present condition of existence, the sense appetites are regarded by the moral theologian as disturbing factors in the moral life. To see the reason for this, we must think for a minute of the concept of *original sin*. This is another point in regard to which moral philosophy may gain in clarity and validity by paying some attention to moral theology.

Every serious observer of human nature knows that there is a certain strife between the human flesh and the human spirit. Psychologists know this in its more extreme forms as emotional maladjustment. Novelists make it the theme of nearly all fictional depictions of the growth of character. Jurists, medical doctors, and religious advisers meet this deformity of personality in recurrent cases. It is hard for a natural scientist to understand this universal human defect.

Let us think of the supernatural explanation that is offered by Catholic theology, not with a view to imposing this doctrine as a matter of dogma in ethics, but with the intention of deriving from it a reasonable understanding of man's present moral condition. Before Adam sinned, we are told by moral theologians, he existed in a condition in which his will was subject to God, and his sense appetites were subject to his rational appetite. This is the condition called "original justice." This original condition was based on an especially advantageous relationship of man to God. The peace and rectitude of this original state of Adam were due not only to the innate goodness of the human creature but also to the special ordering of the whole of man's being to its objective ultimate end, God. It was a condition resulting from a special sort of grace, or divine help. Though Adam was at first in this enviable condition, he remained a free agent. It was possible for him to sin and he did. This first sin meant a turning away from the perfection of God, to the imperfect goods of material creation. It broke the chain of ordered human relations to the Perfect Good. The coordination of man's potencies was lost. The animal nature of man was no longer subject to man's rational nature, for the latter had turned away from its end and was henceforth unable to control, with ease, the urgings of the sense appetite. What was lost by Adam was not any essential part of human nature, but the supernaturally induced order which made it much easier for man to do what is right in his original state of rectitude.

How this defect of original justice is transmitted to the descendants of Adam, to all natural men, we need not discuss. Suffice it to say that we have all inherited this privation of original justice, and its consequent lack of subjection of the sense appetites to reason, in somewhat the same way that children rightfully inherit the wealth and the tribulations of their parents. The *formal* character of original sin consists in the de-ordination of man from his supernatural end. The *material* character of original sin is found in the de-ordination, or disorder, in the internal relations of man's powers. It is this material aspect of original sin which is observable to the psychologist. Of course, it cannot be understood without reference to its formal nature. St. Thomas summarizes this teaching, in the following lines:

Because, therefore, the whole admirably ordered integrity of the state referred to, was caused by the subjection of the human will to God, the consequence was, that when the human will was withdrawn from divine subjection, perfect subjection of the inferior powers to the reason, and of the body to the soul, perished. Whence it followed that man experienced in the inferior sensible appetite, inordinate impulses or concupiscence and anger and all the other passions not in accord with the order of reason, but rather in conflict with it, frequently darkening it, and in a manner deranging it. And this is the opposition of the flesh to the spirit of which Scripture speaks.[54]

In order to understand how man, in his present condition, may rationally control his passions, it is necessary now to review briefly the thomistic metaphysics of man. The human soul is immaterial;

[54] *Compendium Theologiae*, Pars Ia, Tr. II, c. 192; transl. by R. J. Dunn (Toronto, 1934), p. 26. Read, in this translation: pp. 17–41.

but it is united with matter to form the one substance, man. Thus, the soul is the substantial form of the human being. From this point of view, the soul is affected indirectly and accidentally, when the body suffers some physical change, or corporeal passion. For instance, when the body suffers a wound, the human agent may lose consciousness, or strength, and so the soul is influenced in a very indirect manner by this type of "suffering," or passion. Here, the disturbance starts in the material part of man, and the resultant modification of the soul is of no direct moral consequence. In plainer and more concrete terms, if a man is injured in an automobile accident, he is affected in his whole being, and so in his soul. But this kind of "passion" is, in itself, neither morally good nor morally bad.

The sort of passion with which we are dealing in ethics is that which starts in the soul itself. The soul is the moving principle (*motor corporis*) of the human body. A cognitive event occurs in the soul, and as a result of this knowledge the soul feels, emotes, tends toward or away from the object known. Such psychically caused emotions are *passions of the soul* (*passiones animales*), and they are of great moral importance. They are described by St. Thomas, in the following lines:

In the second case, passion takes its origin from the soul, but terminates in the body. This is called an animal passion. Examples are found in anger and fear, and others like them. For, this kind of passion is produced by thought and desire within the soul, and is followed by a change in the body, just as any change of a movable thing follows the working of its mover, in every way that the movable thing is disposed to obey the movement of the mover. Thus, the soul itself is said to undergo a passion, accidentally, when the body is affected by some sort of alteration.[55]

As in the case of all animals, man meets with certain things in his environment which are suitable to his physical welfare; and he encounters other things which are unsuitable and need to be avoided. This is the basic distinction between sense goods and sense evils. This division is not yet a moral one. It is also a matter of simple observation, to note that some goods of sense are easy to attain, and some disagreeable things are easy to avoid. Only mild emotions are stimulated by the perception of these simple objects. The concupis-

[55] *De Veritate*, q. 26, a. 2,c.

cible potency is moved by the sense knowledge of these. It may first be simply inclined to favor such a good, and this is the concupsicible passion called *love*. A movement of this potency to attain such an object is *desire;* and *delight or joy* is the resting of the satisfied appetite in the good which is attained. Parallel to these are three passions of the concupiscible appetite in relation to evil objects: *hate* is opposed to love, *aversion* or *flight* to desire, and *sorrow* to joy.

In another distinct category are the passions of the irascible appetite. If the object perceived by sensation is evil, and if it presents some difficulty or hardship to the agent, then he may be moved by the passion of *fear* (when he feels that he cannot overcome the difficulty), or *daring* (if he feels that he can overcome it). On the other hand, when the object is good but difficult to attain, then the agent may experience *hope* (provided he regards the difficult good as attainable), or *despair* (if he feels that it is impossible of attainment). Finally, there is a fifth irascible passion, anger, from which this potency gets its name (*irascibilis*, from *ira*, anger). The reason why anger was chosen to denominate this potency may be understood from the nature of this passion. The emotion of anger may be one of the most vehement of all passions. Anger is a feeling which has always a twofold object: the good and the evil. Suppose Fred has stolen Joe's bicycle and Joe becomes angry. Joe's emotion is a composite of his feeling that he has suffered something *evil* from Fred, and of his feeling that it is *good* to make Fred pay for his wrongdoing. Because both good and evil enter into the composition of the object of this passion, anger has no contrary. So, while there are six chief passions of the concupiscible appetite, there are but five species of irascible passions.[56]

While the foregoing classification of human passions is already an advance in the clarification of the problem of the human emotions, the matter may be further simplified. Not all the passions of the soul are of the same priority and importance in ethics. The irascible passions are for the sake of the concupiscible ones. That is to say, the struggles and vehement feelings inhering in this irascible appetite find

[56] As a review of this classification of the eleven passions, which should be known from the philosophy of man, read: Appendix to Chap. III, Text Ten: *The Eleven Chief Passions.*

their completion and rest in two emotional conditions of the concupiscible power. Ultimately, one feels either emotional success, which is *joy* in the attainment of the good and in the avoidance of evil, or emotional failure, which is *sorrow* arising from inability to attain the good or to avoid the evil. Thus, we may consider all the passions from the point of view of the basic difference between joy and sorrow.[57]

We have already seen that some types of ethics are called hedonistic because they place man's ultimate end in pleasure. The proper way to consider pleasure, as a moral factor, is in connection with the emotion of joy. There is a kind of pleasure which is directly associated with the body and its sensual satisfactions. This is called natural delight (*delectatio naturalis*) by St. Thomas, but in English this might suggest that the other kind of pleasure is unnatural or supernatural, when it is not. Hence, we will name the pleasure in which all animals, including man, share, *animal pleasure*. Then, there is a kind of pleasure which follows rational desire. This includes not only the desire which is elicited by the will but also the *voluntary* movements of the sense appetites. Part of man's difference from brute animals lies in the human ability to incorporate the operations of the sense potencies into the life of reason. For man, the enjoyment associated with the eating of an apple can be on a much higher level than a pig's pleasure in the same operation. Eating an apple when one is hungry is a biological good; it can also be a rational good. What is necessary is simply the intention, actual or habitual, of performing an action useful to the organism and *moderated by reason*. This is the kernel of truth in Moliere's famous dictum: "We must eat to live, and not live to eat." St. Thomas calls only that pleasure which is moderated by reason, *joy* (*gaudium*).

For we take delight both in those things which we naturally desire, when we attain them, and those things which we desire according to reason. But, the name, *joy*, is restricted to the delight which follows reason. Hence, we do not attribute joy to brute animals, but only delight. Now, everything which we desire according to nature, can be desired in accordance with reason; but the converse is not true.[58]

[57] Read: Appendix to Chap. III, Text Eleven: *The Principal Passions*.
[58] *S.T.*, I-II, 31, 3,c.

The pleasures of the body are not, in themselves, immoral. They may, under the mastery of reason, be moral goods. Sense pleasures are among the most vehement which man experiences upon earth. The strongest are those associated with the sense of touch, with sexual desire.[59] This is not to say that pleasures of the body are the best in kind, or the most noble, for man. All delight or pleasure follows upon action, and it is reasonable to conclude that the best pleasure is associated with the most perfect action possible to the agent. Man's most perfect actions are those of the intellect and will. Therefore, the highest type of human pleasure, or joy, is that which comes as a complement to rational activity.[60]

To try to consider pleasure as an end in itself (*bonum honestum*), as hedonistic ethicians do, is to give up the possibility of ranking pleasures in their degrees of nobility. For, within pleasure itself, there is no satisfactory principle of specification. Neither vehemence of feeling, nor duration of feeling, nor any such determinant, enables the moralist to set one type of pleasure above another. Acts and passions are specified by their objects, and the objects of the passions are presented (as formal not material objects) by the activity with which they are associated. This is why St. Thomas places man's greatest joy in the Beatific Vision.[61]

Sorrow is the passion directly contrary to joy. Pain (*dolor*) is the name of the low-grade passion suffered by all animals, including man, in the face of a sense good which has not been attained, or a sense evil which has not been avoided. Pain is the natural, or animal, passion opposed to animal pleasure. But sorrow is the name of that passion of the human being, who is saddened by his lack of success and who knows this situation by his intellect, or by the interior senses. We may say, then, that sorrow is the kind of pain which is peculiar to the rational animal. "Just as sorrow is one species of pain, so is joy one species of pleasure." [62]

Psychologically and biologically, sorrow has many bad effects. When extreme and uncontrolled, it impedes the work of reason by diverting the agent's attention, as in the case of physical pain. Sor-

---

[59] *Ibid.*, a. 6,c, and ad 3m.   [60] *S.T.*, I–II, 34, 3,c.
[61] *Ibid.*   [62] *S.T.*, I–II, 35, 2,c.

row also disturbs the work of the other human powers and, more than all the other passions, may disrupt the balance of bodily good health. The very name, insanity, a condition in which uncontrolled sorrow may end, suggests a lack of health (*in-sanus*, not healthy).[63] The natural means for the combating of sorrow is joy. The agent's attention must be turned away from the evil to the good. But, from the moral point of view, the agent needs above all to be reasonable. Sorrow is not necessarily a moral evil. It may be turned to good purposes. This is not to say that sadness can be a moral end in itself (*bonum honestum*); turned to good use, such as the avoidance of moral evil, it becomes a morally good means (*bonum utile*).

In general, then, the moral value of the passions of the soul is related to the human act in much the same way as is any operation of man, exterior to the elicited operations of intellect and will. Considered in themselves without reference to the ordering of reason and will, the passions of the soul are neutral in regard to moral good and evil. When they become voluntary, that is capable of rational regulation, the passions are subsumed under the broad nature of the whole human act. Then they are of moral consequence.

Antecedent passion may be the partial cause of the moral act. Such passions cause the act to be less voluntary, by interfering to some extent with the clarity of rational judgment. An otherwise good act is less good, if it springs from uncontrolled passion, than it would be if dictated by reason. Thus, while it is good to do a work of charity because of a feeling of pity for the unfortunate, it is much better to do it because of rational motives, such as the recognition of the basic equality of all human beings in the moral sphere. A morally bad action is also less voluntary, and so less evil, if caused in part by an uncontrollable passion.

Consequent passion is that movement of the sense appetites which is either permitted or chosen by the reasoned will of the agent. Such passion, when not deliberately cultivated, is at least a sign of the intensity of the will-act, and so of its greater voluntariness. When it is deliberately encouraged by the reason and will of the agent, consequent passion increases the total voluntariness of the human act,

---

[63] *S.T.*, I–II, 38, art. 1–4, inclus.

making the human act better or worse, depending on whether it is fitting or unfitting in regard to reason.[64]

Two of the great cardinal virtues are devoted to the work of bringing the emotional movements of man under the sway of reason. In the later study of temperance and fortitude, with their associated virtues and vices, we shall study the moral aspects of the passions in greater detail. For the present it is enough to understand the great need, throughout the whole of the structure of the human act, for rational control. This is to say that the morally good man must regulate all his voluntary actions by reference to right reason. It is the purpose of the next chapter to show how reason is the regulative principle of the moral order.

Circumstances and the Concrete Moral Act

It must always be kept in mind that a moral act is a definite event performed by a human agent under singular conditions. Some of these conditions may constitute part of the very essence of the moral act. Thus, it is essential to the act of stealing, that the thief take something *which belongs to another*. Without the last condition, it would not be this kind of act. But there are some other conditions which are outside the essence of the moral act, yet which are so closely related to it that they modify its moral character. Such contiguous conditions are said to be *circumstances* of the moral act.

In the physical world, we find the original application of the term, circumstances. When a physical change, or motion, occurs, there may be some motions around the place of the central motion. So, a falling stone may be accompanied by air movements, may be deflected by the branch of a tree, and may cause a splash and waves in the water on which it falls. These accompanying motions "stand around" the original motion, and this is the simple, bodily connotation of the word, *circumstance*. So, in regard to place, a thing is said

[64] Read: Appendix to Chap. III, Text Twelve: *Morality of the Passions*. Read also: Gilson, *Moral Values and the Moral Life*, pp. 91–133. Some useful information on the relation of the passions to the human will may be found in: Baker, R. D., *Thomistic Theory of the Passions and their Influence upon the Will* (Notre Dame, Ind. 1941), pp. vii–147 (Univ. Dissert.).

to be a circumstance (*circum stare*), when it is outside an object but touching it, or near it in place. Now, the words which we use to speak about immaterial things are usually transferred from our descriptions of material things. This is the case, here. The circumstances of a moral act are those conditions outside the substance of the act, which touch it in some way. We have seen a similar situation in the metaphysical relation of accidents to substance. Hence, another way of saying this is to call the circumstances the "accidents" of which the human act is the "substance."

One might object that there is an infinite number of conditions associated with the concrete action, and so it is not possible to take all into consideration. However, not all adjacent conditions are morally pertinent. It is necessary to use one's reason, in sifting out the morally important from the morally unimportant. Say, for instance, a man has bled to death as a result of being stabbed by his son with a blue-handled knife. The reasonable person will understand that the facts, that the killer was the victim's son, that the man died a lingering death, that he was stabbed, not injured by chance, are pertinent details. But he will also realize that the color of the handle of the knife is of no moral importance. Hence, only certain details associated with the action are significant in ethics. These details, to the extent that they are known, or should be known, by the agent, are the moral circumstances. They are things which must be considered by the human agent before he can reach a reasonable decision as to whether he should act or not, or in this way or that way.

To bring some order, and so science, into this welter of circumstantial conditions, the ancient moralists tried to make lists of the different *types* of moral circumstances. In connection with his discussion of ignorance and voluntariness, Aristotle enumerated the kinds of circumstances, of which the agent might be in ignorance. This list has had an important influence on ethical theory. It includes these six kinds of circumstances: *who* the agent is, *what* he is doing, *on what* he is acting, *with what* instrument, *for what* purpose, and *how* the action is done.[65] Later, Cicero divided the circumstances of

---

[65] *Nic. Ethics*, III, 1, 1111a3–8.

the moral act into seven classes, under the headings: who, what, where, by what means, why, how, and when.[66] With these lists as a basis, St. Thomas was able to make a more simple and orderly theory.[67]

St. Thomas saw that what is necessary to a moral circumstance is that it "touch" the act in some way. Hence, to understand the kinds of circumstance, we must know the different ways in which they "touch" the moral act. These ways are three. (1) Some circumstances touch the very performance of the act; this may be in terms of the quantity of time or space involved, or in terms of the quality of the action (that is, lightly or with force, the *way* the action is done). (2) Other circumstances touch, or pertain to, the effect of the moral act; this type will pertain to the material object of the act, whether it is large or small, for instance. (3) Finally, there is a group of circumstances touching the cause of the act; these may pertain to the final cause (why the act is done), to the material cause (upon whom or what it is done), to the principal efficient cause (who does it), or to the instrumental efficient cause (by what means).

To illustrate this teaching, let us think of the following case, in which the circumstances are mentioned in the order of the previous analysis. The reader may pick them out as we go along. A soldier volunteers to destroy an enemy ammunition depot. He (1) sets time bombs so that they will explode at dawn, when an attack will be made; and he puts them all around the ammunition dump; he also uses very big bombs, to make sure that there will be nothing left of the ammunition. He (2) places his bombs so that they will destroy not only the ammunition, but also the storage facilities and the trucks which might be used to get more ammunition. Finally, he (3) does this because he wants to do his part in winning the war; he does it knowing that he is going to destroy the enemy guards as well as the ammunition; he does it as a soldier, not a private citizen; he does it with a type of bomb which releases poisonous gas, killing all enemy personnel within a distance of five miles. There is no suggestion in this illustration that the soldier has done a morally bad

[66] *De Inventione Rhetorica*, I, 24.   [67] *S.T.*, I–II, 7, 3,c.

action. In fact, as described it may be a justifiable action. But, if an important circumstance is varied, it can become a bad action. Suppose, the soldier volunteers to do the job to get even with an enemy for the death of his brother in battle. This motive, of private revenge, will make the action bad, because of the circumstance of a bad end of the agent.

Not all types of circumstance are of the same degree of importance. The *end* is by far the most important circumstance. To avoid misunderstanding, we should observe that the end which is a circumstance is not the end which gives the moral act its original species —but another end added to the act. The original specific end of an act of fortitude is the *good* of a courageous action. To this, the agent may add his own purpose; he may act with fortitude, *to save his country*. This additional end gives a new species to the moral act. It becomes an act of patriotism, as well as of fortitude. As St. Thomas says: "Though the end is not of the substance of the act, it is, however, its principal cause, because it moves the agent to do the act. So, the moral act gets its species chiefly from the end." [68] To see this point, we could think of a case of ignorance of the end of the work. Suppose, a country girl comes to the city and is employed in copying the names and addresses of wealthy people. She does not know that the list she so carefully makes is to be used to swindle these people. That this is the real purpose of her work, is a circumstance of which she is ignorant. Her ignorance is antecedent and, let us say in view of her rusticity, invincible. She is not guilty of a moral fault. However, if she learns of this circumstance, she cannot continue with her job and be a good girl.

The second important circumstance is the *material object of the act*. Sometimes this is a person, sometimes a thing. Morally, it is the same *kind* of act to steal five cents and to steal a thousand dollars. But the second is much worse than the first, because of the larger amount of money involved. To kill a man without justification is bad enough. To kill a good president of one's country is more reprehensible. Yet, in these two cases, the difference lies in a change

[68] *S.T.*, I–II, 7, 4, ad 2m; cf. *In III Ethic.*, lect. 3; ed. Pirotta, pp. 143–144, nn. 420–423.

of one circumstance, the nature of the object on which the act is done.[69] The material on which one works is the object of the external act. The end is the object of the internal, will-act.[70]

The other kinds of circumstance vary in moral importance, depending on their bearing on the end and the material object. So, to kill a man with very cruel means, would seem to be related to the end of the agent. The bad means indicate an intention to punish the victim severely. On the other hand, variations of time and place appear to be more nearly related to the material object. To steal from a private home is bad, but to steal the same article from a church may be worse. It is a variation in the circumstance of place which affects the character of the material object stolen. This modification in circumstance may result in a change from simple theft to sacrilegious theft.[71]

Circumstances are of interest at this point as parts of the complex organism which is the moral act. They adorn and qualify the act in an accidental, but real, way. It is not necessary to remind the reader that, when we speak of them as accidents of which the central act is the substance, we are using both substance and accident analogically. The point is simply that circumstances do not form part of the essence of the act but they manifest its peripheral contacts with the field of reality surrounding it. The precise manner in which they affect the goodness or badness of the act will be treated in Chapter IV.

The complete moral action of man has been treated in the foregoing from the point of view of various factors, internal and external to the agent, which may affect its moral quality. Let us remember that the will is not one moral agent, the intellect another, and the sense appetites a third. The whole man is the one real agent. Each of his moral actions is an integral unit, composed of various moments of understanding, volition, emotion and even physical activity—but unified in concrete performance. This whole action must be judged as a unit in a moral evaluation.[72]

---

[69] S.T., I–II, 7, 4, ad primum.   [70] In III Ethic., lect. 3; p. 144, n. 423.

[71] Read: Appendix to Chap. III, Text Thirteen: The Important Moral Circumstances; Text Fourteen: Three Types of Moral Circumstance.

[72] Read: Klubertanz, "The Unity of Human Activity," The Modern Schoolman, XXXVII (1950) 75–103.

Summary of Chapter III

The moral act of a human agent is essentially one operation which includes analytically distinguishable moments of intellection and volition, in relation to the end, the means, and the execution of the act. Twelve such moments, or steps, of the elicited acts of intellect and will are summarized in the *Table of Steps in the Moral Act*. Voluntariness is the most significant characteristic of man's moral act. An action is voluntary when it comes under the possible control of the will; even an omission of action may be voluntary in this sense. Involuntary means against the will. Not-voluntary means outside the control of the will. For an action to be perfectly voluntary, the agent must not only *will* the action, without any repugnance, but he must *know* that the action is directed toward a given end. Elicited acts of the rational potencies (intellect and will) as well as commanded acts of all the human powers capable of being directed by reason may be voluntary actions. Violence is the characteristic of an action which the agent is forced to do, or omit, because of some efficient cause acting from outside the agent. Three internal factors which influence the degree of voluntariness of a human action are fear, concupiscence, and ignorance. Voluntariness is not coextensive in meaning with freedom, for some voluntary actions (*e.g.*, the wishing of an end impossible of attainment) are not simply free. Freedom of choice applies to means, not to ends. Liberty of exercise means freedom to do or not to do something. Liberty of specification means freedom to do, or omit, something in a variety of noncontradictory ways. Moral passions are stimulated by the sense perception of physical objects which may be helpful or harmful to the agent's physical well-being. When capable of being controlled by reason and will, passions become part of the moral act, broadly considered. Joy and sorrow are morally significant passions because they indicate whether or not the agent is in favor of, or opposed to, an otherwise good or bad action. Antecedent passion may decrease voluntariness; consequent passion leaves the act voluntary and may increase voluntariness. Circumstances are those con-

ditions immediately surrounding the concrete moral action, affecting
its moral value in some morally significant way. The two most important circumstances are the *end*, when it is distinct from the
formal object of the action, and the *material object* on which the
act is performed. A proper judgment of the morality of an action
must be based on a reasonably complete knowledge of the morally
pertinent circumstances. Throughout this chapter, it is well to stress
the essential unity of each moral act; such an act is not a mere
aggregation of the activities of distinct agencies but is *one action*
of *one agent*, the man who understands, wills, and feels in regard to
the one thing which he proposes to do, or is doing.

Appendix to Chapter III

¶ TEXT ONE: *The Meaning of Voluntariness.* Voluntariness must
be present in human acts. To show this, we must consider that the
principle of some acts is *within* the agent, or *within* that which is
moved, but the principle of other movements or acts is *outside*. For,
when a stone is moved upwards, the principle of this movement is
outside the stone; but, when it is moved downwards, the principle
of this movement is in the stone itself. Now, some beings which are
moved by an inner principle move themselves; others do not. For,
since every agent or moved thing acts, or is moved, because of an
end, as has been said before, those things are perfectly moved by an
inner principle, in which there is some inner principle by which
they are not simply moved but by which they are moved to an end.

Now, in order that something be done for the sake of an end, some
knowledge of the end is required. Therefore, whatever being so
acts, or is moved, by an inner principle that it has some knowledge
of the end, possesses within itself the principle of its own act, not
only enabling it to act, but also enabling it to act *for an end*. And, in
regard to that which possesses no knowledge of the end, even though
there be in it a principle of action or of movement, the principle of
action or of movement for the sake of an end is not [wholly] within
it, but in some other being, from which the principle of its move-

ment to the end is received. Hence, things of this kind are not said to move themselves, but to be moved by other things.

But, those beings which do possess a knowledge of the end, are said to move themselves; for there is a principle in them, not simply to act but to act for the sake of an end. Therefore, since both factors come from an inner principle, namely, that they act, and that they act for the sake of an end, the movements and acts of these are called *voluntary*. Indeed, this is the meaning of the word voluntary: *that motion and act be from a thing's own inclination.* Hence it is, that the voluntary is said, in the definitions of Aristotle [*Ethic. Nic.*, III, 1, 1111a28] and of Gregory of Nyssa [St. Thomas is referring to Nemesius, *De natura Hominis*, c. 32; PG 40, 728] and of Damascene [*De fide orthodoxa*, II, 24; PG 94, 953], to be not only that, "whose principle is from within," but they add, "with knowledge." Hence, when man knows the end of his work to the greatest degree, and moves himself, then the voluntary character of his acts is present to the greatest degree. (*S.T.*, I–II, 6, 1,c.)

¶ TEXT TWO: *Violence and Voluntariness.* Violence is directly opposed to the voluntary, as it also is to the natural. For, it is common to the voluntary and the natural that both arise from an inner principle, but the violent action is from an outer principle. And, because of this, just as violence does something against nature, in things which lack cognition, so it does something against will, in things capable of knowing. Now, what is against nature is said to be unnatural. Similarly, what is against will is said to be involuntary. Hence, violence does cause involuntariness. [*Ad primum*] The involuntary is opposed to the voluntary. Now, it has been said above that voluntary is predicated not only of the act which immediately pertains to the will, but also of the act which is commanded by the will. Therefore, in regard to the immediate act of the will, as has been said above, violence cannot work upon the will. But, in regard to the commanded act, the will can suffer violence. And violence produces involuntariness, in regard to this latter act. (*S.T.*, I–II, 6, 5,c and *ad primum*.)

¶ TEXT THREE: *Fear and Voluntariness*. Since the good is the object of the will, a thing is voluntary in the same way that it is good. Now, it happens that a thing may be considered good in a general way, but because of some particular circumstance, it may be bad. Thus, to generate offspring is good, but to do this with one who is not one's wife, is bad.

Similarly, it happens that a thing considered evil, from a general point of view, may nevertheless become good because of some particular circumstances. Thus, killing is in itself evil, but to kill a man who is dangerous to society may be good.

Because actions concerned with singulars are judged good or evil (and consequently, voluntary or involuntary), in an absolute way, when the circumstances have been considered, but in a relative way, they are considered in an abstract, general way, therefore those things which are done from fear, when considered *generally*, are bad and involuntary, but if they be considered in the light of their singular circumstances, then they are good and voluntary. Thus, to throw goods in the sea, considered in itself, is bad and not voluntary. But, *in a given case*, it is good and voluntary. Hence, the Philosopher in the *Ethics* (III, 1, 1110a12) says that acts of this kind are a mixture of the voluntary and the involuntary. Absolutely considered, they are voluntary; but relatively, from the necessity of what is done, they are involuntary. (*Quaest. Quodl.*, V, q. 5, a. 10,c.)

¶ TEXT FOUR: *Types of Ignorance*. One kind of ignorance wholly excuses from wrongdoing (*peccatum*); another kind, however, partially alleviates it; and still another kind neither excuses wholly, nor alleviates partially. To make this clear, it should be noted that a threefold division of ignorance may be made.

First, on the part of the knower himself: there are some things which *can* be known by the agent, and ignorance of these is called *vincible*, or *affected*; and there are other things which he *cannot* know, and this is called *invincible* [ignorance]. In the case in which ignorance applies to things which can be known by the agent who is ignorant, there are two possibilities: either (i) it is of something which, *in itself*, lies within the knowing power of the agent, as in the case of the man who is ignorant of any precept which he could know immediately; or (ii) it comes within his power, *in virtue of its cause*, though not in itself, as appears in the case of the intoxicated man, for the intoxication which causes his ignorance was within his power, but not the consequent ignorance, since his use of reason is obstructed.

Second, a division of ignorance is made from the point of view of the knowable object. For, there is a kind of ignorance (a) of that which the agent is obliged to know; this is called, according to the Philosopher, *universal* ignorance, and according to the legal experts, *ignorance of the law (juris)*. This varies with different people, for there are some things which one man is obliged to know and another man is not obliged to know. Another kind of ignorance is (b) of that which the agent is not obliged to know, and this is concerned with the knowledge of the particular circumstances of an act. The Philosopher calls it *particular* ignorance, and the lawyers *ignorance of fact*.

A third division is made in relation to the act. For, one kind of ignorance (1) is that which is the cause of the act; for, if one were not ignorant, one would not do it; and in this case one is said to sin *through* ignorance, and the mark of this [kind] is actual repentance. And another kind of ignorance (2) is that which is not the cause of the act but which is accidentally related to the act; and, according to this, as the Philosopher says in the third book of the *Ethics* (c. 2), one is not said to act through ignorance, but *while* ignorant. Hence, in such an act, he is not repentant. For, example, a man, believing that he is making love to one woman, actually does so to another woman, to whom he would have made love anyhow, even if he were not ignorant of her identity. Still another kind of ignorance (3) is that which sometimes follows upon the affective aspect of sin. For instance, due to the concupiscence associated with a sin, which the will does not repress, the rational judgment concerning a particular and proposed action is swallowed up. This is what is referred to in the fourth book of the *Ethics* (c. 4), when it is said that pleasure corrupts the prudential judgment. This is *ignorance of choice (ignorantia electionis)* and it is in this way that every bad person is called ignorant. (*In II Sent.*, d. 22, q. 2, 2,c; ed; Mandonnet, II, 559–561.)

¶ TEXT FIVE: *Ignorance and Voluntariness.* Ignorance can cause involuntariness in the same way that it takes away the knowledge which is a prerequisite to voluntariness, as has been said above (q. 6, a. 1). However, not every kind of ignorance takes away this kind of knowledge. Therefore, it should be understood that ignorance is related to the act of will, in three ways: concomitantly, consequently, and antecedently.

Ignorance applies to the action, *concomitantly*, in such a way that, even if the knowledge were possessed, the act would nevertheless be done. For, then, ignorance does not lead to the wish that it be done, but it happens that, at the same time that something is done, something is ignored. This is the case in the example given [in the third objection], that is the case of a man who wishes to kill his enemy but does so in ignorance, thinking that he is killing a deer. Such ignorance does not cause involuntariness, as Aristotle observes [*Ethic. Nic.*, III 1, 1110b25], because it does not cause anything that is repugnant to the will; but it does make the act *not-voluntary*, for that of which one is ignorant cannot be actually wished.

Ignorance is related *consequently* to the will, by virtue of the fact that it is voluntary. This happens in two ways, according to the two types of voluntariness given above (q. 6, a. 3,c). In one way, the act of will carries over into the ignorance, as in the case of the man who wishes to be ignorant, either to have an excuse for sin, or so that he may not be restrained from sinning, as is said in Job 21:14, "We do not wish the knowledge of Thy ways." This is called *affected ignorance*. Ignorance is called voluntary, in a second way, when it applies to that which a man can and should know. For, in this case, not to act and not to wish, are called voluntary, as has been said (q. 6, a. 3). Ignorance is spoken of in this way, either when one does not actually think of what he can and should consider, and this is *ignorance from a bad choice*, arising from passion or habit; or, when a man does not take care to acquire the knowledge which he should have; and in this way, ignorance of the universal principles of moral law, which one is obliged to know, is called voluntary, for it arises from negligence. Since this [consequent] ignorance is voluntary in one or the other of the preceding ways, it cannot, absolutely considered (*simpliciter*), cause involuntariness. However, relatively considered (*secundum quid*), it does cause involuntariness, in the sense that it precedes a movement of the will to perform an act which would not be done were the knowledge present.

Ignorance is related to the will *antecedently*, when it is not voluntary and yet is the cause of an act of will, which would not otherwise have been made. This is the case when a man is ignorant of some circumstance of an act, which [circumstance] he was not expected to know, and because of this he does something which he would not have done, had he known; for instance, a man, after having taken all necessary precautions and being unaware that there is anyone going along the road, shoots an arrow which kills a passerby. Such ignorance does cause involuntariness, absolutely. (*S.T.*, I–II, 6, 8,c.)

¶ TEXT SIX: *Free Choice and the Voluntary*. The genus to which election (choice) belongs, is the voluntary, because the latter is always predicated of election and of more than that. Hence, he (Aristotle) says, first of all every act of election is a kind of voluntary act; but election and voluntariness are not wholly the same, for the voluntary is of greater extension. He proves this by two lines of reasoning:

Children and other animals share in voluntariness itself [*i.e.*, imperfect voluntariness], insofar as they operate by their own spontaneous movements. But they do not share in the act of election, for they do not operate as a result of deliberation, which is required for election; therefore, the voluntary is of greater extension than is election.

We call those things, which we do *suddenly*, voluntary, for their principle lies within us. But they are not said to be according to choice (*electio*), since they are not done as a result of deliberation. Therefore, the voluntary applies to more than does choice.

[After showing that choice, or election, is not concupiscence, nor anger, nor opinion, St. Thomas continues:] Aristotle says, first of all, that election is not the will-act, either; though it may seem to be near to the will-act. For both pertain to the one potency: namely, to the rational appetite, which is called will. But will-act (*voluntas*) is the name of the act of this potency, in relation to the absolute good. Election, however, is the name of the act of the same potency, in relation to the good which belongs to our operation, through which we are related to some definite good. For, election is not said to apply to impossible things, because it refers to our operation. And, if anyone says that he chooses impossible things, he will seem to be a fool. But the will-act [*i.e.*, the simple *wish*] can apply to this kind of goods, even to the impossible, for it is concerned with the absolute good. Thus, one may *wish* not to die, which is impossible according to the conditions of this corruptible life. Therefore, election and the will-act are not the same.

Aristotle says that the will-act is more concerned with the end, than with the means to the end. For, we wish the means to the end, for the sake of the end. Now if one thing is for the sake of another, the other is more important. But election is solely concerned with the means to the end, not with the end itself. For, the end is taken as the basis, as already having been determined. The means to the end are investigated by us so that we may deal with them in regard to the end. Thus, we chiefly *wish* health, which is the end of medical treatment. But we *choose* the medicines by means of which we may be made healthy. Similarly, we wish to be happy, which is the ultimate end; and we say that we perform the act of wishing, in regard to it. But it is not fitting to say that we choose to be happy. Therefore, choice (or election) is not the same as the will-act. (*In III Ethic.*, lect. 5; ed. Pirotta, pp. 150–152, nn. 434–446.)

¶ TEXT SEVEN: *On Human Election or Free Choice.* Some people have claimed that the will of man is moved of necessity in the choosing of something; however, they did not maintain that the will is forced. For, not everything that is necessary is caused by violence, but only that whose principle is from without. Hence, some natural movements are found to be necessary and not from violence. For, violence is opposed to the natural, as it is to the voluntary, since the principle of both is from within, while the principle of the violent is from without. However, this opinion is heretical; it takes away the essence of merit and demerit in human acts. It does not seem to be meritorious or demeritorious, to act necessarily and in such a way that one cannot avoid it. So, this is to be reckoned among the extraneous opinions of philosophy, since it is not only contrary to faith but subverts all the principles of moral philosophy.

For, if there be nothing free in us, and if we are moved by necessity in willing, deliberation is taken away, and also exhortation, precept and punishment, praise and blame—which are the subject matter of moral philosophy. Now, opinions of this kind, which destroy the principles of any part of philosophy, are called extraneous positions. For instance, "that nothing is moved," destroys the principles of physical science. Some men have been induced to maintain positions of this kind, partly because of impudence (*protervia*), partly because of sophistical reasonings which they could not solve, as is said in the fourth book of the *Metaphysics* (c. 3, 1005b4).

To get at the clear truth of this question, one should first consider that, just as there is some principle of the proper acts of other things, so also is there in the case of men. Now, this active, or motive, principle in men is properly the intellect and will, as is stated in the third book *On the Soul* (c. 10, 433a10–15). And this principle is partly like the active principle in physical things, and is partly different from it. It is like it, in this way: just as there is in physical things the form which is the principle of action, and also the inclination associated with the form, which is called natural appetite and from which action follows, so too, in man there is the intellectual form, and the inclination of will associated with the apprehended form, from which the exterior action follows. But the difference lies in this: the form of the physical thing is a form individuated by matter, hence the inclination associated with it is determined to one objective (*determinata ad unum*), but the form apprehended by the intellect is universal and many things can be comprehended under it. Hence, since actions belong in the order of singular things, among which there is nothing equivalent to universal potency, the inclination of the will remains in an undetermined relationship to many things (*ad multa*). It is just as if an architect conceives the form of a house universally, and as different shapes of houses are comprehended under it, his will can be inclined to the actual building of a house which is square, or round, or of some other shape.

But the active principle in brute animals occupies a middle place between these two. For the form apprehended through sensation is individual, just like the form of the physical thing, and so an inclination to one act follows from it, just as in physical things. However, the same form is not always perceived in sensation, but now one and again another (but it is the same in physical things, for fire is always hot). For instance, there may be now an enjoyable form, and again a painful one. Hence, at times one flees, at other times one seeks. In this, it [the form apprehended in sensation] is like the active human principle.

Secondly, we should consider that any potency is moved in two ways: in one way from the side of the subject, in another way from the side of the object. On the part of the subject, vision is made more or less clear by a change in the disposition of the organ. And, on the part of the object, vision sees a white thing at one time, and a black thing at another time. The first change pertains to the very exercise of the act, namely, that it be done or not be done, or that it be done in a better or worse way. But the second change pertains to the specification of the act, for the act is specified by the object.

Now, we should consider that the specification of the act of physical things comes from the form; but the act of exercise comes from the agent which causes the motion. Now the mover acts for the sake of the end. Hence, it follows that the first principle of motion, from the point of view of the exercise of the act, comes from the end. But, if we consider the objects of the will and intellect, we find that the object of the intellect is the first principle in the order of formal cause, for its object is being and the true; but the object of the will is the first principle in the order of final cause, for its object is the good under which all ends are included, just as all apprehended forms are included under the true. Hence, the good itself, insofar as it is a certain form capable of being apprehended, is contained under the true as a definite, true thing. And the truth itself, inasmuch as it is the end of the intellectual operation, is contained under the good as a definite, particular good.

Therefore, if we think of the movement of the potencies of the soul, from the viewpoint of the exercise of the act, then the principle of the motion comes from the will. For, the potency to which the principal end pertains always moves into act the potency to which the means to that end pertain. Just as the military man moves the maker of bridles to do his work, so does the will move itself and all the other potencies. For, I understand because I will to; and similarly, I use all my potencies and habitus because I will to. That is why the Commentator [Averroes] defines habitus [*In Aristotelis De Anima*, III, 3; ed. Venetiis, 1550, t. VI, fol. 169v, line 22] as, "that which one uses when one desires."

So also, to show that the will is not moved of necessity, it is required that we consider the movement of the will both in regard to the exercise of the act, and in regard to the determination of the act, which latter is from the object. In regard to the exercise of the act, it is first of all evident that the will is moved by itself; just as it moves the other potencies, so does it move itself. Nor does it follow, on account of this, that the will is both in potency and in act in regard to the same thing. Just as man moves himself toward knowledge, intellectually, by the way of discovery (inasmuch as he proceeds from one thing that is actually known to something unknown, which was merely in potency to be known), so also from the fact that man actually wishes one thing, he moves himself to wish something else, actually. For instance, from the fact that he wishes health, he moves himself to wish to take a drink of medicine: for, from the fact that he desires health, he begins to take counsel concerning those things which lead to health, and then having finished the process of self-counselling, he wishes to take the drink. So, counsel precedes the act of willing to take the drink, and yet it proceeds from the wish of the agent who wills to take counsel. Therefore, since the will moves itself by counsel (and counsel is a certain investigation which is not demonstrative but concerned with alternatives), the will does not move itself of necessity.

However, since the will does not always wish to take counsel, it must be moved by something so that it will wish to take counsel; and if by itself, it is again necessary that a movement of will precede the act of counsel, and an act of counsel must precede the act of will. Since this cannot go on to infinity, it is necessary to maintain that, in regard to the first movement of the will, the will of the agent who is actually wishing, is not always moved by something external which makes the will begin to wish as a result of the process of investigation.

Therefore, some people have maintained that this instigation comes from a celestial body. But this cannot be. Since the will is rational, according to the Philosopher [De Anima, III, 10, 433a10–35], and the intellectual reason is not a corporeal power, it is impossible for the power of a celestial body to move the will itself, directly. Now, to claim that the will of man is moved by the influence of a heavenly body, just as the appetites of brute animals are, is, according to the opinion of these thinkers, to make no difference between intellect and sense. For, it is to these people that the Philosopher [De Anima, III, 3, 427a25] attributes the statement that man's will is whatever the "father of men and of gods," that is, the heavens or the sun, leads man to.

So, it remains, as Aristotle concludes in his chapter, "On Good Fortune," [Ethic. Eudem., VII, c. 18] that what first of all moves the will and intellect is something above the will and intellect, namely God, Who (since He moves all things according to their principles as movable things, for instance the light go upward and the heavy downward) also moves the will according to its own condition, not as from necessity but as being related indeterminately to many objectives.

Therefore, it is clear that, if the movement of the will be considered from the viewpoint of the exercise of the act, it is not moved of necessity. But, if the movement of the will be viewed from the side of the object determining the act of will to wish this or that thing, it must be understood that the object moving the will is an apprehended good which is suitable. Hence, if any good be proposed, which is apprehended under the principle of the good but not under the principle of that which is suitable (*conveniens*), it will not move the will. Now, since acts of counsel and acts of election have to do with particulars, to which action pertains, it is necessary that what is apprehended as good and suitable, be apprehended as good and suitable *in particular* and not merely universally. So, if something is apprehended as a suitable good according to all the particulars which can be considered, it will necessarily move the will. And, because of this, man necessarily desires happiness, which according to Boethius (*De Consol. Philos.*, III, prose no. 2; ed. Stewart and Rand, p. 228, lines 11–12), is a "condition perfected by a gathering together of all goods." Now, I say *necessarily* in regard to the *determination* of the act, since it is not possible to will contraries, but this does not apply to the exercise of the act, since one can will not to think of happiness, for the acts themselves even of intellect and will, are particular.

Now, if there be a good of such a nature that it is wanting in goodness in regard to some particulars which may be considered, it will not move necessarily, even in regard to the determination of the act. For, it will be possible for someone to wish its contrary, even while thinking of it, since it is perhaps good or suitable according to some other particular point which is being considered. Thus, what is good from the point of view of health is not good from the point of view of enjoyment, and so for other things.

And it can happen in three ways, that the will may be drawn to that which is presented to it, more according to one particular condition than according to another. In one way, inasmuch as one particular outweighs the other, the will may be moved according to reason. For instance, a man chooses what is useful to health rather than what is useful to his initial wish. In a second way, insofar as he thinks of one particular circumstance and not of another, such a thought occurs to a man mostly because of some occasion that is presented either from within or from without. In a third way, it happens as a result of the disposition of the man, since, according to the Philosopher (*Ethic. Nic.*, III, 5, 1112b15), the end will appear differently, depending on the kind of man that one is. Hence, the will of an angry man, and the will of an undisturbed man, are differently moved in regard to the same thing, for the same thing is not suitable to both; in the same way, food is differently regarded by a healthy man and by a sick man.

If the disposition, through which something appears good and suitable to a person, were natural and not subject to will, then the will would necessarily choose it, just as all men naturally desire to exist, to live, and to understand. But, if the disposition be such that it is not determined by nature but is subject to will (for instance, when one is so disposed by a habitus or passion that a thing appears good or bad to him in one particular way) then the will is not necessarily moved. For, he could remove this disposition, so that this thing would not appear in this way. Thus, for instance, one may quiet the anger within him, so that he will not judge something, in the fashion of an angry man. However, it is easier to remove a passion than a habitus.

And thus, in regard to some things, the will is necessarily moved from the point of view of the object, but not in regard to all things. However, from the aspect of the exercise of the act, it is not moved by necessity. (*De Malo*, q. 6, art. unicus, c.)

¶ TEXT EIGHT: *Freedom and Necessity in Will-Acts.* One should consider that the will is said to be inclined toward something in a two-fold way: in one way, from without; in another way, from within. From without, [it is inclined] by an intellectually known object, for a good which is apprehended by the intellect is said to move the will. In this way, it is said to move by counsel or persuasion, insofar as it makes something appear to be good. From within, however, the will is moved by that which produces the very act of will. Now, an object proposed to the will does not move the will necessarily: although the intellect may necessarily assent at times to a truth which is presented. The reason for this diversity is that both intellect and will do tend of necessity to that to which they are naturally ordered; for it pertains to the natural to be determined to one thing. As a result, the intellect necessarily assents to first principles naturally known, and it cannot assent to their contraries. In the same way, the will naturally and of necessity desires happiness, and no one can wish for unhappiness. In the area of understanding, it does happen that those things which possess a necessary coherence with first principles naturally known, may move the intellect of necessity. Examples are demonstrated conclusions, when they are evident; for, if they be denied, it is necessary to deny the first principles from which they necessarily follow. But if there be some conclusions not possessing a necessary coherence with the first principles naturally known, for example, contingent truths and matters of opinion, the intellect is not compelled by these to give assent. In the same way, it does not necessarily assent even to necessary truths, which are necessarily connected with first principles, before it *knows* their necessary connection.

Thus also, it appears in reference to the will, that the will is not moved necessarily toward anything which does not clearly have a necessary connection with happiness, which is naturally desired. Now, it is plain that particular goods of this kind do not have a necessary connection with happiness, for it is possible for a man to be happy without any certain one of them. Hence, no matter how strongly one of these is proposed as a good, the will does not necessarily tend to it. However, the Perfect Good, which is God, does indeed have a necessary connection with the happiness of man, because without Him man cannot be happy. Nevertheless, the necessity of this connection is not clearly evident to man in this life, because he does not see God in His Essence. Therefore, the will of man does not necessarily cleave to God, during this life; but the will of those who do see God in His Essence, who clearly know that He is the Essence of Goodness and the Happiness of man, cannot but cleave to God; just as our will, in our present condition, cannot but desire happiness.

Therefore, it is clear that the object does not necessarily move the will; and so, no form of persuasion necessarily moves man to act. It remains true, then, that the perfecting and proper cause of the voluntary act is solely that which works from within. Now this can be nothing other than the will itself, as a secondary cause, and God as a primary Cause. And the reason for this is: the act of the will is nothing but a certain inclination of the will toward what is desired; just as a natural appetite is nothing other than an inclination of a nature to something. The inclination of a nature, however, comes both from the natural form and from Him Who gives the form; hence, it is said that the upward motion of fire is from its lightness [*i.e.*, an accidental form], and from the generator who creates such a form. So too, the movement of the will directly proceeds from the will and from God, Who is the Cause of the will, Who alone works in the will and can incline the will to whatever He desires. But God is not the cause of sin, as is shown above in the first two articles of this question. It remains, then, that nothing else is the direct cause of human sin, than the will. (*De Malo*, q. 3, a. 3,c.)

¶ TEXT NINE: *Liberty of Exercise and Liberty of Specification.* Now, any power of the soul may be in potency to diverse acts, in two ways: first, in regard to action or non-action; second, in regard to acting in this way or that. Thus, the potency of sight sometimes sees, sometimes it does not; and sometimes it sees white, sometimes black. So, it requires a mover for two reasons: namely, in regard to the *exercise*, or *use*, of its act; and in regard to the *determination* of its act. The first of these is on the side of the subject, which is found at times to be acting, at other times not acting. The second is from the side of the object, inasmuch as it specifies the act.

The movement of the subject itself is from some agent. And, since every agent acts for an end, as was shown above, the principle of this movement is from the end. . . . Now, the good in general, which has the formal nature (*ratio*) of an end, is the object of the will. So, from the side of the will, it moves the other potencies of the soul to their acts; for we use the other potencies when we wish. For, the ends and perfections of all the other potencies are comprehended under the object of the will, as some particular goods.

But the object moves by determining the act, in the way of a formal principle, by which action is specified in the things of nature, as the act of heating is by heat. Now, the first formal principle is being and universal truth, which is the object of the intellect. And so, it moves the will by this way of moving the intellect, that is, it presents its object to it.

[Ad 3m] The will moves the intellect in regard to the exercise of its act, because truth itself, which is the perfection of the intellect, is included within the universal good, as a certain particular good. But, in regard to the determination of the act, which comes from the side of the object, the intellect moves the will, because the good itself is apprehended as a special intelligible nature (*ratio*) comprehended under the universal intelligible nature of truth. (*S.T.*, I–II, 9, 1,c and *ad 3m*.)

¶ TEXT TEN: *The Eleven Chief Passions.* So, it follows that the passions are properly called operations of the sensitive appetite, and they involve a modification of the bodily organ, and man is influenced by them.

The sense appetite is divided into two powers, namely, the *concupiscible*, which has to do with the simple good of sense (that is, what is delightful in a sense way), and its contrary evil; and the *irascible*, which is concerned with a good considered as somewhat beyond the powers of the agent (as victory is called a sort of good, though not accompanied by sense delight). And so, whatever passions are concerned with good and evil, in their simple sense, are in the concupiscible power. Some of these have to do with the good, and there are three of these. *Love* implies a connatural inclination to the good as an object of love. *Desire* implies a movement of the appetite toward the good which is loved. And, *delight* implies a resting of the appetite in the good which is loved. And there are some contrary to the above, by virtue of being related to evil; namely, *hate* as opposed to love, *aversion* or *flight* to desire, and *sorrow* to delight.

But those passions which are concerned with the good or evil, considered under the aspect of some difficulty, pertain to the *irascible* power; these are: *fear* and *daring*, in regard to evil; *hope* and *despair*, in regard to the good. The fifth is *anger*, a composite passion which has no contrary. (*In II Ethic.*, lect. 5; ed. Pirotta, p. 181, nn. 292–293.)

¶ TEXT ELEVEN: *The Principal Passions.* There are four principal passions of the soul: namely sorrow (*tristitia*), joy (*gaudium*), hope (*spes*) and fear (*timor*). And the reason for this is that passions are called principal, when they are prior to others and the source of others. Now, since the passions of the soul are in the appetitive part, those passions will be prior which spring immediately from the object of the appetitive part; and this object is good and evil. But others will be, as it were, secondary, because they arise from these as intermediaries.

Now, since a thing is ultimate in the pursuit of an end, to the extent that it is prior in intention and in appetite, those passions spring from good or evil, without depending on any others, which are concerned with the carrying out of the end. Others arise in dependence on these. Now, joy and sorrow arise from the very attainment of good or evil in themselves. For joy arises from good insofar as it is good, and sorrow from evil insofar as it is evil. Similarly, all the other concupiscible passions arise essentially from good or evil. This is so because of the fact that the object of the concupiscible is good or evil, in its absolute nature. But the other concupiscible passions are based on joy and sorrow, as on causes; for the concupiscible good becomes the object of love or desire, because it is apprehended as enjoyable; and evil becomes the object of hate and of repugnance, inasmuch as it is grasped as the object of sorrow. And so, in the order of appetite, joy and sorrow are prior; even though they are posterior in the order of execution.

But in the irascible part not all the passions follow essentially from good and evil; rather, some do essentially and others accidentally. This is due to the fact that good and evil are not the object of the irascible power according to their absolute nature, but according to the condition of *difficulty* which is added. According to this, the good is repudiated as being beyond one's power and there is an inclination to evil as something which one may repel or subject. There cannot be in the irascible power any passion which follows upon good or evil, with nothing intervening; for the good, once possessed, causes no passion in the irascible, as is clear from what has been said in the preceding article; but the evil which is present does cause a passion in the irascible appetite; not however essentially but accidentally, that is, inasmuch as one tends to repel and subject a present evil, as is clear in the case of anger.

And so, it appears from what has been said that there are some passions which primarily and essentially spring from good and evil, for instance joy and sorrow. And there are some which do so essentially but not primarily, for instance the other concupiscible passions and these two irascible ones, fear and hope. The first of these suggests a flight from evil; the second, an approach to the good. Still others do so neither essentially nor primarily, as is the case with the others in the irascible power, namely despair, boldness and anger, which suggest an approach to evil, or a removal from the good.

Thus, the principal passions, from all points of view, are joy and sorrow. But fear and hope are the principal ones of their kind; for they do not presuppose any passions in the potency to which they belong, namely, the irascible. But the other concupiscible passions, love, desire, hate, and aversion, though essentially arising from good and evil, are not however first in their genus, since they do presuppose others existing in the same potency. Thus, they cannot be called principal, either absolutely, or in their genus. (*De Veritate*, q. 26, a. 5,c.)

¶ TEXT TWELVE: *Morality of the Passions.* If, without qualification, we call all the movements of the sensitive appetite passions, then it pertains to the perfection of human goodness that even the passions themselves be moderated by reason. For, since the good of man stands upon reason as its root, then the more things which are suitable to man, to which it [reason] can be applied, the more perfect is this good.

Hence, no one doubts that it pertains to the perfection of the moral good, for an act of an external member to be directed by the rule of reason. And, since the sensitive appetite can obey reason, as has been said above, it pertains to the perfection of moral or human good that even the very passions of the soul be regulated by reason.

Therefore, just as it is better for a man both to will the good and to do it in the external act, so also does it pertain to the perfection of the moral good, for man to be moved to the good not only in his will but also in his sense appetite, in keeping with the statement of Psalm LXXXIII: "My heart and my flesh have rejoiced in the living God," where we may take *heart* to mean the intellective appetite and *flesh* for the sensitive appetite. [*Ad primum*] The passions of the soul can be related in two ways to rational judgment. First, *antecedently:* thus, since they becloud the rational judgment, on which the goodness of the moral act depends, they diminish the goodness of the act; for it is more praiseworthy for one to do a work of charity because of a rational judgment, than because of a feeling (*passio*) of mercy only. Second, they are related, *consequently:* and this may happen in two ways. In one way, by redundancy, for, when the superior part of the soul is strongly moved toward something, the lower part also follows its movement. And thus, passion existing consequently in the sense appetite is the sign of the intensity of the will. And so, it indicates a greater moral goodness. In another way, they may be consequent by choice; that is, when man, as a result of a rational judgment, elects to be affected by some passion, so that he may work more promptly with the cooperation of sense appetite. And thus, a passion of the soul adds to the goodness of an action. [*Ad tertium*] A passion inclining toward evil, and preceding rational judgment, diminishes the sin; but following it in any of the aforesaid ways, it increases it, or signifies an increase of it. (*S.T.*, I–II, 24, 3,c, *ad primum*, et *ad 3m.*)

⁋ TEXT THIRTEEN: *The Important Moral Circumstances.* Circumstance means something standing outside the substance of the act, such however, that it touches it in some way. Now, this may occur in three ways: first, inasmuch as it touches the act itself; second, insofar as it touches the cause of the act; third, insofar as it touches the effect.

Now, it touches the *act*, either by way of quantity (*mensurae*), as of time or place; or by way of quality of the act, for instance the way of acting. From the viewpoint of the *effect*, one considers what a man did. From the side of the cause of the act: in regard to final cause, the reference is to that *for which;* in regard to the material cause, or object, it is that *on which;* in regard to the principal efficient cause, it is *who* acted; and in regard to the instrumental efficient cause, it is *by what means. (S.T.*, I–II, 7, 3,c.)

The motive force and object of the will is the end. And so, the most important of all circumstances is that which touches the act from the aspect of the end, namely that *for the sake of which;* secondarily, it is that which touches the very substance of the act, that is, *what* one did. The other circumstances are more or less important, according as they more or less approach these. (*Ibid.*, 4,c.)

¶ TEXT FOURTEEN: *Three Types of Moral Circumstance.* That is called a circumstance which "stands around" (*circumstat*) the act, as something extrinsic which is considered to be outside the substance of the act. Now, this occurs in one way, from the point of view of the *cause*, either final (when we consider *why* he did it), or from the side of the principal agent (when we consider *who* did it), or from the aspect of the instrument (when we consider *by what* instrument or means, he did it). In a second way, something may "stand around" the act, from the point of view of *measure* (for instance, when we consider where or when he did it). In a third way, from the point of view of the *act itself*, we may consider either the way of doing it (for example, whether he struck lightly or with great force, frequently or just once); or, we may consider the object or matter of the act (for instance, whether he struck his father or a stranger); or also the effect which the action led to (for instance, whether he caused a wound or even death, by striking). All of these are included in the verse: who, what, where, by what means, why, how, and when. (*De Malo*, q. 2, a. 6,c.)

Recommended Readings

Thomas Aquinas, St., *Summa Theologiae,* I–II, qq. 6–7 (in *Basic Writings,* ed. Pegis, II, 225–244); I–II, qq. 11–17 (in *Basic Writings,* II, 266–316).

Bourke, *St. Thomas and the Greek Moralists*, pp. 15–21.

Cronin, *Science of Ethics*, I, 30–46.

Gilson, *Moral Values and the Moral Life*, pp. 52–60, 91–133.

Klubertanz, "The Unity of Human Activity," *The Modern Schoolman*, XXVII (1950) 75–103.

Pegis, "Necessity and Liberty," *New Scholasticism*, XV (1941) 18–45.

Phelan, "Person and Liberty," *New Scholasticism*, XV (1941) 53–68.

Rickaby, *Aquinas Ethicus*, I, 232–244.

Smith, G., "Intelligence and Liberty," *New Scholasticism*, XV (1941) 1–17.

ADVANCED READINGS

Browne, "De intellectu et voluntate in electione," *Acta. Pont. Acad. Rom. S. Thomae* (1936) 32–45.

Gilson, *Le Thomisme*, éd. rev. (1942) pp. 346–351.

Lottin, *Principes de Morale*, I, 61–72, 83–107.

Noble, "L'Action volontaire," *Mélanges Mandonnet*, I, 275–288.

Sertillanges, *La philosophie morale de s. Thomas*, pp. 49–90.

———, *Saint Thomas d'Aquin*, pp. 211–288.

Wittmann, *Die Ethik des hl. Thomas von Aquin*, pp. 73–85.

Topics for Assignment

1. A Good Intention Does Not Necessarily Make a Good Act
2. The Difference Between Involuntary and Not-Voluntary Action
3. Liberty of Exercise and of Specification
4. How Antecedent Passion Affects Voluntariness
5. Aristotle's List of Six Moral Circumstances

The Need of a Standard of Moral Judgment

It has been observed already that, in a teleological approach to ethics, the goodness or evil of human acts depends on the suitability, or conformity, of such action to the ultimate end of the moral agent. Thus, if we regard murder as an immoral action, it is because murder does not advance the agent toward the attainment of his ultimate happiness; rather, it draws him away from his final perfection. This is, of course, a very broad statement. The really practical problem is: *How may man decide whether a proposed particular human act is suitable to the attainment of his ultimate end?*

In attempting to answer this question, the various types of ethics known in the history of philosophy have relied on different standards or norms of moral judgment. It is precisely at this point that each system of ethics finds its distinguishing character. To study the history of ethical theories is beyond the scope of our present work but we may profitably note some of the chief variations of theory centering on this point.[1]

Some thinkers have considered that any action is morally good if it brings *pleasure to the individual* agent, bad if it brings pain to the

[1] Students interested in the history of ethics will find that there is no satisfactory book on this subject, written in English from the point of view of thomistic scholarship. Cronin's *Science of Ethics* includes much historical information, in both volumes, but it is not always historically exact. Brosnahan, T. J., *Prolegomena to Ethics* (New York, 1941), pp. 143–178, offers a brief outline of some historical views on the subject. Though old, the best history of ethics in English, done by a scholar who is not a thomist, is: Sidgwick, H., *Outlines of the History of Ethics* (London, 1931, rev. ed.).

agent. Other ethicians speak of the individual man as having *moral feelings*, by which he may be guided in the performance of his ethical duties. Another variation of this theory, is to suppose that there is in each man an aesthetic sense which perceives the morally good action as beautiful, and the morally bad action as ugly. Associated with this type of theory is a special way of understanding *moral conscience*. In much modern ethics, conscience is regarded as a source of ethical rules, as a sort of "voice," or special faculty, which lays down the law to the individual, in matters of moral duty. This is the "Pinocchio" theory of conscience. It suggests that each moral agent is accompanied by a little spirit who whispers in the agent's ear: "You mustn't tell lies!" or, "You should get up, it's time for school!" We know that this is just a story, and that there really is no "Jiminy Cricket," yet nearly all modern people continue to think of their conscience in this way. Some even believe that religion results from the dictates of such a "conscience."

All the preceding views of moral guidance stress the individual and subjective nature of ethical duty. In its most serious form, this theory is found in the ethics of Immanuel Kant. He was a sincere thinker, and a pious Christian, who tried very hard to explain how the individual man could be the ultimate source of the moral law for himself. The great difficulty in such theories centers in their essential subjectivity. If the individual is the sole source of moral rules or standards, then how can these standards apply universally and necessarily? Kant found an escape from this dilemma by the use of his famous *Categorical Imperative*. He suggested that each man should act in such a way that each of his actions could be used as a universal moral law.[2] This solution was in keeping with his theory of knowledge, but it is hardly a solid basis for ethical judgment. If we are to found an ethics on the pleasure, moral feeling, or conscience of the individual, what are we to do when some individual agent claims that it is his pleasure, or a dictate of his conscience, to murder as many people as he wishes? To this, Kant would say: such an action could not

[2] T. K. Abbott (trans.) *Kant's Theory of Ethics*, sections I and II give Kant's explanation of the categorical imperative; the same text is reprinted in *Kant Selections*, T. M. Greene, ed. (New York, Scribners, 1929) pp. 270–317.

become a universal maxim of morality. It would result in moral chaos. But why?

Realizing the seriousness of the difficulties in an ethics founded on wholly subjective standards, some philosophers of the past two hundred years developed a broader theory. They said that what is morally good is what contributes to the welfare of the greatest number of people. On this basis, we should consider *society* as the starting point of our ethical judgments. If a proposed action is of utility to all, or to the majority, in a social group, then it is good for the individual agent to do it. If antisocial, the action must not be done. This is the theory known as *social utilitarianism*.[3] It has many good features; it stresses unselfishness, service to humanity and to the state. However, we must ask: "Who is to determine what is of value, or utility, to the social group? Suppose one social group decides that another social group is made up of inferior people who have no right to continue living. Which social group is to be considered by the ethician? Or, if we expand it into a universal utilitarianism of humanity as a whole, who knows what is good for all men? We may admit that a high-minded utilitarianism has many things to offer in the area of the ethical relations of the individual to his fellow men, but are there not some ethical problems which pertain to the individual alone? Is it true, as is suggested in a widely syndicated newspaper feature on practical psychology, that, "Science always considers the rights of society to be superior to those of the individual"? Such a view could only be morally true, if the end of man were the happiness of society. But individual human beings are the only realities in human society. Without individual members, human society is nothing. The attainment of the ultimate end, moral happiness, is an individual action. Without adopting a sort of moral totalitarianism, we cannot view it in any other light.

Faced with such objections, modern ethicians have in some cases given up the search for true and unchangeable standards of moral behavior. This amounts to an abandonment of the ethical enterprise, and it takes two chief forms: pessimism and moral evolutionism. The

[3] Cronin, *Science of Ethics*, I, 318–366, offers a lengthy exposition and criticism of various types of utilitarianism.

pessimist says, in effect, "The moral law is so difficult that no ordinary man can conform to it. All that is possible is a sort of resignation to moral failure." This position has been adopted by a few disgruntled thinkers, who have notably failed in the moral direction of their own lives. It is based on a logical self-contradiction, for, if the moral law is what man should do, and if this law is such that man cannot do what it says, then it is not the moral law for man. Pessimism is not a type of ethics, but a destruction of moral thinking. If there is any way in which man may reasonably work to achieve his own happiness, then pessimism may be dismissed from further consideration.

Much the same criticism may be offered in regard to moral evolutionism. In this theory it is maintained that there are moral standards, but that these standards change with the evolutionary progress of the human being. What was right for primitive man is not right for the man of the twentieth century, for they are not the same species of being. This view, of course, implies a radical departure from the thomistic philosophy of being and of man. If man is specifically a rational animal, then he does not change specifically. But, if man is not of one species, then what is mankind—a genus? It is metaphysically impossible for an individual to exist which is a member of a genus but of no species. That would be like having an animal existing, which is neither a dog, nor a cow, nor a horse—just an animal! If all men are not members of the same species, then there can be no one end for all men, and there can be no ethics.[4]

That brings us to the real point of this section. Ethics is a study dealing with right and wrong in human conduct, considered in relation to the ultimate end of man. To judge, or measure, human actions, we must have a standard of judgment. Let us consider another area in which accurate measurement is important. Suppose we are in the business of selling goods to make dresses and suits. If we sell these goods by the yard, then our unit of measurement, the yard, must be constant in value. Customers could not put up with a yard which is sometimes forty inches and sometimes thirty inches. Nor could peo-

[4] See T. J. Brosnahan, *Prolegomena to Ethics* (New York, Fordham U. Press, 1941), pp. 12–13, 167–173, for further discussion of these theories.

ple comfortably wear clothes made by such inaccurate measurement. It is necessary to establish a basic and ultimate unit which will be always of the same length. Such an ultimate unit is called a *primary criterion*, or standard. In this country, the primary unit of linear measurement is kept, as a practically invariable standard, in the Bureau of Standards. But we cannot go to Washington every time we want to sell a yard of goods, so we obtain copies of this original yard-standard, in the form of yardsticks, of wood or of some other material. These many yardsticks are copied from the original, derived from it, and they are called *derivative or secondary standards*. They are not all of precisely the same length but, in good business practice, they are accurate enough.

Now, the ethician does not measure human actions by means of a yardstick. But he does need an ultimate standard of moral judgment; and this will have to be invariable. To be practical, each man must also have near at hand a secondary moral standard, which he will use many times each day to measure the moral worth of his own human actions. What we want to know, then, may be put in this question. *What is the ultimate standard of the morality of human actions, and what is the proximate standard of these actions?*

The thomistic answer to this question is that *reason* is the standard of moral goodness and evil. As *Reason* is present in God, it is the ultimate and unchanging moral standard. As it is found in man, in a particular status known as *right reason*, it is the proximate moral standard. To understand this teaching in a scientific and technical way, we must now apply to the moral area some things which we have learned from the speculative point of view, in metaphysics. That is the work of the two following sections of this chapter. What we want to try to understand is what St. Thomas means, when he says:

In those things which are done voluntarily, the proximate standard (*regula*) is human reason, but the supreme standard is the eternal law. Therefore, whenever man's act proceeds to the end, in accordance with the order of reason and of the eternal law, then the act is right; but when it is twisted away from this rightness, it is then called a sin. Now, it is apparent from what has gone before, that every voluntary act is bad from the fact that it recedes from the order of reason and of the eternal law, and every good act is in agreement with reason and the eternal law.[5] . . . Now, that human reason is the standard, by means of which the goodness of the human will may be measured, is due to the eternal law, which is the divine Reason (*ratio divina*).[6]

Right Reason and the Moral Order

The activity of any being is right and good when such activity is in agreement with the formal nature and end of that being. Bad action is a sort of dynamic "de-formity"; it lacks conformity with the existing nature of the agent. Things in this universe, below the level of man, lack freedom. Their actions tend automatically towards their ends. In plants and brutes, for instance, "bad" action can only mean failure to achieve their specific ends, due to the intervention of external impediments. There is no *moral* good or evil in infra-human agents.

Man must use his capacity for free action, in order to work toward his ultimate end. He must *know* what he should do; *choose* the appropriate means to do it; and then *use* these means. It is the function of reason to order free actions toward an end. Reason is the specific difference of man. His substantial form is rational. When man acts reasonably, he acts in accord with his own formal nature. When he acts unreasonably, consciously doing what he sincerely thinks wrong, he abuses the very power with which his free acts are produced. Just as it is bad and abusive for a wood saw to be used to cut steel, because such use destroys the capacity of the saw to do its proper work, so is it abusive and bad for a man to use his faculty of reason in thinking out and ordering actions which are contrary to human reason. There is something warped and twisted in all immoral action.

By the use of speculative reason, man can know something of the formal natures of all other existing things. He can understand the objective relations of his own nature to other real things in the universe. He knows that there are many kinds of less perfect beings than

[5] *S.T.*, I–II, 21, 1,c.   [6] *Ibid.*, 19, 4,c.

man. He can be shown, by metaphysical reasoning, that this finite universe could not have come into being, and could not continue to work according to very precise scientific formulae, unless there be an existing God, Who causes all things to exist and operate in accord with an intelligent plan. Even men who have had no training in the logical processes of reflecting on the necessary Source of all things have a primitive and natural conviction that there is a Supreme Being Who regulates the universe. There is a real order of beings, in which man occupies a very definite place. It is right for man to know his place and function among other beings. It is right for him to act in conformity with this right knowledge.

One of the things which made the ancient Greeks a great people was their general respect for life in accord with reason. While they did not always succeed in living up to their ideals, the literature, art and philosophy of the Greeks are representative of this high regard for reason. Their moral teachers, Socrates, Plato, Aristotle, and Plotinus, taught that the good man is the reasonable man. Stoicism, beginning three centuries before Christ and lasting for about five centuries into the Christian era, was one of the greatest and most influential systems of natural ethics. The Stoics taught that man should live, "in conformity with nature." They considered nature to be permeated by a universal law of Reason, giving order to all things. This concept was taken over into Roman law and has exerted a great influence on later political and social institutions.

In the Christian Church, great teachers of the early centuries saw that reason is the mark of man's dignity and the stamp of God's Law on the human soul. St. Ambrose adapted Stoic rationalism to the practical use of the Church. St. Jerome, St. Augustine, and St. John Damascene applied it to the life of the individual Christian. A Greek Christian writer, Dionysius the Pseudo-Areopagite, continued this classic tradition, impressing on the mind of nearly every Christian spiritual writer, from the sixth to the fifteenth century, the view that a human act is good when all the pertinent causes or reasons for it are present, and bad when any necessary reason is lacking. Dionysius is the source of the axiom continually cited by St. Thomas: "bonum

causatur ex integra causa, malum autem ex singularibus defectibus." [7]
Commenting on a passage in Aristotle, St. Thomas gives a terse but
very accurate summary of the relation between good action and
right reason:

> The good for any thing whatever consists in the fact that its action is in
> agreement with its form. Now, the form proper to man is that which
> makes him a rational animal. Consequently, it must be that a man's action
> is good from the fact that it is in accord with right reason. For the per-
> version of reason is repugnant to the nature of reason.[8]

The accompanying diagram of *The Rational Order* will help to
explain the nature of right reason. At the top of the diagram is the
Reason of God. That God is the First Cause of all existing and possible beings, is a conclusion of thomistic metaphysics. Hence, all
finite beings, including man, are produced and maintained in being
by God. All beings operate in accordance with the Divine Plan or
Reason. If we could know directly the Eternal Reasons for all things,
we might have a perfect understanding of what is right about every
proposed finite action; we would then be masters of all practical
knowledge. But man on this earth does not know directly what is in
the Mind of God. Nor has God made known the Eternal Reasons
for all things and events, even through supernatural revelation.

However, the moral agent may come to understand enough about
the *reasons*, *i.e.*, the specific natures and objective relations, of things
in this world of nature to comprehend the part which man should
play in life. The long arrow running vertically, at the left of the diagram, suggests that the Eternal Reason is the Source of all the finite
reasons in the world of nature. All natural beings, except man, work
automatically in accord with the Divine Reason.

Thus, while earthly man does not enjoy a direct vision of the Divine Reasons (the exemplary causes) in the Mind of God, he does
know a universe which is rationally contrived, and which works in
conformity with the Divine Plan. This means that the reasoning intellect of each man has some indirect knowledge of God's Reason,

[7] *S.T.*, I–II, 19, 6, *ad primum;* quoting Dionysius, *De Divinis Nominibus,*
c. 4, PG 3, 729.
[8] *In II Ethic.*, lect. 2; ed. Pirotta, p. 89, n. 257.

THE RATIONAL ORDER

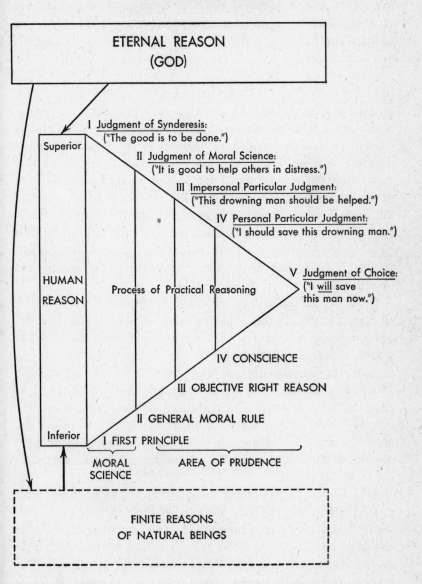

through the direct knowledge which every man has of the way that things exist and act in this world. Such common human knowledge of objective reality is called speculative knowledge. It need not be technical, or "scientific," in order to be right. In speculative reasoning, man thinks out some of the implications of his intellectual experience of the world about him. The conclusions of speculative reasoning may be newly discovered judgments about existing things; or these conclusions may be verifications of judgments, previously held in some tentative manner. Speculative reasoning is not always right but it may be rectified by reference to the world of existing realities which are its objects. Thus, the speculative conclusion that the earth is flat may be tested and proved wrong by reference to more accurate and more extensive sense knowledge of the shape of this earth. That some human beings may continue to reason incorrectly about such a matter, does not mean that the majority of men lack objective certainty on this point. The measure, or standard (*regula*), of rightness in speculative reasoning is the existing and objective nature of real things.

The triangular figure in the middle of the diagram is representative of *human reason*, in this objective order of reason. Man is a real being, existing as part of a rational universe. Human reason is the specific difference of mankind. All finite beings have "reasons," in the sense of formally distinct principles of existence and activity. Men have a "reason," which is the formal principle of human existence; this is the substantial form, the soul, of man. Now, it happens that the nature of man is marked off by its capacity to reason discursively, according to the rules which have been studied in logic. Man is fulfilling his formal role in the universe, when he acts in accord with his reason.

As soon as we begin to think about how to act, we are using *practical reasoning*. It is the same power of intellect that we use in reasoning speculatively or practically. In fact, we must know *what things are* (*i.e.*, use speculative reason) before we can reasonably decide *what to do about these things* (*i.e.*, use practical reason). The process of practical reasoning (more fully to be examined in Chapter VII) is represented by the narrowing down of the triangle in mid-diagram. Practical reasoning may start with general or particular knowledge of things, but it must terminate in a most particular judgment to the effect that the moral agent will (or will not) do a singular action under concrete circumstances.

The ultimate beginning of practical reasoning is found in the first principle of thinking about what should be done. Stated in its most universal form, this practical principle is simply: "The good should be done; evil should be avoided." Every man recognizes the rightness of this rule; though not every man may be able to formulate it. We shall see in the next chapter that it is known through the intellectual habit called *synderesis*. In the same way, every man is guided in his thinking by the first principle of speculative reasoning, which is the principle of noncontradiction. It is not immediately practical to know that the good should be done. What is practical, is to know what things are good and then to do them.

Our initial moral reasonings terminate in universal judgments about actions which are generically good, and so to be done, and actions which are generically evil, and to be avoided. Thus, we may reason to the conclusion: "It is generally good to help others in distress." This kind of practical reasoning is used technically to establish the conclusions of moral science (ethics and moral theology), to formulate positive laws of a society, and also in our nontechnical, but personal, reflections on what is right and wrong in human action. Now, the important point is that general moral conclusions about morality are nearly always rightly made. If we get back to sufficiently universal rules and eliminate misunderstandings due to variations in terminology, we find that human beings agree to a remarkable extent about the general rules of conduct. Most of the rules of the Decalogue are accepted by all peoples, civilized and primitive. Even a thief becomes morally indignant when his own property is stolen.

These general conclusions about what is right and wrong are not made at the whim of the thinker. They depend on our true knowledge (through the speculative intellect) of the natures and relations of objectively existing realities. Nor are these moral rules deduced from a mere analysis of first practical principles. They are formed by the process of practical reasoning about the ever increasing content of actual human experience. The principles are a guide for such reasoning but the content of the conclusions is derived from empirical knowledge. The moral agent must observe the world about him, his own nature and capacities, his place in the whole of things. Such intelligent observation is the basis for the conclusions of right speculative thinking. Right speculative knowledge is the source, in its turn, of right practical knowledge; for practical knowledge is simply the application of speculative knowledge to action. To know whether the act of killing a dog is of the same moral value as the act of killing a man, under identical circumstances, one must first understand *what a dog is* and *what a man is*.

The rightness of practical reasoning, then, depends on the rightness of speculative reasoning. But right action cannot be determined by universal rules alone. The moral agent, in the process of practical reasoning, must move forward beyond the realm of general rules through a series of more and more particular judgments. These judgments are indicated in the triangle of the diagram by the vertical lines, numbered III and IV, and the point which is numbered V. The narrowing down of the triangle to its point, at the right, suggests the decreasing universality of the practical judgments, eventually reaching the singular decision to act or not to act. Each practical judgment is the terminus of a deliberative process of practical reasoning. We shall see later that each process of reasoning to a practical conclusion may be expressed in syllogistic terms.

Judgment III is the first kind of particular operative judgment. At this point we find impersonal judgments about actual moral problems. That is to say, we are now in the area of prudence, of right reasoning about concretely proposed moral actions. The conclusion reached in judgment III is governed by the universal rule in judgment II, but results also from an added definite knowledge of the circumstances of the present moral problem. Such knowledge is acquired through sensation and intelligent interpretation of the sensed situation. In judgment III, one may conclude for instance: "This drowning person should be helped." This judgment is particular, in the sense that it applies to this one moral case; it is still somewhat universal, in the sense that it does not determine the one moral agent who should save him. Such a practical but impersonal moral judgment is usually right, because the thinker is not yet personally involved and his judgment is not likely to be swayed by personal feelings or passions. We may place the end of *objective right reason* at point III.

Judgment IV is personal and particular: "I should save this drowning man." This is the dictate of moral conscience. If made in accord with the rightness of the preceding judgment, this dictate retains the rightness of judgment III. But judgment IV is preceded by a further rational deliberation, including the addition of additional factual information about the circumstances of the agent. Thus, if one decides that a drowning man should be saved, and then observes that there is a good reason why one cannot do this act, the dictate of conscience may quite rightly be: "I should not save this man."

Moreover the judgment of conscience may run counter to the objective rightness of the whole situation. Such a conscience is called *erroneous*. This just means that the personal judgment of the agent is contrary to what a perfect knower would judge to be right in this situation. Now, erroneous conscience may be of two general types; the error in judgment IV may be either voluntary or involuntary. If it is voluntary, then the judgment of conscience is not right, either objectively or subjectively, for the agent is responsible for the mistake which he is making. But if the error is voluntary, then an objectively erroneous conscience is said to be subjectively right. Suppose our potential life-saver has been trained from earliest youth to regard swimming on Sunday as intrinsically immoral, an offense against the law of God. Suppose he has had no opportunity to rectify this mistaken belief. Under these circumstances, his judgment (that he should not save this drowning person) is objectively wrong but subjectively right. We shall discuss in Chapter VI the extent to which an erroneous conscience is obligatory. All that we need note, here, is that objective right reason is not possible for all men to attain at all times. Right reason is the proximate standard of rightness in moral action, but this should not be taken to mean that it is always easy to judge what should be done. To the extent that he is able, man should govern his moral actions by reference to right reason. No type of ethics tries to require the agent to do anything more than is possible, in order to be good.

We should also notice that moral conscience, represented as judgment IV, is the last *purely cognitive* act in the process of practical reasoning. The process of practical reasoning is performed at the volitional initiative of the will of the agent, of course, and it may be stopped, when the agent so wills; but it is essentially a series of intellectual acts. The last of these nonaffective acts of practical judgment is moral conscience.[9] After the judgment of conscience, the decisive act is the act of *election* which goes on in the will, as directed by the practical intellect. Election is rational choice, so there must be a reason, embodied in a *last practical judgment*, for every choice. It is obvious that choice may be in opposition to the judgment of conscience; otherwise choice would not be free and man would not be able to make a bad choice. Hence, there must be a final practical judgment (no. V) in which the agent ultimately commits himself to an object of choice. This last practical judgment presents the proposed object of choice as a real, or apparent, good. Because it is the *last* practical judgment, the power of free choice (essentially, the will) must be governed by this judgment.[10] This means that the last practical judgment is last, *because the will of the agent so determines*. If conscience is right, then its rightness may continue into the last practical judgment which is made in accord with conscience. If conscience is right, and the last practical judgment is opposed to it, then the choice must be bad. If conscience is wrong subjectively, the agent must have some suspicion of this error, and so he must reconsider his reasoning and make a new and right judgment of conscience.

After the choice has been made, there is still another act of the practical intellect (not shown in the diagram which deals only with

[9] *De Verit.*, q. 17, 1, ad 4m: "judicium conscientiae consistit in pura cognitione; judicium autem liberi arbitrii in applicatione cognitionis ad affectionem, quod quidem judicium est judicium electionis." Cf. *In II Sent.*, d. 24, q. 2, a. 4, ad 2m.

[10] *De Verit.*, q. 24, 2,c: "judicium de hoc particulari operabili ut nunc numquam potest esse contrarium appetitui."

the steps of right reasoning leading up to choice) and this is the act of commanding the external operation to be done, which external operation has been chosen. This commanding, or ordering (*imperium*), of the external act is formally distinct from choice, because it is one thing to select a definite course of external action and a different thing to order other faculties (say those of bodily motion) to carry out the external action. The rightness of the act of commanding arises from a conformity between the command and the previous right intention and choice. It is conceivable, of course, that circumstances may change at, or after, the moment of choice, but then a new judgment and choice must be made to precede the act of right command. It should also be clear that command, though an act of practical intellect, is intimately associated with the motive force of will. Hence, a right appetitive inclination, which is essentially a good intention, must underlie the whole process of practical reasoning.

We may observe, by way of summary, that right human reason is the proximate rule of good moral action, but not in the sense of being a standard by which the good is mechanically and automatically distinguished from the bad. Every human being *must think* out his own moral problems. There is no substitute for the personal element in practical reasoning. Yet in this subjective process there is an objective guide. In the progressive and personal application of his moral knowledge to the problem of making a right choice, the agent of good will and right intentions may find rectification, regulation, for his practical reasoning in his right speculative knowledge of the objective reasons of things.

All of this teaching on right reason as the rule of morality presupposes the acceptance of a realistic metaphysics and epistemology. If our theory of reality and knowledge is based on the realistic view that man knows *things*, and not merely his own *ideas*, then we have in such knowledge a real and near-at-hand guide for our decisions about proposed moral actions in regard to these things. If, on the other hand, we are convinced (as have been many modern philosophers) that we never know the objective natures and relations of things, then our only immutable standard of moral judgment is the Reason of God. It is true that actions are right, ultimately, because

God so understands and wills them. But it must also be remembered that man does not possess a natural knowledge of what is in God's Mind. Hence, a modern theistic idealist (such as Immanuel Kant) may retain some conviction that there is a real difference between moral good and moral evil. But a modern non-theistic idealist (such as are many of Kant's followers) is left without any standard of moral judgment, because he no longer believes in a God Who requires man to do his moral duty. In much modern ethics, no real standard of morality can be found, precisely because most modern philosophers think that man cannot know the real truth about things. That is why there are few references to modern books on ethics, in this course. Modern ethicians frequently teach the history of ethical systems, without much attempt to suggest which they think right; or they teach descriptive courses based on surveys of the moral opinions of various classes of people.[11]

The student will find brief explanations of St. Thomas' understanding of the proximate and ultimate rules of morality, in: Appendix to Chap. IV, Text One: *Standards of Morality: Human Reason, Eternal Law;* and Text Two: *The Voluntary Act and the Reason of the Object.* For the best English exposition of the teaching, read: E. Gilson, *Moral Values and the Moral Life,* pp. 79–90. For other references see the end of this chapter.

The Moral Determinants: Object, Circumstances, End

There are three factors, or moral determinants, which must be considered in judging whether a concrete human act is morally good or bad, as a whole. These determinants are: the *formal object* of the action (*ratio objecti*), the *circumstances*, and the *end*.

We have seen that moral goodness always implies conformity with reason. Now, when an agent performs any moral action he *thinks* of the *kind* of act which he may do, and his practical intellect pre-

[11] A recent and quite representative text is: R. A. Tsanoff, *Ethics* (New York and London, 1947). It is a sincere and well-written book. It will show the student the need for personal reflection on moral problems. It offers little help in the solution of these problems.

sents a judgment which *formally* determines the act of choice which he elicits through his will. This act of choice cannot be made unless the general inclination of the will toward goodness is specified by the intellectual knowledge of the agent. This means that one must have some sort of *intellectual motive*, a *reason*, for every moral action.

Let us say that the agent considers the performance of a certain external action: burning another man's finger. We shall see in a moment that this external action is the *material object* of the whole moral action. However, many reasons could be found for burning a man's finger. Some such reasons could make the whole action morally approvable (as in the case of cauterizing a wound) and others could make the action morally bad (as in the case of burning a man's finger with a lighted cigarette for a practical joke). It will be observed that the formal object includes what the agent *intends* to do, as is clear in the above cases, but it goes beyond the intention. We intend ends or purposes, whether they be ultimate or proximate. What makes the cauterization of a wound a good moral action, in some cases, is not merely the intending of a good end (to help the wounded person) but also the rational choice of as good a means as is possible under the concrete circumstances. In contemplating such an action, the agent, already intending a good end, thinks of the *kind of action* which he may do to achieve this intended end. Then he chooses to do this species of action, rather than any other kind, because he judges that it is the best means at his disposal for the attainment of this purpose. If he makes a bad choice, formally, there is some failure on his part to deliberate and judge properly. Granted the goodness of his intention, the agent may clearly be held responsible for the deliberation and choice of the right means to his intended end.

But what is to determine the rightness of the means? Obviously not merely the right intention or purpose of the agent; this is important and will be considered next, under the determinant which is the *end*. Besides intending the right end, the agent must think of a certain species of external action which, in his best judgment, will reasonably attain this end. Such a rationally considered species or kind of action, as understood and chosen by the agent, is his formal motive for performing the external action. This formal motive, or <u>objective reason</u> for the action, is what St. Thomas calls the *ratio objecti*.[12]

Thus, in the example of cauterizing a wound, the agent who intends to help a wounded friend may consider the whole situation and decide that he should burn this man's wound. Let us say that he goes ahead and burns it. If later, a medical doctor tells him that the cauterization harmed rather than helped the wounded person, this does not necessarily mean that the action of cauterizing was morally bad. The doctor's criticism has to do with the success of the external action. The moral problem centers chiefly in the way that the agent deliberated, judged, and chose this species of action. Hence, it is quite possible for an agent to perform an action which is *formally* good (*i.e.*, as he sincerely understands the action it is the best thing for him to do) and which is *materially* bad (*i.e.*, the external action produces harmful results). What determines the moral character of the whole action is the <u>fitness</u> of this kind or species of action to the reasoning agent, having a certain intention under these concrete circumstances. The interior act of will is formally determined, then, by its relation to the reason of the agent. We may say that the rational motive (*ratio objecti*) is simply the way in which a certain species of action is rationally grasped by the agent. So, the moral character of the act of cauterizing would become evil if the agent did it, in order to enjoy the suffering of the wounded person. Not only the intention of the agent is changed here; the formal species of his action is changed. He is now performing an act of torture. Hence, his way of rationally grasping the proposed external act (*i.e.*, his *ratio objecti*) is different from that of the agent who wishes to be helpful.

While the foregoing means that the moral agent must know what he is doing, it does not demand of such an agent a technical knowledge of the "species" of human actions, similar to that technical knowledge which a zoologist should have of the species of animals. As we have noted, the two great moral species are *good* and *evil*.

---

[12] *S.T.*, I–II, 18, 2,c and ad 2m. Read also: Appendix to Chap. IV, Text Three: *Formal Object, End, and Circumstances*.

These we have restated respectively as, conformity to reason, and difformity to reason. So, our present problem is to indicate how acts of certain types are known to be in accord with reason, and how acts of other kinds are known to be in discord with reason.

St. Thomas' suggestion, in regard to the solution of this problem, is that the agent should consider, first of all, the principal virtue to which the matter of the proposed act is related.[13] The general theory of the four cardinal virtues is a necessary part of general ethics for this reason, and it will be studied in Chapter VIII. But, it is justifiable and necessary to anticipate now what is a matter of common knowledge, viz., that there are four basic moral virtues: *prudence, temperance, fortitude*, and *justice*. Most human actions will fall under the species of the last three, because prudence is concerned with right reasoning about any and every moral problem. Now, temperance includes the subject matter of any problem involving the rational regulation of concupiscence. Fortitude covers all the problems presented to reason by the irascible appetite, all cases where there is a question of the reasonable mean in fearing and daring. Justice deals with the exchange and distribution of external goods, in relation to some other person. Similarly, each theological virtue, faith, hope and charity, deals with a distinct subject matter. All that is necessary, then, in determining whether a moral action is good or bad, from the point of view of its subject matter (*materialiter*), is to place it under its proper virtue and then determine whether it is opposed to this virtue, or not. Thus, neglecting circumstances and the end (which are to be considered next), an act of risking one's life may be distinguished from an act of adultery, or of stealing, because risking one's life is related to fortitude. Adultery belongs under temperance (when viewed as an act of concupiscence), under justice (when viewed as the appropriation of another's property). Stealing is an act that is simply related to justice. Of course, various circumstances and ends may place the same act under more than one virtue. Thus a man may steal in order to satisfy intemperate desires, but the original character of stealing remains an act in opposition to justice. So, to judge whether an act is good or bad, in its formal object, one has

[13] *De Malo*, q. 2, a. 6,c.

only to think of it in relation to the moral virtue which covers its subject matter.

Given this material specification of the moral act, there remains another problem. Two acts which are materially the same may differ (*formaliter*) by way of excess or defect. Thus, if we take *eating* as the original act to be considered, then it is morally indifferent, neither good nor bad in itself. But everyone who can reason knows, in general, that overeating is morally bad. Moderate eating is morally good. Here, we get a new species of action (gluttony) by the addition of a <u>significant circumstance</u>. And that brings us to the second moral determinant: *circumstances*.

We have already seen how circumstances are related to the moral action. They modify the concrete act in somewhat the same way that the accidents of a physical substance modify the mode of existence of that substance. A circumstance is not an <u>essential</u> part of the original formal object. Yet, because the whole moral act should be good in all its important features, the circumstances of a given individual act must also be judged in relation to reason. With the addition or subtraction of important circumstances, the act acquires a <u>new</u>, and <u>possibly, morally different, formal object</u>. This new formal object is still the relationship of the act to reason. But the variation of circumstances makes the act being considered less abstract and general, more concrete and individual. Let us consider an example. To transport goods is a species of act which is, of itself, morally indifferent. It has a formal object which is so indefinite that it is not possible to say, at this point, whether it names a good or a bad action. Now we will add a circumstance: these goods are the property of another person. The action may still be morally neutral, but it is necessary, now, to relate this circumstance to reason. Have these goods been improperly (*i.e.*, unreasonably) acquired by the transporter? If they have, then we are dealing with a case which has a new formal object, and we have a name for it, theft. To this, let us add that the stealing has been accomplished by the use of brutal force; this will narrow the action down still more, and will give us a new moral species, or formal object, robbery. If the goods are sacred objects, another specific object is reached, by comparing the whole act with reason; it is a sacrilege.[14]

Continuing the same reasoning, we can see that the third moral determinant, the *end*, is a sort of circumstance. Let us say that the agent considered above, takes away another person's goods so that the agent may keep his own family from dying. The fact that the agent's family is in dire need is an important circumstance; it is also the basis for the good intention of the agent. In this case, he has a good end (to satisfy the extreme needs of his family, which he cannot do otherwise), and his act now has a new formal object. At this point of our consideration, the formal object is the relationship of the act, as now known, to reason. St. Thomas says: "though the end is an extrinsic cause, nevertheless the proper proportion to the end, and the relation to it, is something present within the action." [15]

The three moral determinants are not mutually exclusive. When the individual act is to be judged, it must be viewed as *one act*, to be done or not to be done. Thus, in practice, there is no point to the making of an abstract judgment that the act is good from the point of view of its end (and so, to be done), but bad from another point of view, say of a certain circumstance (and so, not to be done). No action could rationally result from such a pluralization of the morality of the act. What is necessary is that the whole act be considered as an integral unit. This will involve the original formal object, the various pertinent circumstances, and the end for which it is to be done. All taken together and related to reason, in one formal unity, constitute the absolute character of the action. The agent must decide not to do it, if any significant determinant is lacking in reasonable goodness. He may decide to do it, if all are in keeping with reason, and it is a morally optional act. He must decide to do it, if all are good and if the situation is such that he is morally expected to act. If he fails in any of these situations, then he is guilty of an immoral act. Thus, no concrete, individual, moral act is morally neu-

[14] *S.T.*, I–II, 18, arts. 10 and 11,c.
[15] *S.T.*, I–II, 18, 4, ad 2m; see the whole *corpus* of art. 4.

tral: it must be either good or bad, depending on the relation of its circumstances (including the end) to reason.[16]

It might be thought much more simple to say that there is a set of moral rules, or laws, and that the agent, knowing these precepts, may judge his individual action in reference to them. This is partly true. It is a help to have acquired some knowledge of practical maxims of good behavior. However, from the philosophical point of view, as opposed to the legal approach, the question of metaphysical priority must be considered. Is it wrong to murder because there is a law against it, or because murder is an action which is in difformity with rational, human nature? The law is simply a universal formulation of the real relation of the proposed action to the reason of the agent. Beings are metaphysically prior to precepts. Hence, the ethical basis for the distinction of good and evil is not the natural moral law (which will be discussed in the next chapter), but the real nature of the human agent, on which natural moral law is proximately founded. If it be argued that the Law of God is the ultimate foundation for such distinctions, that may immediately be granted. But the point is, that the Law of God is really identical with the Reason and Nature of God. So, even from the ultimate point of view, law is not prior to being. St. Thomas is very clear on this matter, which is not so well understood by a later generation of legalistic moralists:

Nor should it be said, that they [human acts, or more specifically, sins] differ specifically according to the difference of precepts; rather on the contrary, the precepts are distinguished according to the difference of the virtues and vices, for precepts are for the sake of operating in accord with virtue and of avoiding sins. If indeed, some acts were sins solely because they were prohibited, then it would be reasonable for these sins to be specifically differentiated by the differences of the precepts.[17]

The Morality of the Interior and of the Exterior Act

Within the human agent, the potency which proximately gives rise to the moral act is the *will*. Without will, man would be morally

[16] Read: Appendix to Chap. IV, Text Four: *No Individual Human Acts Are Morally Indifferent;* and Text Five: *The Specific Differentiation of Immoral Acts.*

[17] *De Malo*, q. 2, 6,c.

paralyzed. The acts completed within the will we have called *elicited* acts, and they are also called *interior* acts. These may be distinguished from the acts of other potencies, and in particular from bodily acts, which are called *exterior* acts. It is necessary, now, to think of the moral specification, into good and evil, of both interior and exterior acts.

The goodness or evil of the interior act of will depends solely on the formal object. Circumstances which are merely accidental to the external performance of the act have no bearing, then, on the moral value of the will-act, as such. Of course, the end is the object of the will, in the order of intention. Hence, as far as the interior act is concerned, there is no real difference between the goodness or evil which derives from the end and the goodness or evil which depends on the formal object.[18]

Since the formal object of the interior act of will is what is proposed to the will by reason, the foregoing means that the will-act, considered apart from the exterior act, is *good*, if in accord with right reason (the problems associated with erroneous practical reasoning require detailed consideration and will be treated in Chapter VI) and *bad*, if in discord with the rational judgment of the agent.[19]

The question of the effect of good or bad *intention*, on the morality of the interior act, may be subdivided. If the intention precedes the will-act which is being considered, and is the cause of this act of will, then the goodness or badness of the will-act depends on the nature of the intention. For example, if the agent first intends to honor God, and as a result wills to fast because of this intention, the good of the intention carries over into the following will-act. On the same basis, the desire to fast, for the sake of a bad intention, would be vitiated by the evil intention. However, if the act of intending follows the completed will-act, for instance, one wishes to do something and, as an afterthought, relates this to a good intention, the goodness of the intention does not retroact upon the preceding will-act. But such a good intention may make another consequent will-act good.[20] Similarly, a consequent bad intention does not make

---

[18] *S.T.*, I–II, 19, 2,c, and *ad primum*.   [19] *S.T.*, *loc. cit.*, a. 5 and 6,c.
[20] *Loc. cit.*, a. 7,c.

the prior will-act evil, but it does vitiate the will-act which follows.[21]

It is quite possible for two people to will contrary things, and yet both perform morally good interior acts. This point is illustrated by an interesting example, given by St. Thomas.[22] Suppose a just judge decides that a thief must be punished. Next, suppose that the thief's wife wishes that her husband will not be punished. The judge's will-act is good from the point of view of what is reasonable in view of the common good. The wife's will-act is morally good in relation to what is reasonable from the point of view of the good of her family. Since the Will of God is always directed to the common good, the judge's will may be objectively in accord with the Will of God, and the wife's may not be. So, there are cases (as in the wife's instance) where the moral agent may perform a morally good interior act which is not in keeping with the Divine Will. This must be carefully understood. To will something for a private good is not justifiable, unless it also be referred to the common good. Let us say, in the preceding example, that both the judge and the wife formally recognize the need of promoting the common good. They differ *materially*, however, in their willing of the means to this end. The wife may think that the loss of her husband's support will impair the welfare of her family and thus his imprisonment would not be for the common good. Hence, *formally*, both judge and wife would be in accord with the Will of God (in promoting the common good); but *materially*, only one of them would agree with God as to the proper means in this case. Man does not know, by his natural reason, what God would actually will in such a contingent case. Hence, in ethics, we cannot use the Will of God as a standard of the material goodness of an interior will-act.[23]

It should be clearly understood that the interior act is the root and source of the moral quality of the whole moral act. That is to say that, "if the act of the will be good, the external act will also be good; but the latter will be bad, if the will-act is bad." [24] Goodness or evil in the exterior act, which are neither directly nor indirectly willed by the agent, are not voluntary and do not alter the moral character

---

[21] *Loc. cit.*, ad 2m.   [22] *S.T.*, I–II, 19, 10,c.
[23] *Ibid.*, ad *primum*.   [24] *C.G.*, III, c. 10.

of the act, as a whole. That is why the interior act is of primary importance in ethics.[25]

Turning now to the exterior, commanded act, we should notice first that it may be morally good in two ways. Certain of these acts are specifically good, because they are of such a nature that they agree, objectively, with reason. For example, to feed the poor and clothe the naked are good kinds of actions. They may be done for a bad intention, and this will make the whole act bad, *for the agent with the bad intention.* Even in such a case, there remains an objective goodness in these exterior acts (which does not redound to the agent's moral credit, because his act is not willed for the sake of a moral good). Where the interior act is good, and it is completed by an exterior act which has such a goodness of its own, there is obviously a kind of double goodness in the whole moral act. Hence, good deeds are of positive moral value. It is better to do what is good, having willed the good, than just to will to do what is good.[26]

Secondly, there are some *exterior* acts which are in themselves, morally neutral. When commanded by reason and will, these may become either good or bad. Where such an exterior act is morally good, it obtains its goodness from the interior act. There is, in such cases, but one goodness in the whole moral act, interior and exterior. Hence, if some unwilled cause prevents the performance of an objectively indifferent exterior act, the whole moral act is just as good as if it had been carried out externally. Similarly, where the exterior act is morally indifferent, an act which becomes morally bad because of the character of the interior act is just as bad, when the exterior act is prevented by some involuntary cause, as it is when it is externally completed. Of course, in the case of the bad act culminating in an accomplished exterior act, there is a possibility of additional will-acts, say of fruition, which may add to the total evil of the whole action. St. Thomas deals with the complications of such cases with precision:

If we speak of the goodness of the exterior act, which is derived from the goodness of the end, then the external act adds nothing to this goodness:

[25] Read: *Summa contra Gentiles,* III, 10; in Pegis, *Basic Writings,* II, 17–21.
[26] *S.T.,* I–II, 20, 1,c; *De Malo,* q. 2, a. 2, ad 8m.

except in the case where the will, in itself, becomes better in good instances, or worse in evil instances. This would seem to be possible in three ways. First, *numerically*. If, for example, a man wishes to do something, with either a good or a bad end, and then does not do it, and if later he wishes it and does it: the act of will is doubled and so a double good, or a double evil, is done. Secondly, *extensively*. For instance, one man wishes to do something with a good or bad end, and stops because of some impediment, but another man continues the movement of his will until he completes the work: it is evident that [the latter's] will-act lasts longer in regard to the good or evil, and is, because of this, worse or better. Thirdly, *intensively*. There are some exterior acts which, because of their pleasurable or painful nature, are naturally capable of increasing or decreasing the intensity of the will-act. It follows that the more intensely the will inclines to good or evil, the better or worse it is.[27]

Suppose there is some good or evil consequence accompanying the performance of the exterior act: does such a consequence modify the moral value of the human act as a whole? The first point to note in answering this is that certain people are expected to know the regular consequences of certain kinds of actions, because they are experts in such matters. Surgeons should know the ordinary effects of certain surgical operations, for instance, but nonsurgeons are not expected to have such technical knowledge. We distinguish, then, between the man who can reasonably be expected to know the probable consequences of a given action and the man who cannot. The moral responsibility of the expert is greater than that of the nonexpert. This reduces to the question of whether ignorance of such consequences is culpable or not. But where there is no question of culpable ignorance we must make still another distinction in regard to the probability of the consequences. Some results of an action are such that they *rarely* follow; for instance, few men, in proportion to the total number of participants in hunting deer, are shot by mistake. The agent who performs actions with rare bad consequences is not responsible morally for the occurrence of a materially bad result, if he could not reasonably be expected to foresee that it would happen in his particular case. This merely means that it is not evil to hunt deer, even though one knows that there is always some remote possibility of killing someone by such an action. On the other hand, if

[27] *S.T.*, I–II, 20, 4,c.

one knows that a given exterior act is followed by certain consequences, *in most cases*, then even though one is not certain that these consequences will result in *this* case, one is morally responsible for the consequences when they do occur.[28] It is to be noted that, unlike some later types of Scholastic ethics, the thomistic theory places no emphasis on whether these consequences are directly or indirectly intended by the agent. If he knows that the consequences frequently occur, and does the act, he intends them. If he is not sure of the consequences in this particular case but knows that they usually occur, he also intends them. In both cases he is morally responsible for their goodness or evil. If he is not sure that they will follow, and knows that they do not usually follow, he is not morally responsible for them.[29] The moral act must be viewed as a whole, and consequences which are known or should be known ahead, pertain to the original intention of the agent. Any morally bad consequences, then, except those which are purely involuntary, will make an otherwise good act, bad. But good consequences will not make an otherwise bad act, good. The principle always applies: a good act must be good in all its voluntary causes: a bad act is bad because of any single bad feature, provided this defect is voluntary.

We may notice, finally, that three types of moral relations characterize the human act, as a result of its goodness or evil in the order of reason. First, the human act in the relation of rational conformity or difformity with the ultimate end is said to be *right* or *wrong*.[30] It is in this sense that the human act is said to possess the formal character (*rationem*) of rightness or sinfulness. Second, considering right or wrong acts in relation to the responsibility of the agent for his own voluntary acts, we can say that the acts are *praiseworthy* or *culpable*. This second relation deals with what is called the imputability of the moral act.

An act is called culpable or praiseworthy, from the fact that it is imputable to the agent; for, to be praised or blamed is simply that the evil or goodness of his own act is imputed to someone. An act is imputed to an agent, when it is within his power, so that he has dominion over his

---

[28] *S.T.*, I–II, 20, 5,c.   [29] *De Malo*, q. 1, a. 4, ad 15m.
[30] *S.T.*, I–II, 21, 1,c, and ad 2m.

act. But this is the case with all voluntary acts, since it is through the will that man has dominion over his act, as is clear from what has been said above. Whence, it follows that the good or evil of voluntary acts alone constitutes the formal character (*rationem*) of the praiseworthy or culpable, and in these, the bad, the sinful, and the culpable, are the same.[31]

The third moral relationship attaching to the voluntary act is that of *merit* or *demerit*. Every good or bad moral act is of some consequence in regard to some other being than the agent. Thus, justice (which is the virtue dealing with the agent's relations with other persons) applies directly or indirectly to all human acts. It is necessary to think of retribution, or "payment," when an act is considered under justice. The moral necessity set up by a good act, which is helpful to another, is for a reward; such a moral necessity is called *merit*. On the other hand, the moral necessity for punishment, as a consequence of a bad act, harmful to another, is termed *demerit*. As we shall see later (Chapter X), there are two kinds of particular justice: the end of the first kind is the good of one individual, a private good; the function of the second kind of justice (distributive) is the right distribution to individual persons, of things which belong to the community. Now, some acts have merit or demerit from the first kind of justice, because they directly benefit or harm some other private person. If A does work for B, which is worth five dollars, then B is required to pay A five dollars or its equivalent, provided this work has been actually beneficial to that extent. This is a matter of commutative justice.

However, every human agent is a member of some society, whether this social group be some political society or simply the society of all men working for their ultimate end under the government of God. Thus, if A benefits another citizen of his own civil group, or even himself by his own private good act, A merits a reward from this civil society, because he has benefited this civil society by benefiting one of its members. The same is true of demerit in regard to punishment. If A benefits another man, or God (in an analogical sense, for no essential good is produced in God by a

[31] *S.T.*, I–II, 21, 2,c.

good human act), then, even if this other person is not a fellow citizen in a political society, A acquires merit before God, because all men have at least one end in common, the Ultimate End, God. In this latter sense, all human acts have social merit or demerit before God. This is the field of distributive justice, that is to say, of what is owed to the individual agent, in the way of reward or punishment to be meted out by the society to which he belongs as a member. The two ways in which merit or demerit pertain to the human act are precisely described by St. Thomas:

Merit and demerit are spoken of in relation to the retribution which depends on justice. Now, retribution according to justice is accorded to a man because he acts for the benefit or harm of another person. It should be considered that each man living in some society is in some way a part and member of the whole society. Therefore, whoever does something for the good or evil of anyone existing in the society, does something which affects the whole society; just as he who injures someone's hand, injures the whole man, as a consequence. And so, when a man does something good or evil to another individual person, the formal nature of merit or demerit applies to this act, in two ways. First, because retribution is due him from the whole group. Of course, when a man directly relates his act to the good or evil of the whole group, retribution is due him primarily and principally from the whole group, but secondarily, from all parts of the group. And, when a man does something which bears on his own good or evil, retribution is also due him, inasmuch as this has a general bearing, because he himself is a part of the group. Of course, no retribution is due him from the point of view of it being good or evil to the individual person, for he is the same as the agent, unless perhaps we consider him in relation to himself, analogically, insofar as there is a sort of justice of man to himself.[32]

It is apparent, then, that every moral act will have merit or demerit, *in the sight of God*, in two ways. Since God is the objective ultimate end of human acts, all human acts must be either for or against God, considered as an individual Terminus of voluntary action. Again, since God has care of the whole universe, every human act possesses merit or demerit before God, Who is the Ruler of the general society made up of all men.[33]

[32] *S.T.*, I–II, 21, 3,c.   [33] *S.T.*, I–II, 21, 4,c.

This is the point at which we might briefly consider the moral force of *sanctions*. This is the term used by post-thomistic Scholastics to name those rewards and punishments, which make it advisable to obey the moral law. The position of some writers seems to be that the real reason for a man's doing what is right is so that he may attain a positive reward and avoid punishment. It was to this superficial legalism that Immanuel Kant objected, throughout his *Critique of Practical Reason*. Kant's feeling was that an agent who did what was morally good, *because he was going to be paid for it*, was not really a good man. He was convinced that one should do what is right, simply because it is right. Now, setting aside all technical differences between the moral system of Kant and the ethics of Thomism, we may say bluntly that, on this particular point, Kant was right.

It would be a curious distortion of ethics, to say that man should be good because of the sanctions attaching to the natural moral law. The meriting of a reward and the setting up of a moral exigency for punishment (*i.e.*, the acquisition of demerit) are moral consequences which *follow* upon the moral goodness or evil of the human act. The norm or standard, upon which such goodness or evil is to be determined, is not the success of the act in relation to certain sanctions, but rather the relation of the individual act to the order of reason. If we also know that there is a sort of secondary motive for being morally good, namely, that it pays in terms of reward and punishment in a future life, if not always in the present life, this is but a secondary reason for good action. St. Thomas recognized, as Kant did not, that it is reasonable and morally justifiable to work for an ultimate reward; this is another way of saying that every man should do his best to attain final happiness. But, to exalt moral sanctions into primary motives for moral goodness is neither good Kantianism, nor good Thomism. This is the conclusion of a very good interpreter of the moral position of St. Thomas:

It is not in order to receive a reward or avoid a punishment that one should act in such and such a way, but because his reason demands that he so act and subordinate all his acts to his final end, that is, to God.

Whether he does this or not, his act will be followed by a reward or a punishment; sanctions will be a normal consequence of his activity; they will not be its goal.[34]

Summary of Chapter IV

In this chapter, we have faced the problem of the determination of the moral goodness or evil of the individual human act. After looking at various theories of moral standards, we concluded that a valid ethics must have an ultimate, unchangeable criterion of moral value, but that in practice the individual agent must use a proximate and practical standard of morality. The ultimate norm in thomistic ethics is the Reason of God. The proximate norm is human reason, speculatively regulated by the Reason of God, either directly by the immediate influence of God, or indirectly and naturally by man's ordinary intellectual knowledge of the reasons of finite beings. The rational order includes this speculative area of reasoning and also the practical application of the reasons of things to the control of the voluntary acts of man. The diagram of the *Rational Order* summarizes this situation, whereby man is enabled to translate right knowledge into right action. The reason of the object, or formal object, of the human act is the principle, in accord with which the act is judged to be morally good or bad. As man's problems are viewed more and more practically and concretely, it is necessary to make this formal object narrower and more concrete, *i.e.*, by including the morally significant circumstances and the end intended by the agent. Thus, *abstractly*, human acts may be: good, bad, or indifferent. *Concretely*, the voluntary act must be either for or against man's attainment of his ultimate end, or to put it another way, it must be either reasonable or unreasonable. It is the addition of the definite circumstances of the act which makes it impossible for the act to be morally neutral. The kind of act which a man performs may be determined in relation to the subject matter of the different virtues. The moral law is not the source of this distinction of virtuous acts, but its consequence.

[34] M. S. Gillet, O.P., *S. Thomas d'Aq., Somme Théol.*, qq. 6–21 (Paris, 1926), "Notes Explicatives," p. 441.

Distinguishing the interior will-act from the exterior commanded act, we find that each may have a goodness or evil of its own, and that, in cases where the exterior act is morally neutral, it may acquire moral value from the preceding will-act. The interior act is the more important morally, but we cannot neglect the moral quality of the exterior act. As a consequence of its goodness, the moral act is termed: right, praiseworthy, and meritorious—depending on its relation to reason, to the responsibility of the agent, and to a reward. The bad act is similarly called: wrong, culpable, and demeritorious, on the basis of the same relations. Merit in relation to another private individual, and social merit in relation to some society, political or that of all men, are differentiated. Sanctions (rewards and punishments) are not primary motives for good or bad actions.

Appendix to Chapter IV

¶ TEXT ONE: *Standards of Morality: Human Reason, Eternal Law.* Evil is of wider extension than sin, just as good is of wider extension than the righteous. For any privation of good in anything constitutes the essential nature of evil (*rationem mali*), but sin consists properly in an act which is done for some end, when it has not a due ordination to that end. Now, a due ordination to an end is measured according to some standard (*regulam*). And this standard, among things which act according to nature, is the very force (*virtus*) of nature, which inclines to such an end. Therefore, when an act proceeds from a natural force according to a natural inclination to the end, then rectitude is preserved in the act, because the mean of the act stems from the orderly relation of the active principle to the end, and not from the extremes. When, however, any act draws away from such rectitude, then the essential nature (*ratio*) of a sin is present.

And, in those things which are done voluntarily, the proximate standard (*regula*) is human reason, but the supreme standard is the eternal law. Therefore, whenever man's act proceeds to the end, in accordance with the order of reason and of the eternal law, then the act is right; but when it is twisted away from this rightness, it is then called a sin. Now, it is apparent from what has gone before, that every voluntary act that recedes from the order of reason and of the eternal law is thereby bad, and every good act is in agreement with reason and eternal law. (*S.T.*, I–II, 21, 1,c.)

¶ TEXT TWO: *The Voluntary Act and the Reason of the Object.*
Though the act receives its species from the object, it does not receive the species from it considered as a material object, but according to the reason of the object (*secundum rationem objecti*): just as the act of seeing a stone is not specified by the stone, but by the *colored thing* which is the essential (*per se*) object of vision. Now, every human act has the reason [*i.e.*, the formal nature] of a sin, or of a meritorious act, inasmuch as it is voluntary. But the object of the will, according to its proper reason, is the apprehended good; and so, the human act is judged virtuous or vicious, according to the apprehended good toward which the will is essentially attracted, and not according to the material object of the act.

For instance, if, believing that he is killing his father, a man kills a stag, he incurs the sin of patricide. And, on the other hand, if some hunter, thinking to kill a stag, and having taken due care, kills his father by chance, he is quite free from the crime of patricide. Therefore, if something which in itself is not against the Law of God, such as lifting a straw from the ground, or oath-taking, is apprehended by an erring conscience as contrary to the Law of God, and if the will is thus attracted to it, it is plain that the will is attracted to something which, essentially and formally speaking, is against the Law of God, even though, by chance, the act is [objectively] in accord with the Law of God. So, it is evident that there is, in this case, contempt for the Law of God. Therefore, in such an instance, there must be a sin. (*Quaest. Quodl.*, III, q. 12,a. 27,c).

¶ TEXT THREE: *Formal Object, End, and Circumstances.* We are speaking now of the acts of man; hence good and evil in acts, according to our present way of speaking, are to be taken according

to what is proper to man as man. Now, this is *reason*, and so good
and evil in human acts are to be considered according as the act is
in accord with *reason informed by the Divine Law*, either naturally,
or through teaching, or through infusion. So, Dionysius says (*De
Divin. Nomin.*, c. 4) that the evil of the soul is contrary to reason,
and that of the body is contrary to nature.

And so, if to be in accord with, or contrary to, reason pertains to
the species of the human act, one must say that some human acts
are good in themselves, and some are evil in themselves. For, we
say that something is essentially (*per se*) in agreement with another
thing, not only when it agrees with it by reason of its genus, but
also when it agrees by reason of its species. For instance, rational
and irrational are present essentially (*per se*) in animals by reason
of their species, but not by reason of their genus, animal: for an
animal is not, insofar as it is animal, rational or irrational.

Now, if to be contrary to reason, or in accord with reason, does
not pertain to the species of a human act, it follows that human acts
are essentially (*per se*) neither good nor bad, but indifferent, just
as men are essentially neither white nor black. This then, is the
point on which the truth of this question hangs.

To clear this up, we should consider that, since the act receives
its species from the *object*, it is according to some reason of the object (*rationem objecti*) that the act will be specified in reference to
one active principle; and it will not be specified by the same reason, in reference to another [active principle]. For, to know color
and to know sound are different acts, according to species, if they
be referred to the senses (for these are proper sensibles); but they
are not specifically different, if they be referred to the intellect,
for they are grasped intellectually under one common reason of the
object, namely, that of being or truth. Likewise, to sense a white
thing and a black thing are specifically different acts, if they be
referred to the object of vision, but not, if they be referred to taste.
It may be gathered, from this, that the act of any potency is specified according to that which essentially (*per se*) pertains to that
potency, and not simply according to that which pertains to it accidentally (*per accidens*).

If, then, the objects of human acts be considered, which have essential differences *from the point of view of reason*, the acts will be specifically different, according as they are acts of reason, though they may not be specifically different, when considered as acts of some other potencies. For example, to beget children with one's own wife, or to do so with a woman who is not one's wife, are acts having different objects from the point of view of reason, for one's own and what is not one's own are determined according to a rule of reason. However, these differences are accidental, if considered in relation to the generative potency, or even to the concupiscible power. So, the act of procreation, with one's own wife, or with another woman, are specifically different as acts of reason, but not as acts of the generative or concupiscible powers.

But acts are human to the extent that they are acts of reason. And so, it is clear that they do differ specifically, when considered as human acts. Thus, it is clear that it pertains to the very species of human acts, that some are good and some evil. Therefore, we should say, without qualification, that some human acts are in themselves good, or bad, and not that all are morally indifferent (except, perhaps, when they are considered solely in their genus). For, just as one may say that an animal, simply considered as an animal, is neither rational nor irrational, so also may it be said that the human act, simply considered as an act, never possesses the formal nature (*rationem*) of moral good or evil, unless something be added to narrow it down to a species. Nevertheless, even from the fact that it is a human act, and furthermore from the fact that it is a being, it may possess some formal character (*rationem*) of goodness, but not of this moral goodness, *which consists in being in accord with reason;* and that is what we are concerned with, now.

In reply to the second objection, we should say that whatever goes along with the species of a thing is always present in it. Therefore, since an act of man takes its species from the reason of its object, and is, according to it, good or evil, an act thus specified as good, never can be evil; nor can one specified as evil ever be good. Nevertheless, it can happen that, to an act which is good in itself, there may be added some other act which is evil according to some relationship; and because of this sort of evil act, the good is said to produce evil at times, but it is not that it is in itself evil. For example, to give alms to the poor, or to love God, is an act good in itself; but to refer an act of this kind to some inordinate end, namely, to cupidity or vain-glory, is another act and evil. But these two acts are reduced, under some orderly relationship, into one. Now, the good, as Dionysius says (*De Div. Nom.*, c. 4, p. 4) arises from a whole and integral cause, but evil from singular defects. Therefore, whatever of these be evil, either the act or the inordination of the act to the end, *the whole is judged evil*. Moreover, the whole thing is not judged good unless both are good; just as a man is not judged handsome, unless all his members are decorous, for he is judged to be ugly, even if one of his members is deformed. So it is that a bad act cannot be done rightly (*bene*), for, from the fact that it is bad, it cannot be good as a whole; but a good act can be done wrongly (*male*), because it is not necessary that it be evil as a whole, but it is enough that it be evil in some particular way.

In reply to the fifth objection, we should say that circumstances are related to moral acts, just as accidents outside the reason of the species are to natural things. Now, the moral act, as has been said, receives its species from the object according to the way that it is related to reason. So, it is said in a general way, that some acts are good or bad generically, and that the act which is good generically is an act dealing with some proper matter, such as feeding the hungry. But an act which is generically evil deals with improper matter, such as taking the goods of another; for, the matter of the act is called its object. But, over and above this goodness or evil, there may be added another goodness or evil from something extrinsic, which is called a circumstance, of place or time, or a condition of the agent, or the like. For example, one may take what is not his own, from a sacred place, or because of need, or something like that. And, though this kind of goodness or evil does not essentially (*per se*) pertain to the moral act, as something to be considered within its species, nevertheless another goodness or evil does belong to it according to its species, since (as has been said above in the body of the article) there are different formal principles (*ratio*) of goodness, according to various perfections. (*De Malo*, q. II, a. 4,c, and ad 2m, and ad 5m.)

¶ TEXT FOUR: *No Individual Human Acts Are Morally Indifferent.* If we speak of the moral act according to its species, then not every moral act is good or evil, but some are morally indifferent, because the moral act gets its species from the object according to its relation to reason, as was said in the preceding article. Now, there is one sort of object which implies something in agreement with reason, and it makes [the moral act] *good,* in a general way (*ex genere*), for example: clothing the naked. There is another sort of object which implies something in discord with reason (such as, taking what belongs to another), and this makes it *bad,* in a general way. And, there is a third kind of object which neither implies something in agreement with reason, nor in discord with reason (for instance, lifting a straw from the ground, or some act like that), and this kind of act is said to be indifferent. On this point, those people are right, who divide acts into three classes: good, evil, and indifferent.

But, if we speak of the moral act, as individual, then every particular moral act must be good or evil because of some circumstance. For, it cannot happen that the singular act go on without circumstances which make it right or wrong. If anything whatever be done, when it should, where it should, as it should, and so on, then this kind of act is well ordered and good; but, if any of these be defective, the act is badly ordered and evil. This may chiefly be considered in the circumstance which is the end. For, what is done because of a just need, or pious utility, is done in a praiseworthy way, and is a good act; but that which does not have a just need and pious utility is regarded as idle. (*De Malo*, q. 2,a. 5,c.)

¶ TEXT FIVE: *The Specific Differentiation of Immoral Acts.* Since the moral act is the voluntary act proceeding from reason, it is necessary for the moral act to get its species from something in the object, considered in an orderly relation to reason. Thus, it was said in the preceding article, that, if it be in agreement with reason, it will be a specifically good act, but if it be in discord with reason, it will be a specifically bad act. Now, this business of the object being in discord with reason, and the consequent specific differentiation of immoral acts (*peccati*), can be taken in two ways: materially and formally.

Materially, [they may be considered] in opposition to virtue. The virtues differ specifically, according as reason finds the mean in diverse subject matters: thus, justice applies to the cases in which reason establishes a mean in commutations and distributions, and actions of that kind; temperance, however, applies to matters of concupiscence; fortitude, to questions of fear and daring; and so on for the others. . . . And so, immoral acts (*peccata*) differ specifically because of their opposition to the virtues, thus: homicide, adultery, and theft.

But, since there may be specifically different sins, in relation to one kind of subject matter, to which but one virtue applies, it is necessary, secondly, to consider *formally* the specific diversity of sins. That is, one may sin by way of excess or defect; thus does timidity differ from presumption, and illiberality from prodigality; or, according to various circumstances, as the species of gluttony are distinguished according to the items in this verse: "Too quickly, too magnificently, too much, too passionately, too eagerly." (*De Malo*, q. 2,a. 6,c.)

¶ TEXT SIX: *The Goodness of the Interior and Exterior Act.* The exterior act and the interior act of the will are mutually related in this way: each is at times the cause of goodness in the other; and each, considered in itself, has some goodness which it gives to the other. For, the exterior act has a goodness arising from the commensuration of circumstances, according as it is proportionate to the end to be sought by man. And since the exterior act is related to the will as an object, the interior will-act gets this goodness from the exterior act; not indeed from it considered as exercised but as intended and wished; for, insofar as it is exercised, it follows the will-act.

But some formal goodness is present in the interior will-act, in itself, inasmuch as the will is the master of its own acts, and, on this basis, the act has the formal nature (*rationem*) of merit or is praiseworthy; and this goodness proceeds from the interior act to the exterior one. Therefore, speaking of that goodness which the will furnishes to the exterior act, the exterior act adds no goodness, provided the will remains equal from the point of view of the intensity of its act. I say this, because some acts are so capable of arousing pleasure that the will cannot be as intense before the act, as it is while the act is going on. . . . But some acts are difficult, and in these cases, the will becomes less intense while the act is going on; in such instances, the will-act can be more perfect before the act than during the act. But, if we speak of the goodness which the exterior act has of itself, then the exterior act completes the interior in goodness or evil, just as the terminus of a motion completes the motion; for it is related, as has been said, to the will as its object. (*In II Sent.*, d. 40, q. unica, a. 3, c.)

¶ TEXT SEVEN: *The Evil of the Interior and Exterior Act.* If it be asked, whether one who only sins in his will-act, sins as much as he who sins both in will and in the [exterior] act, it must be answered that this can occur in two ways. In the first way, there is equality on the part of the will; in the second way, the will does not remain equal.

Inequality of will may occur in three ways. First of all, *numerically:* thus, if a man desires to sin by one movement of his will, and finds no opportunity to do so, his will-act passes away; but, in another agent, who first has the movement of his will, and then has an opportunity [to sin], the act of will is repeated. Thus, there is a double evil of will, one without the act, another with the act. Secondly, inequality may be observed *in the manner* (*modum*): for instance, one person may have the will to sin but, knowing that he has no opportunity, he desists from such a movement of the will; but another person, knowing that he has the ability to sin, continues the will-act until he reaches the [exterior] act. Thirdly, there may be inequality of will in regard to *intensity:* for, there are some sinful acts which are pleasurable, and in these the will increases by a sort of removal of the control of reason, which was to some extent a restraint, before the performance of the act. Now, in whatever way there may be inequality in the will-act, there will be inequality in the sin.

But, if there be complete equality on the part of the will, then it seems that we should make the same distinctions in regard to sins that we do in regard to merit. He who has the will to give alms, and does not give because he has not the ability, merits just as much as if he had given, from the point of view of the essential reward, that is, of joy concerning God, for this reward corresponds to charity, which pertains to the will. But, in relation to an accidental reward, which is joy concerning any sort of created good, he merits more who not only wishes to give, but gives. For, he will rejoice not only because he has wished to give, but because he has given, by reason of all the good things which came from this giving.

Likewise, if the amount of demerit be considered in relation to the essential punishment, which consists in the separation from God and the sorrow arising from this, then he has not less demerit who sins only with his will, than he who sins in the [exterior] act; for this punishment is the contempt for God, which pertains to the will. But, in regard to the secondary punishment, which is the sorrow connected with any other kind of evil, he who sins both in the act and in his will has more demerit. For, he will have sorrow not only from the fact that he has willed evil, but also from the fact that he has done an evil thing, and from all the evils which result from his evil-doing.

In answer to the twelfth objection, we should say that in both acts, interior and exterior, there is the deformity of a sin; nevertheless, there is but one deformity for the two taken together (*utriusque*). This is so, because the deformity in one of them is caused by the other. (*De Malo*, q. 2, a. 2, ad 8m and ad 12m.)

Recommended Readings

Thomas Aquinas, St., *Summa Theologiae*, I–II, qq. 18–21 (in *Basic Writings*, ed. Pegis, II, 317–365).

Bourke, *St. Thomas and the Greek Moralists*, pp. 21–29.

Brosnahan, *Prolegomena to Ethics*, pp. 12–13, 167–173 (a brief critique of other types of moral theory).

Cathrein, "The Norm of Moral Rectitude," in Leibell, *Readings in Ethics*, pp. 156–162.

Cronin, *Science of Ethics*, I, 318–366 (a criticism of utilitarianism).

Gilson, *Moral Values and the Moral Life*, pp. 79–90.

Kendzierski, "Object and Intention in the Moral Act," *Proc. Amer. Cath. Philos. Assoc.*, XXIV (1950) c. 10 pp.

Murray, "Reason and Morality according to St. Thomas," *Month*, CLI (1928) 417–423.

O'Brien, Sr. M. Consilia, "Recta Ratio in Relation to Moral Truth," *Proc. Amer. Cath. Philos. Assoc.*, XVIII (1942) 120–126.

Rommen, *The State in Catholic Thought*, Chap. 6: "The Idea of Order as the Philosophical Basis of Natural Law," pp. 169–183.

ADVANCED READINGS

Gillet, "Notes Explicatives," in S. Thomas d'Aquin, *Somme Théologique*, I–II, qq. 6–21, pp. 431–432.

Lehu, *La raison règle de la moralité d'après s. Thomas*, 264 pp.

Lottin, *Principes de Morale*, I, 114–132.

Wittmann, *Die Ethik des hl. Thomas*, pp. 282–287.

Topics for Assignment

1. A Critical Appraisal of Utilitarianism
2. Right Reason Compared with Right Intention
3. Why Circumstances Modify the Morality of an Action
4. The Importance of the Interior Moral Act
5. The Nature of Merit and Demerit in Ethics

V · MORAL LAW AND ETHICS

The General Meaning of Law

There are certain principles or causes, *interior* to the nature of the moral agent, which incline man toward moral good or evil. We have seen that these inner principles are the *reason* and *will*, as directed to the attainment of the ultimate end, and the *sensory appetites*, which may incline the agent either to good or to bad action. Included also among these interior sources of human acts are the *habitus of virtue and vice*, which will be examined later (Chapter VIII). There are, in addition, certain principles *exterior* to the nature of man which influence his moral life. In theology, the Devil is regarded as a real cause, soliciting though not compelling, man to evil action. So too, God is a Cause, outside human nature, influencing man to do what is good. In Thomistic morality, God's influence is placed on a twofold basis: by *grace*, man is helped to do what is right in the supernatural order; by *law*, God instructs man so that he may do what is right, if he wishes.[1]

However, we have seen that moral good and evil are to be distinguished, in thomistic ethics, by their reference to the rational order of being. This teaching suggests that, even apart from external reasons, there is in the very nature of man an internal reason for human goodness. Man is so made that he finds his greatest perfection and happiness in reasonable activity. Now, law is concerned with the regulation of operations; hence, it is not something foreign

[1] *S.T.*, I–II, 90, *prolog.*

to reason; rather, it is the expression of what is reasonable, under universal conditions. It is the function of reason to order action. This function is made explicit in law. It is thus that St. Thomas relates law, in general, to reason: "Law is a rule or measure of acts, whereby one is either induced to act, or is restrained from acting. . . . The rule and measure of human acts is reason, which is the first principle of human acts. . . . And so, it follows that law is something pertaining to reason." [2]

If we view law from the side of the reason which initially orders acts (considering the activities of the whole universe, this will be the Reason of God), then we are thinking of law in an active sense, and it is wholly an affair of reason. But law may also be observed in the regulated activities of those beings which are subject to it. In this second case, it is considered as having been received by its subjects, and it is now no longer restricted to the faculty of reason but is shared by all potencies which can be ruled by reason. [3] What has been said so far applies to any kind of law, to the laws discovered by the chemist and physicist, as well as to the laws governing the free acts of man. Law is always regulative of action, whether the action be necessary or free.

The distinctive thing about the rationally free agent is not, as Kant thought, that he is a law unto himself. Man is not the ultimate source or principle of the moral law. Rather, human reason is subject to the laws of reality, which come from the Divine Reason. Speculatively, man is free to think of whatever he wishes; but, if he thinks, he must be governed by the objective and universal truth of things, in order to elicit true judgments. Practically, human reason is, in its turn, directive of human operations; that is to say "the universal propositions of practical reason, ordering actions, have the formal nature (*rationem*) of law." [4] So, man is at once *ordered* by the Law of God, and *ordering* his own free actions. We have already noticed that to issue an order, is not simply the prerogative of will. For the will to command actions that are reasonably calculated to achieve a desired end, it must itself be ordered by reason. It is only under such rational regulation that will-

[2] *S.T.*, I–II, 90, 1,c.   [3] *Ibid.*, *ad primum*.   [4] *Ibid.*, ad 2m.

acts possess the essential character of law.[5] This is the first thing to keep in mind, then, in regard to the general nature of law: *it must be an order issuing from reason.*

The second necessary feature of law in general, is that it be *for the common good.* This is true of all laws, but it may be seen most effectively, perhaps, if we consider the law which governs human acts, that is, the moral law. Reason is the principle of human acts; such acts are not human if they do not stem from reason. Now, the ultimate end is also the first principle of moral action. The ultimate end of man is one and the same for all members of the human species. Thus considered, men make up a huge society or perfect community. All human beings are of the same species and have one specific end; they should cooperate for the attainment of it. The search for happiness is common to all human agents. A rule reasonably directing man to this ultimate end will not be a private and individual regulation; it will have the formal character of law because it orders men, in regard to that purpose or end which is the chief concern of human reason—the common good of all men.[6] A private precept, or rule, may be applied to the gaining of some particular end, of course. What is required for such an order to have the force and obligatory character of a law, is that it be also and primarily for the universal good of men.[7]

It is necessary to understand very clearly what this expression, "the common good," means in this description of law. We have already seen that each moral agent may have his own private purpose for performing a particular act. We have also noted that such private purposes or ends do not make a human act immoral, unless these purposes are definitely opposed to the specific end of human life. Now, a rule of action made for the sake of some private purpose could not be a law, because there would be no reason, in such a case, for the imposition of obligation on the subjects of the law. Suppose there is an absolute ruler who cannot sleep because the trains run past his palace all through the night. He makes a rule that no trains are to run at night. This rule is for his own private good only. It is not a law. To make it a real law, he would have

[5] *Ibid.,* ad 3m.   [6] *S.T.,* I–II, 90, 2,c.   [7] *Ibid., ad primum,* and ad 2m.

to intend the rule to be for the welfare of his whole community. The good for which a law is made must be common in the sense that a plurality of subjects can work for this good as an end capable of being attained by more than one moral agent. As St. Thomas expresses it: "[It is] not with the community of a genus or species, but with the community of a final cause, that the common good is called a common end."[8] Happiness, which means personal perfection in the attainment of the Beatific Vision, is a common good in this sense, *i.e.*, as a final cause to which all men may direct their lives. Happiness is not a common good in the sense of something which must be actually attained by the whole human species before any one man can be said to have it.

A third characteristic of law flows from the first two. If a law must issue from reason, and if it must be for the sake of a common good, it must also be enacted *by an authority* which is greater than that of the private person. The lawmaker must be either the whole community of subjects, or someone who represents this community. A real law must be capable of enforcement. Some external pressure, in the form of rewards and punishments, must be at hand to impel recalcitrant subjects to obey the law. A rule put forth by a private person lacks this coactive force. In some sense, the whole community must approve a rule before it can have the full force of a law. This is what St. Thomas means when he says: "To establish a law pertains either to the whole group, or to a public person who has charge of the whole group."[9]

The fourth and last essential quality of a true law is what is called *promulgation*. A law is a rule of action. This rule is of no avail, unless it be *applied* to the agents capable of such action. In the case of the free actions of man, such application of the law would have to be made by way of knowledge. This means that a law governing human acts would need to be made known, or at least made knowable, to all men. Various laws are published or promulgated in different ways. Every law must be promulgated in some way.[10]

Gathering together the four parts of this analysis, we find the

[8] *Ibid.*, ad 2m.   [9] *S.T.*, I–II, 90, 3,c.   [10] *Ibid.*, art. 4,c.

following general definition of law: (1) an order issuing from reason, (2) for the common good, (3) coming from whoever has charge of the community, and (4) promulgated. Restating this in more acceptable English, we may say: *A law is a reasonable order, promulgated by one who has charge of a community, for the sake of the common good.*[11]

Natural Moral Law in Particular

In the foregoing treatment of law, no attempt was made to differentiate the various kinds of laws. One obvious division of law is into *natural* and *positive*. The distinction, here, may be most easily grasped by thinking of the difference in the way in which these are promulgated. A natural law is applied to its subjects by being made an internal part of their essence or nature. The laws of chemical changes are inserted in the very nature of the elements. Biological or physiological laws are necessary ingredients in human nature. We shall see that moral law is similarly natural to man, but it is not ingrained in his *physical* nature. The natural moral law is implanted in the intellect of man in a way which will be discussed in the next section. A positive law, on the other hand, is promulgated by some manifestation which comes from *outside the nature* of its subjects. Such a law is placed, or posited, before the subjects by someone in authority. This positing may be done by God (as in the case of the Ten Commandments), or by some human legislator (as in the case of the just laws of a state).

That the Reason of God is the supreme standard of right and wrong was explained in Chapter IV. There will be, then, a supreme Law expressive of the Divine Order for all beings and their actions. This is called the Eternal Law. That this is truly a law, is made clear by St. Thomas:

It is evident, considering that the world is ruled by divine Providence, that the entire community of the universe is governed by divine Reason.

[11] *Ibid., ad fin.* Students should read carefully St. Thomas' discussion of law in general, *S.T.*, I–II, 90, arts. 1–4 inclus. It will be found in: Pegis, *Basic Writings*, II, 742–747. Advanced students may read: M. Adler, "A Question About Law," in *Essays in Thomism* (New York, 1942), pp. 207–236.

Therefore, this Reason for the governance of things, which is considered as existing in God as in the Ruler of all, has the formal nature (*ratio*) of a law. And, since the divine Reason conceives nothing from the point of view of time but has an eternal concept, as is said in *Prov.* 8:23, this kind of law should be called eternal.[12]

All beings, potential or actual, come under the regulation of the Eternal Law. This is the same as to say that all things are inclined toward their proper acts and ends by the divine Reason. Men share in this divine regulation, as do all creatures. That part of the Eternal Law in which men participate in a special way, because they are rational, is called the *Natural Law.*[13] To avoid confusion with the law of nature (which would include such things as physical laws), we shall call that part of the Eternal Law which applies especially to the free acts of man, the *natural moral law.* The thomistic definition of this law is: "a participation of the Eternal Law on the part of a rational creature." [14]

Leaving for the next section in this chapter the explanation of the manner in which man participates in the Eternal Law, we can note, now, some of the special characteristics of the natural moral law, and something of its relation to other forms of law. The first thing to observe is that the natural moral law is *not made by human reason,* but is naturally implanted in the reason of man. This point distinguishes the Kantian theory of the autonomy of man's practical reason from the thomistic notion of the discovery of moral law by human reason. "The human reason is not, of itself, the rule of things, but the principles naturally implanted in it [human reason] are the general rules and standards of all things which are to be done by man and which come under the regulation of natural reason, though [man's reason] is not the measure of these things which go on by nature." [15] This is to say that the natural moral law governs only the *free* acts of man, not the acts which man does as a result of the physical and psychic necessity of his nature. A man's heart beats at a certain rate, his digestive processes follow a definite pattern, his body falls according to the law of gravity—these ac-

---

[12] *S.T.*, I–II, 91, 1,c.   [13] *Ibid.*, art. 2,c.
[14] *Ibid.*   [15] *S.T.*, I–II, 91, 3, ad 2m.

tions are natural but not free. Only human acts, in the technical ethical sense, are to be regulated by the natural moral law.

Positive laws, those of a state for instance, are related in two possible ways to the natural moral law. They may be *derived from the moral law, as conclusions are from principles*. Thus, a positive law which states that one should not murder is really a conclusion of practical reason from the more general and obvious principle of the natural moral law: *No evil should be done to anyone*.[16] Other positive laws are *derived from the natural moral law by way of determination*. That is, because the circumstances under which concrete human acts are to be performed vary much with changes of time and place and other contingent conditions, it is necessary that the maker of a positive law give more specific rules than those which can be discovered by the use of ordinary practical reason. For example: any reasonable person would know that in driving an automobile on a public road it is necessary for those driving in the same direction to keep to one side of the road, leaving the other side for those who are driving in the opposite direction. But is it more reasonable to drive to the right, as in America, or to the left, as in England? The answer may depend partly on the construction of the automobiles, but it is clear that someone in authority must make the decision and then all must obey it. If the lawmaker determines that all must keep to the right, then this is a case of the positive law adding something useful to the natural moral law, by way of determination. Many of the determinations of human positive law have to do with the kind of punishment and the manner of assigning punishments to those who break the law.

Those parts of the positive law which are conclusions of practical reason from the first principles of natural moral law are also part of the moral law. Hence these have the force of both the natural moral law and the positive law. On the other hand, those parts of the positive law arrived at by the determination of the human lawmaker have only the force of human law. This means that it is an offense against moral law, as well as state law, to mur-

[16] *S.T.*, I–II, 95, 2,c.

der. But it is not a direct offense against the moral law, but only against the state law, to break a traffic law.[17]

We should note here the meaning of the phrase, *jus gentium*. Literally, this signifies the *Law of Peoples*. There are certain conclusions from the principles of the natural moral law which are such that all men can know them. The ordinary rules of honesty in buying and selling, for instance, do not change with local customs or with variations of nationality. A part of the positive law of any state may consist in a declaration of what these commonly accepted rules are. This is what St. Thomas calls the *jus gentium*, the law which is declarative of what is right for all people. To be distinguished from this law is the other part of positive, state law which is called civil law (*jus civile*). Since civil law includes rules arrived at by the special determination of the rulers of one state, these civil rules are not the same for all men.[18] The modern concept of international law is not quite the same as the *jus gentium*. Since the rise of modern theories of jurisprudence, from the fifteenth century on, various attempts have been made to prescribe a code of conduct to govern the relations between sovereign nations. By international agreement and by the force of popular opinion, it has been possible to develop a set of rules outlawing certain inhuman forms of warfare, prescribing the manner in which international treaties may be ended or amended, regulating commerce between states, and things of this kind. Such generally accepted rules governing the mutual problems of sovereign states make up international law. This law is, of course, good if in accord with natural justice. But, unlike the *jus gentium* which deals with what is generally right for individual moral agents, international law is concerned with what is right in the actions of one sovereign state to another.[19]

Further to clarify the notion of natural moral law, we may next consider whether each and every act of virtue is prescribed by the moral law. This problem is easier to handle when the proper

[17] *Ibid., c, ad fin.*   [18] *S.T.*, I–II, 95, 4,c.
[19] See: Rommen, *The State and Catholic Thought*, pp. 620–625.

and specific fields of the cardinal virtues have been studied. We know, however, that the virtue of justice deals with the external operations of men in regard to other persons. Because more than one person is involved in matters of justice, law applies in its most formal sense to questions of justice. Here, there is always some concern about the common good, and the law looks to the common good. On the other hand, temperance and fortitude deal with questions of private morality, with the rational regulation of the concupiscible and irascible appetites. A man who allows himself to become unreasonably angry is not doing a morally good thing, but as long as he does not exhibit his lack of self-control to others he is not offending the common good of the members of his community. Hence, it is not as easy to promote temperance by positive legislation, as it is to prescribe justice. However, the common good to which the natural moral law directs man is not simply the corporate welfare of the civil society in which he lives. There is what St. Thomas calls [20] the common good of nature. By his specific nature as a rational animal, every man shares in one common end. Private immorality, though not directly involving others, does work against the attainment of the happiness of the moral agent, and so is opposed to the natural common good of man.

Considered as formally virtuous, then, all the acts of all the moral virtues are prescribed by the natural moral law. Expressed in another way: every act in accord with man's formal, rational nature is virtuous; all such acts are in keeping with the natural law. However, if we consider individual acts of virtue, in themselves, it is clear that many good things may be done which are not directly dictated by man's rational nature. A moral agent may often have the opportunity of doing actions which he is not required by his nature, or by his practical reason, to do. Yet, if he does these things, which are useful for a good life but not necessary, the moral agent is acting virtuously but not because he is necessitated by moral law. Some actions are morally good, when done by some men under certain contingent conditions; the same actions may be bad, when

[20] *S.T.*, I–II, 94, 3, *ad primum*.

performed by other men. Acts of this kind are not prescribed by the natural moral law.[21]

There are two types of precepts making up the natural moral law: *primary* and *secondary*. Their difference is succinctly stated by St. Thomas: "First of all, certain most common precepts which are known by all men pertain to the natural law; and there are other secondary and more particularized precepts which are like proximate conclusions from the first."[22] If we ask whether the natural moral law is one and the same for all men, the obvious answer is that it is one and the same for all, in its primary and most easily known rules. However, in regard to its secondary precepts, the matter is more complicated. Some of these secondary rules are rather close in meaning to the primary principles of the moral law: such secondary precepts are right for all men, and are known to all, *in most cases*. In unusual circumstances, such secondary laws may have exceptions. Other precepts are rather remote from the first principles of moral rectitude and these (called *tertiary* precepts by later thomistic commentators) are not easily known by all men. This means that the more particular moral rules, requiring developed capacity of practical reasoning, may be erroneously or inadequately grasped by some men who are led astray by bad reasoning, vicious customs, or corrupt habits. The weight of popular opinion, for instance, is not always on the side of what is morally right. In a corrupt society, even the best people (let us say, well-intentioned cannibals, or those who believe that it is right enough to procure a divorce, because many prominent movie stars do), may not think clearly enough about these tertiary precepts.[23]

If we keep these different kinds of precepts in mind, it is not hard to arrive at a reasonable view of the possibility of change in the natural moral law. It is sometimes said that human nature is always and everywhere the same, therefore the laws of moral rectitude must be permanent and incapable of change. This position is too simplistic and too rigorous. Certainly, the primary and most common principles of moral behavior do not change in themselves.

[21] *Ibid.*, ad 3m.   [22] *S.T.*, I–II, 94, 6,c.   [23] *S.T.*, I–II, 94, 4,c and 6,c.

However, the natural moral law is changed, *by way of addition*, when some rules of divine or human positive law are added to it. But some laws may be changed *by way of subtraction*. Subtractive change cannot apply to the primary precepts of the natural moral law: to say anything else would be to make morality a purely relative and fluctuating standard. But, because contingent circumstances form part of the secondary principles, these more particular conclusions about moral rightness do admit of some change. Secondary principles of moral law remain immutably right *in most cases;* in certain unusual and rare cases, the secondary precepts do change by virtue of special causes which prevent full obedience to the general law.[24] It is evident, for instance, that if God commands something to be done which is opposed to a secondary moral precept, the moral agent is absolved by this special act of God from the application of the ordinary moral law.

By way of summary of these general qualities of the natural moral law, we can conclude that the primary principles of this law are (1) *universal* for all men; (2) *immutable* under all conditions; and (3) *ineradicable* from the minds of men. Also, the secondary precepts usually have these three qualities, though exceptions may occur in special cases.[25]

Synderesis and the Principles of Natural Moral Law

Something has been studied already, in metaphysics and in the philosophy of man, as to the manner in which first speculative principles of reasoning come to be known by men. We have seen that these principles are so true and plain in their meaning that they are accepted and used by all human beings, as soon as the reasoning

[24] *S.T.*, I–II, 94, 5,c, and ad 2m.
[25] Read: *S.T.*, I–II, 94, arts. 1–6 inclus.; these articles should be carefully studied by the student, using the translation in: Pegis, *Basic Writings*, II, 772–781. Secondary aids in the understanding of this section on natural moral law may be found in: Cronin, *Science of Ethics*, I, 633–652; and Gilson, *Moral Values*, Chap. 6: "Law on the Human Level," pp. 193–212. Read also: Appendix to Chap. V, Text One: *Rightness According to Nature and According to Positive Law;* and Text Two: *Natural Moral Law: Can It Change?*

processes of a child's life require them. Almost from the beginning of infant life, a person will make use of the principle of noncontradiction, and of the principle of sufficient reason. A baby, who howls because he is given an empty, instead of a full, milk bottle, does not possess a formal knowledge of the principle of noncontradiction, but he does know that there is something contradictory in the matter. With increased sense experience, a child begins (at different ages for different individuals) to reason in such a way that he shows a working knowledge of these speculative principles. Are they, then, inborn in every man, or are they simply acquired by learning from experience? The thomistic answer is that first principles are partly innate and partly acquired.

It is not possible to prove everything by rational demonstration. Things which are so proved are conclusions, not principles. There must be some first principles which are known to be true by some other kind of act than that of discursive reasoning, otherwise it would never be possible to begin to reason. There are two other acts of the human intellect: simple apprehension and judgment. By simple apprehension, a single meaning is conceived. The simplest concept for man to grasp is that of "thing," or "being." The simplest judgment for man to make is that a thing is a thing, or that a being is not identical with a non-being. This judgment is an elementary formula of the principle of identity and also of the cognate principle of noncontradiction. But these are great truths. How is it possible to explain philosophically the knowing of these first truths? Unlike all the remaining content of natural human knowledge, these principles must be immediately apprehended by the human intellect without demonstration. To do this, the intellect of man must be provided in its very nature with a special quality, technically called a *habitus of first principles*, enabling man to perform the important act of seeing the truth of these principles as soon as the concepts included in the judgment are understood. This habitus must be an inborn, or innate, disposition to make this sort of judgment. At birth, this imperfect habitus must be in the intellect, for there is no way in which such a disposition could be wholly acquired in later life. This does not mean that the *knowl-*

edge of the principles must be in the intellect at birth; it does mean that a special strengthening of the ordinary power of the intellect, empowering it to make this unusual and quasi-angelic act of intuition of first principles, must be part of the native endowment of the human mind. It is in this sense that the knowledge of first principles is partly innate: the special subjective capacity, as yet unused, not actuated, is innately disposing the human intellect to perform this kind of action.

However, the concepts which are identified in the initial judgment which marks the beginning of man's actual knowledge of a first principle are not innately present in the human intellect. Man is not born with any knowledge actually present in his mind. It is necessary for each man to learn the meaning of things by perceiving them with his senses and by interpreting or understanding what he has sensed, with his innate power of intellect. So, to make any judgment, even a self-evident one, the human agent must first have sense experience and then some conception of what he has experienced. The concepts and the consequent judgments are not innate. This is the reason why one's knowledge of first principles is partly acquired.

Now, the situation is much the same in regard to the knowing of *first practical principles*. Here too, some very simple concept must be grasped and from it a judgment must be elicited without demonstration. This judgment must be so elementary that it will be known to be true as soon as its component concepts are identified by intellectual composition. What will this initial practical, or operative, principle be? It will have to be formed from a simple concept, much like *being,* which will have a meaning capable of causing one to think of action. We know from the philosophy of man that it is the function of *appetite* to cause an agent to move itself. An appetite is actuated by the presentation of something which attracts it. A psychic appetite is moved by the apprehension of a being as *good.* We also know from the philosophy of being that being may be conceived transcendentally, that is without limitation by genus or species, as one, as true, and as *good.* Obviously, the most general concept which may be grasped by any man as leading to action, is the concept of *the good*. If one were to judge that the good is the good, this would be a speculative principle, an example of the principle of identity. What is needed to form a first practical judgment, is a proposition which will have the good as its subject and which will relate the good to action, to the doing of something. The simplest form which such a principle could take is: *the good should be done.* It will be observed that this is also a formula of the principle of identity, because in the order of practical thinking, the good *is* what should be done. It would be possible to regard the predicate as a sort of definition of the subject, in this principle.

There are some practical problems to which the foregoing formula of the first practical principle does not directly apply. Sometimes it is not a question of what to do, but of what not to do. If the good is what should be done, then by the principle of noncontradiction, the contradictory of the good (*i.e.*, not-good or evil) is what should not be done. Our complete first practical principle will, then, be: *The good should be done; the evil should not be done.*[26]

Just as the human intellect requires a special stepping-up, or increased strength, in order to be naturally disposed to grasp first speculative principles, so does it need a special and innate quality to increase its power so that it may see immediately the truth of this first practical principle. This strengthening quality of the practical intellect is also a habitus of first principles. Such a habitus will have to be part of the innate endowment of the intellect guiding operations. Traditionally in thomistic terminology, this habitus of first practical principles is called *synderesis*. This name is somewhat like a Greek word (*syneidesis*), used by the Stoic philosophers, to designate an insight into simple matters of common knowledge. The important thing to remember, here, is that *synderesis* is, most properly, not the name of the actual knowledge of first practical principles but of the *intellectual habitus* which makes it possible to acquire such knowledge from experience.

It is well to understand the very clear distinction made in tho-

[26] *S.T.*, I–II, 94, 2,c; see Appendix to Chap. V, Text Three.

mistic philosophy between synderesis and conscience. Both pertain to the intellectual knowledge of practical matters. But synderesis is a *habitus*, whereas conscience is an *act* of judgment. The product of the use of synderesis is a most general and *universal* knowledge of the first principles of practical reasoning. The act which is conscience is not concerned with the universal, but with a *particular* application of practical reasoning to decide a particular moral problem. Conscience should in no way be confused with synderesis.[27]

It is reasonable to inquire whether the principle: *Good should be done and evil avoided*, is the only principle of practical reasoning. If it were, then that would be all that there is to the natural moral law, for this law is known by man through the use of synderesis. The truth is that this general formula can be multiplied into a large number of primary precepts, simply by considering generic or specific instances of moral good or evil and using them as subjects of more limited rules. Thus, if we understand that almsgiving, considered as a species of action without modifying circumstances, is good, then we may immediately see that: *almsgiving is to be done*. Similarly, it is plain that theft (considered as a bad kind of action) is not to be done. Other examples of such primary rules of the natural moral law are: it is good for a being to act in conformity with its nature; it is good for a reasonable being to act reasonably; it is good for a being to act in conformity with its end; it is good to be prudent, temperate, brave, and just; it is bad to injure anyone unjustly; it is bad to tell a lie; it is bad to commit murder.

While it might seem on first thought a good idea to make a complete list of these rules and then say that conformity to these is what makes a good life, this is quite foreign to the theory of ethics which we are studying. It is the function of right reason to develop these general precepts of moral rightness. Much as we would like other people to do our thinking for us, the fact remains that, if we are to guide our actions by reasoning, we must do some reasoning ourselves. Those who are capable of studying ethics

[27] On synderesis, read: *S.T.*, I, 79, a. 12,c; in Pegis, *Basic Writings*, I, 765–766.

should realize this. Of course, people of undeveloped rational powers, and those who are impeded by lack of experience (children, for instance) require some help to know what is specifically right and wrong. For such people, and indeed for all men because no one is perfect in practical reasoning, positive laws are of great help in declaring and determining the content of the moral law. The Ten Commandments are examples of morally good rules; these are positive divine Laws. The just laws of one's country are often declarative of the more commonly accepted rules of morality. But simply to memorize the precepts reasoned to by some other person is not to study ethics philosophically, any more than to memorize the theorems of geometry is to study mathematics.

The Christian concept of charity is expressed in two general precepts: "Love the Lord, thy God," and "Love thy neighbor." (*Matt.* 22:37–39.) These are primary and common precepts of the natural law. They are self-evident to human reason, but not to the mind of just any man. Certain things are self-evident to the trained intellect of the geometrician, for instance, because he has acquired by study a habitus of the speculative intellect enabling him to understand the technical but true principles and conclusions of his science. So too, the law of Christian charity (which was never grasped by the most high-minded pagan moralists) requires a certain preparation of the human intellect. Such preparation includes the acquisition of the intellectual habitus of supernatural faith. The habit of faith is given to man by God. It enables the human intellect to assent to truths which are beyond the natural capacity of man, but which are not opposed to the nature of man's intellect. The supernatural does not destroy the natural, but raises it to a higher level of existence and operation. That is why St. Thomas can say: "These two precepts of Christian charity are primary and common precepts of the law of nature; they are self-evident to human reason, either through nature *or through faith*." [28] This means that the full meaning of some of the most fundamental principles of the moral law can only be grasped by men who are enlightened by the

[28] *S.T.*, I–II, 100, 3, *ad primum.*

habitus of faith. We have here another example of the subordination of natural science to supernatural science.[29]

We make no attempt in ethics, then, to list all the rules of moral law. Any action is morally good, in itself, if it is in accord with the natural inclinations of man. It is possible to consider these inclinations of human nature on three levels. First, man is a substance, and, like any other substance, it is good for him to maintain his continued existence. On this lowest level of consideration, we can see that the good for man lies in the preservation of life and the avoidance of all dangers to his continued existence within his species. Second, there are goods which man shares with all animals: it is natural and good for man to reproduce within his species and to ensure the continuation of the human race by the proper care of offspring. Third, there are goods which belong to man alone, by virtue of that part of his nature which is peculiar to the human species, namely, rationality. The goods of reason would include the pursuit of intellectual truth and the avoidance of error, the use of free choice, the cultivation of virtue, even the supernatural possibility of cooperating with divine grace so as to rise to a friendship with God. It will be observed that what is natural to man is not always so, in the same way. Understanding of human inclinations increases with the acquisition of experience and with the development of intellect. The diverse goods so known suggest precepts of the moral law; all such precepts are rooted in the original principle: *Good is to be done and evil avoided.*[30]

One might properly ask: If synderesis is a natural quality of the human intellect, why is it that some people do not seem to know the first principles of the natural moral law? To answer this, we must recall that synderesis is a habitus, not the act of knowing these principles. If synderesis is used it must be of such a nature

[29] It is for this reason that some Catholic educators are advocating the inclusion of theology in the program of the liberal arts college. See: G. B. Phelan, "Theology in the Curriculum of Catholic Colleges and Universities," *Man and Secularism* (New York, 1940), pp. 128–140; and J. Maritain, *Education at the Crossroads* (New York, 1943), pp. 71–75. Read also: *S.T.*, I–II, 100, 1,c; in Pegis, *Basic Writings*, II, 828.

[30] Read: Appendix to Chap. V, Text Three: *How the First Principles of Natural Moral Law Are Known.*

that it will not be actuated by erroneous principles. The act of understanding the first practical principles may, of course, be prevented by the general loss of the use of intellect. This would be the case with people who are demented. Injury to some bodily organ needed for the exercise of the internal senses would result in such a condition, because the intellect needs the help of the imagination and other senses in order to act during this life on earth. In other cases, where people speak or act in opposition to the natural moral law (this may be true of whole societies; members of a certain religion, for instance, may believe that it is essentially immoral to take an oath), they are not denying that good should be done. They are simply mistaken in regard to the nature of a definite, or even particular, good. Men may be in error in regard to the remote precepts of the moral law, those which are reached as conclusions of practical reasoning. No man is capable of error in regard to the immediately evident principles of the moral law.[31]

Moral Obligation and Legal Sanctions

Law means very little unless it is in some way enforced. Physical laws are obeyed because the bodies subject to these laws are so made that they can only act in one way in a given situation. The nature of physical agents is such that they operate in conformity with their forms by virtue of physical necessity. Such a situation allows for no freedom on the part of physical agents. Positive laws are presented to their subjects as commands coming from an external lawmaker. Their force, or binding quality, or obligatoriness, derives from rewards or punishments. Obedience to positive law is not absolutely necessary. Subjects who disobey them must take the consequences, the loss of certain rewards, the assigning of certain punishments. Thus, the obligation connected with positive laws is not of the nature of physical necessity, for the subjects of positive law are free agents. Rather, the obligation of positive law

[31] Read: Appendix to Chap. V, Text Four: *The Nature of Synderesis;* Text Five: *The Act of Synderesis Is Quasi-Angelic;* Text Six: *Can Synderesis Be Mistaken?;* Text Seven: *Can Synderesis Be Lost by Its Owner?*

is hypothetical; *if* the law is obeyed a reward is gained, and *if* it is disobeyed a punishment is required.

The natural moral law is neither a physical law nor a positive law. The obligatory force which attaches to it is that of moral necessity. When a concrete moral act is perfomed, it is either in accord with the rational ordering of man's life to his ultimate end (and such an act is good), or it is in discord with this ordering to the ultimate end (and such an act is bad). A good act gives origin to a need, or exigency, for some reward; this need is called merit. On the other hand, a bad act requires punishment; this need for punishment is called demerit or guilt. Both merit and demerit are moral exigencies arising from the fact that the moral agent is *responsible* for his voluntary actions. Merit is described by St. Thomas as, "the road to the end which is happiness." [32] Similarly, each case of guilt is a step away from real and ultimate happiness. Thus, the supreme sanction of the natural moral law is the gaining or losing of final happiness. This is a sanction which is applicable only after death; as long as a man is living, it is possible for him, with God's help, to "reform" his life, that is, to begin to act in such a way that his continued effort is "conformed" to the rational ordering of human life to its proper goal: the Beatific Vision. So, the greatest punishment for man consists in the loss of his greatest good: eternal happiness. The greatest reward is the attainment of this highest good. In the light of this supreme sanction, all lesser sanctions are dwarfed to comparative insignificance.

Of secondary sanctions, the gaining or loss of virtue would be next in importance, precisely because virtue is that which is most useful in enabling a man to gain his supreme reward. Next in value are certain goods of the soul: the proper disposition of reason and of the powers subject to it. To lose these is to suffer great spiritual and mental disturbance. Somewhat lower in the scale of human goods are bodily health and integrity; sickness and wounds are temporal punishments which may follow from disobedience to the moral law. Finally, the lowest of human goods consist in all those things which are external to human nature and which are useful to

[32] *In II Sent.*, d. 35, q. 1, a. 3, ad 4m.

a good life on earth. The loss of possessions or of one's good reputation is a form of punishment. But these secondary rewards and punishments pertain to the natural moral law only by virtue of their relation to the supreme sanction. The secondary sanctions are only effective if the punishments therein contained are suffered involuntarily. It is clear that some very good people may give up external things, good health and strength, even the cultivation of their natural powers, for the sake of the one great good: eternal happiness. Such people are exemplified by the great ascetics. Their voluntary loss of temporal goods is not a punishment but a means to personal perfection and the attainment of the greatest good.[33]

In the concrete moral act, obligation is a quality which is associated with the practical judgment (conscience) that one should do or refrain from doing something. Certain human actions are objectively necessary in given circumstances, if the agent is to attain his end; it is the work of man's practical intellect to acknowledge the necessity or obligation to do these actions. Other actions are of such a nature that they must be avoided, if the agent is to achieve his end; here again, obligation stems from the objective character of these actions as known in relation to the end. That is, the moral agent feels his obligation when he is making the judgment which is called conscience. Moral obligation in general should not be confused with duty. If we mean by duty, that which is owed to another, then duty is a term which has only a place in the matter of justice. The problems of personal morality (questions of prudence, temperance, fortitude and charity) require us to think of obligations which are not duties, strictly speaking. Justice covers only one area of morality; there are other areas.[34] There is a tendency to attempt to reduce all ethical problems to those of justice, if we overstress the moral law in ethics. The application of law is easiest and clearest in matters of justice, because both law and justice involve the consideration of the common good. To speak of special ethics as dealing with man's duties to God, to other men, to himself, and in regard to infra-human things, is to fall into this error. The

[33] Read: Appendix to Chap. V, Text Eight: *The Supreme Sanction of Moral Law*. Read also: *S.T.*, I–II, 87, arts. 1–8; in Pegis, *Basic Writings*, II, 708–720.

[34] *S.T.*, I–II, 60, art. 2,c.

moral law is bigger than the field of justice. Its obligations cannot be exhausted by a "legal" treatment of rights and duties. It is true that positive human law deals solely with questions of justice [35] but the eternal law and the moral law cover the acts of all virtues. Many books of morality by modern Catholic authors tend to restrict their discussion too exclusively to the moral law as it applies to matters of justice.

Grace as an External Principle of Human Acts

It will be remembered from the opening lines of this chapter that God helps man to live a good moral life, by means of two forms of external aid. The first, law, has just been discussed. The second divine and external principle of morally good human acts is grace. It is not possible to make a complete study of divine grace in philosophy. Theologians find it a sufficiently difficult topic. However, we may briefly present a few remarks about man's need of grace, so that Catholics may understand a little more of what they believe, and so that those who are not of the Catholic faith may have some information as to what Catholics do think about grace.

First of all, we know that nothing moves in this universe which is not preserved in its being and moved initially in its every movement by God. The finite world is not, *of itself*, a going concern. A First Mover is needed to explain not only how things started to move but also how they continue to move at each instant. Human actions are no exception. Freedom of choice is not opposed to this dependence of all finite agents upon the Infinite Power of God. Granting that man can do nothing without this divine concurrence, we may still understand that man has the natural capacity to direct his own actions to the ends which he intends and to use the means which he elects. As an agent, man is something like an instrument which has its own power to produce certain effects, even when used by a principal agent distinct from the instrument. In this sense,

[35] *S.T.*, I–II, 100, a. 2,c.

no action, good or bad, free or unfree, can be done by man without the general help of God. Applied to moral matters, one conclusion from this may be that no man can be too proud of the fact that he is a "self-made" man. All human agents owe their existence and their capacity for successful work to God. This thought should make men realize that their rights to the product of their labors, to private possessions for instance, are not absolute; no one is wholly independent of God.

But divine grace is something different from this general assistance which God gives to all creatures. We have seen two reasons why man needs some additional and special help from God. The first reason depends on the kind of ultimate end which is open to man. Perfect happiness in the contemplation of God is not a natural end. Such perfection exceeds the natural powers of the human being. To merit this reward of eternal happiness, man needs to be elevated to a plane of life and action which is superhuman. That God freely gives the assistance needed to rise to this supernatural level, is a belief of most Christians, of all Catholics. The Latin name, *gratia*, stresses the fact that grace is a help which is *freely* given by God to man. What grace is, when received within man, is hard to explain, but St. Thomas tried to suggest its nature by saying that habitual grace is a quality, something like a habitus of the soul, but not in the natural order of accidents. To be perfectly happy throughout eternity is obviously a reward which cannot be merited by a few years of good action and by the giving up of a few temporal goods. Just as the winner of a scholarship in school does not "merit" the scholarship in the sense of giving to the donor something equal in exchange for it, so too, man cannot merit perfect and continued happiness by purely natural effort. So, the special help, or grace, of God is a necessary external principle of the acts whereby man may hope to attain to his supernatural end.

A second reason, why man needs grace, lies in the present condition of the human race. We have noted that man is not now living in the same condition of nature which characterized the first man, before his first sin. Man is now in a state of fallen nature. This means that certain preternatural gifts with which Adam was originally endowed have been lost by his descendants. The defect of these gifts and the consequent disruption of the personality of man, internally and in its relation to God, is what Catholics understand by original sin.

Because human nature is now in a troubled state (not that it is positively lacking in any capacity which belongs to it by nature, but because it now is deprived of those special gifts which it once possessed in the state of original justice), it is particularly necessary for man to have the grace of God. Before the Fall, man could at least obey the Ten Commandments, in the sense that he could, without being given any more help, do the kind of works prescribed in these precepts. Of course, even Adam in his original state of integral nature needed divine Charity in order that the manner, or mode, of his action would be acceptable to God. Now, after the Fall, man cannot even do the substance of the acts prescribed in these Commandments, without the special grace of God.

This is not to say that man can do no good things without habitual grace. It is possible for man, now, by means of his natural powers (with the general *concursus* of God), to perform certain naturally good actions: to build houses, plant his crops, and do the ordinary tasks of life. But the point is that fallen man cannot do all the things that would bring him everlasting happiness, unless he is specially aided by divine grace. Thus, as St. Thomas explains it, fallen man needs grace, (1) because of the supernatural character of eternal happiness; (2) because of the defective state of his fallen nature:

The nature of man can be considered in two ways: first, in its integrity, as it was in the first parent before he sinned; second, as it is corrupted in us after the sin of the first parent. In both conditions of nature, human nature needs divine help, as from a Prime Mover, in order to do or wish anything good. But, in the state of integral nature, as far as the sufficiency of operative power is concerned, man could both wish and do, with his natural endowments, the good proportioned to his nature, such as the good of acquired virtue. However, he could not do supernatural good, such as the good of the infused virtues. But, in the state of corrupted nature, man is even defective in regard to that which is within his natural capacity, so that he cannot fulfill the entire good of this kind,

by means of his natural endowment. Still, since human nature is not totally corrupted by sin, to the extent that it is deprived of its entire good,
man can, even in the state of corrupted nature, do some particular good
things by his natural capacities, such as building houses, planting grape-
vines, and like things; but not all the good connatural to him, as if he
were lacking in nothing. A sick man, for instance, can make some movements by himself, but he cannot move perfectly, as can a healthy man,
unless he be healed with the aid of medicine.

And so, man in a state of integral nature has need of a gratuitous
power super-added to the capacity of his nature, for one reason: to do
and wish a supernatural good. But, in a state of corrupted nature, he
needs it for two reasons: to be made healthy; and, in addition, to do the
good which pertains to supernatural virtue, which is meritorious. Moreover, in both states, man needs divine help in order that he may be
moved, from within himself, to act well.[36]

Summary of Chapter V

In general, law is a reasonable order, promulgated by one who
has charge of a community, for the sake of the common good.
Positive law is promulgated by external presentation to its subjects;
natural law is imbedded in the essential being of its subjects. The
natural moral law is a participation of the Eternal Law on the
part of a rational creature. The Eternal Law is the Order, in the
divine Reason, for the governance of all things. State laws, if good,
are either conclusions of practical reason from the natural moral
law, or they are determinations which are not opposed to the natural moral law. Law applies most formally to matters of justice, because law is for the common good, but the natural moral law
governs the acts of all the virtues. The precepts of this law are
primary, if they are so evidently right that no practical reasoning
is needed to establish them; secondary, if they are conclusions,
proximate or remote, from the primary precepts. Primary precepts
are immutable, universal and ineradicable from the minds of men;
secondary precepts usually hold but not in all cases. Synderesis is
the habitus of the practical intellect whereby the primary princi-

[36] S.T., I–II, 109, 2,c. Students should read at least the first five articles of this
q. 109; in Pegis, *Basic Writings,* II, 979–987.

ples of moral reasoning are known immediately to men who have sufficient experience to understand their component concepts. The first principle of all morality is: Good should be done, evil avoided. Other principles use more limited meanings of good and evil. Synderesis cannot be mistaken or lost; it is an innate habitus. Its act may be erroneous, but not in regard to primary principles. Moral obligation is a consequence of moral law, whereby the agent is morally necessitated to obey the law or be punished. The supreme sanction of the natural moral law is the loss of eternal happiness. Other sanctions are effective only in dependence on this one. Grace is a second, external principle of goodness in human acts. It is a special and freely given divine aid, enabling man in his fallen state to work for the complete good of his nature and also for his supernatural end.

Appendix to Chapter V

¶ TEXT ONE: *Rightness According to Nature and According to Positive Law*. The naturally just [right] is that which everywhere has the same power and force to encourage good and discourage evil. Now, this is due to the fact that nature, which is the cause of this sort of justice [rightness], is everywhere and for all men the same. But the just, which depends on the positive law of a state or a ruler, is only virtuous for those who are under the jurisdiction of that state or ruler.

He [Aristotle] shows, in another way, what this justice [natural] is, in its cause, when he says that natural justice does not consist in its being seen, or not being seen. That is, it does not arise from some human opinion but from nature. For, just as in speculative matters, there are certain things naturally known, like the indemonstrable principles and those which are closely related to them (for, some are found out by human investigation and they are closely related principles), so also, in operative matters there are certain naturally known principles which are, as it were, indemonstrable, and there are closely related ones; for example: evil is to be avoided, no one is to be unjustly harmed, one should not steal, and the like. But others are thought out by the efforts of men, and these are just in the legal sense.

It should also be considered, that natural justice is that to which *nature* inclines man. Now, nature may be regarded in two ways, in man. First, from the point of view that he is an animal, and this [nature] is common to him and to other animals. Secondly, nature belongs to man, as something proper to him as man, that is, insofar as he distinguishes between the base and the upright. But the experts in positive law (*Juristae*) only speak of what is naturally right, in connection with what follows the inclination of nature considered as common to man and to other animals; for instance, the union of male and female, the rearing of offspring, and other things like that. That kind of rightness, which is associated with the proper tendency of *human nature* (that is, inasmuch as man is a rational animal) the legal experts call the Law of Peoples (*jus gentium*), because all peoples use it. Examples of it are: that agreements are to be kept, that envoys are safe with the enemy, and like things. Now, both of these meanings are included under natural rightness, as here considered by the Philosopher.

We should also consider that what is right legally, or positively, always takes its origin from the natural, as Cicero says in his *Rhetoric* [*De Inv. Rhet.*, II, 161]. However, something may originate in two ways from the natural law. First, as a conclusion from principles: and it is impossible for what is positively or legally right to arise from the natural law in this way. For, given the premises, the conclusion must necessarily follow, but, since the naturally right is so always and everywhere, as has been said (n. 1018), this cannot be true of the legally or positively right.

And so, it must be that whatever follows as a conclusion from the naturally right must be naturally right. For instance: from the precept that no harm is to be done unjustly to anyone, it follows that one should not steal; and the latter pertains to natural rightness. But something may take its origin from natural rightness in a second way, by way of determination. And it is in this way that all things that are right legally or positively originate from what is naturally right. Thus, that a thief should be punished, is a matter of natural rightness; but, that he should be punished in such and such a way, this is a matter of legal and positive rightness. (*In V Ethic.*, lect. 12; ed. Pirotta, pp. 340–341, nn. 1018, 1019, and 1023.)

¶ TEXT TWO: *Natural Moral Law: Can It Change?* Just and good things can be considered in two ways. First, *formally*, and in this way they are always and everywhere the same; for, the principles of moral rightness, which are in natural reason, do not change. Second, *materially*, and in this way the just and the good are not the same everywhere and for all men; rather, it is necessary that they be determined by law. This happens because of the changeable aspects of human nature and because of the diverse conditions of men and things, according to differences of place and time.

For instance, it is always just that an exchange be made on the basis of equality, in buying and selling; but, in regard to the measure of grain, it is just to give the amount which is customary in a certain place at a certain time, and in a different place or time, not the same amount, but more or less. (*De Malo*, q. II, a. 4, ad 13m.)

¶ TEXT THREE: *How the First Principles of Natural Moral Law Are Known.* The precepts of the law of nature are related to practical reason as the first principles of demonstration are to speculative reason, for both are self-evident principles. Now, a thing is said to be self-evident in two ways: first, in itself; second, in relation to us. Any proposition is called self-evident in itself, if its predicate is derived from the essential meaning of its subject. Of course, it may happen that such a proposition will not be self-evident to one who is ignorant of the definition of the subject. Thus, this proposition: Man is rational, is self-evident according to its own nature, because to speak of man is to speak of what is rational; yet, to one who is ignorant as to what man is, this proposition is not self-evident.

Hence, as Boethius says in his *De Hebdomadibus* (PL 64, 1311), there are certain axioms or propositions which are commonly self-evident to all men, and these are such that their terms are known to

all, such as: Every whole is greater than its part, and: Those things
which are equal to one and the same thing are equal to each other.
But some propositions are self-evident only to wise men who understand the meaning of the terms in these propositions. Thus, to
one who understands that an angel is not a body, it is self-evident
that an angel is not circumscriptively present in place. But this is
not evident to the unlearned, who do not grasp it.

Among those things which fall within the apprehension of men,
a definite order may be found. For, that which first falls within
apprehension is being (*ens*), and the understanding of it is included
in all things whatsoever that one may apprehend. And so, the first
indemonstrable principle is that: One should not, at the same time
and in the same way, both affirm something and deny it. This is
based on the formal nature of being and non-being. And all other
principles are based on this one, as is said in the Fourth Book of the
Metaphysics (III, 9; 1005b29).

Now, just as being is the first thing which falls within apprehension considered in an unqualified way, so also is the good (*bonum*)
the first thing which falls within the apprehension of practical
reason, which is directed toward work. For, every agent acts for
the sake of an end, and this [an end] has the formal nature of the
good. So, the first principle in the practical reason is that which is
based on the formal nature of the good, which is: the good is that
which all seek after. Therefore, this is the first principle of the law:
*The good is to be done and sought after, and the evil is to be
avoided*. And, all the other precepts of the law of nature are based
on it; so that all those things which are to be done (which practical
reason naturally apprehends as human goods), or avoided, pertain
to the precepts of the law of nature.

Because the good has the formal nature of an end, and evil has
the formal nature of the contrary, reason naturally apprehends as
goods, and consequently as things to be sought after in action, all
those things to which man is naturally inclined, and their contraries
[are apprehended] as evils and things to be avoided. Therefore, the
order of the precepts of the law of nature follows the order of
natural inclinations.

First, there is present in man the inclination to good on the level of that nature which he shares with all substances, insofar, namely, as every substance seeks the conservation of its own existence according to its own nature. Those things, through which the life of man is preserved and the contrary is hindered, pertain to the natural law according to this inclination.

Second, there is in man the inclination to some more specific things, on the level of the nature which he shares with other animals. And on this basis, all those things, "which nature teaches all animals" (for instance, the union of male and female, the upbringing of offspring, and such like), belong to the natural law.

Third, there is in man an inclination to the good according to the nature of reason, which is proper to him, thus, man has a natural inclination to know the truth concerning God, and to live in society. And according to this, those things which refer to this kind of inclination (for instance, that man should avoid ignorance, that he may not offend others with whom he is associated, and other things of like reference), pertain to the natural law.

[Ad 2m] All inclinations of this kind, of whatever part of human nature, for example, of the concupiscible and irascible, insofar as they are regulated by reason, pertain to the natural law. And they are reducible to one first precept, as has been said. Thus, there are many precepts of the law of nature, considered in themselves; however, they all share in one common root. (*S.T.*, I–II, 94, 2,c and ad 2m.)

❡ TEXT FOUR: *The Nature of Synderesis.* Since reason has a certain variety, and is in a way mobile, according as it goes in its deductions from principles to conclusions, and deception is possible in this process of reasoning, it is necessary that every act of reasoning proceed from some knowledge which possesses a certain uniformity and stability. This [knowledge] does not come about by discursive investigation; rather, it is presented all at once to the intellect. For, just as reason in speculative matters goes deductively from some self-evident principles, the habitus of which is called understanding, so also must the practical reason make its deductions from some self-evident principles (for example, that evil should not be done, that the precepts of God will have to be obeyed, and others such); and, the habitus of these is synderesis.

Hence, I say that synderesis is distinguished from practical reason, not indeed in the substance of the potency, but as a habitus which is in a way inborn in our mind from the very light of the agent intellect, just as is the case with the habitus of speculative principles, such as: Every whole is greater than its part, and the like. However, we need sensation and memory to make definite our knowledge of these, as is said in the *Posterior Analytics* (II, c. 19; 99b20–100b17). And so, I say that synderesis designates either simply a habitus, or even the potency considered as developed in us by an innate habitus. (*In II Sent.*, d. 24, q. 2, a. 3,c.)

¶ TEXT FIVE: *The Act of Synderesis Is Quasi-Angelic.* The human soul, from the point of view of that which is highest in it, attains to something of what is proper to the angelic nature; namely, it possesses knowledge of some things immediately and without long searching, although in regard to this it remains inferior to the angel, inasmuch as it cannot know the truth of these things without acquiring it from sensation. Now, there is a twofold cognition in the angelic nature: speculative, whereby it intuits the very truth of things, simply and absolutely; and practical, both according to the philosophers (who maintained that the angels are the movers of the heavenly bodies, and that all natural forms pre-exist in their [angelic] knowledge), and also according to the theologians (who maintain that the angels minister to God in spiritual functions, and accordingly their [angelic] orders are distinguished).

Hence also, in human nature, insofar as it attains to the angelic, there should be a knowledge of the truth without long search, both in speculative and in practical matters. Indeed, this knowledge should be the starting point (*principium*) of all consequent knowledge whether speculative or practical, since the principles should be more stable and more certain. Hence, this knowledge should be naturally present in man, since in fact he knows this as a sort of seed-bed (*seminarium*) of all consequent knowledge; just as certain

natural seeds of consequent operations and effects pre-exist in all
physical things. Also, this knowledge must be habitual, so that man
may exist in readiness to use it when there is need. Now, just as there
is a certain habitus of the human soul, whereby it knows the principles of the speculative sciences, which we call the understanding
of principles, so too, there is in it a certain natural habitus of first
principles concerning things to be done, which are the natural
principles of the natural moral law; and this habitus pertains to
synderesis.

Now, this habitus exists in no other potency than reason, unless
by chance we claim that the intellect is a distinct potency from
reason, and the contrary of this has been asserted in the preceding
Question (q. 15, a. 1). It remains, then, that this name, *synderesis*,
either denominates simply the natural habitus which is similar to
the habitus of principles, or it denominates the potency itself of
reason, together with such a habitus. However this may be, it does
not make much difference, for there is no difficulty in this, except
in regard to the meaning of the name. Indeed, it cannot be that
this potency of reason, considered as it knows naturally, would be
called synderesis, without any habitus. Natural knowledge belongs
to reason according to some natural habitus, as is clear in the case of
the understanding of [speculative] principles.

[Ad 9m] Synderesis signifies neither the superior nor the inferior
reason, but something having a common relation to both. For, in
the very habitus of universal principles of the moral law, some
things are included which pertain to the eternal reasons, for instance, something which is a matter of obedience to God; but there
are some things which pertain to inferior reasons, for instance, that
one should live in accord with reason. Now, synderesis is said to
look to immutable things in one way, and superior reason [to look]
in another way. For, a thing is called immutable because of im-
mutability of nature, and it is thus that divine things are immutable;
and in this way the superior reason looks to immutable things. Also,
a thing may be called immutable on account of the necessity of
truth, although it may be concerned with things that are mutable
by nature, as in this truth: every whole is greater than its part, the

immutable is also present in mutable things. It is in this latter way that synderesis is said to look to immutable things.

[Ad 12m] The act of this natural habitus, which synderesis designates, is to spurn evil and to incline to good; and so, man is naturally capable of this act. However, it does not follow from this that man can perform a meritorious act [*i.e.*, in the order of supernatural merit] solely by natural means; for, to attribute this to natural capacity only is the Pelagian impiety.

[Ad 14m] The act of knowledge is not prerequisite to the potency or habitus of synderesis, but to its act. Hence, there is nothing in this to prevent the habitus of synderesis from being innate. (*De Veritate*, q. 16, a. 1, c, ad 9m, ad 12m, and ad 14m.)

¶ TEXT SIX: *Can Synderesis Be Mistaken?* Nature in all her works intends the good, and the conservation of those things which come about through the working of nature. So, in all the works of nature, the principles are always permanent and immutable, and they maintain rectitude; for, it is necessary that principles stand firm (*manere*), as is said in Book I of the *Physics*. For, there could not be any firmness or certitude in those things which flow from the principles, unless the principles were firmly established. Thus it is that all mutable things may be traced back to some first thing which is immutable; hence also, every specific cognition is derived from some most certain cognition, concerning which there can be no error, and this is the cognition of first universal principles in regard to which all these known things are evaluated and from which every true thing receives approval, and every false thing receives disapproval. And, if any error could befall these, no certainty would be found in the entire consequent knowledge. Hence, in human works, to the end that some rectitude be in them, there must be some permanent principle which has immutable rectitude, in terms of which all works are evaluated; thus, this permanent principle resists every evil and assents to every good. And this is synderesis, whose function is to spurn evil and to incline to the good. So, we concede that in it [synderesis] there could not be sin. (*De Veritate*, q. 16, a. 2,c.)

¶ TEXT SEVEN: *Can Synderesis Be Lost by Its Owner?* The extinguishing of synderesis can be understood in two ways. In one way, in regard to the habitual light itself: and in this way it is impossible for the human soul to be deprived of the light of the agent intellect through which first principles in speculative and operative matters become known to us. For, this light belongs to the nature of the soul itself, which is intellectual through it. Concerning this light, it is said in *Psalm* 4:7, "It is impressed upon us as the Light of Thy countenance, O Lord." That is to say, it shows us the good, for this was the answer to the question: "Who will show us the good?"

In another way, [the extinguishing of synderesis may be considered] in regard to the act; and this consideration is twofold. First, the act of synderesis may be said to be extinguished insofar as its act is altogether cut off. Thus, it does happen that the act of synderesis is extinguished in those who do not possess the exercise of free choice, nor any use of reason. This is because of the impediment arising from a lesion of the bodily organs from which our reason needs to receive [help]. Second, there is the possibility that the act of synderesis may be deflected to the contrary; but it is impossible for synderesis to be thus extinguished in regard to universal judgment. However, it may be extinguished in regard to the particular work to be done, whenever there is a sin of election. For, the power of concupiscence then swallows up reason, so that, in the act of election, synderesis does not apply the universal judgment to the particular act. But this does not extinguish synderesis absolutely, only relatively. Hence, absolutely speaking, we concede that synderesis is never extinguished.

[Ad 2m] Among heretics, conscience does not spurn their infidelity, because there is error in their superior reason, whence it happens that the judgment of synderesis is not applied, in this case, to the particular act. The judgment of synderesis in regard to universal matters does stay in them; they judge that it is evil not to believe what is said by God. Now, their error of superior reason consists in this: they do not believe that this particular thing has been said by God.

[Ad 3m] The possessor of the habitus of some vice is indeed corrupt in regard to the principles of things to be done; not in regard to the universal but in regard to the particular thing to be done. He is bereft of reason, by means of the habitus of vice, to this extent: he does not apply the universal judgment to the particular thing to be done, in his act of election. It is in this way that the impious man who has reached the depths of sin is said to contemn [the good]. (*De Veritate*, q. 16, a. 3,c, ad 2m, and ad 3m.)

¶ TEXT EIGHT: *The Supreme Sanction of Moral Law.* Evil is the privation of the good. Hence, the ordering of different punishments should depend on the differences and on the order of goods. Now, there is a highest good for man: *happiness;* and this is his ultimate end. So, the nearer a thing is to this end, the more important is it as a good for man. Virtue is the nearest thing to this; and, if there is anything else which is useful for the good works of men, by which he may attain happiness, it will follow as a due disposition of reason and of the powers subject to it. After this, there are: bodily welfare, which is needed for prompt action; and, lowest of all, are those external things which we may use as aids to virtue.

Thus, the greatest punishment will be for man to be cut off from happiness; after this, the loss of virtue and of the perfection of the natural virtues of the soul inclining to good action; then, the de-ordination of the natural powers of the soul; then, after this, injury to the body; and, at the lowest, the loss of external goods. (*C.G.*, III, c. 141.)

Recommended Readings

Thomas Aquinas, St., *Summa Theol.*, I–II, qq. 90–97 (in *Basic Writings*, ed. Pegis, II, 742–805); I–II, q. 109, arts, 1–5 (in *Basic Writings*, II, 979–987).
Cronin, *Science of Ethics*, I, 633–652.
Gilson, *Moral Values and the Moral Life*, pp. 193–212.
Hart (ed.), "The Natural Law and International Relations," *Proc. Amer. Cath. Philos. Assoc.*, XXIV (1950). Papers by various authors; see

especially the contributions of Father C. A. Hart, C. de Koninck and H. Rommen.

Maritain, *The Rights of Man and the Natural Law*, pp. 59–64.

Rickaby, *Aquinas Ethicus*, I, 264–287.

Rommen, *The State and Catholic Thought*, pp. 184–215.

ADVANCED READINGS

Adler, "A Question About Law," in *Essays in Thomism*, pp. 205–236, 388–410.

Grabmann, "Das Naturrecht der Scholastik von Gratian bis Thomas von Aquin," in *Mittelalterliches Geistesleben*, pp. 65–103.

Lottin, "La loi en général. La définition thomiste et ses antécédents," in *Psychologie et Morale*, II, (Problèmes de Morale, première partie) 11–47.

———, *Principes de Morale*, I, 121–146; II, 33–54.

Renz, *Die Synteresis nach dem hl. Thomas von Aquin* (BGPM, Bd. X. 1–2).

Sertillanges, *La philosophie morale de s. Thomas*, pp. 91–114.

Wittmann, *Die Ethik des hl. Thomas von Aquin*, pp. 318–368.

Topics for Assignment

1. An Explanation of the Thomistic Definition of Law
2. How We Know the First Principles of Moral Law
3. Are Men Morally Obliged to Obey the Laws of Their Country?
4. Rewards and Punishments as Moral Sanctions
5. Why Even the Good Man Needs Supernatural Assistance

The Nature and Purpose of Moral Conscience

Moral law, like any law, consists in *universal* rules of behavior. Human beings differ individually in the kind of lives they lead and so they differ in the way in which the moral law applies to their individual actions. No codification of law could take care of all possible individual moral problems. Some people are in business, for instance, and they need to know what is right or wrong in business transactions. Other people may have little or nothing to do with such affairs. Moreover, one businessman does not face exactly the same moral problems as does another businessman. Even within the lifework of the individual man, the moral problems of yesterday are not identical with those of tomorrow.

The application of general moral knowledge to the particular moral action is a function of the practical intellect of each moral agent. Each man must judge whether each one of his moral actions is right or wrong. No other human being can do this for the moral agent. Only the individual agent is capable of knowing his own intentions, the motivation of his choices, the peculiar circumstances of his particular actions. God knows what goes on within each human consciousness, of course, but God does not directly communicate His moral judgments to man, in the natural course of life.

When we say that each man must judge the morality of his own concrete actions, we do not mean that such judgment is arbitrary, without objective reference. Just as the speculative intellect is governed by the true nature of things, so is the practical intellect

governed by objective rightness. It is as much an error to think
that the killing of a dog is morally equal to the killing of a man, as
to think that two plus three equals four. The original principles, by
which moral right and wrong are distinguished, are rightly known
by the natural power of the human intellect, strengthened by the
inborn habit of synderesis. But the application of these principles to
the concrete action is done by each man's intellect. If his reasoning
is guided by the Law of God (as revealed in the Decalogue, for
instance) he proceeds to make a judgment of the morality of the
concrete action, in terms of *superior reason*. On the other hand, he
may reason to somewhat the same conclusion by using what he
knows of the natural moral law, and in this case he uses *inferior
reason*. The conclusion to such thinking is a practical judgment to
the effect that: *This act is good, right, and should be done*; or, *This
act is bad, wrong, and should not be done*. This judgment is precisely the application of one's practical knowledge to any concrete,
individual moral action. The act is judged with knowledge (*cum
scientia = conscientia*) and so this practical judgment is called *conscience*.[1]

The practical judgment which is moral conscience is quite distinct from the decision which the agent may make, *to do* or *not to
do* a proposed action. This latter decision (which is the *judgment
of choice*) may be made by an agent who refuses or neglects to
consider the moral rightness or wrongness of his proposed action.
Moral conscience is impossible without a consideration of the rightness or wrongness of the action, for conscience is simply the *act of
knowing* that this action is right or wrong. One may know that it
is right to save this man's life (conscience); yet one may decide not
to do it (judgment of choice, in conflict with conscience). So, conscience is merely the cognitive termination of moral reasoning
about a given moral action. We shall discuss the difference between
the kind of practical reasoning which ends with the judgment of
conscience, and that kind of practical reasoning which terminates
in the judgment of choice, in the first section of Chapter VII.

[1] *S.T.*, I, 79, 13,c; in Pegis, *Basic Writings*, I, 766–767; see also the very clear
explanation in Appendix to Chap. VII, Text Two: *How the Practical Syllogism
Functions*. Note that this text is at the end of the next, not the present chapter.

In traditional language, two different functions have been given the name, conscience. One is the act of remembering whether a certain human act has been performed or not; this is a memory function and is sometimes called *psychological conscience*. The second is the act of judging whether a past, present, or future human act conforms to moral rules or not; this is *moral conscience*. We are concerned with this second meaning, here. It may be further subdivided, in view of the time element, into two main parts:

(1) If the act has been completed, the reasoning process starts with the accomplished action and goes back to known moral rules and principles, judging that this act should, or should not, have been done.[2] In relation to such actions of the past, moral conscience is said to *excuse*, to *accuse*, to *torment*, or to *cause remorse*. This is what many people have in mind, when they speak of their consciences bothering them about something they have already done. Such recriminatory judgments may be accompanied by moral feelings of shame, remorse or self-blame, but these feelings are not the conscience. Conscience is an act of the practical intellect.

(2) If the act is proposed to be done, now or in the future, the process of moral reasoning may start with the known moral rules and principles and proceed to a judgment by which the morally appropriate act is discovered.[3] It is in regard to not-yet-accomplished actions that conscience is said to *direct*, to *instigate*, to *induce*, or to *bind*.[4]

The purpose of moral conscience, then, is to enable the agent to know whether an individual moral action is good or bad. By means of such judgments, the agent can decide to improve, or make reparation for, past actions which are judged to have been evil; and he is able to decide rationally whether to choose to do, or not to do, a not-yet-accomplished action. It is not precise to think of conscience as the standard, or norm, of morality. Right reason is the moral

---

[2] Such reasoning follows the pattern of the *via resolutionis*, in thomistic logic; cf. *In Boetii De Trinitate*, q. VI, art. 1, ad 3m, translated in: Sr. Rose Emmanuella Brennan, *The Trinity by St. Thomas Aquinas* (St. Louis–London, 1946), pp. 179–180.

[3] This process uses the *via inventionis;* see *In Boet. De Trin., loc. cit.*

[4] Read: Appendix to Chap. VI, Text One: *Conscience, Application of Knowledge to Action;* and also, *S.T.*, I, 79, 13,c; in Pegis, *Basic Writings*, I, 767.

norm; conscience is the application of this standard, in the very judgment of the value of the action.

The Obligatory Force of Conscience

Conscience is said *to bind* the agent in some way. The Latin words, *ligare* (to bind) and *ligatio* (the binding or bond), are the sources of the English term *obligation*. A person is under an obligation, when he is subject to some kind of necessity. If one is tied up with physical bonds, then he is subject to a physical necessity to remain at rest. This necessity which comes from being bound, or obligated, is distinct from the need of an agent to act in accord with its physical nature. Binding or obligation suggests the imposition of necessity on one agent, *by another agent*.

One agent may necessitate, or obligate, the action of another either by coaction or by hypothetical necessity. Binding by coaction is a case of violence and it has no application to the human will. Man's will cannot directly be forced to act, by the application of external force. The will must produce its own acts, efficiently, or they are not will-acts. The kind of obligation imposed by conscience on the will, then, must be of the nature of *hypothetical or conditional necessity*.

An agent subject to hypothetical necessity is bound to act in a certain way (or to refrain from acting), *if he is to achieve a certain end*. Thus, a ruler may impose a legal obligation on his subjects to pay taxes. If they do not pay the taxes, he will put them in jail. Of course, they may choose not to obey and then they will lose their freedom of movement. The point is that these subjects are not subject to physical necessity. If they were, they could not but pay the taxes. By refusing to pay they may disobey the orders of the ruler but they do not escape their obligation as citizens—for legal punishment will follow such disobedience.

The human agent is not bound by physical, but by hypothetical or moral necessity, to conform to the order of reason. This hypothetical necessity is imposed on the moral agent through the practical judgment of conscience. However, this does not mean that the sole source of moral obligation is one's own conscience. It is really impossible for the agent to bind himself to a certain code of conduct. Kant's theory of the autonomy of practical reason, whereby he attempted to explain the source of moral obligation, is founded on a misunderstanding of the character of obligation. He seems to have confused the necessity of acting in accord with the physical laws of one's nature with the quite different, moral necessity of doing one's duty. Natural necessity is from within the agent but obligation or binding requires the causality of *another agent*. Ultimately, the ground or reason for the obligatory force of moral conscience must be found in a Being Who is in charge of all men. This Being is God. If there were no God, there would be no moral obligation for man.[5]

It is quite clear that, if one's practical judgment of conscience is objectively right (that is, in full accord with the Law of God), then one is obliged to choose and act in accord with this conscience. Right conscience imposes an absolute moral obligation on the moral agent. He acts immorally, if he does not conform to such a conscience.

However, conscience is not always objectively right. In many cases, the agent may err in his practical moral judgments, either through his own fault or not through his own fault. To understand the problem of obligation in such cases, we must examine the ways of making an error in the practical moral judgment.

Before this examination of error in the practical judgment, we may make one general observation. If the agent actually makes a practical judgment that some act should be (or should not be) done by him, here and now, he acts immorally by acting in opposition to this conscience, whether it is objectively right or wrong. This becomes obvious, when we advert to the simple meaning of this statement. It means that, if a man sincerely *thinks* something should be done by him, here and now, and if he does not do it, he is acting against the practical dictate of his own reason. That which is formal

---

[5] Read: Appendix to Chap. VI, Text Two: *The Type of Obligation Arising from Conscience.*

in morality is the way the proposed act is apprehended by the reason of the agent (*i.e.*, the *ratio objecti*). So, to fail to do what one judges must be done, is to fail to conform to the moral order of reason, *as one knows it*. Even an action which is materially good or materially indifferent, becomes evil, if the agent performing it sincerely thinks it to be immoral. Thus, almsgiving is a materially good action and playing cards is a materially indifferent action, but if the agent's practical judgment is that he should not give alms, or play cards, then he does wrong in giving alms or in playing cards.

We took the above case of a person who thinks he should do something and does not do it, but the same reasoning applies to the case in which the agent thinks that he should not do an action, and then does it. In both cases, he is acting against his own practical moral judgment and is doing what is wrong, even though his conscience is erroneous. Let us repeat: "Every conscience, whether right or erroneous, whether in regard to acts which are evil in themselves, or acts which are indifferent, is obligatory; so that he who acts in opposition to his conscience, does wrong (*peccat*)." [6]

The above teaching of St. Thomas must not be misunderstood. It does not mean that one is always morally good, if he acts in accord with his conscience; it does mean that one is always morally evil, if he acts against the dictate of his conscience.

Erroneous Conscience and Moral Obligation

Conscience means the application of knowledge (*scientia*) to an individual moral problem. This knowledge may be of almost any kind, from the general cognition of moral rules to the most particular cognition of the definite circumstances of the proposed action. St. Thomas puts it this way: "When I speak of conscience, I don't

---

[6] *Quodl.* III, q. 12, a. 27,c, *ad fin.* The student may read an expanded exposition of this teaching of St. Thomas, *S.T.*, I–II, q. 19, 5,c; in Pegis, *Basic Writings*, II, 339–341; but the reader should notice that the first half of the *response* outlines a doctrine which St. Thomas cannot accept; his own view begins with the words: "But this is unreasonable."

just mean science (*scientia*), in the strict sense, that is of formal truths only, but knowledge taken in a broad way for any kind of cognition (*pro quacumque notitia*), in which sense we say colloquially that we know (*scire*) everything which forms part of our cognitive experience." [7]

Now, there can be error at two places in this application of knowledge to the concrete problem. First of all, the *knowledge* which is applied may be erroneous. Secondly, it is possible that there be some error *in the practical reasoning* by which it is applied. Just as in the speculative syllogism, so also in the cognitive practical syllogism, the conclusion (which is conscience) may be wrong, either because of error in the premises, or because of a bad process of inference.

As far as the premises of the practical syllogism are concerned, error may occur in any premise except the most primary principles of the natural moral law. Synderesis cannot be mistaken about these self-evident rules. But the agent may be mistaken in the judgments arrived at by superior reason (he may think, for instance, that it is contrary to the Law of God, to undergo any surgical operation); or he may err in the judgments reached by inferior reason (as in the case of a man who is ignorant of the laws of his country, or some technical point in moral science). Apart from error due to ignorance of law, there is even greater possibility of error in the knowledge of the facts modifying the proposed action.

No special explanation need be offered for the possibility of error in conscience, resulting from faulty reasoning. Practical reasoning is less certain than speculative reasoning. It is even possible to make a mistake in the process of speculative reasoning. So, one may sometimes draw the wrong conclusion from right premises in a practical syllogism.[8]

When the agent *voluntarily* makes an error in a practical moral judgment and then chooses and acts in accord with this erroneous conscience, he performs an immoral act. The situation here is much

[7] *De Veritate*, q. 17, a. 2, ad 2m.
[8] Read: Appendix to Chap. VI, Text Three: *Can Conscience Err?* and Text Four: *How Conscience May Be in Error.*

the same as in the case of acting through voluntary ignorance. Error in practical judgment may be either directly or indirectly voluntary. It is directly so, when the agent actually wills to err. It is indirectly so, when the agent neglects to think prudently and rightly but does not actually desire to err. If the agent forms an erroneous conscience by reason of actually willing to do so, or because he neglects to take care to know something which he should know, then he is not doing his best to govern his moral act prudently and he cannot use such error as an excuse for consequent wrongdoing.[9]

However, if the agent falls into *involuntary* error of conscience, arising from ignorance of some circumstance which he could not reasonably be expected to know, then his consequent choice and external act are not immoral, provided they are in accord with his conscience. Involuntary error is in no way the fault of the agent. It only occurs in regard to knowledge which the agent could not reasonably be expected to have in the definite circumstances in which he is making his judgment. It is not possible to be in involuntary error concerning the primary principles of the natural moral law, or of the law of God. Involuntary error is possible in matters of fact, of moral circumstances, or in questions of positive law.[10] Of course, people who are insane or demented would not be able to think clearly about the divine or moral law, and their actions would not be immoral, even if materially opposed to the moral law, because such persons are in a condition of invincible ignorance.[11]

⌘Moral Doubt and Conscience⌘

We must clearly distinguish between an agent who is in moral doubt and one who has made an erroneous judgment of conscience. As long as the agent is in doubt as to the moral value of a performed or proposed action, *he has no judgment of conscience.* In thomistic language, doubt means, "the movement of reason over the

[9] Read: Appendix to Chap. VI, Text Six: *The Conditional Obligation of Erroneous Conscience.*
[10] Read: Appendix to Chap. VI, Text Five: *Ignorance of Fact and of Law.*
[11] Read: *S.T.*, I–II, 19, 6,c; in Pegis, *Basic Writings*, II, 341.

two sides of a contradiction, fearing to make a decision in favor of either one." [12]

It is clear, then, that there is no such act as "doubtful or perplexed conscience." Many moral writers, in the centuries following St. Thomas, devote much space to what they call the problem of the perplexed conscience. These moralists have devised various systems (tutiorism, probabiliorism, equiprobabilism, probabilism and laxism) as an aid to the solution of moral doubts. They offer various rules by which one may turn a perplexed conscience into a subjectively certain conscience. Examples of such rules are: "in cases of doubt one should always choose the safer course"; or "a law does not obligate unless it is sufficiently promulgated"; or "a doubtful law does not obligate." While the proponents of these systems have usually had excellent intentions, they would seem to have abandoned, in some cases at least, the true thomistic teaching on the nature of moral conscience and its relation to practical science. [13]

What should one do who is in doubt as to how to act in facing a moral problem? The first thing to note is that the intellectual condition of doubt offers no rational guidance for a voluntary action. It is morally wrong for an agent to think: I don't know what is the right course of action, therefore I may do anything I wish. Rather, the good man must think: *I am in moral doubt, I must make as good a judgment of conscience as is possible for me in this situation, and then choose to act in the light of that conscience.* To do a morally approvable action, the agent who is in doubt must do something to reach subjective certainty in his moral evaluation of his problem.

Sometimes the agent is in a condition of doubt which he can remove directly by his own efforts. In this situation his doubt results

[12] *In III Sent.*, 17, 1, 4,c: "Primo enim et principaliter [dubitatio] significat motum rationis supra utramque partem contradictionis cum formidine determinandi." Cf. *S.T.*, I, 79, 9, ad 4m, where opinion is similarly defined and contrasted with the intellectual act of judgment.

[13] For a severe criticism of probabilism and associated systems see: Th. Deman, O.P., "Probabilisme," *Dictionnaire de Théologie Catholique*, XIII (1936) 417–619. References to many other studies of this question are given in the excellent work by Dom O. Lottin, *Principes de Morale*, I, 231–240. Father Lottin approves the limited use of probabilism and his interpretation of this system has much to recommend it, for he insists on the prudent use of its rules.

from vincible and voluntary ignorance. Obviously, he must remove this doubt by getting the knowledge needed for a certain and right judgment of conscience. In such cases, the agent can get more accurate knowledge by personal investigation and by consulting other, well-informed people. There is no real difficulty here, provided the agent has a good intention; he will realize what can and must be done and he will do it. Failure to remove such directly vincible doubt is evidence of bad will, or intention, on the part of this agent.[14]

The real difficulty lies in the situation where the agent is in a condition of moral doubt which cannot be removed by direct investigation or consultation. Let us eliminate first the case of the person who is morally perplexed because of a previous immoral action which must be rectified before a new problem may be faced. St. Thomas gives the example of a priest who is under a religious obligation to chant the holy office. Suppose he is in a state of sin, then he does wrong in singing the office in a sinful state and he also does wrong in omitting the singing which he is supposed to do. The way out of this perplexity is clear enough. "He is not absolutely perplexed, because he can do penance and then sing without sin." [15]

In all other cases of moral doubt, where the doubt is not directly capable of solution, certainty in the judgment of conscience must be achieved by indirect practical reasoning. Fundamental to rightness in this process are a *good intention* on the part of the agent and a *prudent reconsideration* of the entire situation. If his initial doubt results from involuntary ignorance of some law which may objectively apply to him, the agent may use the rule enunciated by St. Thomas: *No one is bound by any precept unless he knows the precept.*[16] With this rule, the agent may reason as follows: I do not and cannot know whether this precept applies to me in this case; I am morally obligated only by precepts which can be known by me;

[14] *S.T.*, I–II, 19, 6, ad 3m; in *Basic Writings*, II, 342–343.
[15] *Quodl.* III, q. 12, a. 27, ad 2m.
[16] See the statement and explanation of this rule in Text Two of the Appendix to Chap. VI. Stated in Latin, it is: "nullus ligatur per praeceptum aliquod nisi mediante scientia illius praecepti." For a discussion of this rule, consult: Lottin, *Principes de Morale*, I, 218–222.

therefore, I am not morally bound by this precept. This last statement expresses a subjectively certain moral judgment, which is conscience. The agent may now act in accord with the judgment of conscience.

It should be observed that the preceding method of solving moral doubt based on invincible ignorance of the application of a law should be used only in those difficult cases where no other method of solution is available. Moreover, if the agent suspects that he should conform to a certain law, and that nonconformity may be of serious consequences to his religious life, or to the good of others, then he must judge that the right thing to do is the *safe* thing, that is, conform to the doubtful law. This is the rule of tutiorism: "in doubt always choose the way which is more safe." It should be followed where the consequences of disobedience to the doubtful law are of great moral importance. People who try to lead a life of moral perfection, in whom the moral virtues are highly developed, follow tutioristic reasoning as a matter of course. But the average man is not obliged to live a life of heroic virtue.

While legal writers distinguish between ignorance of law and ignorance of the facts circumstantial to a practical problem, it may be questioned whether this distinction should be rigorously maintained in the discussion of moral doubt. Ignorance of moral law is only possible in regard to secondary moral precepts which include complicated specifications of circumstances, under which the law may, or may not, apply. It is when moral precepts become highly technical that the average agent begins to doubt their application to his own case. Now, there are moral situations in which the average man may be able to form no direct judgment of conscience because he does not wholly understand the facts of the case, or the means available for action.

Suppose two ordinary men, A and B, go alone on a hunting trip. B chokes on some object and appears to A to be dying of suffocation. A has heard that it is possible to cut a hole in a person's throat to enable him to breathe under such circumstances but he does not know the details of such surgery. A faces the problem of trying to perform an inexpert tracheotomy, at the risk of causing the death of B, or of simply letting B choke to death. Here, the doubt does not arise from ignorance of law but from invincible ignorance of the means to help B. It is impossible for A to avoid making a serious decision. If he does nothing, B will probably die; if he tries to do the operation, B may live but he may also die as a result. In such a dilemma, A may finally decide either to try to perform the operation, or not to perform it. As long as his intention is good, either choice is morally good. If B dies, A is involuntary in regard to this consequence. If B lives, such a good result is not wholly due to A's conscious action. A is only voluntary in regard to his decision to help his friend. In effect there is no ground for making a rational choice of the means available. A should not blame himself for being unable to decide a problem which is actually beyond his grasp.

Of course, if A were a surgeon, one who is expected to know about such things and if, through negligence, he were ignorant of the technique of tracheotomy, then his doubt would be culpable. He would be morally guilty of failure to help B under these circumstances.

Concluding this section on moral doubt, we may say that *moral* doubt is always capable of solution, sometimes directly, sometimes indirectly. Where there is no evident solution, then the problem ceases to be a moral one and this is the case in the hunting problem given above. We are only responsible, morally, for those acts which are voluntary. Hence, in those rare situations where we cannot get enough knowledge to form a right conscience we are not responsible for the action performed.[17]

Conscience and Positive Law

Ethical conscience is formally the act of judgment whereby the natural moral law is applied to singular moral problems. We have seen that this moral law is known by man's intellect strengthened by the habit of synderesis and this knowledge may be further developed and made precise by the use of the habit of moral science.

[17] Read: Appendix to Chap. VI, Text Seven: *No One Is Absolutely Perplexed.*

Since the natural moral law is a participation in the eternal law, conscience is also an application of the eternal law to human acts.

Unlike those laws (eternal and moral) which are made known to man through the natural tendency of his intellect to know self-evident truths, either speculative or practical, positive laws are promulgated to man by some sort of external sign and not through his natural, intellectual processes. The laws of one's country, one's Church, of any society of which one is a member, are (if good laws) but restatements of rules of the natural moral law or special determinations reasonably added to the natural moral law. Such positive laws are of great value to the ordinary moral agent, since they express precisely the universal rules of good behavior which he must follow in order to live a good life. He has a moral obligation to inform himself concerning the human positive laws governing his state in life. Because such laws are made for the common good, and disobedience to them tends to disrupt the good of society, he is morally obliged to conform to all positive laws unless he knows positively that they are opposed to right reason, that is, to the natural moral law. So, in this sense, moral conscience involves application of positive law to the human acts which come under it.[18]

There is, however, another type of positive law which is directive of moral conscience and which is needed in order to live a good life. This is called the divine law. It has been promulgated by supernatural revelation, imperfectly in the Old Testament, more perfectly in the New Testament. The Ten Commandments given to Moses are definite examples of its precepts.[19] Four good reasons are given by St. Thomas, to show why man needs this divine law:

First, because man is directed by law to the acts which are proper in relation to his ultimate end. Now, if man were merely ordained to an end which does not go beyond the proportion of the natural faculties of man, it would not be necessary for man to have anything directive in the area of reason, above the natural law and human positive law which is derived from it. But because man is ordained to an end consisting in eternal beatitude which goes beyond the proportion of natural human faculties, as

[18] Read: *S.T.*, I–II, 91, 3,c, et *ad primum*, et ad 3m; in Pegis, *Basic Writings*, II, 751–752.
[19] *Ibid.*, art. 5; Pegis, *Basic Writings*, II, 754–755.

was established above (*S.T.*, I–II, q. 5, a. 5), it was therefore necessary for him to be directed to his end by a divinely given law, above natural and human law.

Second, because of the uncertainty of human judgment, in particular concerning contingent and singular things, it is possible that there may be diverse judgments about the human acts of different men; from which, too, diverse and contrary laws proceed. Therefore, so that man can know without any doubt what he is to do and what to avoid, it was necessary that he be directed in his own acts by a law which is divinely given, of which it will continually be true that no error is possible.

Third, because man can make a law in regard to those things of which he can make a judgment. Now, a man's judgment cannot apply to inner impulses, which lie hidden within, but only to exterior acts which are overt. And yet it is required for the perfection of virtue that man stand in the right, in regard to both kinds of acts. So, human law was not able to restrain and order inner acts adequately, and it was necessary, for this reason, for divine law to be added from above.

Fourth, because as Augustine says in the first book of the treatise *On Free Choice* (c. 5; PL 32, 1228), human law cannot punish or prohibit all things which are done in an evil way, for, as a consequence of its desire to remove all evil, many good things would be taken away and the common welfare which is necessary for human society would be impeded. So, in order that no evil thing might endure unprohibited and unpublished, it was necessary that the divine law, through which all sins are prohibited, should be added.[20]

The insufficiency of the ordinary man's knowledge of the natural moral law, in view of the supernatural end to which his moral actions are directed, is the chief reason why man needs the guidance of divine positive law. This is but another instance of the inferiority of natural ethics to a higher moral science. Man, as a result of the darkening of his intellect consequent upon the sin of Adam, even has much difficulty in discerning the rules of natural virtue. The divine law prescribes the acts of natural and supernatural virtue, definitely and firmly. Unaided natural reason knows the moral obligations of human nature rather vaguely at best, and it could not grasp at all the requirements of supernatural virtue.[21]

[20] *S.T.*, I–II, 91, 4,c; the complete article may be read in Pegis, *Basic Writings*, II, 752–753.
[21] Read: Appendix to Chap. VI, Text Eight: *Natural Reason and the Divine Law*.

Summary of Chapter VI

Moral conscience may be defined as: the act of the practical intellect, applying moral knowledge to the rational judgment of the moral goodness or evil of each singular, voluntary action. It is the cognitive conclusion of the practical syllogism. Conscience *testifies*, when it is the act of recalling previously done moral actions; it *excuses* or *accuses*, when it is the act of judging that such performed actions were good or evil; and it *instigates, induces*, or *binds*, when it is the act preceding choice, presenting a proposed action as something to be done or not to be done. Moral conscience is an act of practical cognition, not of appetition; it differs from free choice, which is an act of the will guided by the intellect. Moral obligation is a kind of necessity, not physical but hypothetical, imposed ultimately by God and mediately by moral conscience, requiring the moral agent to choose certain means and to act externally in a reasonable way, if he is to attain his ultimate end. Unlike the acts of synderesis in knowing the universal rules of morality, the act of conscience is not always right. Conscience may be either morally right, or involuntarily erroneous, or voluntarily erroneous. Right conscience binds the agent without any qualification. Erroneous conscience is conditionally obligatory: as long as it remains the agent is wrong in acting against it but he does not do right in acting in accord with it, unless his error is completely involuntary. Moral doubt is not identical with erroneous conscience; the perplexed agent must do his best to make a morally certain judgment of conscience, either directly or indirectly. One should always have the guidance of conscience in the performance of a moral action. Certain practical perplexities, incapable of clear solution, are not moral problems. Conscience is formally an application of the natural moral law to man's moral problems, but it is also guided by good positive laws, in particular (because of the insufficiency of man's knowledge of morality) by the divinely given, positive law of God, of which the commandments of the Decalogue are examples.

Appendix to Chapter VI

¶ TEXT ONE: *Conscience: Application of Knowledge to Action.*
The name, *conscience*, signifies the application of knowledge to
something; hence, *conscire* means, in a way, to know at the same
time (*simul scire*). Now, any kind of knowledge can be applied to
something; hence, conscience cannot be the name of any special
habitus, or of any potency; rather, *it is the name of the very act
which is the application of any kind of habitus, or of any kind of
knowledge, to some particular act.*

Knowledge is applied to an act in two ways: first, when one considers whether the act is or was being done; second, when one
considers whether the act is right or not. According to the first
kind of application, we are said to have the conscience [*i.e.*, to be
conscious] of an act, inasmuch as we know that this act was done or
not done. Thus, we may say colloquially: this was not done "to my
knowledge" [*de conscientia mea:* as far as my conscience is aware];
that is, I do not (or did not) know whether this was done (or had
been done). And, it is according to this way of speaking that one
understands the passage in Genesis 43:22, "It is not in our consciences, who placed the money in our bags"; and in Eccles. 7:23,
"Thy conscience knoweth that thou hast often spoken evil of others"; and it is according to this usage that conscience is said to
testify to something: Rom. 9:1, "my conscience giving testimony
for me."

But, according to the second way of application, whereby
knowledge is applied to the act, in order to know whether the act
is right or not, there are two possibilities. In one way, through the
habitus of science, we are directed to something which is to be
done, or not done. In another way, after it has been done, the act is
examined in relation to the *habitus* of knowledge, as to whether it
is right or not right. These two ways in the realm of operative
matters are distinguished according to two ways used in speculative thinking: the way of discovery and the way of judgment.
For, the way in which we look, by means of knowledge, to see

what should be done (that is, when we are as it were taking counsel) is like the process of discovery whereby we investigate the
conclusions by going from the principles. But the way in which we
examine and discuss the rightness of things already done, is like the
way of judgment, in which we resolve conclusions into principles.
Now, we use the name, conscience, for both sorts of application.

Inasmuch as knowledge is applied to the act, and is directing it,
conscience is said to instigate, or to induce, or to bind. But, inasmuch as knowledge is applied to the act by way of the examination
of things which have already been done, conscience is thus said to
accuse or cause remorse, when what has been done is found to be
in discord with knowledge, in the light of which it is examined, and
to defend or excuse, when what has been done is found to have
proceeded according to the form of the knowledge.

But, one should understand that, in the first application of knowledge to the act with the purpose of knowing whether it has been
done, the application to the particular act is of sense knowledge,
for example, memory, through which we remember what has been
done; of sensation, through which we perceive this particular act
which we are now doing. But, in the second and third applications,
whereby we take counsel as to what should be done, or examine
what has been done already, the habitus of operative reason, namely
synderesis and the habitus of wisdom (by which superior reason is
perfected), and the habitus of science (by which inferior reason is
perfected), are applied to the act. They may all be applied together, or just one or the other of them. For, we examine what we
did, in the light of these habitus and we take counsel according to
them, concerning things to be done. However, the act of examination is not merely concerned with things done but also with things
to be done; but counsel deals solely with things to be done. (*De
Verit.*, q. 17, a. 1,c.)

¶ TEXT TWO: *The Type of Obligation Arising from Conscience.*
I answer that, undoubtedly conscience does bind (*ligat*). But, to
see how it binds, one should know that binding (*ligatio*), metaphorically transferred from bodily to spiritual things, signifies the

imposition of necessity. For, he who is bound is under the necessity of staying in the place where he is bound, and the power of being turned to other things is taken from him. Hence, it is clear that binding has no place among things which are, of themselves, necessary. For, we cannot say that fire is bound to go upward, though it is necessary that it be carried upward. Rather, binding has a place only among those things which are necessary in the sense that their necessity is imposed by another agent.

Now, there are two kinds of necessity which can be imposed by another agent. One is that of *coaction*, and through this every being is absolutely necessitated to do that to which it is determined by the action of the agent; otherwise it would not properly be called coaction, but rather inducement (*inductio*). The other is a *hypothetical* necessity (*necessitas conditionata*), arising from the supposition of an end. Thus, a necessity is imposed on someone, in the sense that, *if* he does not do this, he will not attain his reward.

The first kind of necessity, which is of coaction, does not apply to the movements of the will but only to corporeal things, because the will is naturally free from coaction. The second kind of necessity can be imposed upon the will, as in the case where it is necessary to choose this, if this good is to be attained, or this evil is to be avoided. For, to be without evil is reckoned the same as to have the good, in these matters, as is clear from the Philosopher in his *Ethics* (V, 1; 1129a12). Now, just as the necessity of coaction is imposed on corporeal things by some action, so too, hypothetical necessity is imposed on the will by some action. But the action, by which the will is moved, is the command of a ruler or governor. Hence the Philosopher says, in Book V of his *Metaphysics* (Cf. *Polit.*, I, 5; 1254b4–5), that the ruler is the principle of motion by means of his command. For, the command of a governor is related to binding in the order of voluntary things (in that kind of binding which can apply to the will) in the same way as corporeal action is related to the binding of corporeal things, by the necessity of coaction. Now, the action of a corporeal agent never induces necessity in another thing unless by the contact of its coaction with the thing on which it acts. Hence, no one is bound by the command of any king or lord, unless the command reaches him who is commanded. Now, it reaches him by way of knowledge. Hence, no one is bound by any precept, except by means of the knowledge of that precept. Therefore, he who is incapable of possessing knowledge is not bound by the precept; and no one ignorant of God's precept is bound to do what is prescribed, except to the extent that he *should* know the precept. If he should not, and does not, know it, he is in no way bound by the precept. Just as in corporeal things the corporeal agent does not act, except by contact, so also in spiritual things the precept does not bind, except by knowledge. Thus, just as it is the same power by which the sense of touch acts, and by which the force of the agent acts (since touch does not act except through the force of the agent, and neither does the force of the agent except by means of touch), so too, it is the same force, by which the precept binds and by which conscience binds. For, the precept may not bind except by the force of knowledge, nor knowledge except by the force of the precept. Hence, since conscience is simply the application of knowledge to the act, it follows that conscience is said to bind by the force of divine precept. (*De Verit.*, q. 17, a. 3,c.)

¶ TEXT THREE: *Can Conscience Err?* As is clear from the statements in the preceding article, conscience is nothing but the application of knowledge to a special act. In this application, error may occur in two ways: firstly, because what is applied has some error in it; secondly, from the fact that it is not rightly applied. Similarly, a twofold mistake (*peccatum*) is possible in syllogistic reasoning, either from the fact that one uses false [premises], or from the fact that he does not syllogize rightly.

But the use of false [premises] happens in some cases, and not in others. For, it has been said above, in the preceding article, that the knowledge of synderesis and of superior and inferior reason is applied through conscience to the examination of the particular act. Now, since the act is particular and the judgment of synderesis is universal, the judgment of synderesis cannot be applied to the act, unless by the assumption of something particular. Sometimes the superior reason supplies this particularity, and sometimes the inferior reason. Thus conscience is perfected by a certain particular syllogism, as it were. For example, if it is suggested from the judgment of synderesis that *nothing should be done that is prohibited by the law of God*, and if the knowledge that *association with this woman is prohibited by the law of God* is taken from superior reason, the application of conscience may be made by concluding that *this association is to be avoided*.

Now, error does not occur in the universal judgment of synderesis, as appears from what is said in the preceding article. But there can be a mistake (*peccatum*) in the judgment of superior reason, as when anyone thinks something to be in accord with the law, or in discord, which is not. This is the case with heretics who believe that oath-taking has been prohibited by God. So, error occurs in conscience because of falsity which was in the superior part of reason.

Likewise, error can happen in conscience from an error existing in the inferior part of reason, as when one errs in regard to civil rules (*rationes*) of the just or the unjust, of the honorable or dishonorable.

Also, error may occur from the fact that the application in conscience is not made in the right way. For, just as it happens in syllogistic reasoning about speculative matters that the proper form of argumentation may not be followed, with the result that falsity occurs in the conclusion, so also does it happen in the syllogism which is needed in problems of action, as has been said.

However, it should be noted that conscience can never err in regard to some things. That is to say, when the particular act to which conscience is applied is intrinsically concerned with the universal judgment of synderesis. Just as, in speculative matters there can be no error about particular conclusions which are considered directly under the universal principles and in the same terms (for instance, no one can be deceived in regard to the proposition: this whole thing is greater than its part, just as in this proposition: every whole is greater than its part), so too, in a judgment such as: God should not be loved by me, or: some evil thing should be done, no conscience can err. The reason for this is, that in both kinds of judgment, whether speculative or operative, both the major which consists of a universal judgment and the minor which states the same proposition in particular terms, are self-evident. It is like saying: Every whole is greater than its part; this thing is a whole; therefore it is greater than its part. (*De Veritate*, q. 17, 2,c.)

¶ TEXT FOUR: *How Conscience May Be in Error.* Conscience, as the name itself suggests, signifies the application of science or human knowledge to some act of one's own. Now, every kind of knowledge which man has can be applied to his act; whether it be memory, as when a man is said to have a conscience testifying that he has done something or has not done it; or even universal or particular knowledge, through which a man can know whether something is to be done or not, and according to this, conscience is said to urge or to hinder.

Now, it is evident that, if we take up the various kinds of knowledge in man, error can be present in some and not in others. Regarding the first principles which are naturally known, whether they be speculative or operative, there can be no error; examples of this sort of knowledge are: "Every whole is greater than its part," or "No injury should be done to anyone." However, in other kinds of more particular human knowledge, whether pertaining to the sense order, or to inferior reason which considers human things, or the superior reason which considers divine things—error can occur in many ways.

Now, it is evident that error arises in the application of many kinds of knowledge to the act, depending on how many erroneous things were present in these kinds of knowledge, just as falsity evidently occurs in a conclusion whenever any of the premises is false. And thus, though there is no error in the cognition of first principles of the natural moral law (*juris naturalis*), nevertheless, because error can occur in other principles of human or divine law, therefore man's conscience can err. It is clear, for instance, that a heretic, who has a conscience that he should never take an oath, has an erroneous conscience because of the fact that he believes all oath-taking to be against a precept of God; however, he does not err in the fact that he thinks nothing should be done in opposition to a divine precept. (*Quodl.*, III, q. 12, a. 26,c.)

¶ TEXT FIVE: *Ignorance of Fact and Law.* [It is argued in obj. 5, that God is more merciful than any earthly ruler, but no ruler would hold a man responsible for what is done out of error.]

From this argument, the conclusion is not that erroneous conscience does not bind in pain of sin, if it be not fulfilled; rather, it excuses from sin, hence the argument is not pertinent. However, the objection does reach a true conclusion, when the error itself is not a sin: for instance, when it occurs as a result of ignorance of a fact. But if it arise from ignorance of the law, then it does not reach a true conclusion, for this ignorance is a sin. For, he who alleges ignorance of a law which he should know, is not excused even before a civil judge. (*De Verit.*, q. 17, a. 4, ad 5m.)

TEXT SIX: *The Conditional Obligation of Erroneous Conscience.* Right conscience and erroneous conscience bind in different ways. The right one binds absolutely and essentially (*simpliciter et per se*); the erroneous one relatively and accidentally (*secundum quid et per accidens*). Now, I say that the right one binds absolutely, because it binds completely (*absolute*) and in every case. Thus, if anyone has a conscience in regard to the avoidance of adultery, he cannot put aside this conscience, without sin, because in the erroneous action of putting it aside he sins gravely. But, while it remains, he cannot actually overlook it, without sin; hence it binds absolutely and in every case.

However, an erroneous conscience binds only relatively and conditionally (*sub conditione*). For, he, to whom conscience dictates that he is obliged to fornicate, is not obliged in such a way that he cannot, without sin, give up fornication, except under this condition, that such a conscience persist. Now, this conscience can be removed without sin. Hence, such a conscience does not oblige in every case; for, something could happen, namely the putting aside of the conscience, and when this does happen, there is no further obligation. What is so in a conditional way only, is said to be relative.

Also, I say that right conscience binds essentially, but erroneous, accidentally; and this is clear from the following. He, who wishes or loves one thing because of another, likes the latter essentially, because it is that for the sake of which he likes the former; and the former is liked accidentally. For instance, he who likes wine for the sweet taste, likes the sweet *essentially*, but the wine *accidentally*. Now, he who has an erroneous conscience and believes it to be right (otherwise, he would not be in error), only adheres to the erroneous conscience because of the rightness which he believes to be in it. Indeed, he does adhere, essentially speaking, to a right conscience, but it is, as it were, accidentally erroneous, insofar as this conscience which he believes to be right, happens to be erroneous. And hence, it is that, speaking essentially, he is bound by a right conscience; accidentally, however, by an erroneous one. This solution may be taken from the words of the Philosopher, in his *Ethics* [*Eth. Nic.*, VII, c. 9; 1151a29] where he asks pretty much the same question, namely: whether that man should be called incontinent, who departs from right reason only, or also he who departs from false. His answer is, that the incontinent man essentially departs from right reason, but from false reason, accidentally; from the first [right reason], absolutely, but from the second, relatively. For, what is so essentially, is so absolutely; but what is so accidentally, is so relatively.

In answer to the first objection, it must be said that, although that which the erroneous conscience dictates is not in agreement with the Law of God, nevertheless it is taken, by the man who is in error, as the very Law of God; and so, essentially speaking, if he departs from this, he departs from the Law of God; although accidentally, it is true, he does not depart from the Law of God.

In answer to the third objection, it must be said that the erroneous conscience, being in error about those things which are essentially evil, dictates things contrary to the Law of God. Nevertheless, it says that those things which it does dictate are the Law of God, and so the transgressor of this conscience becomes a transgressor

of the Law of God; although, in following this conscience and fulfilling it in his action, he sins mortally as one who acts against the
Law of God. The sin was in the error itself, since it happened as a
result of ignorance of what he should have known. (*De Verit.*,
q. 17, a. 4,c, and *ad primum*, and ad 3m.)

¶ TEXT SEVEN: *No One Is Absolutely Perplexed.*   Speaking absolutely and without qualification, no one is perplexed. But, when
some condition has been supposed, then it is not unfitting that, as
long as this condition remains, a man may be perplexed. For instance, as long as an evil intention remains, sin occurs, whether a
proper act in accord with the law be done or not done. Similarly
too, as long as an erroneous conscience remains, sin cannot be
avoided, whatever be done. But a man can put aside the erroneous
conscience, just like the bad intention; and so, he is not perplexed
absolutely. (*In II Sent.*, d. 39, q. 3, a. 3, ad 5m.)

¶ TEXT EIGHT: *Natural Reason and the Divine Law.*   Nature inclines sufficiently to hope for the good proportioned to human nature. But a man must be led by authority of the divine law, partly by
promises, partly by admonitions or precepts, in order to hope for
a supernatural good. Even in regard to those things to which
natural reason does tend, such as the acts of the moral virtues, it
was necessary that the precepts of the divine law be given, for the
sake of greater firmness, and chiefly because the natural reason of
man was darkened by the concupiscences arising from sin. (*S.T.*,
II–II, 22, 1, *ad primum*.)

Recommended Readings

Thomas Aquinas, St., *Summa Theologiae*, I, q. 79, 12–13 (in *Basic Writ-
      ings*, ed. Pegis, I, 765–767); I–II, q. 19, 5–6 (in *Basic Writings*, II,
      339–343).
Cronin, *Science of Ethics*, I, 472–505.
Rickaby, *Aquinas Ethicus*, I, 281–285, 303–307.

ADVANCED READINGS

Lehu, "La recta ratio de s. Thomas signifie-t-elle la conscience?" *Revue Thomiste*, n.s. VIII (1925) 159–166.

Lottin, *Principes de Morale*, I, 148–157, 201–240; II, 149–154.

Sertillanges, *La philosophie morale de s. Thomas*, pp. 385–401.

Wittman, *Die Ethik des hl. Thomas von Aquin*, pp. 275–287.

Topics for Assignment

1. Why Conscience Is Not a Moral Sense
2. The Difference Between Physical Necessity and Moral Obligation
3. Is an Act Contrary to the Law of God Always Bad?
4. The Relation Between Moral Doubt and Ignorance
5. Is One Morally Obliged to Obey the City Traffic Laws?

VII · THE PRACTICAL SYLLOGISM

Right Reasoning About Moral Problems

The act of understanding, whereby the moral agent grasps the general principles and conclusions of the natural moral law, leaves man with a knowledge of certain universal rules of conduct. The moral action which is to be directed by the application of such rules is a particular event. Something must be done to bridge the gap between the *universality* of the rule and the *particularity* of the action. It is the purpose of this chapter to show how this bridge is supplied by *practical reasoning*.

Discursive reasoning is the intellectual process of demonstrating conclusions, either by deriving previously unknown conclusions from known truths, or by relating unverified judgments to known truths. Such rational demonstration has been studied, from the point of view of the correctness of the inference, in logic. The same rational process is treated, in the philosophy of man or rational psychology, from the point of view of its function as the third operation of the human intellect. Man is called a *rational* animal, because his is the only kind of intellect which must use this slow, step-by-step process of demonstrating conclusions.

In the ordinary processes of logical reasoning, the typical pattern is that of the syllogism. There are other forms of mediate inference but they are contractions or expansions of the syllogism. The conclusions of syllogisms are reached with greatest accuracy and promptness by an intellect trained by the habitus of some demonstrative science. A person who knows geometry has a special skill in reaching the true conclusions of his science; similarly the physicist, the philosopher, the theologian, all have acquired intellectual habits which make them adept at demonstrating the conclusions of their respective sciences. All such scientific conclusions are somewhat universal in scope, because every science deals with universal knowledge. Even a practical science, such as ethics, terminates in universal conclusions. Hence, in this chapter we are not going to examine the kind of reasoning which is typical of ethical science but rather the sort of *reasoning which leads up to the performance of concrete moral actions.*

It is imperative for us to grasp the importance and necessity of this most practical kind of reasoning. Every moral act issues from a rational choice. As St. Thomas puts it, "since the act, either of sin or of virtue, is dependent on election, and election is an appetition of the result of previous deliberation, and deliberation is, of course, a rational investigation, there must be some quasi-syllogistic deduction to every act of virtue or sin." [1] So, to direct his own concrete and individual moral actions in a reasonable way, each man must go through a process of practical reasoning. He may not know that he is using syllogisms but he is. The practical syllogism differs from the syllogism studied in logic, in two ways. First, the conclusion of the practical syllogism is *wholly singular.* Second, the minor premise of the practical syllogism must be a *particularized* judgment, such that it will show the logical connection between the general moral rule and the proposed individual action. This kind of syllogism is also called *operative,* or *prudential.*

Syllogistic reasoning is done for the sake of demonstrating a definite conclusion. The nature of the syllogism will depend on the nature of the judgment with which it concludes. Hence, to understand the character of practical moral reasoning, we must note the difference between two kinds of moral conclusions. One of these is a *purely cognitive judgment* about the morality of a concrete action. When we say that it is purely cognitive, we mean that it is essentially *an act of knowing,* performed by the practical intellect under the initial instigation of the will, of course, as are all voluntary acts, but not including a direct participation of the will.

[1] *De Malo,* q. III, a. 9, ad 7m.

This first kind of moral judgment is simply to know that this individual action is right or wrong, to be done or not to be done. This is the judgment of *moral conscience;* it need not result in a concrete moral action. For example, if a beggar asks me for a dime on the street, I may judge: "It is a good act to give this man a dime now." This is conscience in its impersonal form, Or, I may make the personal judgment of conscience: "I should give this man a dime now." In neither form does my judgment of conscience necessarily move me to perform the act of giving him the dime. It is quite possible for me to walk on and not give him the dime. By the judgment of conscience, my will is not committed to the carrying out of the approved, or omission of the disapproved, action. The moral necessity or obligation associated with conscience is not a physical necessity. We know already that a moral agent does not need to act in accord with his conscience.

The second kind of conclusion to a process of moral reasoning is also a *practical judgment,* but it is the sort of decision which leads immediately and necessarily to the act of *choosing* and *doing* the action. This is called the *judgment of election,* or of choice. Continuing the example of the beggar and the dime, I may decide either that I *will* or *will not,* give him the dime. My conscience remaining the same (that I should give him the dime), I may be swayed by passion (for instance, I may dislike his appearance) and voluntarily refuse to do what I think I should do. This judgment of election obviously includes some participation of appetite. The will and also both concupiscible and irascible appetites may affect it. However, the judgment of choice is the termination of a rational process. The reasoning implied in the refusal to help this beggar follows some pattern such as this: "Dirty people don't deserve to be helped. This man is dirty. Therefore, I won't help him." It does not concern us, at the moment, whether this practical reasoning is right. The point to be noted is that both the judgment of conscience and the judgment of choice are preceded by a process of practical reasoning, yet they are two distinct types of practical judgments.[2]

[2] Read: Appendix to Chap. VII, Text One: *Conscience Distinguished from the Judgment of Choice.*

For conscience and the judgment of choice to be right and good, both must be in accord with right reason. The habit of reasoning rightly about proposed moral actions is called prudence. To be prudent, man must not only judge moral actions rightly; he must also *choose* and *do* right actions. Of the three acts which are proper to the virtue of prudence (right deliberation, right judgment, and right preception of action) [3] the third, preception, is not found in the reasoning which may precede the judgment of conscience. But certainly the formation of a right conscience does require prudent deliberation and judgment. Hence, we may conclude that there is one process of practical reasoning, to which the first two acts of prudence apply, but not the third, and this process terminates in the judgment of conscience. Let us call this process ending with conscience the *cognitive moral syllogism*. Secondly, there is another process of practical reasoning, which usually comes after the judgment of conscience, and which terminates in right choice and right action. We shall call this second process the *operative moral syllogism*. (This precision of terminology is not found in the text of St. Thomas, though it is clear that he thought the two processes distinct.)

Let us first examine the *cognitive* moral syllogism. Illustrations of this syllogism are numerous in the writings of St. Thomas. Text Two of the Appendix to Chap. VI, offers the following example:

MAJOR: Every evil is to be avoided (judgment of synderesis)
MINOR: Adultery is evil because prohibited by the law of God
        (a judgment of superior reason)
CONCL: This act of adultery is to be avoided (judgment of con-
        science)

Note that St. Thomas plainly calls this conclusion an act of conscience, in the text cited. Note also that this is a condensed polysyllogism; the formal conclusion to the right syllogism illustrated is: *Adultery is to be avoided*. This conclusion becomes a major;

---

[3] See *infra* and also, Appendix to Chap. VII, Text Fourteen: *The Principal Act of Prudence: Preception.*

the next minor is: *this proposed act is a case of adultery:* and the conclusion of conscience is: *this act of adultery is to be avoided.*

Additional examples of the cognitive moral syllogism are found in Text Three of the Appendix to this present chapter. Observe especially the reasoning typical of the continent man, in which there are two possible majors: (1) *No sin is to be done;* and (2) *Every pleasurable thing is to be sought after.* Because he is continent, he eventually concludes his reasoning by reference to the first major and decides that, *this act of sin should not be done.* The incontinent person allows the second major to dominate and concludes: *this act of pleasure* (though sinful) *is to be done.*

A favorite case of the cognitive moral syllogism, including a faulty minor, is found in many of St. Thomas' discussions of conscience.[4] Here, the conscientious heretic reasons:

MAJOR: It is evil not to believe what God teaches (moral science)
MINOR: This particular thing (say the Divinity of Christ) has not been taught by God (error of superior reason)
CONCL: I should not believe this teaching (erroneous conscience)

Such a judgment of conscience is objectively in error but it would be possible for this judgment to have *subjective* rightness. This would be the situation where the "heretic" is in condition of invincible ignorance in regard to the minor. In this event, he would not be a formal heretic.

The general pattern of the cognitive moral syllogism, then, is that of mediate inference involving two (or more) premises—the major a primary principle or some universal conclusion of moral knowledge, the minor a particular judgment which puts the concrete action within the scope of the major, and the conclusion the judgment or dictate of conscience. It is well to emphasize again that conscience is simply a practical cognitive judgment, that this act is morally good or bad. The judgment of conscience is right, if both premises are right, and if the inference to the conclusion is rightly made. On the other hand, the judgment of conscience may

[4] See for instance, Appendix to Chap. V, Text Seven, the answer to the second objection.

be wrong, or erroneous, if either premise is not right, or if the process of inference is not rightly performed.

The *operative* moral syllogism terminates in the judgment of choice and the consequent doing of the action. This is the reasoning in which all three acts of prudence may be fully used. Here, we find the possibility of right reasoning to the ultimate moral climax, which is rationally chosen right action. In this operative moral syllogism, we may distinguish two general patterns; one includes the judgment of conscience, but the other omits the act of conscience. An example of the first pattern (involving conscience) is suggested by Text Four, in the Appendix to this chapter:

MAJOR: I should not kill my father (judgment of conscience)
MINOR: This man is my father (judgment of particular reason)
CONCL: I will not kill this man (judgment of election leading to the actual omission of the proposed action)

A more complicated illustration of the first pattern of the operative moral syllogism is presented by the reasoning of the incontinent man.[5] Here, the agent is concerned about the morality of his proposed action but he eventually gives in to the passion of concupiscence. Thus we find four propositions in his reasoning:

MAJOR 1: Nothing sweet should be tasted at the wrong time (conclusion of moral science; say the man is a diabetic)
MAJOR 2: Every sweet thing is pleasurable and a good to be sought after (rationalization of faulty inclination of concupiscence)
MINOR: This thing is sweet (judgment of particular reason)
CONCL: I will taste this sweet thing (judgment of election, accompanied by choice and action)

Observe that while conscience is not listed as a part of this reasoning, the judgment of conscience is implied in the fact that the incontinent person is concerned about the morality of his action. In some

[5] See: *In VII Ethic.*, lect. 3; ed. Pirotta, p. 440, nn. 1346-1348. Note that the term, *incontinent*, is used in the strict thomistic sense, here.

such cases, this judgment of conscience may even be spoken,[6] but the incontinent agent does not permit himself to dwell upon the rightness of his conscience. As St. Thomas remarks, "he may even say, 'It is not good for me to seek this pleasure now,' but he does not believe it in his heart." We might think of a fat lady who sits down before a large serving of ice cream; she says, "I shouldn't do it!" and then proceeds to eat the ice cream with great relish. She considers that she has fulfilled her moral obligation by expressing her judgment of conscience, but her intention and decision are contrary to her right conscience. In such a case, the agent will have some spurious reason to justify the bad choice. She may say that, "You must not offend your hostess," or "One more sundae will do no harm." Reasoning from such rules is practical but not prudent.

The second pattern of the operative moral syllogism simply omits the judgment of conscience in a process of reasoning where it should be present. A clear example is found in the reasoning of the intemperate man.[7] An intemperate person simply refuses, or neglects, to consider whether his proposed action is moral or not. This omission of moral consideration arises originally from the habitual intention of an end which is contrary to the intention of man's ultimate end. An intemperate person lives to enjoy things of sense. His choices are habitually made to achieve this end. There is some practical reasoning preceding these choices but such reasoning is defective because of the vice of intemperance. The general pattern of such reasoning is:

MAJOR: Every pleasure should be enjoyed (general rule of concupiscence)
MINOR: This act is pleasurable (judgment of particular reason)
CONCL: I will do this pleasurable act (judgment of election plus the consequent action)

In this process, no universal *moral* rule appears, and no judgment of conscience. The vice of intemperance enables the agent habitually

[6] *Ibid.*, n. 1344.
[7] *De Malo*, q. III, 9, ad 7m, gives instances of four practical syllogisms, including the intemperate cases.

to stifle any possible tendency to think and act in terms of a moral judgment. Of course, all developed vice leads to such a mental state, because all morally bad habits take their root in wrong moral reasoning, that is, in the vice of imprudence. The important thing to remember about this is that imprudent reasoning is voluntary. The error in such bad reasoning is imputable to the agent and he acquires demerit through it. Even if one performs immoral actions resulting from a habit of bad reasoning, one is doing wrong because the bad habit was acquired voluntarily. The intemperate action follows necessarily from the bad choice (unless there be some external impediment) but the agent is free in making the practical syllogism and the choice.[8]

It is quite obvious that the reasoning employed in the practical syllogism is open to error. The moral agent may develop skill in such reasoning, in the form of prudence, a habit of the practical intellect. We shall examine the general character of prudence later in this chapter. Our conclusion in this present section is that prudential reasoning belongs most properly in the process leading to right choice and right action, i.e., in the *operative moral syllogism*. However, the judgment of conscience should be one of the premises of this conclusion; hence, conscience is an essential part of prudential reasoning. There is, in fact, a need for the prudential acts of deliberation and judgment in the formation of a right conscience.[9]

Superior and Inferior Reason in the Practical Syllogism

In the reasoning from the general law to a particular moral decision, man may use either superior or inferior reason. In the terminology of St. Thomas, these words have a highly specialized meaning. Superior and inferior reason are one and the same power (the intellect performing its discursive operation) in man. They are distinguished by the way in which they proceed to their respective

[8] See: *In VII Ethic.*, lect. 3, n. 1346.
[9] Read: Appendix to Chap. VII, Text Two: *How the Practical Syllogism Functions;* Text Three: *Examples of the Practical Syllogism;* Text Four: *The Conclusion of This Syllogism Is Singular.*

conclusions. The superior reason leads to a judgment which is based on the divine law; the inferior reason proceeds according to the standards of natural law. Though not distinct as potencies, they are the subjects of distinct habitus. *Wisdom* is that good habitus, or virtue, which enables the possessor to think in terms of the highest causes. It is a habitus of superior reason. *Natural science* is also a good habitus, an intellectual virtue, which makes inferences according to secondary causes. It is a habitus of inferior reason. The names, *superior* and *inferior*, are derived from the fact that the objects of the first are *above* the nature of the human soul, while the objects of the second are *below* the soul. It is important not to confuse this distinction with the difference between speculative and practical reason. Both superior and inferior reason may be used either speculatively or practically.[10]

To illustrate the respective uses of superior and inferior reason in the practical syllogism, St. Thomas takes the example of a proposed act of adultery.[11] Starting from the universal principle of the moral law: *Every evil is to be avoided*, the agent may find his minor premise either by superior or inferior reason. If he uses the higher reason, his motive for rejecting this proposed act will be found in the specific rule: *This act of adultery is evil, because prohibited by the law of God*. The moral conclusion is clear: *This act of adultery is not to be done*.

The Ten Commandments, for instance are rules of superior reason. Man judges as a result of superior reasoning, when he decides that a proposed concrete action is, or is not, in keeping with a divine command. Also, to decide by reasoning that an act is good or bad because of its conformity or difformity with one's ultimate end, is to proceed according to superior reason. We know that the last end of man is an act of continued, supernatural perfection. It is the work of superior reason to consider rational motives which stem from suprahuman standards of conduct. Since metaphysics deals with ultimate causes, and is a kind of wisdom, moral reasoning

[10] Read: Appendix to Chap. VII, Text Five: *The Distinction Between Superior and Inferior Reason*. Also read: *S.T.*, I, 79, 9,c; in Pegis, *Basic Writings*, I, 759–762.

[11] *In II Sent.*, d.24, q. 2, a. 4,c; see Appendix to Chap. VII, Text Two.

which uses a principle of philosophical wisdom will fall within the sphere of superior wisdom. To demonstrate that God exists, by going from our knowledge of earthly things, is not to use superior reason. But, to use the result of such a demonstration (*i.e.*, the rational knowledge that there is a Supreme Being with infinite attributes) as a higher principle from which to reason, by descent, to the goodness of an earthly action, is to employ superior reason. Thus, the movement of superior reasoning is from some eternal truth (previously accepted by some form of wisdom, whether mystical, theological, or philosophical, or by the light of simple faith) to some temporal truth or rightness which is deduced from the higher principle. The agent who gives alms because he sees in a needy person one of God's deserving creatures, and because he believes that when he benefits a poor man he is manifesting his love of God, is thinking in terms of superior reason. The man who gives alms because of sympathy for a suffering neighbor, or because of a simple motive of humanitarianism, is thinking in terms of inferior reason.

When inferior reason is used to reach a moral judgment, the moral agent is influenced by rational motives of a temporal, earthly, finite character. The goods of inferior reasoning may frequently be of more direct influence on the judgment of man, than those of superior reason. Thus, a person may be impelled to do morally approvable acts because of the force of public opinion, because of the inherent satisfaction or beauty of a naturally good action, or because of the fear of punishment by positive legal sanctions. He may be deterred from evil action by contrary, but earthly, considerations: the natural ugliness of immoral action, the disapproval of friends, and so on. St. Thomas considered that an immoral act (*peccatum*) proceeds from inferior reasoning:

. . . if the deliberation of reason moves on the basis of temporal reasons, for instance, that something is useful or useless, that it is suitable or unsuitable, that it is in accord with the opinion of men. But, if the deliberation is made by means of eternal reasons, for instance, concord or discord with divine precept, the sin may be placed in superior reason.[12]

[12] *De Malo*, q. 7, a. 5,c.

While it is true, then, that either superior or inferior reasoning may lead to the practical judgment which offers rational guidance to man's voluntary actions, this does not mean that both types of reasoning are of the same moral value. Just as man does not reach ultimate truth in speculative thinking, until he reduces his considerations to first principles, so the moral agent does not reach an *ultimate* motive in practical reasoning, until he considers the relationship of his action to his ultimate end which is a first principle in practical reasoning. So, while man may do some naturally good actions for the sake of the attainment of an earthly and temporal good, he does not come to a final decision unless he intend his action toward the ultimate end. Of course, this ultimate end is supernatural happiness and it is viewed in the light of superior reason. The ultimate consent to a proposed act must derive from a process of superior reasoning.[13]

This teaching again emphasizes the inferiority of ethics to moral theology, and of natural prudence to supernatural prudence. To some extent, man must think in terms of the eternal reasons for good action, and he must will his moral acts for the sake of the supernatural good which is eternal happiness. If he does not use superior reason, he cannot merit anything more than a natural reward. So important is this matter, we may well take the occasion to read St. Thomas' mature teaching on the subject:

Consent implies a definite judgment concerning that to which consent is given. Just as speculative reason judges and gives consent in intelligible matters, so does practical reason judge and give consent in matters of action. We should note that the final decision (*sententia*) in every question of judgment pertains to the supreme court of judgment. In speculative matters, we see that the final decision on any proposition is given by means of a resolution to first principles. For, as long as some higher principle remains, the question can be further examined in the light of this [principle]. Hence, judgment is still suspended, as if the final decision were not yet given.

Now, it is evident that human acts can be regulated by the rule of human reason, which is derived from created things which man naturally knows. And further, [they can be regulated] by the rule of divine

[13] Read: Appendix to Chap. VII, Text Six: *Moral Consent Is Ultimately in Superior Reason.*

law, as has been said above (q. 71, a. 6,c). Since the rule of divine law is superior, it follows that the final decision, in which the process of judgment terminates ultimately, pertains to superior reason which looks to the eternal reasons (*rationes aeternas*). Now, when it happens that there is a process of judgment about several things, the last judgment is of that which happens last. In human acts, the act itself happens last and the preamble is that enjoyment which leads to the act. Therefore, consent to the act properly pertains to superior reason, while the preliminary judgment, which is concerned with enjoyment, pertains to the inferior reason which judges on a lower level. However, superior reason can judge concerning the enjoyment, because whatever is submitted to the judgment of an inferior is also subject to the enjoyment of a superior; but not vice versa.[14]

In studying the role of inferior reason in the practical syllogism, we should not forget that man's moral acts are guided by two kinds of knowledge, universal and particular.[15] It is all very well and necessary for the good man to understand the universal rules of moral behavior, but he must also possess enough experience to be able to apply these rules to his own life. Experience of the circumstances of earthly life is built up by repeated sense perceptions retained in imagination and sense memory, and partly interpreted in concrete conditions by the power of sensory judgment, the cogitative sense. We recall from the study of the philosophy of man that the highest of the internal senses is the cogitative power, whereby man may discriminate between those individual sensory objects which are harmful and those which are beneficial to him as an individual. This kind of particular knowledge of the concrete facts of life in relation to the agent himself is of the utmost importance in moral matters. Moral rules can be taught; the theory of good behavior can be grasped by any ordinary intellect. Practical experience cannot be taught; it must be gained by personal sense perceptions, retained and evaluated in the agent. The young may substitute the good advice of their elders for their lack of personal experience. Docility and discrimination in the taking of good counsel are especially valuable to children. But the mature person cannot continue in-

[14] *S.T.*, I–II, 74, 7,c.
[15] *S.T.*, I–II, 77, 2,c; see again, Appendix to Chap. VII, Text Four: *The Conclusion of This Syllogism Is Singular*.

definitely to lean vicariously on the experience of others. With the development of a more perfect prudence, the more adult agent must learn to profit by his own experience.

There is, here, a partial parallel with the behavior of brute animals. These animals guide themselves by instinct, we say, However, their young must learn many things from early sense experience. Once burned, it is a very dull dog that will go too close to a fire a second time. Because they are not rational and not endowed with free choice, brutes soon learn rather automatically to avoid what is harmful and seek what is good for them. Before achieving the full use of reason, children learn to discriminate between sense goods and evils. As they develop in discretion, young people more and more relate this particular knowledge to their increasing knowledge of universal rightness. Technically expressed, their cogitative sense comes to participate in the life of reason. In a way, the power of sense judgment is subsumed under the higher direction of the universal reason, and this sensory power begins to work reasonably. But the cogitative sense always remains a sense, that is, it continues to know the particular, individual, singular features of reality. Directed by universal reason, the cogitative power grows into *particular reason*. It becomes a sort of reasoning power because it shares in the process of going from premises to conclusions, in the practical syllogism. It remains particular because its objects never rise from their concrete individuality to the level of universality.

In thinking over the advisability of performing or omitting a proposed action, the moral agent must marshal his sense knowledge of all the pertinent circumstances governing this action; he must view the whole action as a unit in which nothing significant is to be omitted. This cogitative process requires imagination, too, so that the proposed act may be pictured in advance. The agent must think: If I act at this time and place, with these people present, with these means, in this way, for this particular purpose—the action will be of this character and it will probably have these consequences. In a way, the act is enacted, tried out, in imagination, while it is being considered. We shall see that it is the mark of a prudent man to look ahead in this way. Particular reason has much to contribute to the growth of prudence, for the intellect of itself is not able to deal with such concrete considerations.[16]

How Practical Reason Is Perfected by Prudence

No man is born a scientist, nor is any man endowed with complete natural prudence at birth. The human intellect needs to be perfected by carefully repeated acts of right reasoning. When geometry or algebra are first studied, one reasons to the mathematical conclusions slowly, with evident difficulty and with some inaccuracy. With more study, the intellect acquires greater speed, facility, and accuracy in such thinking. What is really happening is that the intellect of the embryonic mathematician is being developed into a better potency by the acquisition of a quality which is called a habitus. Mental skill consists of the basic, natural potency of the intellect, *plus* habits gained from continued use of the intellect. Where such habits perfect the intellect so that the thinker can reach universal conclusions in a better way than he could at the beginning of his study, these habits are called sciences. But we have just seen that there is another kind of intellectual reasoning, which leads to practical and particular conclusions. Scientific habits of mind are only indirectly useful to the process of reasoning to singular conclusions. It is quite possible for a chemist or a biologist to know scientifically a great deal about the constitution of water and its effects on the organism, and still not know enough to come inside when it is raining.

Practical thinking requires the development of a skill, or habit, in the human intellect too. It is no easy matter to decide the one way of acting which is best for the agent in a given moral case. We have noted the complications arising from the variety of formal kinds of action, from the many pertinent moral circumstances, from the emotional disturbances, which make up the context of any moral action. But the moral agent who does his best to make a good de-

[16] Read: Appendix to Chap. VII, Text Seven: *Particular Reason in the Practical Syllogism;* and Text Eight: *Particular Knowledge of Circumstances and Moral Judgment.*

cision in the face of such complications will find that successive problems of somewhat the same nature are easier to judge. Good use of the practical intellect is slow and painful in the beginning but it improves with repetition. The metaphysical explanation of such improvement is much the same as in the case of the student of geometry. A habit of right reasoning is being acquired. This habit which perfects the practical intellect so that it can solve a concrete problem more quickly, more easily, and more accurately, is named *prudence*.

Prudence is not moral science. The latter is a habit enabling the intellect to know the universal rules of good human action. Neither ethics nor moral theology solves the *individual* problems of human life. These practical sciences prepare the way for the use of prudence, but prudence must be acquired by each moral agent making repeated and continued application of whatever moral science he has, to his own individual moral difficulties.

To understand this point, let us think of a boxer who has a smart manager. The manager tells his fighter about the weaknesses of his opponent. A general plan is outlined for the fight. The boxer is to keep away from his opponent throughout the early rounds, tire him out, refuse to be drawn into close fighting. Then, in the last rounds, he is to take the initiative and knock out the opponent. This is all theory and few such plans work out as preconceived. The opponent may have much the same instructions. The crowd may boo both of them for stalling. The referee may warn them that he will stop the fight and stop payment of their purses, if they refuse to mix it up. Now, the experienced fighter will know how to adapt his plan to such unforeseen developments. He may notice that the opponent is not using his left hand much; it may be broken. His experience (which is also a practical habit gained from repeatedly facing similar situations) enables him to take advantage of the new circumstance and decide quickly on a change of plans. Notice that the manager cannot do all of this thinking for his fighter. The actual fighting must be done by the boxer and each blow must be quickly adapted to the individual circumstances, as well as to the end, which is victory. This means that the fighter must do his own practical thinking. He needs a sort of prudence to outwit his opponent. He does not acquire this prudence simply by listening to his manager. He gets it from his own experience in the ring, if he is smart enough to remember it and profit by it.

Moral victories follow the pattern suggested by this example. The theoretical advice of the manager is like the conclusions of moral science. These conclusions cannot be preadapted to the new circumstances of each individually distinct moral problem. The agent faced by these concrete circumstances needs to apply the theory to the individual problem. Like the fighter, the moral agent needs experience to do this well. Prudence is the habit which coordinates moral theory, moral experience and the particular knowledge of a novel moral situation. It does not automatically suggest the right decision. The prudent agent still has to puzzle over his problems, but he is a skillful fighter who is well prepared to judge his own proposed actions, as quickly, easily, and accurately as the circumstances permit.

Prudence may be defined, then, as *the intellectual habit enabling the agent to reason to right conclusion to his moral problems*.[17] It is precisely the skill needed to bring the practical syllogism to its proper conclusion. As such, it is always *right*. Unlike conscience, which may be erroneous, prudence is essentially right reasoning (*recta ratio*).

Moreover, prudence is a *practical* wisdom. This means that it must carry over into the domain of right moral action. The agent is not prudent, who thinks out his problems accurately enough, but does not do the right things, the appetites, sensory and intellectual, are the efficient sources of complete moral actions. Unlike brute animals, whose appetites are naturally and instinctively directed toward their concrete and individual good actions (for this reason, brutes have no moral problems), man desires naturally the good-in-general. Human appetites need to be determined, specified, definitely ordered to individual acts of goodness by the personal use of practical reason. Skill in right reasoning (prudence) is the root of all the natural moral virtues of the appetitive powers of man. To

[17] Read: *S.T.*, I–II, 57, a. 4–6; in Pegis, *Basic Writings*, II, 434–439.

be temperate, brave and just, the human agent must first be prudent. We can even say that a temperate, brave or just action, *which does not issue from prudence*, is not a truly human act. A human act must be done knowingly, and the agent who does what is objectively right, without thinking that it is right, is not entitled to moral credit for his action. This can be put briefly, in another way. All naturally virtuous actions observe a certain *golden mean*, a middle position between excess and defect. Practical reasoning must be used to judge the mean in each case of moral action. To observe the mean, without having thought out the nature of this middle position, is to act from chance, or physical necessity; such action is not human action.[18]

Moral Deliberation, Judgment and Preception

Right reasoning about moral problems may be divided into three different acts. It is necessary, first of all, *to deliberate*, or take counsel, concerning the means and circumstances of the proposed act, considered in relation to the ultimate end. Secondly, the agent has *to judge* whether the action is to be done or omitted, and with what means, and under what circumstances. Finally, the prudent man must be prepared intellectually *to prescribe*, or *to order* (*praecipere*) that the proposed action be done or omitted, and in this or that way. These three acts of right reason are: deliberation, judgment, and preception.[19]

Moral deliberation, as the name implies, is an intellectual process of weighing the various possible actions which may be done, under the actual circumstances which can be foreseen, in the light of the end to be attained. This is precisely the moment of counselling. In this act, one's efforts must be directed to the discovery of all the

[18] Read: Appendix to Chap. VII, Text Nine: *Prudence As Right Reasoning About the Goods of Any Appetite;* and Text Ten: *Prudence Is Not Moral Science;* also see: O'Neil, C. J., "Prudence, the Incommunicable Wisdom," in *Essays in Thomism* (New York, 1942), pp. 187–204.

[19] Read: Appendix to Chap. VII, Text Eleven: *The Three Acts of Right Reason.* That these intellectual acts are not isolated from concomitant will-acts, is rightly stressed by Gilson, *Moral Values,* pp. 70–78.

important relationships of the proposed action to the end in view. It is not merely a question of the moral fitness of the kind of act which is contemplated, but of the concrete circumstances which accompany the action in this definite situation. If quick action is demanded, then it is not morally right to delay the process of deliberation. Nor is it right to speculate about hypothetical cases, when a moral situation demands the consideration of a definite and real problem. Deliberation must be as thorough as the circumstances permit, and yet prompt enough to guide the action which is required in a given case.[20]

Let us think of two examples, briefly. A man is bringing home his pay check to his family, which needs this money. He is asked for help by a deserving beggar. It is not enough for this man to think: This man is in need; I have some money. Almsgiving is always an act morally good in its species. He must also think: This money is not mine to give away; my prior duty is to the family of which I am the natural supporter. Of course, if he observes that the beggar is about to die, if not fed, this circumstance must be considered in his complete act of deliberation. Such a circumstance, together with the state of need of his own family and the possibility of aid to the beggar from other sources, cannot be overlooked by the prudent agent. Proper deliberation under these circumstances may take some time.

In a second case, let us consider a lifeguard on duty at a bathing beach, who hears a cry for help from a burning house nearby. If he leaves his post, someone may drown. If he does not respond to the appeal for help, someone else may die in the fire. He cannot spend hours in deliberation. Immediate action is required. Still, there is opportunity for quick consideration of the clash of two opposed duties. He must think of the consequences of a decision to stay at his post, and of a contrary decision to leave his work and try to rescue the person in the fire. Here other circumstances would need to be considered, but the essential thing is that the lifeguard find some good reason for his ultimate decision. This is the kind of case

[20] Read: Appendix to Chap. VII, Text Twelve: *The Nature of Good Deliberation.*

for which no hard-and-fast moral rule can be made. If the guard thinks it over quickly and does his best to discover the right thing to do, and then does it, he is acting in a morally good way. But he must *think* the matter out, himself.

Moral judgment brings deliberation to a close. Deliberation may offer a plurality of moral possibilities. One thing must be done at a time. To decide which thing must be done, or omitted, is to make the moral judgment which precedes a rational choice. The results of deliberation may be so clear that this act of practical judgment becomes obvious and almost routine. Many situations conform to standard moral rules, or laws, and can be judged without too much difficulty. The rarer, exceptional cases require more deliberation, but a judgment must eventually be rendered and this decision must be made in the light of the unusual circumstances which hold in each such problem. Not even moral laws are made to cover exceptions. Personal good judgment is the only aid to the decision of exceptional problems.

To conclude right reasoning about an ordinary moral case, which conforms to the known rules of morality, the habit of *ordinary practical judgment* (*synesis*) may be acquired. For people who are rather frequently faced with exceptional problems, a special habit of *good judgment in unusual problems* (*gnome*) may be developed.[21]

The final act of practical reasoning is the chief act of the virtue of prudence: this is the act of *preception*. Before the act of choice (essentially an act of will directed by reason) there must be a *last practical judgment*, by which the will is formally (but not efficiently) determined to elect certain means. This last practical judgment is the judgment of election. If this judgment of election is in accord with the previous prudential acts of right deliberation and right judgment, then the judgment of election which formally commits the agent to one choice will be identical with the act of preception (*praecipere*); but if the judgment of election is not in accord with right reason, it is not identical with the preceptive act of

[21] Read: Appendix to Chap. VII, Text Thirteen: *Ordinary and Exceptional Practical Judgment.*

prudence, for a bad judgment of election is an act of imprudence. While preception implies a certain element of intellectual commanding, it should be observed that the final imperative (*imperium*) by which the intellect directs the execution and use of the means chosen, must *follow* the act of choice. Hence, the act of *preception* precedes choice, while the act of *commanding the use* of the means comes after choice.[22]

Summary of Chapter VII

Practical reasoning about moral problems should follow the pattern of the practical syllogism, in which the first premise is a universal moral principle, the second premise a particular moral proposition, and the conclusion is wholly singular and concrete. This singular conclusion is threefold: cognitively, it is the practical judgment; appetitively, it is the act of free choice (election); executively, it is the moral action itself. To reason from motives gathered from experience of the working of secondary causes in the finite world is to use inferior reason. To reason from principles of action known by a consideration of primary causality, *i.e.*, of God and the Eternal Law, is to be guided by superior reason. In order that a moral act be meritorious in relation to man's supernatural end, some reference to the motives of superior reason is necessary. Training of the interior sense potencies, especially the cogitative power and the imagination, is needed in order that the moral agent may grasp the concrete and individual circumstances of his own moral problems. When the cogitative sense moves to a judgment under the control of practical reason, this sense rises to the level of particular reason. Prudence is the good habit of the practical intellect, which unifies this complex of practical intellectual power and internal sense power, enabling the agent to judge, to choose, and to act rightly. Moral science terminates in universal conclusions

[22] *S.T.*, I–II, q. 17, 3, *ad primum;* read also Appendix to Chap. VII, Text Fourteen: *The Principal Act of Prudence: Preception;* and Text Fifteen: *Counselling, Judging, and Preception.* On the relation of intellect and will in the situation surrounding choice, read Klubertanz, "Unity of Human Activity," *The Modern Schoolman*, XXVII (1950) 94–103.

about questions of morality; prudence terminates in good action. That is why moral science (either ethics or moral theology) can be taught to another, but prudence cannot. It is only by personal effort that prudence may be acquired. Prudence is the root from which the good acts of all the moral virtues must spring. There are three acts of prudent reasoning: counsel (or deliberation) is the act of reasoning rightly about the various possible means and circumstances related to the attainment of an intended end; moral judgment is the intellectual conclusion as to what means are preferable for the attainment of this end; finally, preception is the ultimate prudential directive which dictates right choice formally but not efficiently, to the will which makes the choice. Preception, the principle act of prudence is to be distinguished from the intellectual commanding (*imperium*) of the use-act following choice.

Appendix to Chapter VII

¶ TEXT ONE: *Conscience Distinguished from Judgment of Choice.* It should be said in answering the fourth objection that the judgment of conscience and that of free choice differ in one way and are similar in another. They are alike in the fact that each deals with this particular act. This is true of the judgment of conscience in the process of examination. On this point, both judgments differ from the judgment of synderesis.

But the judgment of conscience and that of free choice differ, because the judgment of conscience falls within the area of pure knowledge, while the judgment of free choice consists in the application of knowledge to affective inclination (*ad affectionem*); of course, this latter judgment is the judgment of election.

Thus it sometimes happens that the judgment of free choice goes wrong, when that of conscience does not. For instance, a man may examine some immediately proposed action, and judge (taking at this point a sort of theoretical view in relation to principles) that *this action is evil*; for example, to have sexual intercourse with this woman.

But when he begins the application to the actual doing, then

many circumstances pop up on all sides of the act—for example, the
pleasure associated with such intercourse—as a result of which,
reason may be overcome (*ligatur*) by concupiscence, so that the
dictate of reason cannot break through and effect the rejection of
the act.

This is the way a man may err in the act of choosing and not in
the act of conscience. Of course, he does it against his conscience
and he is said to do this act with a bad conscience, inasmuch as the
deed is not in accord with the cognitive judgment. Thus, it is clear
that conscience must not be identified with the judgment of free
choice. (*De Verit.*, q. XVII, 1, ad 4m.)

¶ TEXT TWO: *How the Practical Syllogism Functions.* We should
note that, as the Philosopher says (*Eth. Nic.*, VI, 8), reason uses
syllogisms in its acts of choosing or refusing. Now, there is a threefold consideration in the syllogism, according to the three propositions, the third of which is the conclusion from the first two. And
the same thing happens in the present matter, when reason, in dealing with operations, develops a judgment about particulars, syllo-
gistically from universal principles. And, because the universal
principles of moral law (*juris*) pertain to synderesis, while the
reasons which are more proper to the [particular] work pertain to
the habits by which superior and inferior reason are distinguished,
synderesis supplies, as it were, the major of this syllogism, and the
consideration of this is the act of synderesis; but either the superior
or inferior reason supplies the minor, and the consideration of it is
their act; but the consideration of the conclusion which is elicited,
is the consideration of conscience.

For example, synderesis offers this proposition: "Every evil is to
be avoided"; superior reason states this minor: "Adultery is evil,
because it is prohibited by the Law of God"; or, inferior reason
might supply the minor: "It is evil, because it is unjust or dishonest"; but the conclusion: "This act of adultery is to be avoided,"
pertains to conscience, and it makes no difference whether the act
be present, past, or future. For, conscience both spurns things that
have been done and speaks against things to be done. That is why

it is called *conscience* (*conscientia*) as if it were derived from *cum alio scientia*, that is, knowledge applied to something else; for, universal knowledge is applied to the particular act; or also, because through it one is conscious of those things which he has done or intends to do. For this reason, too, it is called a decision (*sententia*) or dictate of reason. Also for this reason, it happens that conscience may be mistaken, not because of an error of synderesis, but because of an error of reasoning. This is evident in the case of the heretic whose conscience dictates that he may permit himself to be burned before he will take an oath. His superior reason is perverted on this point; he believes that oath-taking is absolutely prohibited.

In this way, it is apparent, how synderesis, the natural law, and conscience differ. The natural law is the name of the universal principles themselves of moral rightness (*juris*). Synderesis, however, designates the habitus of these [principles], or the potency along with its habitus. And conscience is the name for any application of the natural law to some proposed action, after the fashion of a conclusion. (*In II Sent.*, d. 24, q. 2, a. 4,c.)

¶ TEXT THREE: *Examples of the Practical Syllogism.* There must be a sort of syllogistic deduction in every virtuous or sinful act. However, the temperate man syllogizes in one way, and the intemperate in another; the continent man in his way, and the incontinent in another.

For, the temperate man is moved only in accordance with rational judgment. He uses a syllogism containing three propositions, reasoning deductively, as it were, in this way: No fornication is to be committed; This is an act of fornication; Therefore, this should not be done.

The intemperate man is wholly given over to concupiscence. And so, he too, uses a three-termed syllogism, reasoning after this fashion: Every pleasure is to be enjoyed; This is a pleasurable act; Therefore, it should be done.

But, both the continent and the incontinent man are moved in two ways: according to reason, with the purpose of avoiding sin; and according to concupiscence, with the purpose of committing it. In the case of the continent man, however, rational judgment gains the victory; but, in the incontinent man the movement of concupiscence wins. Hence, both use a syllogism with four propositions but contrary conclusions.

The continent man syllogizes thus: No sin is to be done; he proposes this according to rational judgment, but according to the movement of concupiscence, he turns around and says within his heart: Every pleasurable thing is to be sought; but, since rational judgment wins the victory in him, he makes his consideration and reaches his conclusion from the first proposition: This is a sin; Therefore, it should not be done.

However, the incontinent man, in whom the movement of concupiscence wins out, makes his consideration and conclusion under the second major: This is pleasurable; Therefore, it is to be sought after. Such a man is properly of the sort who sins out of weakness. So, it is clear that, though he may know in a general way, he does not know in the particular case, for, he does not make his consideration according to reason but according to concupiscence. (*De Malo*, q. III, a. 9, ad 7m.)

¶ TEXT FOUR: *The Conclusion of This Syllogism Is Singular*. It is to be noted that reason directs human acts according to two kinds of knowledge, universal and particular. For, the agent, in reasoning about proposed actions, uses a syllogism whose conclusion is a judgment, either a choice or an operation. Now, actions go on in the realm of singulars. Hence, the conclusion of the operative syllogism is singular. A singular proposition cannot be concluded from a universal, unless through the mediation of some singular proposition. Thus, a man may be restrained from the act of patricide, by knowing that: One's father should not be killed, and also that: This man is his father. Ignorance of either could cause the act of patricide; that is, either of the universal principle which is the rule of reason, or of the singular circumstance. (*S.T.*, I–II, 76, 1,c.)

¶ TEXT FIVE: *The Distinction Between Superior and Inferior Reason.* Superior and inferior reason are distinguished in this way. Some natures are superior to the rational soul; others are inferior. Since everything which is understood is understood after the manner of the agent who is understanding, the understanding of the things above the soul is in the rational soul as something below these objects of understanding; but for those things below the soul, there is in the soul an understanding which is higher than these things, for these things have a more noble existence in it [the soul] than they have in themselves. Thus, it has a different relationship to each kind of things, and from this it receives different functions (*diversa officia*).

For, according as it looks up to superior natures, either simply contemplating their truth and nature, or receiving from them a reason and a sort of pattern (*quasi exemplar*) of action, it is called *superior reason*. But, according as it is turned to inferior things, either gazing upon them contemplatively, or being disposed to action, it is called *inferior reason*.

Both types of objects, those of superior and of inferior reason, are apprehended in the human soul by a common principle of rationality: the superior insofar as it is immaterial in itself, the inferior insofar as it is denuded of matter by the act of the agent intellect. Hence, it is plain that superior and inferior reason are not the names of different potencies but of one and the same potency in relation to different things according to a diverse manner. (*De Veritate*, q. 15, a. 2,c.)

¶ TEXT SIX: *Moral Consent Is Ultimately in Superior Reason.* It is apparent that any act may be attributed to reason in one of two ways. First, *immediately*, thus it is elicited from reason itself, as in the act of inference about matters of action or of knowledge. Second, *through the mediation of the will*, which is moved by its [reason's] judgment.

Now, just as the appetitive movement which follows the judgment of reason is attributed to reason, so the appetitive movement following the deliberation of superior reason is attributed to su-

perior reason. This is the case, when there is some deliberation
about matters of action, based on the fact that something is acceptable to God, or prescribed by Divine Law, and so on. And, it is
attributed to inferior reason, when the appetitive movement follows the judgment of inferior reason, as in the case of a deliberation
concerning matters of action, in terms of inferior causes. Thus, one
might consider the ugliness of the act, the worthiness of the reason,
the offense to men, and things like that.

These two considerations are arranged according to this order.
The end, according to the Philosopher [*Ethic. Nic.*, VII, c. 8],
stands as a principle in matters of action. Now, in speculative
sciences the judgment of reason is not completed until the reasons
are resolved to first principles. So too, in matters of operation, it
is not completed until there is a reduction to the ultimate end; for
then, only, will reason give the final decision (*ultimam sententiam*)
concerning the operation. This decision is the consent to the work.
Hence, consent to the act is attributed to the superior reason, which
looks to the ultimate end. But, joy, or the pleasure of enjoyment or
consent, is attributed by Augustine [*De Trinitate*, XII, c. 12] to
the inferior reason. (*De Veritate*, q. 15, a. 3,c.)

¶ TEXT SEVEN: *Particular Reason in the Practical Syllogism.* So,
he [Aristotle] says first, that the imagination of the object of sensation (as is clear from what has been said) is also present in other
animals; but that (imagination) which results from deliberation is
found only in rational beings—since, to consider whether this
should be done, or to perform the act of deliberation, is the work
of reason. And, in such a consideration, it is necessary to take some,
one rule, or end, or something like that, in terms of which one may
measure what is best to be done. For, it is plain that man "imitates,"
that is *desires*, what is greater in goodness, and what is better. Now,
we always judge what is better, by means of some measure. Therefore, it is necessary to take some standard, in deliberating as to what
it is better to do. This standard is the mean from which practical
reason syllogizes to what should be chosen. Hence, it is evident
that the deliberating reason can make one phantasm out of several,

let us say, out of three; and one of these may be chosen in preference to a second, and the third is a sort of measure which establishes the preference. This is the reason why animals do not possess opinion, though they have imagination. They cannot use the syllogism which would enable them to prefer one thing to another. But rational deliberation does possess opinion, otherwise it could not make one out of several phantasms. So it is, that the lower appetite, following upon imagination, does not possess deliberation. Rather, it is moved to passions of concupiscence and irascibility, without deliberation, for it follows upon sensory imagination.

This is the natural order: that the superior appetite move the inferior appetite. . . . [an astronomical example of the supposed influence of the higher spheres on the lower, is given to illustrate the point]. Likewise, the inferior appetite, though retaining something of its own movement, is nevertheless moved in a natural order, by the movement of the superior appetite, and by the movement of the deliberating reason. But, if the contrary occur, and the superior appetite is moved by the inferior, that is against the natural order. Hence, this causes a sin in moral matters; for, sins are like monsters in nature.

First, it must be noted that speculative reason, which Aristotle calls scientific, *does not move but is at rest*. It has nothing to do with desiring (*imitando*) or fleeing, as was said above. But practical reason is sometimes universal, sometimes particular. It is universal, when it says that such a thing should be done in such a way; for example: a son should honor his parents. But, particular reason says that this individual is such a thing, and that I am such a person (for instance, that I am a son) and that I should at this moment pay this honor to my parent.

Now, this opinion is a source of movement, but not the reason which is universal. Or, if both cause movement, then the one which is universal moves as a first cause remaining at rest, but the particular moves as a proximate cause, in some way applied to the thing moved. For, operations and movements are in the area of particular things; hence, it is necessary that universal opinion be applied to particular things, in order that a movement follow. Because of this, then, a sin occurs in actions, when opinion in regard to a particular work to be done is corrupted by some pleasure, or by some other passion, which does not corrupt a universal opinion of this kind. (*In III De Anima*, lect. 16; ed. Pirotta, pp. 272–273.)

¶ TEXT EIGHT: *Particular Knowledge of Circumstances and Moral Judgment.* It should be noted that two kinds of knowledge which can prohibit sin, govern moral acts. One kind is universal, and by it we judge that an act is right or wrong [generally]. . . . The other kind of knowledge, which governs moral acts and which can prohibit sin, is particular knowledge, namely, of the circumstances of the act itself; for universal, without particular, knowledge does not move to action, as is explained in Book III of the treatise *On the Soul*. [See: Text Six, *supra*, where this passage from Aristotle is explained by St. Thomas.]

Now, it may happen that a man will be withheld, in an unqualified way (*simpliciter*), from sin, by the knowledge of some circumstance. And, in another case, he may not be altogether kept by the knowledge of some circumstance from sinning, but only from committing a certain kind of sin. For example, if an archer knew that a passerby were a man, he would not shoot. But, because he does not know that it is a man and thinks it is a stag, he kills a man when he shoots his arrow, and thus the ignorance of a circumstance causes a homicide which is a sin (unless this be the kind of ignorance which completely excuses).

But, if the archer does will to kill a man, but not his own father, (that is to say, if he knew that a passerby was his own father, he would not shoot the arrow at all), then, not knowing that the passerby is his father, he shoots and kills him, in this case, this ignorance clearly is the cause of the sin of homicide. However, he is not guilty of patricide, in every such case. And so, it is clear that ignorance may be, in various ways, the cause of sin. (*De Malo*, q. 3, a. 6,c.)

¶ TEXT NINE: *Prudence As Right Reasoning About the Goods of Any Appetite.* [After explaining that brutes are instinctively inclined to seek their specific and individual goods, St. Thomas continues:] But man is capable of many diverse operations. This is due to the nobility of his active principle, namely his soul, whose power is in a way infinitely extensive. Therefore, the natural appetite for the good is not sufficient for man, nor is natural [*i.e.*, instinctive] judgment enough to ensure right action, unless it be further determined and perfected.

Of course, man is inclined by natural appetite to seek his proper good, but since this is diversified in many things, the natural appetite for this determinate good could not be present innately in man, according to all the conditions required in order that it be a good for him; for this [good] is diversified in many ways depending on various conditions of persons, time, place, and like things. It is for this same reason that a natural and uniform judgment [*i.e.*, one which is instinctive] does not suffice in the search for this kind of good.

Hence, it is by means of reason, whose work is to make inferences between diverse things, that man must find and judge his proper good, determined according to all its conditions as something to be sought after, here and now. To do this without a perfecting habitus, reason is in much the same position as reason without a habitus of science (trying to judge some conclusion of that science) is in speculative matters; for, this can be done only imperfectly and with difficulty. So, just as speculative reason must be perfected by a habitus of science, in order to judge the scientific matters pertaining to any science, so must practical reason be perfected by a habitus, in order to judge rightly concerning the human good in singular actions.

This virtue is called prudence, and its subject is practical reason. It perfects all the moral virtues which are in the appetitive part, each of which gives an appetitive inclination to a special kind of human good. Thus, justice gives an inclination to the good which lies in an equality of things pertaining to the social life; temperance has to do with the good of restraint in regard to matters of concupiscence; and so on, for each of the virtues.

Now, it is possible for any one of these to work in many ways, and in different ways, in different people; hence, prudence of judgment is needed in order that the right way may be established. So, rightness and the fulfillment of goodness in all the other virtues come from it [prudence]. That is why Aristotle says [*Nic. Ethic.*, II, c. 6, 1106a25–1107a7] that the mean in moral virtue is determined according to right reason. And, since all the habits of appetitive virtue get their formal character (*rationem*) from this rightness and fulfillment of goodness, that is why prudence is the cause of all the appetitive virtues. (*De Virtutibus in Communi*, a. 6,c.)

¶ TEXT TEN: *Prudence Is Not Moral Science.* Prudence means more than moral science. What pertains to practical science is a universal judgment concerning matters of action: for instance, that fornication is evil, that one should not steal, and the like. Even where this science is present, it is possible for the rational judgment to be impeded in the particular act, so that a right judgment is not made. For this reason, [moral science without prudence] is said to be of little value to virtue, for even where it is present man may sin against virtue.

But right judgment about singular matters of action, insofar as they are now to be done, pertains to prudence. This judgment is destroyed by any sin. Therefore, as long as prudence remains man does not sin. Hence, it (prudence) is not of little, but of great, importance to virtue. In fact, it causes virtue, as has been said. (*Ibid.*, *ad primum.*)

¶ TEXT ELEVEN: *The Three Acts of Right Reason.* Diverse acts are ordered on different levels to the one ultimate end, which is the complete act of good living. For, counsel or deliberation (*consilium*) comes first, then judgment (*judicium*) follows, and finally comes preception (*praeceptum*) which is immediately concerned with the ultimate end, while the other two acts are remotely related to it. But these have also their proximate ends: counsel pertains to the intending of the things which are to be done, while judgment has to do with the ascertaining [of these things]. (*S.T.*, II–II, 51, 2, ad 2m.)

¶ TEXT TWELVE: *The Nature of Good Deliberation.* What is required in a process of good deliberation (*ad bene consiliandum*) is not only the discovery, or thinking out, of the means suited to the end, but also of the other circumstances. That is, [one must consider] the fit time, so that one may be neither too slow nor too quick in one's deliberations; and the manner of deliberation must be such that one is firm in his deliberation; and there are other proper circumstances of this kind, which sinners do not observe when they sin. Every virtuous person is one who possesses good deliberation in regard to those things which are means to the attainment of the end of virtue—though, perhaps, he may not have good deliberation in regard to other particular affairs, such as business matters, or military matters, or other things like that. (*S.T.*, II–II, 1, ad 3m.)

¶ TEXT THIRTEEN: *Ordinary and Exceptional Practical Judgment.* It is evident that goodness in the act of deliberation and goodness in the act of judging cannot be reduced to the same cause. There are many people who are good at deliberating but who have not good sense, that is, they do not judge rightly. The same situation is found in speculative thinking: some people are good at searching for information, because their reason is prone to run through a variety of things (this would seem to be due to a disposition of the imaginative power enabling one quickly to form a variety of phantasms); yet people of this kind sometimes lack good judgment, because of a defect of understanding (which is due, chiefly, to a bad disposition of the common sense, which does not judge well). So, over and above good deliberation, there must be another virtue which provides for good judgment. This is called *synesis*. (*S.T.*, II–II, 51, 3,c.)

Sometimes a situation comes up in which something must be done which is an exception to the common rules of action. Thus, a deposit [St. Thomas is thinking of weapons] need not be returned to the enemy of one's country, and so on. So, one must judge such cases according to principles which are higher than the ordinary rules, whereby synesis judges. In keeping with these higher principles, a need is set up for a higher virtue of judgment, and this is called gnome. This signifies a perspicacity of judgment. (*Ibid.*, 4,c.)

¶ TEXT FOURTEEN: *The Principal Act of Prudence: Preception.* Prudence is right reason about things to be done, as has been said before. So, the chief act of prudence must be the principal act of reasoning about things to be done. Now, there are three acts pertaining to it. The first of these is to deliberate (*consiliari*), and this pertains to discovery; for, to deliberate is to make a search, as was explained above. The second is to judge (*judicare*) the things which have been discovered; this even speculative reason can do.

But practical reason, which is directed to action, proceeds further. So, its third act is to command by way of precept (*praecipere*), and this act consists in the application of the results of deliberation and judgment to action. Since this act is nearer to the end of practical reason, this is the principal act of practical reason, and consequently of prudence. (*S.T.*, II–II, 47, 8,c.)

¶ TEXT FIFTEEN: *Counselling, Judging and Preception.* It belongs to reason to prescribe (*praecipere*) what must be done, for the other powers obey reason in some way. Now, reason does not prescribe unless it first be perfected within itself in regard to what pertains to it—just as no thing moves before it becomes perfected. The perfection of practical reason, as also of speculative reason, consists in two things: in discovering, and in judging what has been discovered.

Now, discovery in regard to problems of action is called counsel [or deliberation]. Therefore, it is necessary that a virtue, whereby reason may perform the act of counselling, be possessed. This is eubulia, which is rightness of deliberation, according to Aristotle [*Ethic. Nic.*, VI, c. 10; 1142b16]. By it, one seeks the good by means which are suitable according to propriety of time and other circumstances.

It is also necessary that a virtue, enabling one to judge of the results of counselling, be possessed. This is *synesis* and *gnome*, whose differences will be explained. [See *infra*, last paragraph.]

It is necessary, also, that a virtue, which is properly preceptive, be possessed. This is prudence, which Aristotle says in the same place, is preceptive. But, since, in regard to practical problems, knowledge is directly related to the work, therefore both counsel and judgment of the results of counselling lead to the preception of the work, as to their end. Because of this, prudence is the employer, and chief, in relation to the other acts, and these others participate in it to some extent, as has been said.

In answer to the third difficulty, we say that right judgment in regard to problems commonly covered by the precepts of law, belongs to synesis. So, synesis is the judicative habit for problems of action. But, right judgment, in regard to the problems which the law does not wholly cover and which present a special difficulty, pertains to gnome. These are equity problems. Hence gnome, according to Aristotle [*Ethic. Nic.*, VI, c. 11; 1143a20], is the right judgment characteristic of an equity judge. (*In III Sent.*, d. 33, q. 3, a. 1, qla. 3, resp. et ad 3m.)

Recommended Readings

Thomas Aquinas, St., *Summa Theologiae*, I–II, q. 57, 4–6 (in *Basic Writings*, ed. Pegis, II, 434–439).

Brennan, Sr. R. Emmanuella, *The Intellectual Virtues According to the Philosophy of St. Thomas*, pp. 65–76.

Childress, "The Prudential Judgment," *Proc. Amer. Cath. Philos. Assoc.*, XXII (1947) 141–151.

Farrell, *Companion to the Summa*, III, 141–162.

Gilson, *Moral Values and the Moral Life*, pp. 70–78.

O'Neil, "Prudence, the Incommunicable Wisdom," in *Essays in Thomism*, pp. 187–204.

Smith, G., "Intelligence and Liberty," *Proc. Amer. Cath. Philos. Assoc.*, XVI (1940) 69–85; also in *New Scholasticism*, XV (1941) 1–17.

ADVANCED READINGS

Thomae Aq., S., *In II Sent.*, 24, 3, 3; *In VII Ethic.*, lect. 3 (Pirotta, n. 1344–1348); *De Malo*, q. III, 9, ad 7m; *S.T.*, I–II, 77, 2, ad 4m.

Garrigou-Lagrange, "La prudence. Sa place dans l'organisme des vertus," *Revue Thomiste*, n.s. IX (1926) 411–426.

Gundlach, "Klugheit als Prinzip des Handels," *Gregorianum*, XXIII (1942) 238–254.

Lottin, *Principes de Morale*, I, 252–266.

Pieper, *Traktat über die Klugheit* (Leipzig, 1937).

Topics for Assignment

1. The General Pattern of Practical Reasoning
2. Why There Cannot Be Rational Choice Without Practical Judgment
3. Superior Reason and Moral Deliberation
4. How Prudence May Be Acquired
5. The Difference Between Prudent Judgment and Preception

Virtue as a Good Habit

The moral agent is, of course, the individual person. Each human being is a supposit, a complete substantial being existing as an individual. Moral actions are imputable to this complete being. Moral science often treats the sources of human action analytically, distinguishing various principles which concur in the production of such action. This is done for the sake of clarity of understanding. Rational analysis of the background of the moral act is not intended to break up the very real unity of the moral person.

There are two kinds of principles which contribute to the performance of moral action: *internal* principles and *external* ones. Internal principles are so called, because they reside within the moral agent either as part of his personal endowment at birth or as acquisitions of his nature during the course of his life. External principles are outside the moral person and yet exert some influence on the performance of his moral actions. There are two kinds of internal principles: potencies and habits. In discussing the moral act, we have already seen that four operative potencies may be directly involved in this act: *will, intellect, concupiscible appetite,* and *irascible appetite.* The will is the power whereby the moral agent proximately and efficiently produces every moral act. The intellect is the proximate source whereby the agent formally determines the moral quality of his action. These two potencies are always rational and they concur in the performance of every moral action. We have also seen that the movements of the irascible and concupiscible appetites are passions, or emotions; passions become of moral consequence when they come under the possible control of the essentially rational potencies. These two sense appetites are then said to participate in the life of reason.

The second kind of internal principle of the moral act is called a *habit*. Certain qualities may be added to any of the above four potencies, disposing them permanently to some kind of operation which is more definite or limited than the operation proper to the bare potency. These added qualities, or habits, are of great importance in the development of a mature moral character. All human beings are born with the four potencies which may enter into the moral act, but each man acquires in the course of his life a somewhat distinct and individual structure of moral habits. His moral personality, or character, is constituted by the addition of a set of habits to his native powers. The mature moral agent is somewhat like an organism which has grown and developed many specialized functions, only present in rudimentary form, if at all, at birth. Much of the present chapter will be devoted to the study of these moral habits.

The external principles influencing the moral act are also two: the *devil* and *God*. It is a teaching of Catholic theology that the devil is a fallen angel who incites, or attempts to instigate, evil actions on the part of men. By forming certain images in the imagination of man to perceive things other than as they are, the devil may tempt the human agent to perform immoral acts. It is not possible for the devil to force man's will to act evilly. Nor is it necessary to believe that all sins, or immoral actions, are due to diabolic instigation. It is enough to keep in mind the real possibility of such interference in moral life, by a principle of evil.[1]

God works as an external principle of moral action in two ways: through *law* and through *grace*. That the natural moral law is but a rational participation in the law of God, and that God is the supreme Reason for all determinations of the rational order, we have noticed already. By law, God instructs man so as to incline him toward the good. Grace is a kind of help or supernatural assistance

[1] Read: *S.T.*, I, q. 114, a. 1–5; in Pegis, *Basic Writings*, I, 1048–1054.

offered to man by God, for the same purpose. We shall notice its bearing on the moral life of man, at the end of this chapter.[2]

The nature of habit formation has been studied in the philosophy of man. We may recall that some operative potencies are *active;* these can have no habits added to them, because such potencies are not perfected, or improved, by acting. They are always at the peak of their power and that means that these potencies are virtues. The Latin word *virtus* (virtue) means a potency which is perfected, that is, in a condition of peak capacity. In man, the agent intellect and the physical forces working in his body are active potencies. No habits are formed in these powers.

A second kind of operative potency in man is wholly passive. Such a potency is capable of being moved by another agent; when it is so moved, it undergoes a passion; when the motion stops, the passion ceases and the passive potency reverts to its original condition. No habits are formed in these potencies, either. They are perfected by the extrinsic action of another agency but they do not retain any perfecting quality, after such actuation has ceased. In less metaphysical language, these wholly passive potencies are not permanently improved by use. The external senses are the best examples of such potencies as found in man. One's power of hearing, or of seeing, for instance, is not in itself perfected by being used. A man may learn to control his power of sight better than he did as a child; this is an improvement in the use of his reason, not in his basic power of vision. He sees no better at the age of forty than he did at the age of ten.

But there is a third type of potency found in man which is *partly active* and *partly passive.* This sort of potency is able to operate imperfectly, from the beginning of its period of use. When used however, it tends to improve, to become more perfect in itself. It acquires some quality which is added to it by repeated use and which renders the original potency capable of operating more promptly, more easily and more accurately. These added qualities are *habitus;* they remain in the power after it has been used and

---

[2] Read: Appendix to Chap. VIII, Text One: *Enumeration of the Principles of Human Acts.*

dispose it to perform its operation in a perfect manner. When this kind of potency is thus habituated, it is called a virtue. Several virtues may be found in one and the same basic potency, because this kind of potency is not determined by its nature to just one sort of act; such a potency is open to a plurality of specifically different uses. When used regularly and well in any of these ways, it becomes permanently disposed to more perfect operation. Obviously, these potencies of the third kind are spiritual powers, for the non-spiritual, or physical, potencies are all determined to one and only one kind of action.

There are only four operative potencies in man which are habit-forming in this sense: the possible intellect, the will (or intellectual appetite), the concupiscible, and the irascible appetite. Each of these can be perfected or improved by the addition of a perfecting quality to it. Each is a potency which is partly active and partly passive by nature. We know from studying the philosophy of man that the intellect and will are rational, and so spiritual, powers. We also know that the two sense appetites, though not in themselves rational, can come directly under the control of reason in man, and so they are rational in this sense of being able directly to participate in the operations of reason.

It should be clear, then, that the philosophy of St. Thomas does not regard all moral virtues as habits of the will. There are four operative potencies which need to be perfected by moral virtue. Good habits of the practical intellect, concupiscible appetite, irascible appetite, and the will are moral virtues. Each of these four powers is a separate and distinct subject which may be perfected by its own characteristic kind of virtue.[3]

To sum up the general meaning of virtue, we should notice that, at the time St. Thomas Aquinas taught, there was current in the Catholic schools a definition of virtue, gathered from the writings of St. Augustine. This definition was: "Virtue is a good quality of the mind, by which one lives rightly, which no one uses badly, and

[3] Read: Appendix to Chap. VIII, Text Two: *The Potencies Perfectible by Virtue;* also read carefully: *S.T.*, I–II, qq. 55–56; in Pegis, *Basic Writings*, II, 412–429.

which God works in us but without us." [4] The last clause of this Augustinian definition must obviously be excluded from a general definition of virtue, because this clause restricts the definition to virtues which are supernaturally infused. It should be observed that, while the natural way of acquiring virtue is by the repeated good use of a rational potency, it is also quite possible for God directly to instill any moral virtue by supernatural action. Such virtues are said to be *infused* and, because of their superior mode of origin, they confer a capacity on the moral agent which is more perfect than that of the naturally acquired virtues.

However, infused virtues are not the only kind and a general definition must be broad enough to cover all types of virtue. St. Thomas also remarks, in commenting on the Augustinian definition, that the term, habit (*habitus*), is more precisely descriptive of the genus of virtue than is quality. He also understands the remainder of the Augustinian definition as expressive of the two parts of the specific difference: (1) that a virtue perfects the potency in which it resides, and so is a perfectant of the *being* of the moral agent; and (2) that a virtue perfects the *act* of the potency in which it is, *i.e.*, a virtue inclines the agent to perfect operation. Point 2 means two things: that a virtue, if used, must be used in a good way; and that a virtue cannot be used to perform a vicious act. Gathering together these elements of a thomistic definition, we may conclude that: *human virtue is a good habit perfecting man in any of his rational potencies and inclining him to the right and perfect use of his potencies.*[5]

The Cardinal Virtues

There are several kinds of virtue which man can possess. The student will probably be familiar with the *intellectual virtues*. These

[4] St. Thomas approves this definition but suggests some revisions of its archaic terminology, in *S.T.*, I–II, 55, 4,c; Pegis, *Basic Writings*, II, 417; and in *De Virtutibus in Communi*, q. unica, art. 2,c.

[5] An excellent modern explanation of the general nature of virtue may be read in: Gilson, E., *Moral Values and the Moral Life*, (St. Louis, Herder, 1941), pp. 135–150. See also: V. J. Bourke, "The Role of Habitus in the Thomistic Metaphysics of Potency and Act," in *Essays in Thomism*, pp. 103–109.

are habits of the possible intellect of man which enable the agent to perform acts of intellectual knowing in a way that is more perfect than is possible to the unhabituated potency. The speculative intellect (whose function is simply to know the truth without attempting any application of the truth to actions) may be perfected by three habits of virtue: (1) the *understanding of first principles;* (2) *science;* and (3) *wisdom.* At birth, man's possible intellect is endowed with a native disposition, or a special quality added to the basic power of the intellect, which imperfect (*habitus*) inclines the agent to understand the truth of first principles of reasoning, as soon as the agent has sufficient experience to grasp the meaning of the terms of these principles. Thus, as soon as a child can understand what "whole" and "part" mean, he naturally and immediately judges that: "A whole is greater than its part." This is an example of the use of the habit of understanding first principles. Since some such principles are purely speculative and some are practical, the virtue of understanding first principles may be subdivided into the habit of knowing *speculative* principles and the habit of knowing *practical* principles. The latter is also know as *synderesis* and has been examined earlier in our course. Since it springs partly from an innate disposition and partly from repeated good use of the intellect, the virtue of understanding first principles is not wholly an acquired habit; it is called a *natural virtue, i.e.,* one which is imperfectly present in man when he is born (*natus*).

The second virtue of the speculative intellect perfects man for the act of reasoning demonstratively from principles to conclusions. In this sense, science is a habit of the possible intellect, acquired by repeated acts of reasoning in terms of what is ultimate in any given genus of knowledge. Thus, geometry is a science, an intellectual virtue, enabling its possessor to reason to true conclusions in that genus of knowledge which includes the properties of mathematical points, lines, planes, solids, and so on. There are as many different kinds of science, and so scientific virtues, as there are kinds of generically distinct knowledge. So a man may acquire the habit or virtue of one kind of scientific reasoning, without necessarily acquiring the habit of another science.

Wisdom, the third virtue of the speculative intellect, is like science in that it also perfects man so that he may reason to true conclusions. However, wisdom differs from science in the fact that wisdom does not reason in terms of the principles and causes of one genus of knowledge but in terms of the *first* and *highest* causes. It is because of this that the virtue of wisdom confers the ability to order, or prescribe the fields and methods of the various sciences. Wisdom even includes the ability to investigate and defend the truth of first principles. Metaphysics and theology are examples of wisdom.

The practical intellect (whose function is to know in such a way as to be able to prescribe right action) can acquire two virtues: (4) *art*, and (5) *prudence*. Art is the habit of reasoning rightly about the making of things. It requires a perfected intellect to plan and control the execution of a work of art. Any object which is well and intelligently produced is an art object. The perfection of the habit of art is judged by the perfection of the art product. A good carpenter has one kind of art; a good cook possesses another kind of art; and a good poet has still another kind of art. Notice that certain subjects may be both sciences and arts: medicine, for instance, is a science if studied just for the sake of knowledge, but it is an art when used by the practising physician. We should not be surprised that such things are called virtues, because carpentry, cooking, poetry, and the medical art are acquired habits which perfect the human intellect for right use.

Prudence, the last of the intellectual virtues in this enumeration, is that habit of the practical intellect which enables man to reason in such a way that he will act rightly. Where art is concerned with *making things*, prudence is concerned with *doing*. We have already seen the important role of prudence in the performance of a good moral action.

Of these five kinds of intellectual virtue, only prudence is a moral virtue. The understanding of first practical principles is necessary for a good life; but it is through the use of prudence that this understanding is applied to moral problems in the concrete. The other intellectual virtues may make important contributions to morality but a man does not need to be a scientist, or a philosopher, or an artist, to live well. He must, however, be prudent and this requires some understanding of first principles.[6]

Another distinct set of virtues are those which are called *moral*. These are all habits which incline man's appetites to actions which are good, in relation to his desire to attain his ultimate end. It is easy to see why they are called moral: they are concerned with human *mores*, with patterns of human action. In the course of time, men have given names to a large number of moral virtues. There are so many known to civilized man that it became quite a problem to classify the moral virtues and to deal with them in a scientific way. However, there is a very old and very sound theory (found in the writings and oral tradition of many ancient peoples and also in the Old Testament and in Aristotle) which maintains that there are four *principal virtues:* prudence, temperance, fortitude, and justice. In was in the twelfth century of the Christian era that these came to be commonly known as the *cardinal virtues*.[7]

They were called *cardinal* because man's moral life depends on these virtues, as a door hangs on its hinges (*cardines*). To extend the metaphor a little, one might say that a man enters into a good life through the doorway of virtue and his whole moral career turns on these cardinal virtues. St. Thomas gives three reasons why there should be four principal virtues for moral action. Firstly, because there are four potencies which require to be perfected. We have seen that these include the three human appetites: intellectual, concupiscible, and irascible. The practical intellect is the fourth moral potency; it does not immediately tend to action, as do the appetites, but its cardinal virtue (prudence) is concerned with matters (moral actions) which are practical. So, prudence in its essence is an intellectual virtue, but in the subject matter to which it applies, it is a moral virtue.[8]

---

[6] On the intellectual virtues, read: *S.T.*, I–II, q. 57, arts. 1–5 inclus.; in Pegis, *Basic Writings*, II, 429–437; also Sr. R. Emmanuella, *The Intellectual Virtues*, pp. 77–110.

[7] Cf. Lottin, "La théorie des vertus cardinales," *Mélanges Mandonnet*, pp. 233–259.

[8] *S.T.*, I–II, 58, 3, *ad primum*.

The second reason for a fourfold division of the principal moral virtues is found in the formal principles of virtue. In its definitive essence (*ratio*), every virtue must be the source of a human act which is: done with *right knowledge* (the work of prudence); properly *ordered in regard to things external* to the moral agent (the work of justice); *well measured* or *moderated* in regard to the desire of sensible goods (the work of temperance); and done *with firmness and strength* in the face of sensible evils (the work of fortitude). While these four formal characteristics belong in a general way to every moral virtue, each characteristic is specifically distinct and is proper to the perfection of a different moral potency. *Prudence*, or right practical reasoning, belongs especially to the practical intellect. *Justice*, or right desire of the good to other persons for rational motives, pertains to the will. *Temperance*, or reasonable moderation of one's concupiscible passions, resides in the concupiscible appetite. *Fortitude*, or reasonable firmness in one's irascible passions, perfects the irascible appetite.

A third reason why there are four cardinal virtues is to be found in the natural division of the subject matter of morality. There are really four kinds of natural moral problems. Some ethical difficulties lie in the area of practical thinking. Before he can be appetitively inclined, *by some reasonable motive*, to any moral act, the agent must first deliberate, judge, and foresee the consequences of his proposed action. To find the right cognitive direction for his appetitive acts is a special kind of problem for man. Such problems make up the subject matter of prudence. All the other moral problems that man faces are appetitive ones. Now it is easy and natural to desire what is reasonably good for oneself. Without any trouble, the agent can think of all kinds of reasons why other people should pay their debts to him, for instance. So, the human will, which is the appetite for the universal good of reason, has no moral difficulty in desiring the personal good of the agent. Where one has some trouble, is in desiring the reasonable good of other persons. It is always a little hard to wish other persons as much good as one naturally desires for oneself. This, then, is another special area of moral difficulty. The human will needs to be perfected by justice, the virtue which enables the agent to wish the good of other persons to the same reasonable extent that he desires it for himself. Since man only deals with other persons through his external actions, the problems of justice always involve the difficulty of maintaining objective rightness in the transfer and handling of extramental things or services.

A third kind of problem consists in the difficulties caused by the objects of concupiscence. Attractive food and drink, and the pleasures associated with sexual stimulation, tend to arouse inordinate passions in the average human agent. To keep these feelings within reasonable bounds, and to undergo them for morally good purposes, is no small problem. Moderation, or reasonable control of such emotions is a problem of personal morality and positive law is not of much help in this area. Temperance, as a habit rendering the concupiscible appetite submissive to the control of reason, is the chief virtue required for such problems. Finally, there are difficulties stemming from one's tendency to become discouraged by sensible dangers. Man naturally recoils from pain and suffering and death. Sometimes reason requires him to suffer these things as firmly as is reasonably possible; sometimes it is reasonable to fight strongly to overcome them. His irascible appetite needs strengthening for this kind of problem. This rational firmness in the irascible power is the fourth cardinal virtue, fortitude or courage.

In all these ways, we see the appropriateness of distinguishing four major virtues in the moral order: prudence, temperance, fortitude, and justice. The fact that moral problems fall into these four classifications is to be stressed because this gives us the principle of division of the subject matter of the second Part of this course in ethics. In special, or applied, ethics we make a more detailed study of the different moral problems which man encounters. In thomistic philosophy, these are treated as problems of prudence, of temperance, of fortitude, and of justice. One of the things an agent must do, in order to determine the formal object of a proposed action, is to decide under which cardinal virtue the proposed action, or problem, falls. Some actions will come under one virtue only; others are related to two or more virtues. Still other actions, which are directly related to God, will also come within the subject matter of the theological virtues: faith, hope, and charity. These theological virtues will be examined next.[9]

The Theological Virtues

If man had a purely natural ultimate end, and if he were not impeded in any way in the use of his natural powers, the cardinal virtues and their associated subordinate virtues would be sufficient to enable him to achieve this natural ultimate end. We have seen, however, that man's real purpose in life is to attain to that supernatural end which is the Beatific Vision. This is one reason why the human agent requires a higher kind of virtue. The soul and its natural operative potencies are the principles of naturally good actions, when these potencies are perfected by acquired and morally good habits, and when there is no impediment to good use. But the attainment of a supernatural end demands supernatural action; that is, the operations by which man may merit the vision of God exceed the capacity of man's natural powers. What man needs, in order to be able to perform such supernatural actions, is not a new set of operational potencies; for, if man were given potencies specifically different from human intellect and will, he would become a member of a new metaphysical species and would not merit his reward *as a human being*. Rather, it is necessary for God to raise the human intellect and will to a higher level of action, by infusing certain habits into the rational powers of the human soul. Unlike the natural virtues which dispose man to know and to choose the right *means* to a good life, the divinely infused theological virtues habitually perfect man so that he may know and incline toward his one, ultimate *End*, Who is God.

We may define the theological virtues, then, as *good operative habits of the rational potencies of the human soul, infused in man by God alone, directing human acts immediately to God as an End,*

[9] Read: Appendix to Chap. VIII, Text Three: *Why There Are Four Cardinal Virtues;* and also, *S.T.,* I–II, q. 61, arts. 1–4 inclus.; in Pegis, *Basic Writings,* II, 466–472.

and serving as the principles of right action in relation to man's supernatural End.[10]

It should be emphasized that the theological virtues are *principles,* or beginnings, of supernatural actions for man. There is, in the supernatural order, somewhat the same situation that we have observed in the sphere of natural virtue. The natural light of the human intellect, perfected by the habit of understanding first principles, is the source of man's knowledge of first principles of judgment and practical action. Then, flowing from these first principles, there may be many acquired moral virtues which further perfect man's rational powers for the naturally good operations of human life.

Similarly, in the supernatural order, there are the theological virtues, which give man a start, as it were, in supernatural action, but there are other *infused moral virtues* which follow upon the reception of the theological virtues, complementing the supernatural organization of man's character. These additional infused moral virtues have, in most cases, the same names as the corresponding, natural moral virtues. Thus, there may be infused prudence, temperance, fortitude, and justice. While the infused moral virtues parallel, in name, the naturally acquired virtues, it should be remembered that each infused virtue is a different species of habit from its corresponding natural virtue. The natural virtue of temperance, for instance, is a certain habit of moderation in the concupiscent passions, established by the rule of human reason. On the other hand, infused supernatural temperance is a habit of moderation in the same concupiscent passions, according to a mean which is directly established by Divine Reason. To put this point in a more practical way, we may say that naturally acquired temperance disposes man to use enough food and drink to maintain his health and strength, so that he may work to the best of his ability in this life on earth. But infused temperance may dispose the good man further to curb his natural desires, even to mortify his body,

---

[10] Read: *S.T.,* I–II, q. 62, arts. 1 et 2,c; in Pegis, *Basic Writings,* II, 475–477; also Appendix to Chap. VIII, Text Four: *How the Theological Differ from the Moral Virtues.*

by abstaining from food and drink at times, for the sake of super-natural merit.

The virtue of chastity, for example, may be difficult to under-stand and justify, if treated in terms of purely natural reasoning. But, viewed in the light of supernatural faith and love of God, chastity becomes a highly reasonable habit. For certain human be-ings to renounce all desire for carnal pleasure, even that pleasure which is naturally enjoyed within the bonds of matrimony, is quite reasonable to those people who believe in the real possibility of attaining a higher joy in the supernatural love of God. Notice that chastity is not a negative, or unmotivated, virtue. To give up the enjoyment of natural pleasure for no reason at all is irrational and not conducive to moral merit; to renounce the enjoyment of nat-ural goods, *for the sake of a definite supernatural reason*, is a logical and morally approvable action. We should not understand this to mean that the infused moral virtues supplant and eradicate the ac-quired moral virtues. The part of man's character which is consti-tuted by supernatural habits, even including habitual grace which we shall come to discuss presently, is a superstructure built on the foundations of a naturally good character. With the infused vir-tues, both theological and moral, man's acquired virtues remain and are elevated to a higher level of motivation and action, but the supernatural does not destroy the natural. Just as man's bodily ac-tions retain their own physical goodness and acquire a new rational goodness, when they are motivated by rationality, so do man's natural operations of reason (his human acts) keep their natural goodness and receive an additional supernatural goodness, when motivated by the theological virtues.[11]

Not only are the theological virtues distinguished by the fact that they order man's actions directly to God as an End, and by the fact that they must be infused by God and cannot be acquired by human effort, they are also marked off by the special way in which they become known to man. The theological virtues are known only through divine revelation. The greatest of the Greek

[11] On the relation of the infused moral virtues to the theological virtues, read: *S.T.*, I–II, 63, arts. 3 et 4,c; in Pegis, *Basic Writings*, II, 485–487.

philosophers knew a good deal of the principles and nature of the acquired virtues; no philosopher, without supernatural revelation, has grasped the significance of theological virtue.[12]

Supernatural motivation of human action requires both cognitive and appetitive perfection. Man must *know* God in a special manner, in order to rise above the confines of natural action. For such knowledge, the human intellect is given the habit of *faith*. The act of faith is essentially cognitive, and so it belongs to the intellect. However, to believe is to accept as true something which is not clearly understood; hence the will must move the intellect to assent to a truth of faith. That is why St. Thomas formally defines supernatural faith as: "*a habit of the mind* (mentis), *by which eternal life is begun in us, making the intellect assent to things which are not apparent.*" [13]

In regard to his will, man needs to be inclined appetitively to his supernatural end, as to something which he trusts may be attained. For this act of intention, he is disposed by the theological virtue of *hope*. Thus, we may define hope, the theological virtue, as: *a divinely infused habit of the will inclining man to expect eternal happiness in union with God, as a good only to be obtained in the future and with difficulty, but possible of attainment through the help of God.*[14]

The greatest act of the human will is that of love of an object which has been attained. Unlike the action of the human intellect which is inward-going, reaching its peak in the intentional union of the known object with the knower *within the soul*, the act of the human will is *outward-going*, reaching its climax in the real union and identification of the lover with the thing loved. Thus, while the will may properly love imperfect goods for rational motives, the supremely good act of will must consist in a love of a Perfect Good, for the sake of that Good. Further, to understand

---

[12] *S.T.*, I–II, 62, 1,c, *ad. fin.*
[13] *S.T.*, II–II, q. 4, a. 1,c; students may read a brief account of the habit of faith, in: St. Thomas, *The Trinity*, transl. by Sister Rose E. Brennan, pp. 80–81.
[14] This definition has been gathered together by the present writer from the analysis of hope, made by St. Thomas in: *S.T.*, II–II, q. 17, a. 1,c; and *Quaest. Disp. De Spe*, q. unica, art. 1,c.

the nature of the supernatural love of God, we should consider the three possible types of friendship, because friendship designates the highest type of mutual love between persons. There is one kind of friendship which is founded on blood relationship; among the members of a family, there is a special love not simply between individuals but of the whole family and each individual member, which family love arises from the unity and reciprocity of persons who belong to the natural society which is the family. Notice that family love must be more than a love of concupiscence, for the good of the family is not merely a sensible good but is a *common good*, known by the intellect and loved by the will. A second kind of friendly love is found among members of a civil society; a good citizen loves his fellow citizens, individually and collectively, for the sake of the common good of his country. This is a higher type of common good than that of the family, and patriotism or love of country is even farther removed from concupiscent love than is love of the family.

The highest kind of human society is the union of all men in that society whose common good is God Himself. In the communion of those who love God as the commonly shared Principle of eternal life and divine friendship, there is no place for concupiscent love but there is the purest kind of volitional love. This love of God for His own sake and of all other things for the sake of God issues from the theological virtue of *charity*. If we understand friendship as he did, we can see the force of the short definition of charity, given by St. Thomas: *charity is the friendship of man for God.*[15] A less terse statement of the essence of this theological virtue is: *charity is a divinely infused habit of the will, by which man is enabled to love God for His own sake, in intimate union with Him, desiring the good to Him and rejoicing in the mutually returned love of God.*[16]

[15] *Caritas est quaedam amicitia hominis ad Deum:* see, *S.T.*, II–II, q. 23, a. 1 et 3,c. For an explanation of the manner in which charity "informs" the other virtues, perfecting them and organizing man's life into a supernatural unity of character, see: Klubertanz, "The Unity of Human Activity," *The Modern Schoolman*, XXVII (1950) 75–85.

[16] Read: Appendix to Chap. VIII, Text Five: *God as the Object of the Theological Virtues;* and on the interrelations of the moral and the theological

There are, then, seven great virtues which may serve as habitual principles of good human action. These we have seen to be the three theological virtues: *faith, hope,* and *charity;* and the four cardinal virtues: *prudence, temperance, fortitude,* and *justice.* Each of these virtues has a formal object by which it is defined and which makes it a distinctly different specific principle of moral action. Also, each great virtue has its own characteristic subject matter, or moral field. It is important to understand this last point, for we are to use the differentiation of subject matter, or of the various fields of virtue, in organizing the treatment of the problems of special ethics.

The problems of prudence center in the difficulty of discovering, judging, and applying right knowledge to human action. Temperance covers the field of the agent's concupiscent passions, just as the problems of fortitude fall in the area of the agent's irascible passions. Justice applies to all of man's voluntary dealings with other persons and so its problems involve the rightness of man's external actions. If man had a merely natural end in life, these four fields of virtue would exhaust the possibilities of moral difficulty. But, considering human life as directly ordered to God, in the supernatural order, we find three new species of moral problem. There are special difficulties in the area of truths which have some immediate relationship to God and which cannot be known clearly by purely natural reasoning; this is the field of faith. To look forward and firmly maintain one's aspirations for eternal life with God is another field of moral difficulty; it is the field of problems to which hope applies. Finally, there are many problems concerned with the loving of God for His own sake, and of rational creatures as participants in this society of those whose wills are supernaturally ordered to God; this is the field of charity.

We come to realize more fully the significance of these seven special areas of moral problematics, when we examine in detail the

---

virtues, see: *S.T.,* I–II, q. 65, arts. 2–5 inclus.; in Pegis, *Basic Writings,* II, 498–504. The student will find a good exposition of the nature of the virtues, in: Sister M. Rose Emmanuella Brennan, *The Intellectual Virtues According to the Philosophy of St. Thomas* (Washington, 1941), Chap. IV, pp. 77–110.

vices and possible kinds of offenses against these different virtues. This is not part of the work of ethical theory and it will be left to special or applied ethics.

Before closing this section, we should also notice that there is another habitual principle of supernatural life for man; this is *grace*. Probably the simplest explanation of divine grace is to say that grace is a special help given man by God to enable man to know and to act, and so to exist, in the supernatural order. For the natural operation of man's intellect and will, God has given man a natural tendency to truth (the "light" of the human intellect) and a natural inclination to goodness in general (the natural "appetite" for happiness). Moreover, in the regular course of natural events, God extends to all creaturely agents enough divine assistance to enable them to exist and to operate naturally; without such divine cooperation, man and other creatures would be unable to continue to exist and do things. This "ordinary" help given to man by God is only ordinary in the sense that the divine conservation and cooperation is ever present in nature.[17]

Now, if God's help is needed by natural agents to produce their natural effects, it is clear that a special divine help is necessary to enable man to perform supernatural actions. But actions do not happen unless there be an existing real agent, capable of performing them. Man must remain human in his essence and yet be raised to a higher-than-natural manner of existence. That is why St. Thomas defines grace as: "a perfection elevating the soul to a certain supernatural existence" (*quaedam perfectio elevans animam ad quoddam esse supernaturale*.[18] Because sanctifying grace does not confer a new substantial essence on man, it is classified as an *accident* of the human soul. It is *like* a quality of the first species, that is, a habit; but it is not a proximate principle of operations (the theological virtues are proximate principles of supernatural ac-

---

[17] Students who do not remember this teaching, from their study of primary and secondary causality in the philosophy of being, and from the discussion of free choice, in the philosophy of man, may read with profit: *Summa contra Gentiles*, III, cc. 64–67; in Pegis, *Basic Writings*, II, 113–121.

[18] See *De Veritate*, q. 27, 3,c; see also *S.T.*, I–II, q. 111, 2,c, *ad fin.*; in Pegis, *Basic Writings*, II, 1006.

tions), so grace is what the later Commentators on the thought of St. Thomas call an *entitative habit*.[19]

The perfection of the human soul by sanctifying grace does not remove the necessity for the development of the natural virtues. As St. Thomas puts it: "The rectitude of grace does not exist without the rectitude of nature."[20] Grace builds a superstructure on the edifice of natural being and virtue. Through grace man attains a new dimension of existence and functioning; but grace does not destroy what is natural to man. It is precisely because of this that there is a unity and continuity between the life of nature and the life of grace in the moral agent. It is also for this reason that moral science must take cognizance of the possibility of the elevation of human nature by grace, without pretending to give an adequate account of the nature of divine grace. Fully to grasp the importance of grace, one would have to study theology.[21]

Vice and Immoral Action

We may now take a brief look at the principles, or sources, of immoral action. These are to be studied so that we may know how to avoid such action. In general, there is but one efficient cause of bad actions and that is the *will*. Whenever the human will acts in opposition to the order of reason, or in opposition to the divine law, immoral action (sin) results. The will cannot be forced to perform immoral acts. Nor can the will act solely for the sake of evil. In every case of immoral action, the will is attracted to some *apparent good*, when it can, and should, be motivated by a real good.[22] This is well summed up in the following paragraph:

The proper principle of an act of sin is the will, for every sin is voluntary. Hence, nothing can be the cause of sin directly, except that which

[19] Thus, Sylvester of Ferrara suggests that grace, "can be called a *habitus ad essendum* inasmuch as it constitutes man in a supernatural *esse*, making him formally worthy of eternal life." *Comment. in III Contra Gentiles*, c. 150.

[20] *De Malo*, q. 4, art. 2, *ad primum in contrarium*.

[21] At the discretion of the professor, good students might be directed to read the *Treatise on Grace*, S.T., I–II, qq. 109–113; in Pegis, *Basic Writings*, II, 979–1037.

[22] S.T., I–II, q. 75, arts. 1 et 2,c; in Pegis, *Basic Writings*, II, 617–620.

can move the will to act. Now the will can be moved by two things, as was said above: first, by the object, as an apprehended object of appetite is said to move the will to act; second, by that which inclines the will from within to the will-act. This latter is, of course, either the will itself, or God, as was indicated above. Now God cannot be the cause of sin, as we have said. So, the only remaining possibility, from this point of view, is that the will of man is alone the direct cause of its sin.[23]

However, there are other things which can be the indirect causes of immoral action. We can think of three such principles within the agent. These internal causes of sin are: *ignorance, passion,* and *malice*.[24] The influence of ignorance and passion on the voluntariness of the human act has been studied at an earlier point in this course (Chapter III). We understand that ignorance is the privation of knowledge. Now, not every kind of ignorance is an indirect cause of immoral action. It is only in the case of ignorance which deprives one of knowledge that would prevent the immoral act, that we have ignorance as a principle of moral evil. Suppose we have a man who takes a valuable book which belongs to the school library, and *he does not know that it is not his own book*. This is objectively an act of injustice. If he would take it anyhow, even if he knew that it is not his, his ignorance is not the cause of his bad act; it is merely incidental or what is technically called concomitant. But if he would not take the book, unless he were ignorant of its ownership, then his ignorance is an indirect cause of the unjust act; it is antecedent ignorance.[25]

We have also seen that the passions, or movements of the sense appetites, may influence the voluntariness of human acts. It is clear, then, that some passions may be the indirect causes of immoral action. Passion may influence the will to act badly, in two ways. First of all, the soul in the grip of a passion tends to become distracted from the proper act of the will, and so to lose sight, as it were, of the rule of reason. Secondly, a passion may influence the judgment of reason by emphasizing some sensory good or evil, to the detriment or exclusion of a rational motive. Thus, the will is not offered

[23] *S.T.,* I–II, q. 80, 1,c.
[24] Discussed by St. Thomas, in *S.T.,* I–II, questions 76, 77, and 78, respectively; in Pegis, *Basic Writings,* II, 623–650.
[25] *S.T.,* I–II, q. 76, 1,c.

a proper object of choice. In both these ways, passion can contribute to the performance of an immoral act.[26]

It has already been noted that extremely violent passions may remove completely one's ability to reason and to choose freely. Acts flowing from an agent in such a condition are not voluntary and, if evil objectively, they are not morally imputable to the agent. That is to say that a man who acts as a result of a very strong passion, which he could not be expected to control, can do no wrong. But, in most cases, the will can retain reasonable control of its acts, even when the agent suffers some passion. Antecedent passion diminishes the guilt of immoral action, to the extent that it diminishes voluntariness. Consequent passion increases the guilt of immoral action, because such passion follows the act of will and increases the general voluntariness of the action. This is just to say that, if you beat another man unreasonably and voluntarily and then sit back and enjoy his discomfort, your pleasure is a mark of your continuing approval of a bad action. If you are immediately sorry, then your sorrow does not remove the guilt of the original bad act but it does indicate that you have stopped desiring to injure the victim.[27]

Malice means a disorder in the will itself. When the agent knowingly and willfully chooses a lesser good, in a situation where he should choose a greater good, his will is subject to the disorder of malice. The agent who acts from malice is not influenced by ignorance or passion but deliberately and with a clear mind chooses a mutable good, say sense pleasure, in preference to a known immutable good, say eternal happiness. It is even possible for the malicious person to choose a spiritual evil in preference to a spiritual good, if the choice of the spiritual good would deprive him of some temporal good.[28] It is possible for malice to be either actual or habitual. Actual malice is the disorder of will which is found in isolated evil acts, of the type just described; habitual malice is a permanently acquired disposition which remains as a quality of the will of the agent, inclining him to repeated acts of malice.[29]

[26] *S.T.*, I–II, q. 77, 1,c.   [27] *S.T.*, I–II, q. 77, art. 6,c.   [28] *S.T.*, I–II, 78, 1,c.
[29] *De Malo*, q. 3, a. 14, ad 7m; and *S.T.*, I–II, q. 78, 1, ad 3m; in Pegis, *Basic Writings*, II, 645.

We have noted that virtue is a morally good habit. It is helpful to contrast virtue with its contrary forms of evil, in order to understand the principles of immoral action. Thus, to the virtuous act there is opposed the evil act which the theologian calls *sin*, and which we have been calling *immoral action*. To the goodness which is a consequence of virtue, there is opposed the evil of a bad moral action; this moral evil is called *malice*. Finally, to the good moral habit which is the essence of virtue, there is the contrary bad habit, which is called *vice*.[30] Habitual malice, then, is almost equivalent to vice. Just as virtue is an internal principle of morally good action, so is vice an acquired internal principle of evil action.

Turning for a moment from the consideration of moral vice, we may look briefly at the two *external* principles of immoral action. These are: (1) the devil, and (2) original sin. We have already noted at the beginning of this chapter (p. 257), that the devil is a bad angel who attempts to incite man to immoral action. The devil is not a direct cause of man's evil action but may be an indirect cause, in the sense of persuading or suggesting immoral activity.[31] Original sin is an external principle of evil action inasmuch as it is a disorder in the human agent which finds its origin in the act of another man, that is, in Adam.

Before his first sin, Adam is believed to have existed in the condition known as original justice or rectitude. By special grace, his will was subject to God. As a result of this ordering of man's highest appetite to the Supreme Good, the other potencies in Adam's person were ordered to his will and intellect; his sense appetites, for instance, were especially submissive to the rule of reason and to the law of God. With the Fall of Man, this supernatural ordination of the human will to God was lost by Adam, and by his descendants. This loss of original rectitude is essentially a privation of this special ordering of the will to God. It is this privation which is the *formal* character of original sin. On the other hand, the resultant disorder in the potencies of the soul of Adam, and of his descendants, whereby the lower powers lack their original submissiveness

[30] *S.T.*, I–II, q. 71, a. 1,c; in Pegis, *Basic Writings*, II, 560.
[31] *S.T.*, I–II, q. 80, arts. 1–4; in Pegis, *Basic Writings*, II, 658–663.

to the higher, rational potencies, is the *material* character of original sin. Since this material character is equivalent to a habitual tendency to turn away from the immutable good to the mutable goods of the senses, original sin is materially identified with concupiscence.[32]

The effect of the sacrament of baptism is to restore the individual recipient to the state of original justice, to the extent that his rational potencies are again turned to God but not to the extent of restoring the submissiveness of man's lower potencies to his higher powers.[33] Hence all human beings, subject to original sin, retain something of the disorder of concupiscence and this is an indirect cause, external in its origin, of actual sin or immoral action.

Vice is a morally bad habit. It might be thought that the principal vices would be simply the habits directly contrary to the principal virtues. But the formal principle of specification of the vices is not the same as that of the virtues. Each chief virtue is related to the order of reason in a special way. Vices are formally distinguished, however, by the ordination of the appetites to different species of mutable goods.[34] We may then distinguish seven *capital vices*, as seven habits of seeking the good inordinately, or of avoiding the contrary evils inordinately.

Habitually to seek the goods of the soul, such as honor or praise, in an unreasonable way is to possess the vice of *pride* (or *vainglory*). The habit of inordinately desiring the goods of the body which pertain to the preservation of the individual (*i.e.*, food and drink) is *gluttony;* and for the bodily good which pertains to the preservation of the species (*i.e.*, sexual acts), the vice is called *lust*. In regard to external goods, wealth for example, the inordinate habit is called *covetousness*. All four of the foregoing types of goods may also be desired unreasonably for the pleasures which are associated with them.

There are three bad habits in regard to the avoidance of goods because of some evil which accompanies them. Thus, the habit of

---

[32] *S.T.*, I–II, q. 82, a. 3,c; in Pegis, *Basic Writings*, II, 676–677; see also: Appendix to Chap. VIII, Text Six: *Original Sin and Concupiscence*.

[33] *De Malo*, q. 4, art. 2, ad 10m, et ad 2m in contrarium.

[34] *S.T.*, I–II, q. 84, 4, *ad primum;* in Pegis, *Basic Writings*, II, 691.

avoiding a spiritual good because its attainment requires the suffering of some bodily discomfort is the vice of *sloth*. The habit of feeling sorry that another person is possessed of more good or excellence than oneself, without having any intention of injuring or seeking vengeance on that person, is called *envy*. The same unreasonable feeling, when accompanied by the inclination to seek vengeance, is the basis of the bad habit of *anger*. Notice again, that all seven capital vices prompt one also to attack the evils contrary to their respective goods, but in an unreasonable fashion.[35]

Each capital vice is a head (*caput*) to which many minor vices may be ordered. A morally bad character is habituated to desire and to act against the order of reason and of God. Just as virtue does not necessitate good action, so vice does not force one absolutely to immorality. The vicious person retains freedom of choice but the acquisition of vice makes it increasingly difficult to will the good, in conformity with reason. The natural way to get rid of a vice is to stop using it and to perform good actions which will introduce a corrective virtue.[36]

Summary of Chapter VIII

This concluding chapter of Part One has treated the development of moral character in the human agent. Will, intellect, concupiscible, and irascible appetites are four moral powers in man; but the will is the efficient cause of every moral action. God and the devil influence the performance of moral actions from outside the agent. Habit is a perfection of a rational potency. Virtues are good moral habits. There are four cardinal moral virtues: prudence, temperance, fortitude, and justice. With the exception of prudence, the intellectual virtues are not moral virtues. The theological virtues order man's moral life directly to God as an End; they are three: faith, hope, and charity. Sanctifying grace is not

---

[35] *S.T.*, I–II, q. 84, 4,c; in Pegis, *Basic Writings*, II, 691–692; read also: Appendix to Chap. VIII, Text Seven: *The Seven Capital Vices*.

[36] The student will find a brief and excellent treatment of the sources of immoral action, in: Gilson, E., *Moral Values and the Moral Life*, pp. 178–192.

identical with the theological virtues but is the habitual principle which elevates the soul to supernatural existence. Vice is a bad moral habit. Bad actions are directly caused by the human will acting in discord with the rule of reason and the law of God. The indirect causes of immoral action may be: ignorance, passion, malice, the devil, and original sin. Habitual malice, or vice, is of seven chief kinds: pride, gluttony, lust, covetousness, sloth, envy, and anger. Just as a good moral character is an organism of virtues, natural and supernatural, growing out of the native endowments of man aided by divine grace, so also is a bad moral character an organism of habits of vice which turn man's will away from God and eternal happiness to the inordinate pursuit of temporal pleasure and moral evil.

In the eight chapters of this part of ethics, which is called ethical theory or general ethics, we have studied the universal principles on which the practical science of ethics is based. What remains to be seen in ethics is the manner of applying the rule of reason, and ultimately of God's law, to the typical fields of moral problems. This will be the aim of the second part, which is called special or applied ethics. Throughout the chapters to follow, we shall see the application of the simple and very true conclusion of our just completed study:

Since human acts are called moral in relation to reason, which is the proper principle of human acts, those moral acts are termed good which are in keeping with reason, and bad which are in discord with reason.[37]

Appendix to Chapter VIII

¶ TEXT ONE: *Enumeration of the Principles of Human Acts.* After acts and passions, it is necessary to consider the principles of human acts: first, the intrinsic principles, second, the extrinsic principles. Now, the intrinsic principles are potencies and habits. But, since potencies have been treated in the First Part [qq. 77–83], the consideration of habits now remains: firstly, their general na-

[37] *S.T.*, I–II, q. 100, art. 1,c.

ture, and secondly, the virtues and vices and other habits of this kind which are principles of human acts. (*S.T.*, I–II, q. 49, Prolog.) Following this, we must consider the exterior principles of acts. Now, the exterior principle which inclines to evil is the devil, whose tempting has been spoken of in the First Part [q. 114]. The exterior principle which impels to the good is God, and He instructs us by means of law, and helps us by means of grace. (*S.T.*, I–II, q. 90, Prolog.)

¶ TEXT TWO: *The Potencies Perfectible by Virtue.* Virtue, as it is essentially in man, designates the perfectant of a potency (*potentiae complementum*). Hence, it is also called a power (*vis*), inasmuch as anything possessed of complete capacity (*potestas*) can follow through on its impulse or motion. Virtue, etymologically, indicates the perfection of a capacity; hence, the Philosopher says in the first book *De coelo et mundo* [281a14] that a virtue is the peak of power in a thing.

Because potency is spoken of in relation to act, the perfection of a potency is found when it takes on the capacity of perfect operation. Because operation is the end of the operating agent, (since everything exists for the sake of its operation, as for a proximate end, according to the Philosopher in the first book *De coelo et mundo*) each thing is good inasmuch as it possesses a perfect ordination to its end. Hence it is that virtue makes its possessor good, as is said in the *Ethics* [*Eth. Nic.* II, 6, 1106a16]. And in this way, it is apparent that it is a disposition of the perfect to what is best, as is said in the *Metaphysics* [cf. *Physic.* VII, 3, 246a13]. All of these things apply fittingly to the virtue of any kind of thing. For the virtue of a horse is what makes him good, and his work too; similarly for the virtue of a stone, or a man, or any other thing.

There is a difference in the manner of perfection (reading *completionis* for *complexionis*) of potency, and this depends on the kind of potency. For, one kind of potency is solely acting and another is solely acted upon or moved, and a third kind is both acting-and-acted-upon. So, the potency which is solely acting does not need anything added to it in order that it be the principle of an act;

hence, the virtue of such a potency is nothing other than the potency itself. Such a potency is the divine, the agent intellect, or the physical powers (*potentiae naturales*). Hence, the virtues of these potencies are not any habits but the very potencies which are perfected in themselves.

Those potencies which do not act unless moved by others are the solely moved ones. They have not the capacity to act and not to act, rather they act in dependence on the impulsion of a moving agent which is a virtue. Examples of these are the sensory powers considered in themselves. Hence, in the third book of the *Ethics* [*Eth. Nic.*, VI, 2, 1139a19], it is said that sense is the principle of no act. These potencies are perfected for their acts by something which is added, but this is not present in them in the way of a form dwelling in a subject but simply in the manner of a passion, as a species is present in the pupil of the eye. Hence, the virtues of these potencies are not habits; rather, they are the potencies themselves, insofar as they are passively actuated by their agents.

Those potencies are acting-and-acted-upon which are so moved by their agents that they are not determined by them to only one way of acting. Rather, they are able to act, in the same sense that powers, which are rational in some way, can. These potencies are perfected for action by something added to them, which is not present in them merely in the way of a passion but in the manner of a form which is at rest and which remains in a subject; so that the potency is not forced by them [to act] in one way, for then the potency would not be in control of its act. The virtues of these potencies are not the potencies in themselves, nor passions as in the sense powers, nor qualities acting by necessity as are the qualities of physical things. But they are habits by means of which one can act when he wishes, as the Commentator says in his commentary on the third book *De Anima* [Averrois Cordubensis, In *Aristotelis de Anima*, III, 3; see Aristotelis, *Opera*, Venetiis apud Juntas, 1550, t. VI, fol. 169v, line 22]. Augustine too, in his book *On the Conjugal Good* [c. 21, PL 40, col. 390], says that a habit is that whereby one acts when it is time to do so.

Thus, it is clear that virtues are habits, and how habits differ from the second and third species of qualities as they similarly differ from the fourth species, for they [habits] are ready [for action]. Figure [an example of the fourth species of quality] does not imply, in itself, an ordination to act.

From the foregoing it can become evident that we need habits of virtue for three reasons. Firstly, so that there may be uniformity in their operation; for, things which depend on operation alone are easily changed, unless they be stabilized by some habitual inclination. Secondly, so that there may be a readiness for perfect operation; for, unless a rational potency be inclined in some way by a habit to one thing, it will always be necessary, when it becomes necessary to operate, to first go through a preliminary investigation concerning the operation, as is evident in the case of the man who lacks the habit of science and wishes to make a scientific consideration, and also in the case of the man who wishes to act in accord with virtue but lacks the habit of virtue. . . . Thirdly, so that the perfect operation may be completed in an enjoyable way. Which is indeed accomplished through habit, which renders the operation proper to it rather natural and consequently enjoyable, since it is a sort of [second] nature. For, suitability (*convenientia*) is the cause of enjoyment; that is why the Philosopher [*Eth. Nic.*, II, 2, 1104b3], puts down enjoyment of work as the mark of habit. (*De Virtutibus in Communi*, q. unica, a. 1,c.)

¶ TEXT THREE: *Why There Are Four Cardinal Virtues.* Cardinal is derived from [the Latin word for] hinge (*a cardine*); that is, that on which a door turns, as in Proverbs 26:14, "as the door turns on its hinges, so does the sluggard on his couch." Hence, the cardinal virtues are those on which human life is based and through which entrance is gained. Human life is that which is proportionate to man.

Now, in man there is, first of all, a sensitive nature by which he is in agreement with brute animals, practical reason which is proper to man on his own level, and speculative reason which is not present perfectly in man as it is in the angels but according to a participation of his soul. Therefore, the contemplative life is not properly human but superhuman, and the voluptuous life which cleaves to sense goods is not human but bestial. And so, the life which is properly human is the active life which consists in the exercise of the moral virtues. So, those virtues are properly called cardinal, on which the moral life turns and is founded; for, they are like principles for such a life. This is the reason why virtues of this kind are called cardinal.

Now, it is necessary to consider that four things stand out as essential to the virtuous act. One of these is that the very substance of the act be moderated within itself. From this, the act is called good, in the sense that it deals with proper subject matter or that it is adorned with proper circumstances. The second is, that the act be related to the moral agent (*subjectum*) in the proper way. Due to this, it inheres firmly in the subject. [Translator's note: the subject is the potency which is the immediate principle of the act.] The third is, that the act be proportioned in a proper way to some external thing, as to an end. These three belong to that which is directed by reason. But the fourth is on the side of reason itself which is directive, that is, knowledge.

The Philosopher treats these four points in the second book of the *Ethics* [c. 3, 1105a30], where he says that it is not sufficient for virtue that things be done justly or temperately, for this pertains to the moderating of the act. But three other things are required on the side of the agent. First of all, he must be knowing, and this pertains to the directive cognition. Then, he must be choosing, and again he must choose for the sake of a proper end; this pertains to the rightness of the act in relation to some external thing. The third is present, if he *adheres firmly* and unswervingly to his task.

Therefore, these four: directive cognition, rightness, firmness and moderation, though required in all virtuous acts, are each possessed of a special importance in some specific kinds of subject matters and acts. On the part of practical knowledge, three things are required. The first of these is deliberation; the second is judgment of the results of deliberation. Just as in speculative reasoning there is discovery or search for knowledge, and judgment. But, since the practical intellect prescribes flight or approach, which the speculative intellect does not, as is said in the third book *On the Soul* [*De Anima*, III, 10, 433a12–18], therefore it pertains, thirdly, to practical reason to think ahead of time about problems of action. This third is the main function and the other two are subordinate to it. Man is perfected in regard to the first, by the virtue of *eubulia*, which means good counsel. Man is perfected in regard to the second, by *synesis* and *gnome*, by which he acquires good judgment, as is said in the sixth book of the *Ethics* [c. 10–11, 1142b32–1143b15]. But reason is made properly preceptive by prudence, as is explained in the same place. Hence, it is clear that the principal role in directive knowledge belongs to prudence. So, from this side, prudence is put among the cardinal virtues.

Similarly, the rightness of the act in relation to some external thing possesses, indeed, the nature of the good and the praiseworthy, even in the case of things which pertain to one agent in himself. But it is highly regarded chiefly in the case of things which pertain to another; that is, when a man rectifies his act not merely in regard to those things which belong to himself but also in regard to those things in which he shares some common interest with others. For, the Philosopher says in the fifth book of the *Ethics* (c. 1, 1129b25–1130a13) that many people can use their own things virtuously, but cannot do the same in regard to things which belong to others. So justice, for this reason, is placed among the principal virtues; for, by it a man cooperates and maintains equality with others, with whom he has some common dealings, in a proper way. Hence, those things are said, in common talk, to be just which are mutually balanced in a due fashion.

Moderation or restraint, however, is most important and has the rational character (*rationem*) of a good, chiefly in the area of impulses of passion, which reason should restrain so that one may attain the mean of virtue. Passion is strongest in seeking the pleasures of the sense of touch; and so, from this point of view, temperance is put among the cardinal virtues. It represses the desires for the pleasures associated with touch.

Firmness has its chief importance and the rational character of a good, in regard to those things which chiefly arouse the passion which moves one to flight. This is principally the case with very great dangers, the dangers of death. So, from this point of view, fortitude is placed among the cardinal virtues. Through it, man may boldly face the dangers of death.

Now, of these four virtues, prudence is in the reason, justice is in the will, fortitude is in the irascible power, and temperance is in the concupiscible. These are the only potencies which can be the principles of human acts, that is, of the voluntary. From this, the rational essence of the cardinal virtues is clear, both from the modes of virtue which are like formal principles, and also from the subject matter, and from the point of view of the subject. (*De Virtutibus Cardinalibus*, q. unica, art. 1,c.)

¶ TEXT FOUR: *How the Theological Differ from the Moral Virtues.* Just as man acquires his first perfection, namely his soul, from the action of God, so also does he possess his ultimate perfection, which is the perfect happiness of man, immediately from God. And in Him does he find his rest, which is evident from the fact that man's natural desire can find rest in no other being, but in God alone. For, it is inborn in man to be moved, by a desire arising from things caused, to seek the causes. And this desire does not rest until he arrives at the first cause, Who is God.

Therefore it is necessary that, just as the first perfection of man (which is the rational soul) exceeds the capacity of corporeal matter, so the ultimate perfection which man can reach (which is the happiness of eternal life) exceeds the capacity of human nature in its entirety. And because everything is directed to its end by some operation, and the means to the end must in some way be proportioned to the end, it is necessary that there be some perfections of man, by which he will be directed to his supernatural end which exceeds the capacity of the natural principles of man.

Now, this cannot be, unless some supernatural principles of operations be infused into man by God, over and above the natural principles. The natural principles of operations are the essence of the soul and its potencies, that is, intellect and will which are principles of the operations of man, as man. Nor can this be, unless the intellect possess the knowledge of principles through which he may be directed in regard to other things, and unless the will possess a natural inclination to the good proportioned to nature, as has been said in the preceding question (arts. 8–9).

Therefore, there is divinely infused into man, so that he may carry out the actions ordered to the end of eternal life, *grace* first of all, through which the soul is possessed of a certain spiritual existence, and then, *faith, hope,* and *charity.* [This is done] so that the intellect will be illuminated through faith concerning some supernatural things to be known, which occupy the place in this order that the naturally known principles have in the order of connatural operations. Through hope and charity the will acquires an inclination to that supernatural good, to which the human will is not sufficiently ordered by natural inclination. And just as, over and above these natural principles, habits of virtue are needed for the perfection of man according to the manner natural to him, as was said above (preceding art.), so man may attain from divine influence, not only the foregoing supernatural principles but also some infused virtues, whereby he is perfected in regard to operations ordered to the end of eternal life. (*De Virtutibus in Communi,* q. unica, a. 10,c.)

¶ TEXT FIVE: *God as the Object of the Theological Virtues.* It should be considered that the good of both the intellective and the appetitive part is twofold: namely, the good which is the ultimate end, and the good which is for the sake of the end. Nor is the essential nature (*ratio*) of the two the same. Therefore, over and above the foregoing (cardinal) virtues, whereby man attains the good in the area of means to his end, it is necessary that there be other virtues whereby man will be well disposed in regard to the ultimate end, Who is God. Hence these are called theological, because they have God not only for their end but also for their object.

In order that we may be moved rightly to the end, this end must be both known and desired. Desire of the end requires two things: namely, *trust* that the end may be obtained, for no wise man is moved to that which he cannot obtain; and *love* of the end, for it is not desired unless it be loved. Therefore, the theological virtues are three: namely, *faith*, by which we know God; *hope*, whereby we hope that He will be attained by us; and *charity*, by which we love Him. Thus then, it is clear that there are three kinds of virtue: theological, intellectual, and moral, and each kind has several species under it. (*De Virtutibus in Communi*, q. unica, a. 12,c.)

¶ TEXT SIX: *Original Sin and Concupiscence.* Concupiscence, as it pertains to original sin, is not actual but habitual concupiscence. But it should be understood that from a habit we are made apt (*habiles*) to something. Now, any agent can be apt in doing something, in two ways: first, from some form which inclines to this thing, as a heavy body is inclined downward by its form which it gets from its producer; second, from the removal of an impediment, just as wine flows out of broken rings which impeded its flowing, and a spurred horse runs quickly when the bridle, by which he was controlled, is broken.

Thus concupiscence can be called habitual in two ways: first, as any disposition or habit tending to the act of sense desire, for instance, in any man the habit of concupiscence may be caused by frequent, actual concupiscence, and this is not the way in which concupiscence is called original sin; second, habitual concupiscence may be understood as that inclination, or aptness, to the act of sense desire, which is due to the fact that the concupiscible power is not perfectly submissive to reason, when the bridle of original justice has been removed. In this way, original sin, materially speaking, is habitual concupiscence.

Nor yet does it follow, if habitual concupiscence positively understood lacks the formal nature of actual sin as caused by personal action, that, because of this, habitual concupiscence negatively understood has not the formal nature of original sin, inasmuch as it is caused by the act of the first parent. For, original sin is not called a sin for the same formal reason that actual sin is. Actual sin is situated in the voluntary act of some person, and so, what does not belong to such an act has not the formal nature of actual sin. But

original sin belongs to a person, according to the nature which he
has received from another, in his origin. Thus, every defect in the
nature of the offspring, found to be derived from the sin of the
first parent, possesses the formal nature of original sin, provided it
be in a subject capable of guilt. For, as Augustine says, in the first
book of the *Retractations* (cf. *De Nupt. et concup.*, I, c. 23), concupiscence is called a sin because it has been made by sin. (*De Malo*,
q. 4, art. 2, ad 4m.)

¶ TEXT SEVEN: *The Seven Capital Vices.* Those vices are called
capital that have ends which are chiefly capable of arousing appetition in themselves, so that other vices may be ordered in relation to these ends. It is to be considered that it is for the same reason
that one seeks a good or avoids the opposed evil. Thus, a glutton
seeks the pleasure of food and flees from the discomfort arising from
the absence of food. The same is true for the other vices.

Hence, the capital vices can be distinguished suitably according
to the differences of good and evil. Thus, wherever there appears
a special reason for desire or aversion, there is one capital vice distinct from the others. So, it must be considered that the good attracts the appetite to itself, according to a proper principle, but it
is according to a special principle considered in relation to this
kind of good that the appetite flees from such a good. Hence, the
capital sins must be considered according to these special principles, rather than according to those ordered to the seeking of a
good.

Now, the good for man is threefold: the good of the soul, the
good of the body, and the good of exterior things. So, to the good
of the soul, which is a good pictured in the imagination, such as
the excellence of honor and glory, *pride*, or vainglory, is directed.
To the good of the body, which pertains to the preservation of the
individual, such as food, *gluttony* is directed; while to the good of
the body, which pertains to the conservation of the species, such as
sexual indulgence, *luxury* [lust] belongs. *Avarice* refers to the
good in external things.

Now, a good may be avoided because it is an impediment to

some other good which is inordinately desired. In regard to such a good, insofar as it is an impediment, the appetite has a double movement: that of flight, and that of attack. As to the movement of flight, two capital vices may arise, depending on whether the impediment of the desired good is considered in oneself, or in another person. Within oneself, a spiritual good may prevent rest or bodily pleasure, and in this case there is *sloth*, which is nothing but a sorrow concerning some spiritual good, insofar as it is an impediment to the good of the body. In another person, the good of the other may impede one's own excellence; and in this case there is *envy*, which is sorrow concerning the good of another person. *Anger*, however, means rising up to attack such a good. (*De Malo*, q. 8, art. 1,c, in med.)

Recommended Readings

Thomas Aquinas, St., *Summa Theologiae*, I–II, qq. 49–67 (in *Basic Writings*, ed. Pegis, II, 366–526).

Bourke, "Habitus in the Thomistic Metaphysics of Potency and Act," *Essays in Thomism*, pp. 101–109.

Brennan, Sr. R. Emmanuella, *The Intellectual Virtues*, pp. 77–110.

Cronin, *Science of Ethics*, I, 593–632.

Garrigou-Lagrange, *Christian Perfection and Contemplation* (St. Louis, 1937).

Gilson, *Moral Values and the Moral Life*, pp. 135–150.

Klubertanz, "The Unity of Human Activity," *The Modern Schoolman*, XXVII (1950) 75–85.

ADVANCED READINGS

Bernard, "Renseignements Techniques (La Vertu)" in S. Thomas d'Aquin, *Somme Théologique*, I–II, qq. 49–60; qq. 61–70 (Paris, 1933) t. I, pp. 381–460; t. II, pp. 397–486.

Chenu, "La surnaturalisation des vertus," *Bulletin Thomiste*, IX (1932) 93 *–96.*

Lottin, *Principes de Morale*, I, 268–276, 309–315; II, 201–211.

Sertillanges, *La philosophie morale de s. Thomas*, pp. 115–156.

Wittmann, *Die Ethik des hl. Thomas von Aquin*, pp. 217–317.

Topics for Assignment

1. How Moral Virtues Help a Man to Live Well
2. Why There Are Four Cardinal Virtues
3. The Supernatural Does Not Destroy the Natural but Builds on It
4. Charity as Friendship of Man toward God
5. How to Get Rid of Bad Moral Habits

Part Two

ETHICAL PROBLEMS

INTRODUCTION TO PART TWO

Ethical theory studies the broad, universal principles of moral right and wrong. There is need of a more detailed investigation of typical moral problems which come up in the everyday life of man. It is not the purpose of this course to solve the actual moral problems of the student. No science can do that, because these problems are concretely situated in a context of contingent circumstances varying somewhat with each individual case. Rather, the purpose of this course is to enable the student to acquire such skill in moral reasoning that he may, by his own further efforts, develop enough personal prudence to solve his own ethical problems properly.

The order of procedure in treating the problems of this course depends on the matter of the virtues. We shall discuss first the problems of prudence, temperance, and fortitude (Chapter IX). Then we shall take up man's problems under justice (Chapters X–XIV). Following this, come questions associated with special careers, conditions, or types of life (Chapter XV). Finally, because it is not enough for man to lead a *naturally* good life, for this will not adequately prepare him for a supernatural, ultimate end, we shall briefly study the problems connected with the practice of the theological virtues: faith, hope, and charity (Chapter XVI).

In the following passage, St. Thomas Aquinas explains the content and arrangement of this advanced course in moral science:

After the general consideration of the virtues and vices, and other things pertaining to moral matters, it is necessary to consider singular problems in a special way. For, universal statements about moral problems are not very useful, since actions go on in the area of particulars.

Now, anything connected with moral matters may be considered in a special way, from two points of view. In one way, from the aspect of the moral matter itself; thus we may think of this virtue or that vice. In another way, in relation to the special states of different men, we may, for instance, consider those who come under someone's authority and prelates, or the followers of the active and the contemplative life, or whatever other differences there are among men. Therefore, we shall first of all consider, in a special way, those things which pertain to the common state of all men; secondly, in a special way, those things which pertain to determinate states of life.

We should consider, in connection with the first, that if we have determined certain points above [*i.e.*, in general moral theory] concerning virtues, gifts, vices and precepts, a great deal more must be said about them now. For, he who wishes to treat, in an adequate way, the precept: "Thou shalt not commit adultery," must study, in regard to adultery, the kind of sin that it is, and how the knowledge of it depends on the knowledge of the virtue to which it is opposed. Therefore, the method of consideration will be more complete and more expeditious, if at the same time and in the same treatise consideration be given to the virtue and its corresponding gift, to the opposed vices, and to the affirmative or negative precepts.

This method of consideration will be suitable to the vices taken in their proper species, for it has been shown above that vices and sins are specifically diversified according to their matter or object, and not according to other distinctions of sins, for instance, of the heart, of the mouth, and of deeds, or according to weakness, ignorance, and malice, and other differences of this kind. It is the same matter in regard to which a virtue operates rightly, and in regard to which the opposed vices recede from rectitude.

When the whole matter of morals is thus reduced to the consideration of the virtues, all the virtues are to be reduced further, to seven: three of these are the theological, which must be treated first; and the other four are cardinal, and they will be treated afterwards. One of the intellectual virtues is prudence, and it is included and numbered among the cardinal virtues. But art does not pertain to moral science, which is concerned with things that can be done, since art is right reason in regard to things which can be made, as has been said above. And the other three intellectual virtues, wisdom, understanding, and science, have the same names as some of the Gifts of the Holy Spirit; hence, consideration will be given them at the same time that the Gifts corresponding to the virtues are being considered. The other moral virtues all reduce in some way to the cardinal virtues, as appears from what has been said above; hence, in the consideration of each cardinal virtue, all the virtues pertaining in any way to it, and the opposed vices, will also be considered. And in this way nothing will be overlooked in the field of morals.[1]

[1] *Summa Theologiae*, II–II, Prolog.

IX · PROBLEMS WITHIN THE INDIVIDUAL AGENT

We are concerned, in this chapter, with the various moral problems which do not necessarily entail actions in regard to other persons but which have to do with private and personal goodness. A little reflection will reveal that a man will have some moral problems, even if he is living apart from other people. So also, when he lives in association with others, he will undergo certain experiences which may not directly affect his associates but which will be of much moral importance.

These private and personal moral questions may be reduced to three general types: the use of the practical intellect, the feeling of certain movements of concupiscence, and the feeling of certain movements of irascibility. When we think about practical matters, we do so more or less reasonably. We shall discuss some of the aspects of right practical reasoning, in the first part of this chapter, in connection with the virtue of *prudence*. It will not be necessary to take up the question of *willing* what is good for oneself, for a person always tends to do that naturally and necessarily. The later chapters in this Part will be devoted to the many problems of willing what is good to other persons.

Another area in which we find personal moral difficulties is that of the passions, or emotions. Sometimes, we allow ourselves *to feel* in unreasonable ways, without necessarily translating these feelings into overt actions. This sort of problem has much to do with "peace of mind," on which so much has been written in recent years. Some of these emotional problems center in the control of our simple desires and aversions for sensible goods and evils. We shall treat these problems in connection with the virtue of *temperance*.

Thirdly, there are some moral problems associated with those emergency passions by which we feel, or react affectively, in regard to the obstacles, or hardships, which sensible objects sometimes present. Here, the usual human tendency is to feel a certain discouragement. What is ordinarily needed is a certain stiffening of our affective responses, so that we may not be overcome by these threats to our well-being. This is the sort of problem which will be considered under the heading of *fortitude*.

Prudence and Man's Moral Problems

In ethical theory, we have seen that prudence is a habit of the practical intellect enabling man to reason rightly about matters of moral action. It is an intellectual virtue because it is developed as a special quality, or skill, permanently disposing its possessor *to know* a definite kind of subject matter (things to be done and things to be avoided). It is a moral virtue because it goes beyond mere knowledge; it carries over into the sphere of moral actions, directing and guiding its possessor in *reasonable activities*. The process of practical reasoning, from universal rules of good behavior to a definite decision that this kind of act should be done by *me*, here and now, is complex and difficult for an untrained intellect. Each concrete moral problem is somewhat different from every other problem. The many variable circumstances peculiar to each new problem make it hard to think of the whole action as a unit, and so decide, for or against, its performance. Practice in right practical reasoning strengthens and perfects the human intellect so that it eventually comes to make moral decisions promptly, accurately, and with some ease. The prudent man is possessed of this special skill which is prudence. It is the root and source of all the other moral virtues, because good action in any area must stem from good thinking in the moral agent.[1]

· The general nature of the virtue of prudence has been treated in Part One.[2] We must now examine in greater detail the various

---

[1] *S.T.*, I–II, 57, 4–6; in Pegis, *Basic Writings of St. Thomas*, II, 434–439.

[2] As a review, the student might read: *S.T.*, I, 22, 1,c; in *Basic Writings*, I, 229–230; see also, II–II, 48, 1,c. An English version of the *Secunda Secundae* is to

"parts" of this virtue. Since the same terminology will be used later, in discussing the other moral virtues, we may note here the general meaning of the "parts" of any virtue. In thomistic usage, the component factors into which any virtue may be divided by internal analysis are called *integral parts*. (Thus, the integral parts of any apple are the seeds, pulp, juice, skin, and so on. None of these parts is an apple but they combine to constitute one apple.) Secondly, the different species, or types, of the same general kind of virtue, are called the *subjective parts* of this virtue. (Thus, winesaps, Jonathans, Delicious, and crabapples would be subjective parts of the fruit which is generally called an apple. Note that each of these subjective parts is a complete apple; so too, each subjective part of a virtue is a complete virtue.) Finally, the various virtues which partially resemble a principal virtue, without fully realizing the definition of the major virtue, are called *potential parts*, or simply associated virtues. (Thus, the "golden apples" of the ancient world, which were tomatoes, and the "apples of the earth" of the French, which are potatoes, are potential parts of this fruit. Note here that each of these examples is a complete "fruit" but not exactly a species of apple. Potential parts of a virtue are themselves virtues but not exactly true species within the strict genus of the major virtue.)

Of the eight integral parts of prudence,[3] five are factors dealing with the *knowing* of the moral problem, in its concrete circumstances. *Practical memory* (*memoria*) is the ability to retain and profit by past moral experience. *Practical understanding* (*intelligentia*) is the developed capacity to grasp the moral significance of a concrete situation. *Docility* (*docilitas*) is the ability to take good moral advice and instructions from other people. *Practical ingenuity* (*solertia*) is the ability to make a right estimate, or reasonably quick judgment, of a moral situation by one's own effort. The fifth integral part, *practical reasoning* (*ratio*), is most essential to the habit of prudence; it consists in the capacity to apply universal principles and particular knowledge to the singular moral problem by making a right inference.

be found in the translation made by the English Dominicans: *The Summa Theologica* (London, 1912–1926).

    [3] *S.T.*, II–II, 49, arts. 1–8.

Where the preceding five parts are primarily cognitive, the remaining three are preceptive; they deal with the *ordering*, or *prescribing*, of the right action. Thus, *foresight* (*providentia*) is needed to order, or direct in advance, what is to be done, so that it will actually be suited to the attainment of the end in view. *Circumspection* (*circumspectio*) is the ability to prescribe an action, in the given circumstances which now obtain, which is reasonable under these circumstances. The final part is *carefulness* (*cautio*) and it consists in the ability to order the performance of those acts only, which are (for the most part) productive of morally good results. Where there is some possibility of morally bad results as well as good ones, one may follow the rule [4] that an action may be done, if one knows that *in most cases* it is not productive of bad results. Notice that this distinguishes St. Thomas' moral position from extreme tutiorism, which holds that an action may never be done if it is suspected to be productive (even in rare cases) of bad results.

The subjective parts of prudence are really the different species of this virtue. Five kinds of prudence may be distinguished, with reference to five different fields in which moral problems are found. *Individual prudence* (*monastica*) is the habit of reasoning rightly about one's own personal problems, of a private nature.[5] This skill is needed by all moral agents, whatever kind of life they may choose to live. The remaining forms of prudence are needed only by certain people who may have to think in terms of the common welfare of a group of persons, in addition to the private good of their own personal lives. *Domestic prudence* (*oeconomica*) is a skill in reasoning about the problems encountered in family life. Many of these difficulties are associated with the provision of the necessities of home life; hence, the original name of this virtue, *economics*, is used in modern times to designate the study of the management of wealth and associated matters. Parents require domestic prudence in order to direct the activities of the family group; children need this virtue in order to cooperate reasonably with parental direction.[6] *Regnant prudence* is the skill in practical reasoning which should be possessed by the leaders of a political community, *i.e.*, a city,

[4] *S.T.*, II–II, 49, 8, ad 3m.   [5] *S.T.*, II–II, 48, 1,c.   [6] *S.T.*, II–II, 50, 3,c.

state, or nation. By extension, a somewhat similar virtue would be required in the directors of any organized group of people, larger than the family. A school, a religious community, a business organization, and other such societies, must have leaders who will think in terms of the common good of all members.[7] *Political prudence* (*politica*) is a similar virtue needed by any citizen, or ordinary member of a society, so that he may think well concerning those problems which are the concern of the group as a whole. Such members should be reasoning and free men who will be prepared to work in an intelligent manner under the direction of their leaders. Obviously, this virtue is essential in a democracy.[8] *Military prudence* (*militaris*) is a fifth type and is concerned with thinking of the preservation of the common good by force of arms. Principally needed by military commanders, who must issue reasonable orders, this habit is also necessary, secondarily, to those who are to carry out these orders.[9]

It is clear that military prudence is only required by those engaged in a special kind of work. Other special types of prudence might be similarly distinguished: those of a physician, a lawyer, a businessman, and so on. St. Thomas does not discuss such kinds, for they are not entirely distinct from individual prudence. Military prudence is distinct, for the protection of the common good by force is not a private problem.

In turning to the examination of the *potential parts* of prudence, it will be helpful to recall the three special acts of the virtue of prudence. The prudent man should be able, first of all, *to deliberate well* about moral matters. This act of good counsel (*consiliari*) deals with the preliminary consideration of the moral propriety of various means in relation to a given end. It is an act of discursive reasoning. The second act of prudence is *to judge practically* (*judicare*). This is the cognitive termination of the previous process of deliberation. In the act of judging, one comes to a final practical decision about what is to be done. What makes prudence a truly moral virtue is the third act: *to order* that the action be done (or omitted) and that this be carried out in a reasonable way. This is the function of

[7] *Ibid.*, art. 1,c.   [8] *Ibid.*, art. 2,c.   [9] *Ibid.*, art. 4,c.

preception (*praecipere*) in which right reason is brought to bear on the action itself. Combined with the active and moving force of will, the practical intellect issues the command (*imperium*) that prescribes the very doing, or not doing, of something.[10]

Now, any habit of the practical intellect which enables the agent to do *all three* of these acts well will be an example of real prudence. But it is evident that some people develop an ability to do some of these actions better than others. A person might excel in the function of deliberation, or in that of practical judgment, yet fail miserably in the final act of ordering himself to do good actions. We know that many people can give prudent advice to others, yet they cannot manage their own actions well. Thus, we see that there are certain habits of the practical intellect which govern good deliberation and good judgment but which do not achieve the full stature of prudence, because they do not reach to the critical act of actually prescribing that right actions be done. Of course, if one has the habitual ability to order one's own actions reasonably this means that one is possessed of true prudence.

The *potential parts* of prudence are three virtues which perfect the agent in regard to the performance of either of the first two acts of prudence, without extending to the commanding of right action. We may give the name *good counsel* (*eubulia*) to the habit of deliberating well before making a practical judgment. This is simply skill in making an adequate rational investigation of the various moral aspects of a proposed action. Good counsel is an acquired habit of the practical intellect; it is useful; it is like prudence; but it lacks something of the full essence of the cardinal virtue.

The other two potential parts, or associated virtues, deal with the act of practical judgment. Some people develop a special facility in making good moral judgments *about ordinary moral problems*. As long as their difficulties have nothing unusual about them, as long as the regular rules of conduct apply, they know what to do. Let us call this habit of the practical intellect: *practical decisiveness*. In Latin it is called *synesis*, which simply means good judgment, or good common sense. The possessor of practical decisiveness does

[10] *S.T.*, I–II, 57, 6,c; in Pegis, *Basic Writings*, II, 438–439.

not hesitate to make a moral decision, when the circumstances demand it, and he makes a good decision.[11] However, we rather frequently face moral difficulties which do not fit into the ordinary pattern; they are unusual in the sense that they would be badly handled if they were decided on the basis of a strict and rigorous application of the ordinary moral rules. It is a special attribute of an intelligent moral agent to be able to see when an exception should be made. A law is a universal proposition; it cannot prescribe for all possible contingencies. Our knowledge of moral laws is imperfect. So, it is reasonable, at times, to make unusual decisions when faced with exceptional problems. This habit may be termed: *practical sagacity*. The Latin name for it is *gnome*.[12] To clarify this point, let us consider a classic example. Ordinarily, it is right to return a thing left in our charge by its proper owner, when he asks for it. But, if an insane or intoxicated man demands that we return his gun, it is more prudent to break this rule, because of these exceptional circumstances. What *gnome* enables one to do, is to think in terms of the spirit of the law, rather than the letter. We shall see that there is a kind of justice, namely *equity*, which applies to exceptional cases.

Special Difficulties in the Field of Prudence

We can more easily understand the kind of problems which come into the area of practical reasoning, if we consider certain bad habits, or vices. Natural virtues always observe a mean, or middle position, between extremes of excess and defect. Both extremes are vicious, and it is often possible to do too much or too little, in several different ways. That is why more vices than virtues are possible. The general name for vices opposed to prudence is *imprudence*.

Four bad habits, which are *defects of prudence*, may first be considered. These are all habitual tendencies to give too little thought to moral problems. *Precipitation* is the bad habit of omitting some of the necessary steps in the process of moral deliberation, or counselling. In good moral reasoning, one must remember past experience, understand the present situation, make an estimate of future

---

[11] *S.T.*, II–II, 51, 1–3,c.   [12] *Ibid.*, art. 4,c.

consequences, bring all these together into an orderly sequence of inference. To rush through to a moral decision by omitting any essential steps in the process of deliberation is to be imprudent by way of precipitation.[13] A second vice is *inconsideration*, which is the habitual failure to make good practical judgments. This is a defect in relation to the second act of prudence, *i.e.*, the act of good judgment.[14] Thirdly, there is a vice called *inconstancy*, which consists in the habit of failing to carry through a moral act to its proper conclusion. This is a defect of the practical intellect in regard to the third act of prudence, *i.e.*, that of ordering the action to be done. Inconstancy is a vice of the practical intellect but it is due to some interference on the part of other powers of the agent, chiefly from the passions, in the final stage of prudent thinking. The intellect should remain constant in pointing out right action; when it gives in to some other motivation, it is inconstant.[15] There is still another possibility of habitual failure, on the part of the practical intellect, to order right action. This will be the case in which the will habitually fails to make the necessary choice promptly and, as a result, the intellect permits a delay or omission of the inner act of preception. The name of this fourth vice is *negligence* (thought to have been derived from *nec-eligens:* not choosing). It amounts to a lack of promptness in directing one's actions, because of inertia in the will.[16] Notice that inconstancy is due to the positive influence of the appetites upon the practical intellect, whereas negligence arises from a negative influence of the will.

As a matter of fact, the first three of these vices of the intellect indicate ways in which man's reason may be swayed by his passions. That is why St. Thomas related the foregoing bad habits to over-indulgence in sense pleasures. He pointed out at some length the possible influence of lust (*luxuria*) on the work of the practical intellect. The person who experiences great difficulty in thinking out his moral problems may need to stop and ask himself whether repeated acts of intemperance (to be discussed later in this chapter) are contributing to his inability to reason well.[17]

---

[13] *S.T.*, II–II, 53, 3,c. [14] *Ibid.*, 4,c. [15] *Ibid.*, 5,c.
[16] *S.T.*, II–II, 54, 2 et 3,c. [17] *S.T.*, II–II, 53, 6,c.

We may next examine three forms of *excessive prudence*. While we cannot be too prudent in regard to important moral questions, it is clear that we may give too much thought to matters which are relatively unimportant, or which are directed to immoral ends. *Prudence of the flesh* is a habitual disorder in moral reasoning, due to excessive consideration of some good of one's own body (beauty, strength, sensual pleasure). True prudence deals with the rational direction of action in view of the attainment of ultimate happiness. Some mistaken people may order their whole lives very carefully and cleverly toward some proximate end, treating it as if it were the ultimate purpose for man's existence. A man who devotes most of his thought to the development of rippling muscles and a perfect body, a woman who thinks only of the cultivation of personal beauty of body—these are examples of people possessed of this unfortunate vice.[18]

A second kind of excessive prudence is fittingly named *astuteness*. This is the vice of reasoning, or planning, to attain some end, whether morally good or bad, *by the use of improper means*. The astute person may achieve his purpose very cleverly. His end may even be good in itself. His ways of reaching this end are immoral. The successful thief, who steals in order to support his family decently, is astute but not prudent.[19]

The last of these vices is *solicitude for temporal things*. It consists in the habit of giving excessive consideration to the finite goods of this world. Other than the goods of the body (mentioned under prudence of the flesh) there are many external objects of desire (*e.g.*, wealth, fame, political power) which can be mistakenly regarded as the ultimate end of a person's life. It is possible to give too much thought to the acquisition of such things. One may also be overconcerned about the possibility of losing temporal goods.[20]

Here again, it may be noted how easily the practical intellect is led to distorted conclusions, if it permits itself to be moved from the rational consideration of moral rightness under the influence of the passions or emotions. Excessive ambition and misplaced hopes are powerful urges which tend to distort the work of reason. Avarice

---

[18] *S.T.*, II–II, 55, 1 et 2,c.   [19] *Ibid.*, 3,c.   [20] *Ibid.*, 6,c.

is a primary source of excessive prudence. Though a form of injustice, the vice of avarice impels its possessor to think too much about temporal possessions. Its cognitive resultant is a derangement of prudence.[21]

Temperance and Its Divisions

The impression is rather widespread that all moral virtues are qualities of the human will. The corollary of this opinion is that the development of a good character is simply a question of training the will. This point of view is not in keeping with the thomistic metaphysics of man. There are four psychic powers in man which can be perfected by morally good habits. We have seen how the various forms of prudence do this for the practical intellect. The three other potencies which can share in the performance of the moral act are the concupiscible, the irascible, and the intellectual appetites. The latter is what is called will. Each of these appetites can develop its specific virtue. In this part of the present chapter, we shall examine the manner in which the virtue of temperance may perfect the concupiscible appetite.

Let us recall that concupiscible appetite is that potency whereby man inclines toward, or away from, sensible objects which are known through sense perception. The movements of this appetite are the concupiscible passions. These are our feelings, emotions, or affections, in regard to sensibly attractive or repulsive aspects of physical things. We should be clear on this important point: the objects of sensory appetition are individual goods or evils; the objects of intellectual appetition (*i.e.*, of the will) are universal goods or evils. Unlike the irascible appetite which is aroused by sensible objects presenting some *difficulty* to the perceiver, the concupiscible is moved by objects which are *simply* attractive or repulsive.[22]

[21] *Ibid.*, 8,c.

[22] *S.T.*, 1, 81, 2,c; in Pegis, *Basic Writings*, I, 772–774. Students may review this matter in: Klubertanz, *Philosophy of Human Nature*, Unit IX; Brennan, *Thomistic Psychology*, pp. 147–168; or Baker, *Thomistic Theory of the Passions*, pp. 43–47.

The following are the six chief movements, or passions, of the con-cupiscible appetite:

Simple Sensible Good	*Simple Sensible Evil*
Love (amor) affective approval, or liking, of the good	*Hate* (odium) affective disapproval, or dislike, of the evil
Desire (desiderium) affective movement toward the good	*Aversion* (fuga, aversio) affective movement away from the evil
Joy (delectatio, gaudium) affective satisfaction in the attained good	*Sorrow* (dolor, tristia) affective displeasure in an attained evil

There is nothing essentially wrong, or immoral, about the under-going of any of these passions. Considered in themselves, the con-cupiscible passions are morally neutral; they may become morally good or bad by their assumption into voluntary action and by the addition of suitable or unsuitable circumstances. To desire food when it is needed by the living body, is morally good (unless there are other bad circumstances); to desire food when it is not needed at all, is irrational and morally bad. Clearly then, the good man must try to control his concupiscent emotions by following the directions of his reason. Reasoned passions are good passions. So, prudence is required here, as it is in every type of moral problem.

There is a special source of moral difficulties through concupis-cence: the concupiscible appetite in the morally undeveloped person does not take kindly to the rule of reason. Like a wild horse, it tends to kick over the traces and fight against the guidance of prac-tical reason. This anti-rational tendency of both sense appetites is explained in moral theology (as we have seen in ethical theory) as an effect of original sin on the whole human race. What the con-cupiscible potency needs, in the moral order, is to develop the ac-quired quality of tractability, docility, moderation. When this habit is gained, its passions become reasonable and useful to the general well-being of the moral agent. We should see that this habit of *moderation,* which is the virtue of temperance, is needed right in the concupiscible appetite, not in the will or any other power. Again to use Plato's comparison, it is the horse which needs the training, if it is wild, not the rider.[23]

[23] *S.T.,* II–II, 141, 3,c.

Temperance is the *good habit of the concupiscible appetite enabling it to be moderated by reason.*[24] Moderation, or reasonable self-restraint, is of the essence of this virtue. Of course, moderation applies to all the natural virtues. In a general way, this is true of the essential condition of each cardinal virtue; each contains a characteristic goodness which must be found in every virtuous act. Reasonableness (from prudence), moderation (from temperance), firmness (from fortitude), and a general rightness in view of a common end (from justice)—all four conditions are found in the exercise of any virtue. That is one reason why these four habits are cardinal, or principal, virtues; we can do nothing good without them.

However, temperance is a special virtue. It must have a definite type of problem to which it chiefly applies and by which it is formally differentiated from other types of virtue. The greatest moral difficulty, in the area of concupiscence, is found in the control of the passions aroused by the pleasures of the sense of touch. This somatic sense is most basic to the preservation of the individual and his species. There are animals which appear to lack all senses except that of touch. Man, in particular, is most vehemently and inordinately attracted by the pleasures of the act of reproduction and of the taking of food and drink. That is why temperance is most needed for the restraint of human tendencies toward sexual disorders, and immoderation in eating and drinking.[25] In a secondary way, other objects of the senses arouse passions requiring the use of temperance.

The concept of the golden mean is especially useful when applied to the problems of temperance. Every natural virtue is a habit of feeling or operating according to a middle position between excess and defect. If we consider eating, for a moment, we can understand that it is reasonable to avoid the use of too much food, and it is also reasonable to avoid the extreme of taking too little food. Examples of this *golden mean* are frequently taken from the area of temperance, because nearly everyone can see its application in that field. We may distinguish two *component feelings* (integral parts) which constitute the one habit of temperance:

Shame (*verecundia*) is a fear of that which is morally ugly (*turpis*)

[24] *S.T.*, II–II, 141, 1–8.   [25] *S.T.*, II–II, 141, 4,c.

and reprehensible. It is a passion, not a virtue, because the perfectly virtuous agent would not do anything from which he might fear the disapproval of other good people; however, shame is a good passion.[26]

Uprightness (*honestum*) is a love of the spiritually beautiful for its own sake. This is not identical with the modern meaning of honesty, which is usually associated with the notion of justice; *honestas* is a contrary to shame, for uprightness means an attraction to that which is morally beautiful (*decorum*) while shame means a repulsion from the morally ugly.[27]

To cultivate the virtue of temperance, then, one must feel the ugliness of the indecent and immoderate, and also feel the attractiveness of decency and moderation. These feelings are not virtues but they combine to constitute the cardinal virtue of temperance.

Three special types of sense object strongly attract the concupiscible appetite: the pleasures of eating, of drinking intoxicants, and of sex functions. Thus, three *species of temperance* (*i.e.*, subjective parts) are possible.

Abstinence is the good habit of desiring food in reasonable moderation. Absolute abstinence would mean complete nonuse of food; this is not reasonable for a living human being and is not a virtue. Refraining from the use of food for a time, or absolute abstinence from some particular kind of food, *for rational motives*, is the virtue.[28] *Fasting* (*jejunium*) is a special act of this virtue, provided it is done within reason; it is not virtuous to fast so much that one's health is seriously impaired, or to the extent that one is unable to fulfill his duties.[29]

Sobriety is the good habit of *desiring* intoxicating drinks in reasonable moderation. Excessive use of intoxicants disturbs the reasoning processes and is morally bad. Unlike the case of total abstinence from food, it is possible for most people to live well without intoxicants, so this virtue includes nonuse. In fact, some individuals may be so constituted that they are easily intoxicated; for them the mean is nonuse. But it is not wrong to take intoxicants moderately

---

[26] *S.T.*, II–II, 144, 1,c.   [27] *S.T.*, II–II, 145, 4,c.
[28] *S.T.*, II–II, 146, 1–2,c.   [29] *Ibid.*, q. 147, 1,c, et ad 2m.

(unless there be some other bad circumstance). Certain people have a particular obligation to remain sober, children obviously. St. Thomas thought that women should stay away from wine, because "they have not enough strength of mind to resist concupiscence," also men whose work requires clear thinking: teachers, bishops, and priests, and rulers of states.[30]

Chastity is the good habit of moderation in desiring the use of the faculty of sexual reproduction; "that one use bodily members moderately, according to the judgment of reason and the choice of will, pertains to chastity." Chastity does not mean complete abstinence from the reproductive act; this function is good when rationally regulated.[31]

Associated with chastity, are two other special virtues: *Modest reserve (pudicitia)* is rational moderation in regard to certain actions associated with the function of reproduction. These associated conditions of sexual pleasure include kissing and caresses. This is not precisely a separate virtue, but is chastity in relation to special circumstances.[32] *Virginity* is perpetual abstinence from the act of reproduction and its associated pleasures; materially, a wholeness of body; formally, an integrity of mind which is not broken by any thought of sexual pleasure.[33] For all human beings to practice virginity would not be for the good of the species, but there is little danger of this. For certain people devoted to the life of religious contemplation, virginity is a virtue of perfection. It does not mean abstinence from all sensible pleasure, only from that associated with sexual functions.[34] As a state of life, virginity is superior to chaste married life, just as the life of contemplation is superior to that of action.

It is to be remembered that all these species of temperance signify a moderation in the psychic movement of the appetite in relation to its object, and are not primarily concerned with the external operation which involves the physical use of this object. The temperate person is one who *feels* the attraction of sensible goods and the repulsion of sensible evils, in moderation. Because positive laws govern external operations, overt acts, it is not always possible to produce

[30] *Ibid.*, q. 149, 2,c, et 4,c.   [31] *Ibid.*, q. 151, 1–3,c.
[32] *Ibid.*, q. 151, 4,c.   [33] *Ibid.*, q. 152, 1,c.   [34] *Ibid.*, 4,c.

the habit of temperance in people by legislating against intemperance. Of course, where public acts of intemperance become offensive or harmful to other people, it is quite justifiable to curb such offenses by positive laws, for intemperate operations are also potential offenses against justice and the common good.

Many good habits do not exhibit the complete essence of temperance, but share somewhat in the nature of moderation or in the control of concupiscence. They are, then, *potential parts* of temperance. Of course, all these parts are virtues.

Continence (*continentia*) is a good habit of the human will enabling its possessor to follow the rule of reason, even when he is strongly moved by passions arising from the pleasures of touch (eating, drinking, sexual acts). This differs from temperance in that the temperate man has no great disturbance in his concupiscible appetite; the continent man is passionate but by force of will he controls the passions which he does feel. Continence is not as perfect a virtue as temperance.[35]

Gentleness (*mansuetudo*, *clementia*) is a good habit of the will enabling one to control the passion of anger. Actually this is a double virtue: *mansuetudo* is a sort of sweetness or mildness of disposition moderating the feeling of anger within one; *clementia* is concerned with the moderating of the external operations issuing from anger, such as the giving of punishment, and is also a part of justice.[36]

Modesty (*modestia*) is a generic good habit of moderation in regard to objects of desire, other than those of the sense of touch.[37] Modesty includes within its matter several subordinate virtues: *Humility* is a good habit of will restraining one's tendency to immoderation in the desire of higher things, or of excellence (honors, for instance); not all desire of honor is bad. The virtue of *magnanimity* governs the reasonable pursuit of honors; humility controls the unreasonable craving to be outstanding.[38] *Moderation in study* (*studiositas*) is a good habit of will controlling the unreasonable desire for knowledge (curiosity). This is *not* a habit of studying well, in the sense of knowing how to do it, or of applying one-

[35] *S.T.*, II–II, 155, a. 1–4.
[36] *Ibid.*, q. 157, a. 1–4.
[37] *Ibid.*, q. 160, 1,c.
[38] *Ibid.*, q. 161, 1,c.

self to the task; it is simply self-control in regard to an excessive and unreasonable pursuit of knowledge.[39] *Moderation in the exterior actions of the body* (*modestia in exterioribus motibus corporis*) is a good habit of acting moderately either at work or at play. St Thomas had a genial interest in the subordinate virtue of good play habits (*eutrapelia*); even in his lighter moments a man should behave reasonably. It is possible to be inclined to play too much and also too little; virtue lies in the mean.[40] *Moderation in the adornment of the body* (*modestia circa exteriorem ornatum*) is a good habit controlling the tendency to excess or defect in the wearing of clothes, ornaments, and other bodily decorations. Local custom, if at all reasonable, should be followed in these matters. Women may dress attractively to please their husbands, or prospective husbands, but those who do not have or want husbands should not dress so as to attract men. Of course, it is not seriously immoral to wear finery because of "lightness of mind or vanity"; rouging or whitening the face is a form of deception, permissible to those who are terrifyingly ugly or seriously ill.[41] A woman with no hair should wear something on her head, for instance. *Simplicity* (not wanting too fine clothes) and *being satisfied with what one normally has* (*per-se-sufficientia*) are minor parts of this virtue.

Liberality (*liberalitas*) is a good habit of moderation in the desire for wealth; it belongs in the concupiscible appetite. Liberality is the mean between miserliness and profligacy. When it is a question of the reasonable use of money for the good of others, liberality is a part of justice.[42]

Affability (*amicitia, affabilitas*) is a good habit of feeling kindly to others; the external manifestation of such social agreeableness is a part of justice.[43]

Veracity (*veritas*) is a good habit of wanting to signify one's true thoughts to others and to appear to others as one is. Externally manifested, it is a part of justice.[44]

It will be seen how extensive is the field of the moral problems re-

[39] *Ibid.*, q. 167, a. 1–2.   [40] *Ibid.*, q. 168, a. 1–4.   [41] *Ibid.*, q. 169, a. 1–2.
[42] *S.T.*, I–II, 60, 5,c; II–II, 157, 1,c; on the relation of these virtues to justice, see *infra*, Chap. X.
[43] *S.T.*, I–II, 60, 5,c.   [44] *Ibid.*

quiring reasonable moderation. Aristotle distinguished ten kinds of virtue having to do with the passions [45] and most of these were concerned with the moderating of various forms of concupiscence. It is well to realize how many questions of *personal morality* do not directly involve other people, and so are not controllable by positive law. There are more problems in ethics than in jurisprudence.

Problems of Temperance and Associated Virtues

It is by studying the various vices connected with the field of temperance that we may get some notion of the vast area of moral difficulties arising from the concupiscible passions. We shall examine the major cases of such vice.

¶ *Vices Opposed to the Cardinal Virtue of Temperance.* Insensibility (*insensibilitas*) is a general disinterest in sensible goods needed for the reasonable care of the health, strength and welfare of the individual or of the race of men; this is the *defect* of temperance.[46] *Intemperance* (*intemperantia*) is a habitual superfluity of concupiscence, especially in regard to those tactual pleasures which are not directed to the natural good of the individual or of the human species; this is *excess* in regard to the objects of temperance.[47]

¶ *Opposed to Abstinence.* Gluttony (*gula*) is the habit or act of inordinately desiring food; Molière's epigram, "one should eat to live, not live to eat," expresses the situation very well.[48]

¶ *Opposed to Sobriety.* Drunkenness (*ebrietas*) is the habit or act of inordinately desiring intoxicating drinks. Intoxication is not blameworthy, if it happens by chance, without negligence. It should be noted that one is not responsible for a materially immoral act performed while intoxicated, if one has not voluntarily become intoxicated; but if one is voluntarily intoxicated, immoral actions done in that condition are culpable, though not as much so as if done with full use of reason.[49]

[45] *Ethic. Nic.*, II, 7; 1107a32.
[46] *S.T.*, II–II, 142, 1,c.
[47] *Ibid.*, art. 2,c.
[48] *Ibid.*, q. 148, 1–6.
[49] *Ibid.*, q. 150, a. 1, and 4.

¶ *Opposed to Chastity.* *Luxury* (*luxuria*) is the habit or act of un-reasonable sexual indulgence. Subordinate vices growing out of lux-ury are: loss of mental capacity, inconsideration, precipitation, in-constancy, selfishness, hatred of God, concern for this life, and horror of the future life.[50]

Many species of luxury are discussed by St. Thomas. It will be sufficient to consider four. *Fornication* (promiscuous sexual relations between two unmarried people) is immoral because it renders rea-sonable and proper care of offspring impossible. The practice of artificial contraception is an abuse of the reproductive faculty, be-cause the act is performed in such a way as to render impossible the attainment of its natural purpose: the procreation of children. *Adul-tery* (illicit sexual relationship in which at least one participating party is married to a third person) adds to the evil of simple fornica-tion, an act of injustice to the aggrieved third person, and an act of irreligion, where marriage has been solemnized by the sacrament of matrimony. *Incest* (illicit sexual relationship between close relatives, bound to each other by blood or spiritual ties) is wrong because of natural horror of such actions, because of disturbance of good order within the home, and because it prevents the making of friends out-side the home circle, which is useful in promoting the common good. *Sacrilege* (sexual abuse of a person dedicated to the religious life) adds a special act of irreligion to the immorality of intemperance.[51]

¶ *Opposed to Continence.* *Incontinence* is a lack of reasonable control over strong concupiscible passions. The incontinent man is a weak man who is responsible for his own weakness. Unike the in-temperate man who wills to enjoy sensual pleasure, the incontinent man fights a losing battle against his passions. One may also be in-continent in regard to the passion of anger.[52]

¶ *Opposed to Gentleness.* *Anger* is an immoderate movement of the irascible appetite, not justified by circumstances; moderate anger directed against some evil object is not vicious.[53] *Cruelty* is a love for the giving of excessive punishment. This covers acts of torture and other forms of brutality; external acts of cruelty are acts against

[50] *Ibid.*, q. 153, a. 1–2, and 5,c.   [51] *Ibid.*, q. 154, arts. 2, 8, 9, 10,c.
[52] *Ibid.*, q. 156, 1 and 4,c.   [53] *Ibid.*, q. 158, 1 and 3,c.

justice; here we deal with the sadistic *desire* to punish too severely.[54]

¶ *Opposed to Humility.* *Pride* is the habit or act of desiring what is quite above or beyond one's status or powers; this involves an inordination between the appetites and their objects; the subject of pride is the concupiscible, plus the irascible, plus the intellectual appetite. This vice of pride is the principle from which all sins flow, in some sense.[55]

¶ *Opposed to Moderation in Study.* *Curiosity* is an inordinate desire of knowledge, either of the senses or of the intellect; this will be intended for some improper use.[56]

¶ *Opposed to Moderation in Play.* Here we find two possible forms of vice for which there are no established names. They consist simply in *habitual excess* or *habitual defect* in the desire for amusement.[57]

¶ *Opposed to External Modesty.* Here again, we may simply distinguish between *habitual excess* and *habitual defect* in the desire for adornments of the body.[58]

It should be noted, finally, that offenses against liberality, affability, and veracity, will be discussed later (in Chapter X) in connection with justice. The reason for this is that these vices are nearly always translated into external operations involving other persons. However, feelings of illiberality, unfriendliness, and the desire to deceive others are in themselves opposed to rational moderation and are to be avoided.

Fortitude and Its Divisions

Some of the sensible objects and situations which man must face in the course of his life present special difficulties. These are of the nature of threats to his physical well-being. Such difficulties, known through sense perception, cause emotional movements in the soul of man. These movements can be the source of much moral disturbance. The irascible appetite is the power whereby man may feel and

---

[54] *Ibid.*, q. 159, a. 1–2,c.   [55] *Ibid.*, q. 162, a. 1–3,c.
[56] *Ibid.*, q. 167, a. 1–2,c.   [57] *Ibid.*, q. 168, 3–4,c.   [58] *Ibid.*, q. 169, 1–2,c.

react affectively to the impact of these sensible hardships. What is recognized in modern psychology and psychiatry as a maladjustment of personality is frequently, in thomistic language, a distortion of the natural passions of the irascible appetite. Excessive and ill-founded fears, unreasonable daring, uncontrolled anger—all these give rise not only to psychological but also to moral problems. Just as concupiscence, when not moderated by reason, tends to disturb man's moral character, so does irascibility, uncontrolled by reason, reduce the moral agent to the activity level of the beast.[59]

The five chief passions of the irascible appetite may be presented in the following summary. It is to be noted that the fifth, *anger*, is related both to good and evil sense objects.

Difficult Sense Good	*Difficult Sense Evil*
Hope (spes) feeling that an absent good may be attained in spite of difficulty	*Audacity* or *daring* (audacia) feeling that an absent evil may be overcome in spite of difficulty
Despair (desperatio) feeling that the difficulties associated with the attainment of an absent good cannot be overcome	*Fear* (timor) feeling that the difficulty of avoiding an absent or present evil is too great to be overcome

Anger (ira) feeling which is concerned with both good and evil, at the same time; by this emotion with a composite object, one is impelled to the *good* of overcoming some difficulty, and one reacts affectively to the *evil* which is the possession of some harmful object, or the non-attainment of some difficult good

These irascible passions are morally neutral in themselves. When they are voluntarily entertained and are accompanied by unsuitable circumstances, they become unreasonable and immoral. Morally speaking, the "difficulty" associated with an object of irascibility consists in some element of physical danger, real or apparent. This does not include the concept of spiritual danger, such as the loss of ultimate happiness, for such immaterial danger is not a sense object. The danger of death is like no other sensible threat. It gives rise to two chief irascible passions. *Fear* is a passion which is morally significant, since it may render the agent completely involuntary. Ac-

---

[59] *S.T.*, I, 81, 2 et 3,c; in Pegis, *Basic Writings*, I, 772–776. See the references to Klubertanz, Brennan, and Baker, in footnote [22] of this chapter.

tion done in such a condition is not a moral problem. More frequently, fear makes the agent partly involuntary; he is weakened by this passion and what he needs is a certain strength and firmness in the irascible power. Fortitude is the name of this habit of irascible firmness.[60] The second passion which may be felt in the presence of physical danger is *daring*. This movement of the appetite also requires a firmness, so that it may be maintained at a reasonable level. The same virtue, fortitude, regulates the movement of daring.[61] Actually, fortitude is a mean between the tendency to excessive fear (which implies a defect of daring) and excessive daring (which implies a defect of fear).

Fortitude (courage, bravery) may be defined as the good habit of the irascible appetite enabling its possessor to suffer and to attack physical danger, firmly and reasonably.[62] It is to be emphasized that firmness is of the essence of fortitude; the word means strength, literally. A man must be prepared to remain calm and reasonable, even in a situation in which his life appears to be in danger.[63]

Two acts of the virtue of fortitude are possible. They should be clearly distinguished from the two original passions of the irascible appetite. All persons experience fear and daring. Only the morally developed perform the acts of fortitude. The first act is *to suffer danger reasonably* (*sustinere*). It is not possible for man to avoid all sufferings and physical threats. Even in undergoing physical suffering, he must be a man; use his rational powers to stand up firmly to danger. The second act is *to attack such dangers reasonably* (*aggredi*). Passive resistance is not always enough. The good moral agent is required to use all reasonable means at his disposal to avoid and overcome dangers, particularly that of death.[64]

While sufferance is the principal act of fortitude, because it is always possible where fortitude is, nevertheless thomistic ethics is not in agreement with the notion of Mahatma Gandhi, that passive resistance is the only real bravery. Within reason, one should be permitted to use any morally good means to attain ultimate happiness. Physical force can be such a means for the avoidance of danger,

[60] *S.T.*, II–II, 125, arts. 1–4,c. [61] *Ibid.*, q. 127, arts. 1–2,c.
[62] *Ibid.*, q. 123, 2,c. [63] *Ibid.*, q. 124, 2, *ad primum*.
[64] *Ibid.*, q. 123, 6,c.

and so for the continuation of one's efforts toward happiness. It is reasonable and virtuous to use such force in many cases of actual danger. This is not to deny that it may be a mark of superior virtue to refrain from violence under certain conditions where it is possible to use it.

Nor should we conclude that the brave man suffers no fear. It is excessive, unreasonable fear which is opposed to the virtue of fortitude. We shall see that it is a vice to feel no fear in a situation which actually threatens one's life. Controlled fear is a natural protective device, calling forth special effort and strength in the well-developed moral personality.

Not all the movements of the irascible appetite come under the virtue of fortitude to the same extent. Anger requires a kind of temperance (i.e., gentleness) as its moderating virtue. Then, a moderated anger can be a condition or basis for the acts of fortitude. Not all anger is morally bad; only that which is unreasonable.[65]

What we are discussing at present are the natural moral virtues; fortitude, as a perfection acquired by man's own efforts in his irascible appetite, is one of these. All four of the cardinal virtues may be engendered in the human soul, in a more perfect way, by the action of divine grace. Such moral virtues are said to be *infused*. They form a supernatural superstructure of moral character, building on the natural foundation of the acquired natural virtues, and making supernatural action possible to man. *Martyrdom* is a special act of supernatural fortitude. To suffer death as a witness to one's religious faith, or even in testimony to one's opposition to some great evil (as St. John the Baptist did, in dying to manifest his reprehension for adultery) is the act of a very brave person.[66]

Four inclinations of the irascible appetite combine to constitute natural fortitude. They are its integral parts.[67] Two of them deal with the act of attacking danger. *Confidence-as-a-feeling* is a strong hope, based on firm opinion, prompting one to attack danger. *Magnificence-as-a-feeling* is a strength within the irascible appetite, impelling one to execute a great deed. It is not the external doing of the deed but the internal "greatness" of daring which makes the

[65] *Ibid.*, q. 123, 10,c.   [66] *Ibid.*, q. 124, 5,c.   [67] *S.T.*, II–II, 128, 1,c.

difficult action possible. On the other hand, for the act of suffering danger, two other integral parts may be found. *Patience-as-a-feeling* is a condition of the concupiscible appetite, where sorrow is felt. This moderated feeling of sorrow is a sort of concupiscible adjunct to fortitude. It is not identical with the virtue of patience.[68] *Perseverance-as-a-feeling* is a condition of the irascible appetite enabling one to persist firmly through a long period of suffering. The length of the suffering is the special difficulty faced by this feeling.

In the foregoing description of the integral parts, the hyphenated terms are used to distinguish them from the potential parts which bear the same names. Let us recall again that the integral parts are not virtues but component elements of one virtue. They are the results of an internal analysis.

Turning to the question of the subjective parts of fortitude, we find that there is really only one kind. No other physical danger is on a par with that of death. The cardinal virtue of fortitude enables one to face this danger. There are, strictly speaking, no plural species of fortitude.[69] If the thought occurs that there are other forms of suffering (such as the bearing of a pain which is not fatal) and that there should be virtues to perfect man so that he may endure these, it may be said that this is true enough. These virtues which are somewhat like fortitude are its potential parts.

When a man has to be firm in relation to difficulties in the sense order which present some element of danger, the virtues connected with fortitude, but lacking the complete essence of that cardinal virtue, are required. There are six of these *potential parts*.

Magnanimity (*magnanimitas*) means "great-mindedness." This virtue strengthens the irascible power in its aspiration for important honors. It is good to desire and hope for honor which is reasonably possible. Magnanimity is a sort of strength in facing the obstacles and difficulties associated with the quest for reasonable esteem from others.[70]

Magnificence (*magnificentia*) is literally the capacity "to make something great." As a potential part of fortitude, this virtue is a

[68] *Ibid.*, q. 136, 3,c.   [69] *S.T.*, II–II, 128, 1,c.
[70] *S.T.*, II–II, 129, 1–4,c. On the difference between the integral parts of fortitude and the potential parts, see q. 140, 2, ad 3m.

perfection of the irascible power enabling its possessor to execute some important project, such as a building for public use, with strong hope and firm confidence. The chief real difficulty in such matters is the financial one, so the magnificent man has the ability to spend large sums of money for a good purpose, *with a feeling of reasonable confidence*. While the external actions of magnificence would seem to be those of men of wealth and power, it is quite possible for a poor person to contribute his mite to some great enterprise in a way which is, for him, magnificent.[71]

Patience (*patientia*) is a virtue enabling the agent to bear up under the impact of evils other than that of death. The loss of a job, of one's money, of personal beauty or strength, and other such things, requires much forbearance. The difficulty here consists in the possibility of excessive sorrow, and from this point of view, patience consists in a moderating of the concupiscible appetite. However, there is also the possibility of becoming discouraged (*i.e.*, the passion of despair) and thus patience requires a special firmness in the irascible appetite. (As a supernatural virtue, patience results from the action of grace in the soul and is directed toward suffering in the spiritual order.)[72]

Perseverance (*perseverantia*) is a virtue enabling one to persist in a reasonable way, where the difficulty is really the *length of time* which must be endured before the end is attained. Notice that a passion of sorrow gives rise to the need for patience, but the inability to achieve an end, as soon as one hopes to, requires perseverance. This virtue of perseverance is a perfection of the irascible appetite.[73]

Longanimity (*longanimitas*) is literally "long-mindedness." By this virtue, one is enabled to keep one's intention fixed on some distant objective. It differs from perseverance, in that perseverance implies continued struggle against long-lasting obstacles, whereas longanimity provides for the difficulty of waiting a long time before one's hopes can be fulfilled. On the other hand, patience simply enables one to bear serious and grave evils, without respect to the time element.[74]

---

[71] *Ibid.*, q. 133, 1,c; q. 134, 2–3,c.
[73] *Ibid.*, q. 137, 1,c; et *ad primum*.
[72] *Ibid.*, q. 136, 1–2,c.
[74] *Ibid.*, q. 136, 5,c.

Constancy (*constantia*) is the last of these virtues connected with fortitude. It is to enable one to persist in the face of external obstacles to a good work. Though much like perseverance, constancy implies a firmness of feeling in regard to circumstantial difficulties.[75] Thus, we would say that a pioneer in the development of some new scientific technique, such as Louis Pasteur, might be magnanimous in aspiring to the fame which might come with the accomplishment of his great work, magnificent in devoting his personal fortune to the discovery of something which might be of help to all future men, persevering in his refusal to be daunted by the continued lack of success of his early experiments, longanimous in his realization that it would take years to convince other scientists even after his experiments had been brought to a successful termination, and constant in his refusal to be swayed from his work by the discouraging criticism of other scientists.

In each of the foregoing associated virtues, a degree of firmness in either the suffering or attacking of evils other than death is to be noted. Some, such as patience, endure in the soul even after death. Even in the beatified soul, spiritual patience might be found; in such a case, it would be simply a firmness in the enjoyment of its reward.[76]

Moral Difficulties in the Field of Fortitude

We can better understand the importance of this virtue by examining the excesses and defects of moral firmness in the various types of subject matter to which fortitude and its associated virtues apply. These vices indicate the nature of a special group of problems of personal morality.

¶ *Vices Opposed to the Cardinal Virtue of Fortitude.* *False Lack of Fear* (*impaviditas*) is the habitual absence of fear where one's life may be in real danger. This is a condition which is neither natural nor reasonable. Absolute fearlessness is a defect in the natural love of life; it entails a failure to resist danger. Such unusual fearlessness

[75] *Ibid.*, q. 137, 3,c.   [76] *Ibid.*, q. 136, 1, *ad primum*.

is not to be confused with true fortitude or courage. The man who feels no fear at any time is abnormal.[77] *Foolhardiness* (*audacitas*) is habitual excess in daring. In the case of this vice, there is not enough reasonable control of the movement to attack danger of death. Foolhardiness is based on a lack of prudent reflection in a situation which is possibly dangerous to one's life.[78] *Cowardice* (*timiditas*) is a habitual excess of fear, out of rational proportion to the danger which is faced. It also implies a lack of daring in situations which call for rationally controlled audacity.[79]

The chief problem under fortitude, then, is to maintain a mean in the irascible appetite between a defect of fear and an excess of daring. Man has a moral obligation to use all the means possible to the average person to protect and continue his life on earth. In emergencies, he must avoid being overcome by the original impact of suffering and he must be prepared to attack the difficulty actively, where such action is morally possible.

¶ *Opposed to Magnanimity.* *Presumption* (*praesumptio*) is the habitual tendency to aspire to the performance of works greater than those possible to one's individual capacity and training. It is a special case of presumption to endeavor to perform virtuous deeds without the help of God; this vice is a form of excess of the work attempted in relation to one's powers.[80] *Overambitiousness* (*ambitio*) is the habitual striving for unreasonable honors. This may be immoral on three bases: (1) because honor is aspired to, which is due to some excellence lacking in the agent; (2) because the agent thinks only of the honor and not of the assistance given by God to attain it; (3) because the agent craves only honor and not the usefulness of his act to others; this vice comes close to the modern notion of selfishness.[81] *Vainglory* (*inanis gloria*) is the habitual desire for unreasonable fame or praise. This habit may be bad in at least three ways: (1) because of the unworthiness of the thing for which one wishes to receive praise; (2) because of the unworthiness of those from whom glory is sought—men of poor judgment, for instance;

[77] *S.T.*, II–II, 126, 2,c.   [78] *Ibid.*, q. 127, 1–2,c.
[79] *Ibid.*, especially art. 1, *ad secundum*.   [80] *S.T.*, II–II, q. 130, art. 1–2,c.
[81] *Ibid.*, q. 131, art. 1–2.

(3) because the agent who seeks glory has a bad purpose, in opposition to the honor of God or the welfare of his neighbor.

Subordinated to vainglory are a number of vices whose meanings are indicated by the names: rebellion, exaltation of self, hypocrisy, habitual search for novelties, contention (*i.e.* always to get one's own way in argument), pertinacity (always preferring one's own intellectual judgments to those of others), discord (always wanting one's own will to prevail).[82]

Small-mindedness (*pusillanimitas*) is the habitual tendency to wish to do less than that of which one is naturally capable. This is directly opposed to magnanimity and is rather like a culpable inferiority complex. This vice may be due to partial ignorance, to laziness, or to fear of failure; it is only a vice when the condition is voluntary.[83]

¶ *Opposed to Magnificence.* Parsimony (*parvificentia*) is literally "the doing of things in too small a way." This vice is the habit of desiring to do or make either a small or a great work without providing sufficient money for the task. It is to be distinguished from *miserliness* which is stinginess in regard to the ordinary expenses of living; parsimony is stinginess in regard to unusual and difficult projects. A wealthy man who lived well in his own household but habitually gave too little to philanthropic projects would not be a miser but he would be parsimonious.[84] *Extravagance* (*consumptio*) is the habitual waste of wealth on the part of one who continually pays too much for things. This is the contrary of parsimony and is just as unreasonable as stinginess.[85]

¶ *Opposed to Patience.* While no vices are discussed by St. Thomas, in opposition to patience, it would seem quite possible for a moral agent to incur the following bad habits:

Defect of sorrow—an unreasonable lack of feeling for suffering (particularly on the part of others); this would amount to a habitually unsympathetic attitude, and would be related to justice, in its external manifestation.

---

[82] *Ibid.*, q. 132, art. 1, and 5.
[83] *Ibid.*, q. 133, art. 1–2.
[84] *Ibid.*, q. 135, art. 1–2.
[85] *Ibid.*, q. 135, art. 2.

Excess of sorrow—a habitual tendency to be unreasonably morbid. (Why St. Thomas refrains from an exposition of these vices is not entirely clear, see: *In III Sent.*, d. 33, q. 3, a. 3, qla. 1, resp.; and *S.T.*, II–II, q. 136 *in toto*. It is possible that he thought sorrow the natural tendency of man not elevated by grace, because patience is a supernatural virtue.)

¶ *Opposed to Perseverance. Spinelessness* (*mollities*) is the habit of giving up too easily in the face of difficulties.[86] *Stubbornness* (*pertinacia*) is the habit of persisting in face of difficulties which the reasonable person would not try to overcome.[87]

Summary of Chapter IX

Problems of practical reasoning usually stem from appetitive disorders. In itself, the human intellect tends to elicit true and right judgments, even in the difficult field of particular moral problems. Passions may incline one to judge too quickly, or under the influence of some irrational motivation. The agent has little trouble desiring the good for himself but he finds it difficult to deliberate on, judge, and prescribe right conduct. Prudence in its various forms is the habit of doing this practical thinking rightly.

If, to be morally good, the agent must follow the dictates of prudence, this advice is especially true in the case of concupiscence. Passions of this appetite may easily upset the life of reason. Moderation is the keynote of the virtue of temperance, by which excesses and defects of concupiscence are to be regulated. Rational restraint in the desires for food, drink, and the use of the faculty of reproduction is required of all human beings.

Dangers of death and other threats to man's physical well-being tend to arouse disturbing affective responses in the irascible appetite. These passions may need, at times, to be moderated by virtues akin to temperance but by far the greatest problem in the irascible appetite is that of standing firm in the face of serious difficulties. Forti-

[86] *Ibid.*, q. 138, art. 1.   [87] *Ibid.*, q. 138, art. 2.

tude is the virtue which strengthens this appetite so that the agent may undergo reasonable feelings, and be impelled to react in reasonable ways, to the hardships, real or apparent, of physical existence.

Recommended Readings

ON PRUDENCE

Thomas Aquinas, St., *Summa Theologiae*, I–II, 57, 4–6 (in *Basic Writings*, ed. Pegis, II, 434–439); II–II, qq. 47–56 (this special treatise on prudence may be read in the *Summa Theol.* literally translated by the English Dominican Fathers).

Brennan, Sr. Rose E., *The Intellectual Virtues*, pp. 65–76.

Cronin, *Science of Ethics*, I, 598–604.

Farrell, *Companion to the Summa*, III, 139–162.

Gilson, *Moral Values and the Moral Life*, pp. 233–245.

O'Neil, "Prudence, the Incommunicable Wisdom," in *Essays in Thomism*, pp. 187–204.

ON TEMPERANCE

Thomas Aquinas, St., *Summa Theologiae*, I–II, 56, 4; 60, arts. 2, 4 and 5 (in *Basic Writings*, II, 423–424, 458–465); II–II, qq. 141–170 (see the English Dominican translation).

Baker, *Thomistic Theory of the Passions*, 143 pp. (No specific treatment of moral problems but useful for the distinction of the movements of sense appetites and their relation to will.)

Cronin, *Science of Ethics*, I, 616–618; II, 59–66.

Farrell, *Companion to the Summa*, III, 403–422 (Chap. 16: The Human Animal); 425–445 (Chap. 17: The Freedom of Purity); 449–469 (Chap. 18: The Fullness of Truth); 473–491 (Chap. 19: Modesty and Miracles).

Gilson, *Moral Values and the Moral Life*, pp. 288–308.

ON FORTITUDE

Thomas Aquinas, St., *Summa Theologiae*, I–II, 56, 4; 60, 4; 61, 4 (in *Basic Writings*, II, 423–425, 461–463, 470–472); II–II, qq. 123–140 (see the English Dominican translation).

Aristotle, *Nicomachean Ethics*, Book III, Chaps. 6–9, 1115a5–1117b21 (in *Basic Works of Aristotle*, ed. McKeon, 974–980).

Cronin, *Science of Ethics*, I, 618–621.

Farrell, *Companion to the Summa*, III, 357–400.

Gilson, *Moral Values and the Moral Life*, pp. 276–287.

ADVANCED READINGS

Thomae Aquinatis, S., *Q. D. de virtutibus cardinalibus*, ed. Parmae, VIII, 626–638.

Gilson, *Le Thomisme*, 5me éd., pp. 377–423.

Meier, *Die Lehre des Thomas von Aquin "de passionibus animae,"* (Münster, 1912) BGPM XI, 2.

Noble, *Les passions dans la vie morale*, 2 vol., 300 et 328 pp.

Sertillanges, *La philosophie morale de s. Thomas*, pp. 294–384 (the most useful secondary work).

Topics for Assignment

1. The Worst Kind of Imprudence
2. Is It Possible to Be Overprudent?
3. Temperance and the Golden Mean
4. Modesty and Its Problems
5. Why the Brave Man Must Feel Some Fear
6. The Difference Between Miserliness and Parsimony

X · RIGHT ACTION IN REGARD TO OTHERS

The problems which we have already examined involve matters of *individual morality*. That is to say: a single human being living in complete isolation from all other persons would need prudence, temperance, and fortitude in order to live his own private life in a good way. There is another vast field of moral matters; this is the sphere of what we might call *social morality*. As soon as the individual human agent is brought into association with other persons (as he must, in the natural course of human life), his external actions relate him in a special moral manner to these other persons. Man has these social relations *with other human beings* and, we shall see, with God. All the questions of moral good and evil, arising from man's associations with *other* persons, are problems within the fields of *justice* or of *charity*. In the last chapter, we shall study the virtue of charity.

Why Justice Is Needed in the Human Will

To understand why the virtue of justice must be a habit of the will, we may review briefly our knowledge of the nature of human appetites. From the philosophy of man, we know that man is possessed of two types of appetitive faculty: *sensitive* and *intellective*. The distinction between the movements of these two levels of appetition depends on the prior distinction of the object of sense knowledge and the object of intellectual knowledge. Sense perception grasps the *individual* qualities of things in the material world.

Sensitive appetition is moved by way of attraction or repulsion to the sensible goodness or evil of these *individual material things*. Thus, if I am hungry and smell a good piece of steak cooking, I desire it by the passion of concupiscence. My passion of desire, in this simple case, is apparently much the same as that which occurs in a brute animal (say, a dog), under similar circumstances. We have already discussed the moral need of temperance and fortitude in the undergoing of these passions of sense appetite.

On the other hand, intellectual apprehension grasps primarily the *universal* natures of things. By intellect, man becomes aware of the generic or specific character of things previously sensed, or suggested by previous sensation. The object of the human intellect is not primarily the individual thing or quality but the *general, abstract, universal* essence. Intellectual appetition (the appetitive movement of the will) is moved to embrace or reject any universal object of the intellect presented to the will *as a universal good*. Man does, of course, desire individual things by means of his will, as well as by means of sense appetite. But the will is not attracted by the individual goodness of the thing. The will is moved by rational motives, by some intellectually apprehended, universal goodness. Thus, I might desire the aforementioned steak because I know that it is good to maintain my health by eating the proper food. This is a *reason* for eating the steak and no brute animal is moved by such universal reasoning. It is essential to remember, in this chapter, the universal character of the object of the human will.

The human agent has no moral problem in regard to willing the universal good *for himself*. We noticed at the beginning of the course on ethical theory that all men desire happiness in a general way. This is the same as to say: it is completely natural for a human being to be attracted by general goodness. Automatically, by the very texture of its nature, the will moves toward the good-in-general. But notice that such a natural desire is, in a sense, egoistic or even selfish. I want the good for myself; you, as an individual agent, want the good for yourself. Moral problems arise, however, when the human agent considers the claims which other persons have to the attainment of the good-in-general. It is not easy to will that other persons achieve reasonable success in their moral lives.

In order to get this continued altruistic outlook, this constant willing of the good-in-general to other persons, the human will must be developed or perfected by an acquired quality. This quality is a habit of desiring that other persons may achieve true happiness, the same true happiness which one desires naturally, and without any effort, for oneself. To acquire this altruistic habit of will, it is necessary to be very reasonable, to look at things from the point of view of the other person, to perform repeated acts of altruism—so as to build up a permanent disposition to will as much good to the other person as to oneself. The name of this acquired habit of will is *justice*.

The Cardinal Virtue of Justice

Justice is the habit enabling one to give each and every person his own right (*jus*) because of a constant and perpetual act of will on the part of the possessor of this habit.[1]

This is a very precise definition but it requires some explanation in order to be understood. It is evident that the term, justice (*justitia*), is dependent on the shorter Latin word, *jus*, which means *right*. Now, right is the name of a relation. A relation is a situation in which one thing is connected with another thing in some specific way. This meaning of relation has been studied in logic and in metaphysics. Relation is one of the nine accidental categories of being. One primary relation is that of *equality*. This is one of the first ideas, or principles, used in mathematics. Two plus two *equals* four. Like any first principle, equality cannot be explained. Equality is a starting point for much human reasoning. Now, in any external operation or deal, between two persons, the question of equality of the object in the given circumstances may arise. In a simple example, if I buy a candy bar from another man, I must transfer to him an amount of money which is practically equal to the value of the candy under the given circumstances. Where such equality is observed, the buying-selling contract is right (*jus* or *justum*). This objective deno-

[1] *S.T.*, II–II, q. 58, 1,c.

JUST

OBJECT — CANDY
MONEY

tation is the primary meaning of right. So, a situation is <u>objectively right,</u> when one thing is, in some sense, equal to another thing.

Considering this from the personal, or subjective, side, we find a <u>derivative</u> meaning for right. This derived meaning is important in ethics. When A sells candy to B (where A and B are two distinct persons), it is objectively right that the value of the candy should equal the value of the payment for it. On the part of the seller, A, there is clearly a sort of moral claim to this objective rightness. This <u>moral claim or exigency</u> is called a *subjective right*. As soon as A transfers the candy to B, B has a debt (*debitum*) to pay. And A has a subjective right to <u>demand such a payment of the debt,</u> so that objective equality, or right, will be restored. Also, of course, B has a subjective right to demand that the candy be equal to the value of his payment. This is an example of a simple commutation, an exchange of one thing for another.[2]

Let us notice the several elements in this example. There must be *two distinct persons* involved. It is not morally possible for a man to sell something to himself. This is true of all questions of rightness (note that *justitia* literally means rightness); unless two persons are involved there is no problem of moral rightness, or justice. Secondly, there must be some *matter* which is the object of the deal. This matter need not be concrete material things (as in the foregoing contract: candy bar equals five cents); other, less tangible things, may be the objects or matters of such dealings between persons. Thus, if I give a candy bar to a poor child who cannot pay for it, I may have a right to expect something other than a payment of money in return from the child. He should, at least, be appropriately grateful. I have a right to expect thanks from the child. It is objectively right that he feel thankful. Thirdly, there is a correlation of rights and debts. In our buying-selling example, A has a subjective right to equality of payment, and A has a debt, or duty (*debitum* in its general sense is commonly called duty, in English) to give full value in his candy bar. On the other side of the deal, B has a subjective right by which he may demand that A fulfill his duty as a seller, and B has his own debt or duty, to pay for his purchase on

[2] *S.T.*, II–II, q. 57, 1,c.

the basis of objective equality. Fourthly, it is not right, or just, for either person simply *to will* to pay his debt and then do nothing more about it. This will to do what is right must be translated into external operations; A must give the bar to B, and B must give the five cents to A, or justice has not been done. Justice is the only virtue which requires external actions for its perfection. One can be prudent, temperate, and brave, *within himself*. It is impossible to be just without *doing right actions to other persons*. Justice has to do with objective rightness, with an equality in external actions involving at least one other person. Finally, we may again stress the need for some sort of *equality* (we shall see that arithmetical equality is not always possible or morally necessary) in the relationship of justice.

Some books on ethics, written by Catholic scholars who follow a different tradition of terminology, include a section on "Duties to Oneself." Such books give a broader signification to the term, duty, than is used in the present exposition. So used, duty becomes the equivalent of any *moral obligation*. The thomistic concept of debt or duty (*debitum*), as something owed to another distinct person under justice, cannot reasonably be used to designate moral obligations under prudence, temperance, or fortitude. Nor can one, strictly speaking, have a debt or duty under justice to himself, unless justice be used metaphorically.[3] Man has duties of justice to other men, individually or collectively, and to God. These are the only *persons* (*i.e.*, complete substances having the use of intelligence) with whom man can have earthly dealings, or external operations. If man could do anything externally in regard to angels, there would be moral duties to angels; but there are no such operations possible. So, there are no natural moral duties to angels.

The attempt to make all moral obligation a question of duty is the result of the attempt to find the ultimate basis of ethics in positive law. The positive law of the Catholic Church (canon law) and the positive law of one's country deal, or should deal, with problems of justice. Important though justice is, there is more to morality than the field of justice. When Rousseau suggested (in his novel, *Emile*)

[3] *Ibid.*, q. 58, 2,c.

that one might abolish all immorality by the simple expedient of abolishing all positive laws, he was merely bringing the purely legalistic tradition of ethics to its logical and absurd conclusion. Beyond the positive law is the natural moral law, and beyond that the Law of God. These laws cannot be abolished and so the possibility of immorality cannot be abolished. Man has some *positive rights and duties;* these depend proximately on the justice of positive law. Man also has some *natural rights and duties;* these flow from the natural moral law, and ultimately from the Law or Reason of God. The following definitions will serve as a summary:

Subjective moral right is a person's claim under justice to do, to possess, or to exact something in regard to another person. (It is in this sense that certain rights were declared unalienable by the founders of the United States. One may be deprived of the external use of the rights to life, liberty and the pursuit of happiness. No man can be deprived of his moral claim to these goods.) (1) Such rights are *natural*, when they flow from the rational nature of the person possessing them, or (to say the same thing in another way) from the natural moral law which depends ultimately on the Law of God. (2) Rights are *positive*, when they depend on the contingent legislation of a lawmaker. (Thus, one's right to live is a natural right, but one's right to live as a citizen of a certain country enjoying, let us say, the privilege of voting, is a positive right.)

Moral duty is a person's exigency, or moral necessity, to respect the just rights of another person. (Thus, if A has a right to live, then B has a duty to permit A to live, as long as A does not forfeit the exercise of this right by endangering the equal or greater rights of others.) (1) *Natural moral duties* are obligations under justice, stemming from the natural moral law. (2) *Positive duties* are obligations under justice, stemming from the positive laws of a society. Positive duties are moral duties, provided the law on which they depend is not opposed to the natural moral law.

It is to be remembered that the *subject* or possessor of a moral right or duty, and the *term*, or one in regard to whom the right or duty is directed, are *necessarily persons*.

The *cardinal virtue of justice* is, then, the habit of will enabling a person to fulfill his moral rights and duties (as previously defined) in a good way. If we consider justice in a very general manner, simply as moral *righteousness*, then justice covers all the moral virtues. We have seen previously that this is true of all four of the cardinal virtues. Each shares in the essential character of the other three. So, it is right and just, in a general way, to be prudent, temperate, and brave. Thus considered, *general justice* is not a special habit or virtue of the human will, but is a broad moral condition of rightness in relation to any species of virtuous action. This general condition of rightness is not the cardinal virtue (for it is not a virtue at all) but approximates to the notion of moral goodness.[4]

Since justice, as a special virtue, consists in a habitual willing to do what is right in regard to one's neighbor, there are two *integral parts* of this virtue: *to do what is good* for one's neighbors, individually or collectively; and *to avoid doing anything harmful* to one's neighbors, individually or collectively.[5]

Again we should recall that these integral parts are not themselves virtues but the complementary dispositions which make up the one virtue of justice. To do good to others is the principal integral part, for it covers formally all the acts of justice. To avoid doing evil to others is secondary, but it does not mean a pure negation of action. Rather, it requires an active repudiation of evil, where it might affect other persons. It is evident that one may act unjustly: *by transgression*, that is, by a positive infringement of the just rights of other persons; and *by omission*, that is, by failing to do one's duty to other persons.[6]

We must now consider the four possible species (subjective parts) of this virtue. In the first place, it is necessary to distinguish two broad forms of justice:

General legal justice is the habit of the human will whereby one wishes and does what is right, *in relation to the common good*, formally considered. This virtue is not the same as general justice (moral righteousness). Legal justice is marked off from the second broad type (particular justice) by its *term*, which is the good of a

[4] *S.T.*, II–II, q. 58, 6,c.   [5] *S.T.*, II–II, q. 79, 1,c.   [6] *Ibid.*, arts. 2 and 3,c.

community, of a society of persons considered collectively. Laws are not made for the good of the individual, primarily, but for the good of a whole community. So, *legal* justice looks to the advancement of the common good. In the precise terminology of St. Thomas: "legal justice is a special virtue, from the point of view of its essence, inasmuch as it is concerned with the common good as its proper object." [7] Legal justice is general, in the secondary sense, because it does prescribe the acts of all the other virtues, *insofar as they may affect the common good*. Thus, intemperance is not in itself an act of injustice, but it may easily render a man socially harmful so it is indirectly a matter of concern for the just lawmaker and the just citizen.

It may be remarked that the concept of "social justice," which finds no precise parallel in the terminology of St. Thomas, but which figures prominently in the encyclicals of recent Popes, is partly connected with legal justice. However, social justice seems also to cover in part the area of distributive justice, which we shall discuss later. As often used, social justice is not the name of a personal virtue but of an objective rightness in social life.

We may also notice that an act performed under the virtue of legal justice will also be an act coming under some kind of particular justice. Thus, when an employer pays proper wages to his employees, he is doing his duty under commutative justice,[8] but he is also doing his duty under legal justice, for this payment of wages contributes to the common good as well as to the individual good of the employee. This is well explained by St. Thomas: "An act, such as the avoidance of adultery, may be performed by the same agent, both because of legal justice and because of some other virtue; but not for the same reason. This is true, for where there is some special formal object, even in regard to general subject matter, there should be a special habit. That is why legal justice is a definite virtue which derives its species from the fact that it looks to the common good." [9]

Particular justice is the habit of will whereby one wishes and does what is right, *in relation to another person*, considered as a *single*

[7] *S.T.*, II–II, q. 58, 6,c.   [8] See *infra*.
[9] *In V Ethicorum*, lect. 2; ed. Pirotta, p. 301, n. 912.

individual with a right to his own *private good*.[10] Again St. Thomas makes this distinction clear: "while legal justice is directed to an object which is the common good, particular justice is directed to another object: *that which pertains to some private person.*" [11]

Each of the foregoing broad types of justice must be further subdivided into two subordinate species, with the result that we have four distinct species, or *subjective parts*, of justice.

Equity (*epieikeia*) is the first kind of general legal justice. It is the habit of judging, willing, and doing what is right to others, in those unusual cases which do not come under the formulation of moral law. A legal formula is a universal proposition made to apply to the usual cases. Many propositions of moral law may admit of exceptions. It is, at times, in the interest of the common good to break the letter of the law (as it is imperfectly known to man) in order to maintain its spirit. The ability to know when to make a moral exception is that potential part of prudence which we have called practical sagacity (*gnome*). The ability to will and do what is decided by practical sagacity is the present kind of justice, which is called equity. (The example of refusal to return a deposit of arms to a demented owner is an example of equity as well as practical sagacity.)[12]

Common legal justice (*legalis justitia*) is that habit of the will whereby one is inclined to will and do what is for the common good of others, in accord with the ordinary interpretation of the moral law. This virtue is actually secondary to equity, which latter habit is directive of, and superior to, common legal justice. Common legal justice is a sufficient virtue for the average problem; by it one wills to act for the common good, as prescribed by the letter (and possibly, the intent) of the law. By means of equity, one wills to do what is simply right.[13]

Commutative justice (*commutativa justitia*) is the first division of particular justice, and is the third subjective part of this virtue. Recalling that particular justice is directed to the private good of

---

[10] *S.T.*, II–II, q. 58, 7,c.   [11] *In V Ethic.*, lect. 3; Pirotta, p. 304, n. 918.

[12] *S.T.*, II–II, 120, 1–2,c. See also the reference in the next footnote.

[13] *S.T.*, II–II, 120, 2,c.; et *ad primum; In V. Ethic.*, lect. 16, pp. 359–362, nn. 1078–1090.

another person, we may say that commutative justice is the habit of
the will whereby one wills to do what is right in any exchange between persons, where the objective rightness is to be determined by
the simple equality of whatever is exchanged, and where no attention is to be paid to the possible inequality of the persons involved.[14]

Distributive justice (*distributiva justitia*) is the second division of
particular justice and the fourth subjective part of justice. By the
virtue of distributive justice, the agent wills to apportion things
which belong to a community to individual persons who are parts
of that community. Notice that distributive justice looks to the
private good of the individual person; that is why it belongs under
particular justice. In distributions, one must consider not only the
value of the "things" apportioned but also the unequal value to the
community of the persons who are the recipients. The rightness
(*justum*), here, is not a simple arithmetic equality of things but an
equality of ratios, *i.e.*, a proportion. This distributive proportion
will follow the following pattern: A:B :: C:D, where A represents
the value of one thing that is distributed, B the value of another
thing distributed, C represents the rank within the community of
one person who receives distribution A, and D represents the rank
of another person in the community who receives distribution B.[15]

Because this is a matter of primary importance for the understanding of the problems in the remainder of our course, and because
there are few accurate expositions of the point in English, we may
look at the following explanation given by St. Thomas.

In distributive justice, a thing is given to some private person, insofar
as that which belongs to the whole is due to a part. And the value of that
which is given depends on the rank of the part within the whole. So, in
distributive justice, a man is given the amount of community goods which
is equal to the rank of that person in the community.

This rank (*principalitas*) is determined in an aristocracy, according to
virtue; in an oligarchy, according to wealth; in a democracy, according
to freedom; and in other forms of government, by other standards.

[14] *S.T.*, II–II, 61, 2,c.

[15] *S.T.*, I, 21, 1,c; in Pegis, *Basic Writings*, I, 223–224. *In V Ethic.*, lect. 4; ed.
Pirotta, pp. 308–311, nn. 927–937. Consult also Martinez, M. L., "Distributive
Justice According to St. Thomas," *The Modern Schoolman*, XXIV (1947) 208–
223.

Therefore, the mean is not taken, in distributive justice, according to an equality of thing with thing, but according to a proportion of things to persons. Thus, as one person is more excellent than another person, so is the thing which is given to one person greater than that which is given to another. So, Aristotle says that such a mean is based on a geometric proportionality,[16] in which equality is considered not according to quantity but according to a proportion. It is as if we say: six is to four as three is to two; for, in both there is the proportion of one and a half to one, the first term is greater than the second by half of the first. But, it is not a question of equality of the amount by which one exceeds the other, for six is two more than four, and three is one more than two.

However, in commutations, a thing is transferred to an individual person because of some thing which has been received from him. This is clearest in buying and selling, where the essential notion (*ratio*) of a commutation is found primarily. So, it is necessary to equate one thing with another thing. Thus, to the extent that a man possesses more than is his own (and this means that he has something which belongs to another man), he must make restitution to him whose property it is. Thus, equality is based on an arithmetic mean, which is determined according to a simple equality of the amount of excess. For instance, five is the mean between six and four, because it is one greater and one less.

Therefore, if two people have five to start with, and one man takes one of the other's possessions, then one, the taker, will have six and the other will be left with four. There will be justice, if both are brought back to the mean. Thus, one may be taken from the man who has six, and given to the man who has four. For, then, both will have five which is the mean.[17]

It is easy to understand the justice or rightness of simple equality in matters of commutation. Distributive justice is a little more difficult, for a proportion is harder to understand than is a simple equation. Let us examine a case in which a judge would have to distribute punishments. Suppose we have two thieves who have each taken ten dollars from a store. One thief is an adult with a criminal record; the other a small child who has not stolen before. As far as commutative justice is concerned, the store should get its money back in full, in both cases where possible. From the point of view of legal justice, both are offenses against the law of the community and some adequate punishment must be given, in order to protect the common good. But, should the amount of punishment be arithmetically equal?

[16] *Ethic. Nic.*, V, 3; 1131a29.   [17] *S.T.*, II–II, q. 61, art. 2,c.

This is a question of distributive justice. It is necessary to think of the *persons* who have stolen. The circumstance which changes these cases is: *Who* did it. The adult has greater moral guilt and responsibility, because he is possessed of the full use of reason and he has experience in these matters. The child has no backlog of experience and may not fully understand what he has done. It is right and just, according to distributive justice, for the judge to give the adult a bigger punishment than the child. It is not just, *according to commutative justice*, for the judge to let the child keep half of the money he took, and to make the adult restore all the money he took.

Notice two things, in the foregoing example: (1) The same case or problem may require the use of different kinds of justice, to settle different aspects of the problem; (2) We only apply distributive justice to a situation in which some thing which belongs to the community (here, punishment) is allotted to individual members of the community on the basis of some personal rank which they have in the community and which is relevant to the case in hand. Not all conditions of personality are relevant. It would not be just for the judge to give a heavy sentence to his personal enemy and a light sentence (for the same crime) to his brother. Good, practical judgment (*i.e.*, prudence) is needed to decide what personal considerations are morally relevant to a given case. "The equality of distributive justice is of a special kind: unequal things are given to unequal people. Compensation by means of punishments and rewards would not be just, if all rewards and all punishments were equal." [18]

¶ *Chief Offense Against Distributive Justice*. *Personal Favoritism* (*personarum acceptio*) is the vice directly opposed to distributive justice. The man who habitually gives out things belonging to the community, for some personal reason which is not rightly relevant to the particular case under consideration, is the subject of this vice. (*E.g.*, a teacher has a duty under distributive justice to allot the right grades to the students in his, or her, class. To do this, it is necessary to judge the personal attainments, *in the work of the class*, of all the students. Their ranking should depend on their respective perform-

[18] C.G., III, 142.

ances in the classroom, in examinations, and in other actual tests. If the teacher is consciously influenced in the distribution of grades by considerations, such as the prominence of the student's family, friendship, dislike of the student, the athletic prowess of the student, and other such incidental personal matters, then the teacher is guilty of the moral offense of personal favoritism.) *Nepotism* (giving good jobs, community funds, or honors, to relatives simply because they are relatives) is a particular form of personal favoritism.[19]

¶ *Divisions of Commutative Justice.* The principal act of commutative justice is called *restitution*, the restoring of the simple equality of "things" which constitute the matter of a mutual transaction (commutation) between persons. Voluntary failure to make such restitution is the general name of offenses against commutative justice.[20]

From one point of view the matter of distributive and commutative justice is the same. That is to say: all justice has to do with the external operations of the moral agent in relation to other persons. These operations are of three types: (1) *The use of things* consists in taking away, or returning, or doing something to, the material possessions of a person. *The use of persons* is the conferring of some personal benefit (honor, for instance), or injury (beating, for instance) upon another person. (3) *The use of deeds or services* (*opera*) consists of the doing of some work for or against another person.[21]

All three kinds of external operations can be considered from the point of view of the *distribution* of community goods (distributive justice), or from the point of view of an *exchange* between private persons (commutative justice). So, while the following division of operations is primarily applied to commutative justice, a similar division may be made for the acts of distributive justice. It is well to notice that a commutation may justly take place between more than two persons. If two partners, A and B, sell me a book, there are three individual persons involved in the deal. However, the partnership of A and B makes up a legal "person," with whom I make

[19] *S.T.*, II–II, q. 63, a. 1–3,c.   [20] *S.T.*, II–II, q. 62, 1,c.
[21] *S.T.*, II–II, q. 61, 3,c.

the contract. What is essential to a commutation is that the exchange be made between two "persons" [individuals or groups] who act primarily for the sake of their *private* good. I may sell building materials to a government agency and expect payment according to commutative justice; here, the government represents the community but, under ordinary conditions, it deals according to commutative justice. Under extraordinary circumstances, the government agency may, *for the sake of the common good*, expropriate my building materials. This is no longer a question of commutative justice but of legal justice and of distributive justice. So too, when a civilian works for his government and is paid the standard wages for his services, it is a commutation; when he is conscripted for military service and is paid only a nominal wage, it is a question of legal justice.

Involuntary commutations occur when one person appropriates or uses the possessions, person, or services of another person against the will of that other person. Such involuntariness may be due to an appropriation which is either secret or violent.

Secret or *hidden* commutations (in Latin they are said to be done *occulte*) are fraudulent and immoral. This term covers injurious operations such as stealing, adultery, poisoning, misappropriation of possessions, seduction and false testimony.

Violent or *open* commutations (in Latin they are said to be done *manifeste per violentiam*) consist in the forcing of some exchange upon another when he does not agree to it. These include open injuries to *persons* (beating, incarceration, and killing, for instance); injuries to another through his *possessions* (robbery, killing of relatives, and kidnaping); and injuries to another person by means of *deeds* (false accusation, contemptuous treatment, *i.e.* contumely).[22]

Voluntary commutations consist in willingly and knowingly handing over possessions, persons, or services to another person, with the understanding that the other person incurs a duty to recompense the first person. Simple donation of a gift is not an act of justice but of a virtue associated with justice, liberality.

Three chief types of voluntary commutation may be distinguished.

[22] *S.T.*, II–II, 61, 3,c; and *In V Ethic.*, lect. 4; Pirotta, pp. 308–309, n. 929.

Buying-and-selling is the absolute exchange of one thing for another of approximately equal value. Renting and lending are commutations by which something is handed over to another person, with the understanding that the owner will be compensated for temporary use. There is a moral difference between the renting of things which increase in value with the passage of time (say a flock of sheep), which is called *usufructus*, and the renting of something (say an automobile) which does not increase in value (*accomodatum*). *Handing over goods with a view to their recovery* may be (1) in order to preserve the goods, as in the case of a deposit; (2) in order to fulfill some obligation, as in pawning or mortgaging, or in giving bond.[23]

Obviously, there is always some possible injustice attaching to an involuntary commutation. A voluntary commutation is in accord with commutative justice, when there is simple equality in the exchange. Of course, all the pertinent circumstances of a commutation must be morally good, or it is not a morally approvable action. It is not necessary to discuss at length the properties of a legal contract (these commutations are contracts), for we know what is necessary to a morally good action, from the point of view of circumstances. So, a man cannot justly sell the property of another, or rent a building for immoral use, or marry a person who does not know that she is entering into this contract. The rules governing the six types of circumstance, studied in ethical theory, apply to commutations. (Further discussion of moral problems connected with the exchange of things and services will be found later, in Chapter XII.)

¶ *Just and Unjust Judgment.* When used in connection with a discussion of justice, *judgment* means the determination of what is right.[24] In the logical sense, judgment is an act of reason. Questions of justice need to be decided by a judge who possesses not only the prudence to make a correct and practical intellectual judgment but also the appetitive, or voluntary, inclination *to will what is right.* This appetitive inclination is supplied by the virtue of justice.

An inclination to make unjust judgments habitually stems from the vice which is most directly opposed to the cardinal virtue of justice,

---

[23] See: *S.T.*, and *In V Ethic., loc. cit.*   [24] *S.T.*, II–II, q. 60, 1,c.

i.e., from *injustice*.[25] There is a special vice of injustice which is a contempt for the common good. In a broad sense, all immoral acts may spring from this kind of injustice, because to do anything which is wrong is to express contempt for the natural moral law. Materially, then, injustice of this kind is the root of all wrongdoing. A more limited meaning of injustice is that which considers it as the special vice opposed to particular justice. In this case, injustice is the habit of willing inequality in regard to the good or evil of another person. The unjust person habitually wills to have more wealth and honors, and less work and losses, than he is entitled to in relation to another person. The many problems of injustice will be discussed in the next two chapters.

Virtues Associated with Justice

There are certain moral habits which deal with operations in relation to another person, yet which do not possess the full nature of the justice which is a cardinal virtue. These are the potential parts of justice. In the following brief exposition of the problems covered by these connected virtues, the order of presentation used by St. Thomas [26] is reversed; theology often reasons from the highest to the lowest, but philosophy proceeds from that which is easiest to understand to that which is most difficult. Thus, while St. Thomas begins with the virtue of religion, we end with it. Eight potential parts of justice may be distinguished.

Liberality is the good habit of using and spending material wealth rightly, not only for one's own benefit but for the good of others. The name, liberality, is derived from a Latin word meaning "free," or "freely." This virtue denotes a certain mental freedom from the excessive love of wealth (and from this, liberality has a connection with temperance, which has been noted already); it also indicates a freedom in the dispensing of wealth to others; and this externalized operation makes liberality a part of justice.[27]

Though the chief act of liberality is that of *giving* to other per-

[25] *Ibid.*, q. 59, 1,c.   [26] *S.T.*, II–II, qq. 81–119.   [27] *S.T.*, II–II, 117, 1–2,c.

sons, this virtue should not be confused with "charity." We shall see later that charity is a supernatural virtue raising its possessor to a loving friendship with God. To give money to another man, as a result of the virtue of liberality, is to act for the sake of a rational and natural good (the welfare of one's neighbor, or of civil society); to give out of real charity is to act for a supernatural motive, *for the love of God*. Much philanthropy, in the modern sense, is naturally good (because an expression of liberality) but not really charity, in the Christian sense.[28]

Friendliness (*amicitia, affabilitas*) is the habit enabling one to speak and to act in regard to other persons in a fitting way. This means much more, of course, than etiquette or superficially good manners. The friendly person observes the mean between fawning adulation and churlishness. In the old and mellowed civilizations of the Orient, great store was set in the approved forms of social intercourse. Aristotle devoted a large part of his *Nicomachean Ethics* (most of Books VIII and IX) to the discussion of friendship (*philia*).[29]

Veracity (*veritas sive veracitas*) is the habit of speaking or acting in accord with the truth. It is by external operations that man signifies his thoughts to others. He need not tell or show all that he thinks or feels, but, if he does express his thoughts, he should do so rightly, *i.e.*, truly. It is even necessary to take care to dress and act in such a way as to give, under ordinary conditions, a true manifestation of one's personal attainments, wealth, social position, and intentions.[30]

Vindication (*vindicatio*) is the habit of willing that another person who has committed a moral offense be rightly punished, for his own good, or for the sake of restraining him from further evil-doing, or for the peace of others and the preservation of justice, or for the honor of God. Vindication is a vice, if one wills that another be punished because one hates him. The line of demarcation between true vindication and personal vengeance is quite clear. Revenge issues from a bad intention; vindication from good motives.[31]

Gratitude (*gratia, gratitudo*) is the habit of will enabling one to be duly thankful for some benefit received from another person.

---

[28] See *infra*, Chap. XVI.
[30] *S.T.*, II–II, q. 109, 1–3,c.
[29] *S.T.*, II–II, q. 114, 1,c.
[31] *S.T.*, II–II, q. 108, 1–2,c.

Three degrees in the act of thankfulness may be distinguished: (1) the receiver may recognize within his own consciousness his indebtedness to another (this is essential to gratitude); (2) the receiver of a benefit may openly acknowledge to others his indebtedness, by saying that he is thankful; and (3) the receiver may repay the benefaction by returning something of actual, though not necessarily equal, value to the benefactor. The last two acts are not always possible, but one can always at least feel thankful for a favor received.[32]

Respect for persons (*observantia*) is the habit of will enabling one to acknowledge the excellence of some private individual who is worthy of such honor. Aside from God, parents, and civil rulers, there are people whose public position or private attainments in virtue or science require some acknowledgement from the reasonable person. The external expression of respect is a sort of debt; thus respect for such persons is like justice but not a matter of strict justice. By this virtue, one may manifest his esteem for a good civic official, a soldier for his commander, a student for a good teacher, any human agent for a person of superior dignity.[33] Subordinate to this virtue of respect, are two minor virtues: *Respect for those in immediate authority over one* (*dulia*) originally meant the honor to be paid by a slave to his master; by extension, it came to mean the inclination to honor any man in a position of authority, other than a parent or the head of one's country;[34] *obedience* (*obedientia*) is habitual willingness to carry out the just commands of a human superior.[35]

Piety, or *respect for one's family and country* (*pietas*) is the habit of will enabling one to show due honor or esteem to those persons to whom one owes the opportunity to live, as a member of a family, or as a citizen of a state. This virtue is subdivided into two parts. *Filial piety* is the habit of showing love, honor and respect to parents and to relatives. The reason for this virtue is found in the debt which each person owes to his natural progenitors, who are the natural and proximate sources of his individual existence. *Patriotism*,

[32] *Ibid.*, q. 106, 1,c; q. 107, 2,c.   [33] *S.T.*, II–II, 102, 1–2,c.
[34] *S.T.*, II–II, 103, arts. 1–2,c.   [35] *Ibid.*, q. 104, 1,c.

or *love of country* is the habit of showing respect for the leaders and founders of one's political state, and for one's fellow citizens, to whom is owed the right to live as a citizen.[36]

Religion, or *piety to God* (*religio*) is the habit of acknowledging and showing by external acts one's debt to the Supreme Author of one's existence. This is not religion, in the objective or institutional sense (in which we might speak of Catholicism or Judaism as a religion). This virtue is an acquired quality of the individual will, perfecting man so that he may rightly pay his debt to God, insofar as this is possible to a creature. Because of its importance, a special chapter (XIII) will be devoted to the virtue of religion.[37]

Problems Connected with These Associated Virtues

Our purpose in this section is to consider the vices and difficulties connected with the practice of the first seven potential parts of justice. We shall not deal, at this point, with offenses against commutative justice, or against the virtue of religion.

¶ *Vices Opposed to Liberality.* Miserliness or *avarice* (*avaritia*) as a vice consists in an inordinate desire to possess more material goods than are reasonably necessary to one's condition in life. This is an offense of *excess*, in relation to things which may be owned. Miserliness is offensive in three ways: first, as a disorder of the concupiscible appetite (thus, it has been seen to be connected with intemperance); second, as depriving others of possessions which they might use; third, as an offense against God, for it overstresses the importance of material things to the detriment of divine things (in the last two ways, it is a sort of injustice).[38] Miserliness gives origin to a brood of ugly minor vices: hard-heartedness, acquisitiveness, solicitude for wealth, violence in attaining wealth, perjury, and fraud.[39]

Prodigality (*prodigalitas*) is the habitual lack of reasonable concern for the acquisition and retention of a reasonable amount of this

[36] *S.T.*, II–II, q. 101, arts. 1–3,c.
[38] *S.T.*, II–II, q. 118, 1,c, and ad 2m.
[37] *S.T.*, II–II, q. 81, arts. 1–4,c.
[39] *Ibid.*, art. 8,c.

world's goods, resulting in too much spending or giving away of one's possessions. This is obviously opposed to avarice, both from the point of view of intemperance and injustice. However, as far as other persons are involved, prodigality is not as serious and offensive as miserliness. The prodigal man may benefit others though not himself; the avaricious man is of no help to anybody, because he will not use things reasonably even for his own livelihood.[40]

¶ *Opposed to Friendliness.* *Adulation* is the habit of paying excessive honor to others by words or deeds; this vice, which is also a form of lie, is actually advocated by some contemporary "applied psychologists" as a method of making friends and getting on in the world! To compliment people, when there is no occasion for it, is immoral.[41] *Quarrelsomeness* (*litigium*) is the habit of making oneself as disagreeable as possible to other people, by contradicting them continually. The fawning practitioner of adulation is too friendly; the quarrelsome person is not friendly enough.[42]

¶ *Opposed to Veracity.* *The habit of lying* (*mendacium*) inclines one to use signs in order to enunciate, or manifest, what is thought to be false. It is possible to tell a lie by means of words, actions, or the omission of words or actions in a situation which requires true words or actions. The formal nature of a lie consists in the difformity between what is judged to be true within the intellect and the voluntary enunciation of what is judged to be false. (So, it is possible for a person to lie, because he intends to signify what is false, even though his sign is objectively, or materially, in conformity with the true state of things.)

A secondary effect of lying is the *deception of others*. This is not of the essence of the act of lying. Irrespective of its external effects, good or bad, upon other people, a lie is a wilful unconformity of a sign and the judgment which it is supposed to signify. This means that *every lie is an immoral act.* Some moral actions are bad in their very kind (*malum ex genere*). This is because such actions, in every case, contain an unreasonable disorder between the primary purpose of the potency eliciting the act and the formal end of the act itself.

[40] *Ibid.*, q. 119, 1–3,c.   [41] *S.T.*, II–II, q. 115, 1,c.
[42] *Ibid.*, q. 116, art. 1–2,c.

The power to will to convey the truth to others is always misused, or abused, when it is voluntarily used to convey what is judged to be untrue. Lying is a perversion within the moral agent, and is as essentially evil as any other unnatural and self-destructive use of a moral faculty.

Considering the consequences of a lie, we find that some acts of lying are harmful to others (called *pernicious* lies), some are intended to be helpful to others (*officious* lies), and some are intended for the amusement of others (*jocose* lies). These names and divisions have nothing to do with the formal essence of the lie; the lie is morally bad in itself, irrespective of its possible effects upon others. A pernicious lie is *accidentally*, or circumstantially, worse than an officious or jocose lie. But one is no more justified in lying for a good secondary purpose, than one is in committing a murder in order to help a third person. This is not to say that a lie is always a great immorality; to speak the precise language of theology, a lie is not in every case a mortal sin.

What may one do, then, in a situation which will result in very bad consequences, if the truth is told? First of all, one may not formally will to convey falsity (*i.e.*, tell a lie), in order to avoid these consequences. In some such situations, it is possible to avoid committing oneself in any way. In other cases, where some answer must be given to a question and the truth would have very bad effects, it is morally right to use a *prudent dissimulation*. This consists in the use of a sign which does not convey the whole truth, but which is not formally opposed to the truth.

Let us think of a modern example. I am driving home in my car. At a stoplight, a hitchhiker asks me: "Are you going west?" Of course, I am going west; but, if I answer, "Yes," he will open the door and sit in the car. Now, suppose that I am going to pick up my ten children on the way home and will have no room for this hitchhiker. Must I stop and explain the whole deal to him? I may simply say: "No." This is not a lie, though it is deceptive, for the hitchhiker is really inquiring: "May I have a ride with you?" The right answer to this implied question is, "No!"

This is really the same example as the classic case of assassins who chase a friend of mine, whom I hide in my house. If the assassins come to my door and ask: "Is Joe here?" I may simply say, "No." The whole situation is such that my negation should be understood to mean: "Not to you."

Notice that such dissimulation is deceptive and it must be used *prudently*. The questioner must be one who is not entitled to know the whole truth; the situation must be such that a wholly truthful answer would produce very bad results; the answer given must be equivocal, *i.e.*, have one meaning which is in accord with the truth of the whole context of circumstances, even though it has another meaning (which may be taken by the questioner) which is not materially true.

We should exclude from this question *conventional responses* which have a highly specialized meaning. Thus, for a maid to tell an unwelcome caller that the mistress of the house is not at home, when the lady is really in the house, is not a lie. This is a conventional answer, meaning that the caller will not be received at this time. It is the caller's error if the statement is taken too literally. The same may be said about a guilty criminal who pleads *not guilty*, in a court of law. Such a plea means that the criminal wishes to defend himself, and it is not a lie.[43]

St. Thomas' teaching on lying is summed up in the following passage: A lie is not simply immoral (*non solum habet rationem peccati*) by virtue of the harm which it works upon one's neighbor, but by virtue of its inordination, as has been said [in the main response to the article]. One may not use something illicit, by way of inordination, in order to prevent harm or loss to others; just as one may not steal in order to give alms, unless by chance in a case of necessity, when all things become common. So, it is not right to tell a lie, in order to preserve someone else from some danger. However, it is permitted to conceal the truth prudently, by means of a dissimulation, as Augustine says in his book, *Against Lying* [c. 10; PL 40, 553].[44]

Lying promises are those made with the intention of not keeping them. This is, of course, a lie. One made with the intention of keeping it need not be kept, if (1) what is promised is illicit; or, (2) if

[43] *S.T.*, II–II, q. 110 *in toto*.   [44] *S.T.*, II–II, q. 110, art. 3, ad 4m.

circumstances have changed so considerably that it would not be prudent to keep it. Otherwise, to fail to keep a promise is to make it into a lie, after the fact.[45]

Secrets are not ordinarily to be divulged; it is immoral to attempt to keep something secret by telling a lie, however. There is no case in which a lie becomes morally approvable, not even in an instance where it would procure a very great good. In the next chapter,[46] we shall examine the types of secrets and the cases in which they should be revealed.

Jokes or something which is materially untrue signified for the sake of amusing others, constitute a lie. Exception may be made for the case in which it is plainly understood by everyone concerned that the speaker does not intend that his words be taken in their literal sense. Evident fictions are not, then, lies. The reason for such exclusion is that the speaker does not formally intend to signify something opposed to what he thinks to be true.

Erroneous statements uttered unconsciously, are not formal lies; here, the falsity of the sign is not intended.

Simulation (*simulatio*) is a lie employing an action, or deed, as its sign. All that has been said about lying applies to simulation.[47]

Hypocrisy is a special kind of simulation, in which the agent simulates the person of another. This is also a lie, expressed in deeds. The case of an immoral person who pretends to be just is the typical instance of hypocrisy.[48]

Boasting (*jactantia*) is the use of words to exalt oneself above what one actually is. This, too, is a kind of lie.[49]

Self-belittlement (*ironia*) is the use of words to make oneself appear less worthy than one actually knows oneself to be. This is the original meaning of *irony*, and it is the sense in which we speak of "Socratic Irony," because Socrates habitually pretended to be less wise than he actually was. Were he sincere in his profession of ignorance (as he may have been), then he was doing nothing immoral.[50]

[45] *Ibid.*, ad 5m.
[46] See *infra*, Chap. XI, pp. 360–361.
[47] *Ibid.*, q. 111, 1,c.
[48] *Ibid.*, q. 111, 2,c.
[49] *Ibid.*, q. 112, 1,c.
[50] *S.T.*, II–II, q. 113, 1,c.

¶ *Opposed to Vindication.* *Vengeance* is the vice of seeking to punish an offender, with the *intention of harming him* as the dominating motive.

Failure to cooperate in the just punishment of offenders is a long name to indicate the defect of the virtue of vindication.[51]

¶ *Opposed to Gratitude.* *Ingratitude* is habitual failure to feel and exhibit due thankfulness to a benefactor. One may be ungrateful in three ways: (1) by doing evil to a benefactor; (2) by not expressing thanks, or by claiming that a benefactor is a malefactor; and (3) by not recognizing a benefaction as such. An excess of gratitude is also admitted to be possible (and is also called *ingratitudo*, by St. Thomas), but it is not a common vice.[52]

¶ *Opposed to Respect for Persons.* *Disobedience* is habitual unwillingness and failure to carry out the just commands of superiors; various grades are possible, depending on whether the commands depend on the Law of God, the will of a religious superior, the law of one's country, or the authority of one's parents.[53]

¶ *Opposed to Piety.* *Defect of honor for parents or country* is the vice which inclines children to neglect their parents and close relatives, particularly when these latter are in dire need. Lack of real patriotism is shown by the citizen who fails to do something for the defense or improvement of his country, when there is need for such action.

Excess of honor for parents or country is also a possible type of injustice, consisting in the tendency of some persons to overemphasize their duties to family and country at the expense of other duties, to God for instance.[54]

In conclusion, we might notice that a human being has a group of duties to other persons, which are not strict duties under the cardinal virtue of justice, but which are nevertheless real moral obligations. There is a just and reasonable medium to be observed in all our social relations to other persons. The general moral problem, here, is to

[51] These vices are not named by St. Thomas, in his treatment of vindication, *S.T.*, II–II, q. 108; however, they are implied in his discussion of the virtue.

[52] *S.T.*, II–II, q. 107, arts. 1–2,c.   [53] *S.T.*, II–II, q. 105, arts. 1–2,c.

[54] These vices are not named in St. Thomas' discussion of the virtues, *S.T.*, II–II, q. 101, arts. 1–4,c.

determine the precise mean of virtue in the individual case (by means of prudence) and to act voluntarily in accord with this reasonable mean (by the use of the potential parts of justice). In present-day language, *honesty* has taken on the general meaning of justice. We can say, then, that honesty demands that we not only pay our debts in money but also do our best to be liberal, friendly, truthful, just in the prosecution and punishment of those who have offended us, grateful to benefactors, respectful and obedient to all worthy persons. Later, we shall examine the duties of a human agent to God.[55]

Summary of Chapter X

We have observed the necessity of an acquired habit of the human will, to enable the human agent so to act in regard to other persons that his rights and their rights will be properly respected. Justice is this habit of the human will. Its essence lies in a certain equality in external operations which interrelate persons. A subjective right is a claim, or moral power, to do, possess, or exact something in regard to another person. Moral duty is the cognate term designating the moral necessity or obligation to respect moral rights. Legal justice differs from particular justice in the distinction of the *termini* of these virtues. Duties owed for the sake of the common good belong under legal justice. Duties owed for the sake of the private good of another come under particular justice. Commutative justice deals with the problem of maintaining a right equality in exchanges between persons, where the private good of both parties is the primary concern. Distributive justice deals with the assignment of things belonging to a community to the individual members of the community. Under distributive justice, equality of distribution is not arithmetical but proportionate to the value of the recipient in the community. Not strictly possessing the full nature of justice, but closely allied to it, are the virtues of liberality, friendliness, veracity, vindication, gratitude, respect for persons, piety to family and country, and piety to God (religion). Under each of these virtues, man's moral problems consist in the difficulty of acting in accord with right

[55] See *infra*, Chap. XIII.

reason in each contingent case, and of avoiding any excess or defect
in his external actions.

Recommended Readings

Thomas Aquinas, St., *Summa Theologiae*, I–II, 60, 2–3 (in *Basic Writings*,
    ed. Pegis, II, 458–461); II–II, qq. 57–63 and 80–120 (see English Do-
    minican translation).
Cronin, *Science of Ethics*, II, 80–86.
Farrell, *Companion to the Summa*, III, 165–189.
Gilson, *Moral Values and the Moral Life*, pp. 246–256.
Martinez, M. L., "Distributive Justice According to St. Thomas," *The
    Modern Schoolman*, XXIV (1947) 208–223.
Rommen, *The State in Catholic Thought*, pp. 319–326.

ADVANCED READINGS

Bésiade, "La justice générale d'après saint Thomas d'Aquin," *Mélanges
    Thomistes*, pp. 327–340.
Gemmel, "Die Justitia in der Lehre des hl. Thomas," *Scholastik*, XII
    (1937) 204–228.
Gilson, *Le Thomisme*, 5me éd., pp. 424–434.
Hering, "De genuina notione justitiae generalis seu legalis juxta S.
    Thomam," *Angelicum*, XIV (1937) 464–487.
Hugon, "De Epikeia Seu Aequitate (II–II, q. 120)," *Angelicum*, V (1928)
    359–367.
Lachance, *Le concept de droit selon Aristote et saint Thomas*, 453 pp.
Lottin, "Notes sur la vertu de justice," in *Psychologie et Morale*, III,
    284–313.
Phelan, "Justice and Friendship," *Maritain Volume of the Thomist*, pp.
    153–170.
Sertillanges, *La philosophie morale de s. Thomas*, pp. 167–181, 191–242.

Topics for Assignment

1. A Comparison of Legal and Particular Justice
2. The Nature of Distributive Justice
3. What Is a Commutation?
4. Why Every Lie Is Immoral
5. My Country, Right or Wrong?

XI · JUSTICE AND THE PERSONS OF OTHERS

Since the problems of justice are many (for all moral acts become questions of justice, when they issue into external actions which may involve other persons), it is difficult to find an orderly method of treating these problems. However, St. Thomas has set up a threefold division of the matter of justice [1] based on the use of (1) persons, (2) things, (3) services. This and the following two chapters will be devoted to some typical moral difficulties in these divisions. These chapters are not intended as a catalogue of solutions to all moral problems of justice. Their purpose is, rather, to illustrate the way in which a prudent person may apply right reason to the solution of his own moral difficulties in the field of justice.

We have seen that a moral right is some kind of *claim* upon an-*other* person. There is always something which is claimed and this is the *matter* of the right. Such matter includes not only material things but actions and omissions of action. In the present chapter, we shall consider the right to personal integrity, to a certain wholeness of body and soul which is required by the dignity of man.

The Right to Life

One of the most basic of human rights is the claim to life. This is not a positive but a natural right. It is not granted by any state or society, but flows from the nature of a free living being who is entitled to the means necessary to work for the attainment of his ultimate end. Life is the most fundamental natural means to this end.

[1] *S.T.*, II–II, 61, 3,c.

Ultimately, this right to life comes from God, as does everything else which man has.

¶ *Is Killing Necessarily Unjust?*   If we define killing, generically, as the taking of the life of any living being, then it becomes clear that this act is not intrinsically immoral. In the order of nature, the imperfect is for the sake of the perfect, the irrational is to serve the rational. Man, as a rational animal, is permitted to use things below him in this order of nature for his proper needs. He needs to eat plants and animals in order to maintain his life and strength. To eat plants and animals, they must be killed. So, killing is not, of itself, an immoral or unjust act.

The reason for stating this rather obvious truth is that there have been and are some religions and philosophies in which it is claimed that it is wrong to kill any living thing. Manicheism had such a belief (third to twelfth centuries) and some forms of modern Hinduism have it. This results in an aversion to all types of killing, even of flies or germs, and puts man on the level of the lowest living creature.

It is also to be noted that there are cases in which the killing of a plant or animal is unjust. To kill another man's cow, against the will of the owner, is unjust in ordinary circumstances. This is a moral offense against the owner (a person), not against the cow.[2]

¶ *Is It Unjust to Kill an Innocent Man?*   For one person to take the life of another person, when the victim has done nothing to require such punishment, is a plain act of injustice. Corresponding to the right of the victim to life, there is a duty on the part of other persons to do all that is morally possible to permit him to live. Murder is a very serious infraction of natural justice.

The case of a judge who is required by the processes of law to sentence a man, whom he knows to be innocent but who has been convicted on false testimony, to death, is a most difficult one. St. Thomas thinks the judge should carefully examine the evidence with a view to freeing the innocent man; he should turn it over to a higher court, where this is possible; but, if no other legal recourse is possible, the judge may pronounce the death sentence and the false witness becomes morally responsible for the death.

[2] *S.T.*, II–II, 64, 1,c, et ad 3m.

To kill an innocent person, *on the authority of God*, is not unjust. It is necessary, however, to be quite certain that one does have the authority of God.[3]

¶ *Is It Wrong to Kill an Unjust Aggressor?* A person is morally justified in killing another who is actually attacking the life, or any important good, of the person subject to unjust attack. The right of self-defense is a necessary correlative of the right to life. The attacker, by his unjust act, forfeits his right to consideration as a rational being. In order that his act be just, the one attacked may kill the aggressor only at the time of actual aggression (not before or after); he must be morally certain that no other less serious means of defense will suffice; he must know that the good which he is protecting (his life, that of another innocent and defenseless person, his life savings) is sufficiently great to warrant the use of extreme means. Most important, the primary purpose (end of the agent) of the defender must be to protect this good and he must not intend primarily the death of the attacker. (This involves what becomes known in later Scholastic ethics as the principle of double effect: where a moral action results in two consequences, one evil and the other good, the action *may be done morally*, if the good is in some reasonable proportion to the evil, if the good cannot be attained without the evil, if the two consequences are concomitant, and if the good is directly intended and the evil only permitted.)

An officer of the law may kill a criminal, when in a situation in which positive law grants him that authority, but such an officer is unjust if he kills from private malice, even under such conditions.[4]

¶ *Is the Chance Killing of a Human Being Unjust?* To kill a human being by chance is not, in itself, a moral act; hence, it is not an act which is unjust in its species. However, accidental killing may be unjust by virtue of related circumstances. Homicide resulting from the performance of an immoral act is culpable. For example: a robber who accidentally kills a victim, when committing a robbery, is guilty of an act of unjust killing, though not to the same extent as he would be, had he directly intended the killing. The accidental killer is also guilty of injustice, if he is not sorry after learning the

---

[3] *Ibid.*, art. 6,c, ad 3m et *ad primum*.   [4] *Ibid.*, art. 7,c.

results of his act. One is bound to exercise due care not to cause the death of another person.[5]

¶ *Is It Unjust to Kill Oneself?* To kill oneself on one's own authority, with the primary intention of causing one's own death, is called suicide. We have seen that man is required by fortitude, "to use all the means possible to the average person to protect and continue his life on earth." In relation to self, then, suicide is immoral because opposed to fortitude; not because it is opposed to justice. However, if other persons are adversely affected by the suicide, self-killing is also an act of injustice to these persons. We shall see later that suicide constitutes an infringement of the dominion of God over human life, and is consequently an act of irreligion. St. Thomas also points out that suicide is an offense against legal justice, because it deprives the community of one of its citizens. He adds, too, that it is an offense against charity, for it is right and natural for a man to love and care for himself as one of God's creatures.

Man is the master of those acts to which his free choice applies. To pass from this life to a future one is not properly subject to man's choice but to the power of God. It is not reasonable to kill oneself to avoid life's miseries; these are minor compared to death. Nor may one justly kill oneself as a punishment for one's sins; this would prevent the doing of temporal penance and is contrary to the need of a public trial of a criminal. Nor may a woman kill herself to avoid violation of her chastity; the injury to her body is not comparable to that of death; she need not sin, if she refrains from consenting to the attack. Nor may one kill oneself to avoid future sins; this is to do evil in order to attain a good, and is an act of despair.[6]

¶ *Is Capital Punishment Justifiable Morally?* A state (i.e., a perfect society, see Chap. XIV) may kill a criminal who has seriously offended against the common good of the community. Just as it is reasonable to cut off a diseased member of the human body, when this member threatens the welfare of the whole body, so is it reasonable to permit the body politic to cut off a bad member of society for the sake of the good of the whole society.

[5] *Ibid.*, art. 8,c, ad 2m, et ad 3m.
[6] *Ibid.*, art. 5,c, *ad primum*, and especially ad 3m.

Capital punishment may also be justified on the reasoning that a serious criminal has receded so far from the order of reason that he is no longer worthy of treatment as a rational being.[7]

¶ *Is a Private Person Permitted to Kill a Criminal?* It is not just for a private person to kill a criminal, simply on his private authority. There must be a public trial to determine that a man is a criminal and a serious offender against the common good, before he can be executed. The punishment of such offenders against the common good is the work of those who have charge of the community. A soldier killing the enemy, or a public executioner executing a condemned criminal, act on the authority of the state and not on private authority. Mob lynching of a supposed criminal is a serious act of injustice.[8]

¶ *Is It Just to Kill a Hopelessly Ill Person?* This question reduces to the principle: it is never just to kill an innocent man. If the sick person begs to be killed, he may be either voluntary or not voluntary in making this request. If voluntary, his choice is tantamount to that of the suicide. If not voluntary (*i.e.*, made in a condition in which he cannot reason and will clearly), then his choice is not a moral problem, in itself, but other persons are unjust if they aid in killing, when requested by a much distracted person.

If the sick, or suffering, person does not ask for death, then the one who kills him in order to "put him out of his misery" is taking over a right, which belongs only to God, *i.e.*, absolute dominion over human life. To kill, in order to cure pain or suffering, is to use a bad means to attain a good end. This can never be justified. Hence, euthanasia, or so-called mercy-killing, is an offense against justice.

¶ *Is It Just to Kill an Unborn Child?* Voluntary abortion, the killing of an unborn child, is unjust because the child is an innocent person. It is immoral to advise, or assist in, an operation or treatment for this purpose. The situation, in which a choice must be made between saving the life of a mother or that of an unborn child, is a highly technical case in the ethics of surgical practice. Circumstances differ widely and this sort of problem is best left to treatises on medical ethics.

---

[7] *Ibid.*, art. 2,c, et ad 3m.   [8] *Ibid.*, art. 3,c, et ad 2m.

¶ *Is a Priest Permitted to Kill Under the Same Conditions as a Lay Person?* St. Thomas gives two reasons why priests should not kill human beings, even in circumstances in which a lay person would be justified in doing so: (1) priests are devoted to the ministry of the altar, in imitation of Christ, Who did not strike back, when struck; (2) priests are devoted to the ministry of the New Law of Christian charity, in which the punishments of killing and mutilation are not used.[9] It will follow, then, that priests are not expected to serve as combat soldiers, nor as public executioners.

Problems Involving Bodily Injuries

There are some questions of justice centering in injuries to the physical integrity of the human person. Mutilation of the body, restriction of freedom of movement, and the infliction of physical pain, are the chief types of bodily injuries.

¶ *Is Mutilation of the Human Body Morally Permissible?* In its simplest form, mutilation means the act of cutting off some member of the human body. By extension, it would include other acts which render an organ incapable of functioning, or productive of malformations or abnormalities of structure and function. Thus, mutilation differs from other types of bodily injury inasmuch as it produces a permanent physical disability. In general, we may observe that mutilation of one's own body, without good reason, is an offense against temperance or fortitude; while unreasonable mutilation of the body of another is an act of injustice. Bodily integrity and strength are means to the living of a good life on earth.

Two chief reasons may be given for permitting mutilation in some moral cases: (1) if the removal of an organ is necessary for the good health of the whole body; (2) if the common good of society requires this as a drastic form of legal punishment. The first reason applies chiefly to the ethics of surgical operations. Where demanded by the condition of the patient, surgery is quite justifiable, if done with consent of the patient, or of his guardians in cases in which the

[9] *Ibid.*, art. 4,c.

patient is unable to consider his case reasonably. In emergencies, a surgeon may presume consent of his patient, if the circumstances clearly indicate that an operation is the only prudent means to be used. Surgical operations for cosmetic purposes (*e.g.*, facial surgery) are not justifiable, if done from a motive of vanity; but, if done to remove an impediment which is a handicap in one's life work, they may certainly be justified. No one should be forced to submit involuntarily to an excessively painful operation.

Mutilation of the reproductive organs to prevent sins against chastity is not justifiable. Better means are available to encourage chastity, and such operations do not prevent mental offenses against chastity. The sterilization of physically, mentally, or morally defective persons is not just. The right to reproduce one's kind is for the sake of the good of the human race, not for a private good. Legal punishments by a state should not be detrimental to the common good of the human species. If it be argued that certain families should not be allowed to continue to reproduce because of serious hereditary defects, it may be granted (though not necessarily) that such families are exceptional threats to the common good. However, ethical rules are not based on exceptional cases; to approve eugenic sterilization, even under state control, is to open the door to widespread denial of the natural rights of the individual person.

The second reason for permitting some types of mutilation is to protect the common good of society. St. Thomas argues that, if the state has a right to inflict the penalty of death on serious criminals, it has also the right to inflict the lesser punishment of mutilation. Extreme forms of torture can hardly be justified, however, even when used by state officials, for they are offenses against temperance and unworthy of a rational being. Whipping, which might leave permanent marks, may be justifiable in extreme cases, for instance. It is a form of minor mutilation, if it leaves permanent injuries. That St. Thomas would not justify all forms of mutilation, as legal punishments, is clear from his criticism of castration.[10]

It should be evident that cutting the hair or fingernails, while in some sense a mutilation, is not morally objectionable. Such practices

[10] *S.T.*, II–II, 65, 1,c, *ad primum*, ad 2m, et ad 3m.

do not injure the body and may be required for proper health and use of the body.

¶ *Is Whipping a Justifiable Form of Punishment?* Whipping (*verberatio*), or the infliction of temporary physical pain, is an act of injustice, when done without good reason. The good people of the Middle Ages no more approved sadistic torture than do the good people of any other period. St. Thomas was a mediaeval man and he states quite plainly, in his discussion of this point: "No injury may be done to another person, except as a punishment which is in accord with justice." [11]

Hence, physical and temporary pain may be justly used as a form of legal punishment by a state. The right to use this type of minor punishment may also be granted to the head of a family for the correction of his children. However, it is an offense against temperance and justice for a father to spank his children immoderately. Because his authority is limited to the rule of an imperfect society (the family), a parent is not justified in mutilating, or killing, his children for offenses against the good of the family.

Except when subject to unjust aggression, a private person may not justly beat, or inflict temporary pain or injury on, another person not under his care. The reasonable way to settle grievances in an organized society is to appeal to law-enforcement agencies. Private fights are offenses against the good order of society, that is, against legal justice.

¶ *Is Incarceration a Justifiable Form of Punishment?* Incarceration may be taken to mean the act of depriving a person of liberty of movement. In this connection, St. Thomas lists three orders of personal goods of the body: (1) integrity of body; (2) pleasure or repose of the senses; and (3) movement and use of bodily members.[12] Killing and permanent injury take away the first type of good; they constitute a most serious form of punishment, reserved to the use of state authority. Whipping and other forms of temporary pain take away the second kind of good; this sort of punishment may be used by the state and the heads of families. Incarceration deprives one of freedom of bodily movement, is of a temporary and minor

[11] *Ibid.*, art. 2,c.   [12] *S.T.*, II–II, 65, 3,c.

character, and so is a punishment which may be used, within reason, by state and family rulers and even by private individuals.

It is wrong to incarcerate another person, except for the sake of justice. Incarceration is one of the most reasonable types of legal punishment. It may also be used justly, in emergencies even by a private person, to prevent another person from doing evil. Generally speaking, the right of incarceration should be used only by those who have charge of others.[13]

¶ *Is a Bodily Injury More Unjust If It Affects Many People Indirectly?* To kill or injure one person is a direct act of injustice against that person, if there is no good reason for such injury. But the dependents and associates of the injured person may be adversely affected by such injury. The murderer of the father of a family deprives that family of its natural means of support. His offense is a greater act of injustice, because the injury extends to more than one person. For this reason, it is a greater crime to kill the head of a state (on whom many people are dependent for their political welfare) than to kill a private person. However, other circumstances (such as the way of killing, or the purpose) also increase or decrease the seriousness of such an injury. So, it is not an absolute rule, that the offense affecting more people is always more serious than that affecting a smaller number of people.[14]

Injuries to the Mental and Moral Integrity of Others

Every moral agent has a natural right to use the necessary means to achieve his ultimate happiness. Unreasonably to deprive him of the use of such means is always an act of injustice. Besides that integrity of body and of bodily movement already discussed, the means needed for a morally good life include a wholeness of mind and moral character. Mental and moral integrity may be disrupted in several ways. Unlike bodily injuries, which may at times be inflicted as just punishments, mental and moral injuries are not just forms of punishment.

[13] *Ibid. ad primum* et ad 3m.   [14] *Ibid.*, art. 4,c.

¶ *Is a Lie an Unjust Injury to Mental Integrity?* We have seen that lying is a bad act, because it is contrary to the virtue of veracity, which is a potential part of justice. Under this virtue, we have a duty to use signs which are not consciously opposed to what we think to be true. To misinform others is to injure their mental integrity, in the sense that the liar provides the occasion for others to think what is wrong.

Moreover, there are many situations in which strict justice demands the truth. To tell a lie in a court of law is to offend against the common good, and so against legal justice. The judge, the accuser, the accused, the witness, and the lawyer—each has an obligation under justice to see that sufficient information is made public to provide the basis for a just judgment of a case in court. It is not necessary for all people to tell all they know. But when a witness is asked a question pertinent to the case in trial, he must answer truthfully and as fully as prudence would require in the circumstances. The problem of secrets will be discussed in the next question.[15]

¶ *Is It Permissible to Divulge a Secret?* A priest may never reveal what has been learned in the confessional. Knowledge gained in the practice of a profession, other than that of the priest, should not be revealed unless the keeping of such secrets is detrimental to the public welfare, or seriously harmful to another individual. No one should promise to keep secret information which is required for the common good, or for an important private good. Secrets which come to be known in the ordinary course of life, should not be revealed without good reason. St. Thomas' discussion is brief and to the point:

Under no circumstances is a priest to reveal things which are conveyed to him in the secrecy of confession. The reason for this is that he does not know such things as a man, but as a minister of God. The bond of the sacrament is stronger than any precept originating from a man.

Concerning things secretly conveyed to a man, in any other way, this distinction must be made:

Sometimes, these things are such that a man is bound to reveal them

[15] St. Thomas has a long treatment of the obligations of persons in a court of law; those interested in this special field of professional ethics may read: *S.T.*, II–II, qq. 67–71.

as soon as they become known. This is the case, if they pertain either to the spiritual or physical corruption of the people at large (*multitudinis*) or to the serious harm of any person, or if there is anything else like this, which one is required to reveal as a witness or as an accuser. No one can be obliged, by a secret committed to him, to offend against this duty, for to accept such an obligation would be to break the faith which he owes to others.

Sometimes, these things are such that one is not obliged to reveal them. In this case, one may be obligated by the fact that these things are conveyed to him in secret. Then, he is in no way required to reveal them, not even by the order of a superior. The reason for this is that to keep faith is a matter of natural right, and no order can be given a man which contravenes a matter of natural right.[16]

¶ *Is It Justifiable to Lie for the Sake of a Good End?* There are practical situations, in which circumstances would seem almost to force the moral agent to tell a lie. First of all, it may happen that the apparent results of telling the truth may at times be bad. Suppose one is asked by a sick mother whether her son is well, and one knows that he has just been killed in an accident. To tell the truth bluntly may kill the mother. To say that you do not know, or that the son is well, is to tell a lie. To say nothing, is practically impossible, because the mother may suspect the worst. The first thing to do, in such a case, is to avoid telling a lie. Not even these extreme circumstances will make a lie good. It is never right to use a morally evil means, even for a good end. The next thing to do is to try to tell the truth in the most prudent and least shocking way. It is not always necessary to answer immediately. Nor is it necessary to tell the whole truth immediately. One might tell the mother that her son has met with an accident and that you will tell her more about it later. If she asks bluntly: "Is he dead?" there is nothing to do but tell the truth. If physical evil (even death) results from your truth-telling, that is not your fault. In no case may one use a lie to evade evil consequences.

Secondly, there are many situations in professional work (doctor, lawyer, nurse, political leader, and so on) in which a person has

16 *S.T.*, II–II, 70, 1, ad 2m.

privileged information which may cause harm if made public. The professional person has, in fact, an obligation to keep such information secret from the ordinary questioner. It is quite just for the professional person to refuse to answer private questions, and, where a blunt refusal is impossible, he or she may say that the answer is not known. Thus, if a statesman knows that war has been declared on another country, but is not yet to be announced, he may tell a reporter, in answer to a blunt question, that he does not know whether war has been declared. This should be taken to mean that he does not know anything which can be made public. This is not a formal lie, for it is true that the statesman does not know anything which he is permitted to tell the reporter at this time. So, though he may not justly tell a lie, the professional person may *prudently* give a partial answer which is true in some sense, though not necessarily in the sense in which it will be understood by every listener. This is what St. Thomas calls a prudent hiding of the truth by means of a dissimulation.[17]

A formal lie is the use of signs *with the intention of conveying what is not true*. Such an act is always morally evil (*malum ex genere*). No circumstances will justify the telling of a formal lie. "It is not licit to tell a lie for the sake of saving a person from danger of any sort." [18]

¶ *Is It Unjust to Harm the Moral Character of Another?*   Obviously, it is an act of injustice to do anything which positively contributes to immoral action on the part of another person. This is true of offenses previously listed as forms of luxury under temperance; they are acts of injustice insofar as they involve other persons in the external act. One may also be unjust in preventing others from doing their ordinary moral duties. An employer, for instance, who makes it impossible for an employee to fulfill his religious obligations (where such action is quite possible) is not just.

[17] "Licet tamen veritatem occultare prudenter sub aliqua dissimulatione . . . ," *S.T.*, II–II, 110, 3, ad 4m; see also the prudent evasion of a questioner who has no right to an answer, *S.T.*, II–II, 69, 2,c.
[18] *S.T.*, II–II, 110, 3, ad 4m; cf. *Quaest. Quodl.*, VIII, q. 6, art. 14,c.

Certain injuries to character, apart from unjust accusation in a court of law, involve the use of words harmful to another. Five species of injustice in speaking against another may be distinguished chiefly by the intention of the speaker: (1) *contumely* is the use of words (or other signs in place of words) openly derogatory to the honor of another person; (2) *detraction* is the secret use of words derogatory to the reputation of another person; (3) *alienation of friends* (*susurratio*) is the use of words secretly to prejudice one friend against another; (4) *derision* is the use of words with the intention of ridiculing, causing shame to another person; and (5) *cursing* (*maledictio*) is to express by words a command or desire that some evil befall another person, with an evil intention.[19] Of course, all of these are offenses against charity, and one (cursing) is an act of irreligion, if God is asked to call down evil on another unjustly; the point, here, is that they are also acts of injustice. They unjustly deprive others of the right to a good name in society.

¶ *Is It Unjust to Induce Another to Immoral Action?* To use, or sell, or advise the use of drugs, intoxicants, contraceptives, and other things which contribute to the moral delinquency of another person, is an injury to the moral character of that person. It is not necessarily immoral to manufacture or sell articles, such as liquor or drugs, which may be used in a morally good way. However, the maker, or seller, is under a moral obligation to obey the regulative laws of his state, and to take ordinary precautions against the misuse of such articles.

Much the same reasoning applies to proprietors of places of entertainment. They are obliged in justice to take care that their enterprise is not of such a character as to provide an occasion for immoral action, on the part of the average customer. Such a proprietor is not unjust, if in rare cases some customers misuse his facilities or product. However, to conduct a business which, in most cases, leads to immoral actions, is not only an offense against commutative justice (*i.e.*, against the private good of the customers) but also an

---

[19] These acts of injustice are treated by St. Thomas, at some length, in *S.T.*, II–II, qq. 72–76, in the order cited.

offense against legal justice (*i.e.*, against the common good) and against charity.

Summary of Chapter XI

In this chapter we have examined some problems concerning the use of persons. Each human being has a natural moral right to personal integrity, to a wholeness of body and soul. Personal goods of the body are of three kinds: (1) integrity of body; (2) repose of the senses; and (3) use of bodily members. It is unjust to deprive a person of any of these goods, without reason. The state may, for the sake of legal punishment, take away the use of any of these goods. The head of a family may not punish by destroying bodily integrity, but he may inflict temporary pain, or incarcerate, those under his care, when they deserve punishment. The private person may not, ordinarily, punish another; in emergencies, he may prevent another from doing evil, but only by the use of incarceration. Mental and moral integrity are unjustly disrupted by lying and by actions derogatory to the good character of another. Injuries to mental and moral integrity are never justifiable forms of punishment.

Recommended Readings

Thomas Aquinas, St., *Summa Theologiae*, II–II, qq. 64–76 (see English Dominican translation).

Cronin, *Science of Ethics*, II, 93–112.

Farrell, *Companion to the Summa*, III, 193–233.

Gilson, *Moral Values*, pp. 254–259.

ADVANCED READINGS

Thomae Aq., S., *In I Sent.*, d. 39, 2, 2; *In IV Sent.*, d. 25, 2, 2, 2; *Summa c. Gent.* III, 29, 112, 146; *De duobus praeceptis caritatis* (Op. IV) translated as: *The Commandments of God*, by L. Shapcote (London, 1937) pp. vii–89.

Gilson, *Le Thomisme*, éd. 5me, pp. 434–446.

Sertillanges, *La philosophie morale de s. Thomas*, pp. 180–184, 187–190.

Topics for Assignment

1. The Importance of Personal Integrity
2. The Moral Difference Between Homicide and Killing an Animal
3. Is It Right to Use Physical Force in Self-Defense?
4. Spare the Rod and Spoil the Child?
5. When Must I Reveal a Secret?

XII · JUSTICE AND MATERIAL THINGS

The moral problems to be considered in this chapter are grouped together because they are concerned with the use and management of the goods of this world. These goods are chiefly material things (excluding human bodies which we have dealt with in the previous chapter) but they also include intangible forms of earthly wealth, such as money, credit and other items of economic value. It is to be remembered that we are not concerned with the study of economics, in the modern sense, but with the *moral aspects* of the use and management of economic goods.

The Right to Use the Goods of This World

The first point to be noticed is that the *use* of things is different from the ownership and management of the same things. Use is the employment of something in such a way that the object is either consumed or, if not consumed, the object used is either wholly or partially taken over by the user, to the whole or partial exclusion of other users for some length of time. Thus, food is used when it is consumed; a violin is used but not consumed when it is played (such use excludes all but the one user at one time, normally); and a house is used when it is lived in (such use does not exclude others wholly but partially). Possession will be discussed later, but we may observe now that the use of a house is not identical with its possession. A renter uses a house and quite properly may be required to pay for that use, because such use does not consume the house. In the case of food, where use is ordinarily identical with consumption, one does not pay for the use but for the possession of the food. Things may have plural uses, of course, but one use will be the primary one and others secondary. Thus, the primary use of money is to spend it (a consumptive use) but a secondary use is as an item of bodily adornment, in cases where coins are incorporated in jewelry (a non-consumptive use).[1]

With this precise meaning for *use*, we may proceed to consider a group of typical moral problems:

¶ *Has Man a Moral Right to Use Things?* This is such a basic question that one may not understand immediately why it should be asked. Let us put it this way: most men unhesitatingly take over things and use them at will, killing animals and plants, destroying or altering inanimate things. How may this be justified in reason? The answer would seem to lie in a brief metaphysical consideration of man's place in the physical universe. Man is the most perfect of physical beings; in relation to man, all else is imperfect in the bodily world. Now, the imperfect exists for the sake of the perfect. Since man cannot live a bodily life and work for the attainment of his ultimate end, without using material things, he must have the moral right to use these things.[2]

There have been fanatical thinkers who have tried to restrict man's rights to the use of inanimate beings only. This appears to have been the belief of the Manichees. However, St. Thomas sums up the argument giving man the right to use all infra-human things, to satisfy his needs, in these lines:

Man, indeed, uses all kinds of things for his needs: some for food, and some for clothing. That is why he was made nude at birth, for he is able to procure clothing for himself from other things. So too, nature prepared no special food for him (other than milk), for he can obtain food for himself from other things. Some things [he may use] as a means of transport, for man is found to be weaker than many animals, in regard to speed of movement and the strength for long labor—so, there are other animals ready to help him. Moreover, man uses all sensible things for the perfection of intellectual knowledge.[3]

[1] *De Malo*, q. XIV, a. 4,c, et ad 15m. [2] *S.T.*, II–II, q. 66, a. 1,c.
[3] *Summa contra Gentiles*, III, c. 22 *ad fin.*

¶ *Should One Man Use or Keep More than He Needs, When Other Men Are in Want?* This is a very important moral question. Since the middle ages, an exaggerated concept of the priority and absolute character of the right of ownership has grown up. Many people now think that if they have acquired property legitimately, they have no obligation under justice to share its use with any other men. The modern man often has the conviction that to share the use of his excess property with others is exclusively an act of charity. This modern attitude is quite erroneous.

The right to use things takes precedence over the right to possess. Possession is for the sake of use, but use cannot be for the sake of possession. Food is to be eaten, clothing to be worn, houses to be lived in. That is, things are primarily to be used when there is need. Possession is not use, but the procuring or management of something for the sake of use. It is, then, unreasonable and immoral to possess or hold useful things, without using them, when other persons need them. The right to use things is one of man's most basic and natural rights; the right to possess things privately, as we shall see, is not a primary right but a reasonable determination of positive law.[4] This teaching is expressed as follows by St. Thomas: "The other thing which pertains to man in relation to exterior things is the use of them. And in regard to this, man should not hold exterior things as private (*ut proprias*) but as common (*ut communes*), in order that one may easily share them with others in need." [5]

Two points may be emphasized in this thomistic view of the use of things. Firstly, *this is not communism* in the modern sense. Unlike modern communism (to be discussed later in this chapter) which stresses group or social ownership and management of productive goods, thomistic ethics stresses the primacy of the common right to use economic goods. In a group practising strict communism, there could be no rich people. In a social group practising the rules of thomistic ethics, there could be rich persons, in the sense that some people could have charge of possibly large quantities of utility goods; these possessors would be morally right in using as much of

[4] See the next topic: *The Right to Manage the Accumulation and Distribution of Material Things.*

[5] *S.T.*, II–II, q. 66, 2,c.

these goods as they need, within reason; they would also have the moral obligation under justice to distribute the excess of these goods to other people who are in need, where such distribution is reasonably possible. As in all questions of external moral action, circumstances here play an important part in the determination of what is reasonable.

That brings us to our second point. The rich person is not morally obliged to feed and clothe all the needy people in the world, only those whom he may assist within reason. "A man is not required to look throughout the world for the needy whom he may help; it is enough if he does works of mercy for those with whom he comes in contact." [6] Circumstances of time and place may prevent me from giving of my abundance to some poor person in China. Changes of these circumstances may make it morally obligatory on the rich to share with such a poor person. This means that it is not wrong to be rich but the rich person takes on greater obligations under justice as his riches increase. He is in charge of things which others may need. He must be constantly on the alert to fulfill his just obligations as a steward of this world's goods. "The rich man does not act in an illicit way, in taking possession of a thing which was common [*i.e.*, not owned privately] from the beginning, provided he also share it with others (*si aliis etiam communicat*); he does sin, however, if he imprudently prohibits others from using this thing." [7]

¶ *May a Man Give Up This Right to Use Things?* This question is asked so that we may see clearly the difference between possession for use and possession for management. We are here thinking of possession for use; that is, we are considering the exercise of the right to use. Of course, no natural right may be given up but the actual *exercise* of the right may be given up in some cases. Thus, every human being has the right to procreate children but he, or she, need not exercise it. The use of material things cannot, however, be given up completely by human beings on this earth. Vows of poverty, as taken by religious, are promises to God to give up the exercise of the right to possess things as owner and manager but not

---

[6] *S.T.*, II–II, q. 71, a. 1,c.
[7] *S.T.*, II–II, q. 66, a. 2, ad 2m; see also: *Summa contra Gentiles*, III, c. 127.

to forfeit the use of these things. The use of things may be restricted to the bare necessities of life, for a religious or otherwise reasonable motive, but no man can reasonably forfeit completely the use of material things in this life.

A formal and very thorough discussion of this question is found in one of the shorter works of St. Thomas, *Against the Attackers of the Religious Life*.[8] Here, St. Thomas is defending the right of human beings to live in accord with the vows of poverty, chastity, and obedience, in a religious Order or Congregation. He points out that it is a work of perfect virtue to give up certain things which are naturally good, for the love of God. He is emphatic in stating that a person in the religious life is reasonably justified in giving up all exercise of the right to possess earthly things as owner and manager: "Potest enim sine dominio possessionum terrenarum natura conservari cum spe divini auxilii multis modis, unde quantumcumque ei subtrahatur, non erit superfluum si propter Deum fiat." [9] But he is equally emphatic in reminding the reader that no man, in this life, can entirely give up the *use* of temporal things and remain virtuous.[10] In objection twenty, it is pointed out that a Christian is commanded to say the Lord's Prayer and, in it, he is to ask for temporal things. St. Thomas' comment is: "In answer to the twentieth objection, it must be said that we are commanded to beg temporal things from God for the necessary uses of nature, hence we ought not give up temporal things but rather use them for the needs of the body, in food and clothing." [11]

¶ *Can This Right to Use Things Be Abused?* In answering this question, we should remember that material things are not persons (except in the case of human bodies, which are parts of persons and which we have considered in the previous chapter) and so, are not the terms of any moral duties. That is to say, man owes no moral duties to animals, or plants, or inanimate things. Abuse, or unreasonable use, of these things must be considered in relation to the moral agent and to the other human beings concerned.

[8] Not available in English: *Contra Impugnantes Dei Cultum et Religionem*, c. 6 *in toto;* in *Opuscula Omnia*, ed. Mandonnet (Paris, 1927), IV, 74–93.
[9] *Ibid.*, ad 10m, p. 88.   [10] See *Ibid.*, ad 6m to ad 19m, pp. 86–92.
[11] *Ibid.*, p. 93; cf. *S.T.*, II–II, q. 186, a. 3,c, et *ad primum*.

If a man uses material things in some unreasonable way, and this abuse causes no possible harm to other people, then this abuse is an offense under temperance or its related virtues. Gluttony and insobriety are examples of such abuse. We have already discussed them.

If a man uses material things inordinately, and thereby deprives other people of the use of these things to satisfy their natural needs, this is a form of abuse which is an offense against justice. The owner or manager of things is morally obliged to use them reasonably for his own needs and to share the surplus with others who are in need.[12] This is an obligation under justice. From the point of view of charity and the practice of the perfection of virtue in the religious life, even more generosity may be expected, and the distribution of goods must be done out of love of God. But we have not yet discussed the virtues of religion and charity.

The Right to Manage the Accumulation and Distribution of Material Things

We come now to the question of ownership. Proper treatment of this moral problem demands rigorous precision in the use of concepts and terms. Possession (*possessio*) is a generic term denoting, in the active sense, the act or state of holding power or control over something. Dominion (*dominium*) means the act or state of holding supreme power over something; to make this unambiguous, St. Thomas uses the phrase, principal dominion (*principale dominium*). Ownership (*proprietas*) meant, originally, private possession; hence, to speak strictly, private ownership is a redundant expression, and common ownership, or common property is an illogical combination of terms. However, ownership is often used in modern English as identical with possession.

Since God is the First Cause and Supreme Power of the universe, the *principal dominion* over all things belongs to God. Whatever dominion any man has over the material things of nature, then, will be *secondary* and derivative from the supreme dominion of God.

[12] C.G., III, c. 127 *ad fin.*

This is to say that no man can have absolute and unlimited power over the goods of this earth. Because man has been made by God, with a corporeal nature requiring the use of food, drink, clothing, and other things for continued existence, man holds natural dominion over these things, in the sense that he is naturally equipped by his reason and will to make use of these things.[13]

According to the natural moral law, then, or according to the practical order of reason, man has the right or moral power to possess material things for the purpose of satisfying the reasonable needs of human nature. Note that this is a dominion for the sake of use. The following statement by St. Thomas puts this clearly: "God has the principal dominion over all things. And He, according to His Providence, has ordered some things for the bodily support of man. And because of this, man has natural dominion over things, in regard to the power to use them (*quantum ad potestatem utendi ipsis*)." [14]

¶ *Is This Natural Dominion Identical with Private Possession?* This natural dominion over things, in regard to the power to use them, belongs to man as a species. All men share this right in common. It is not identical with private possession. In the order of time, it is clear that before an individual man can use a thing he must get it. This "getting" of things is the exercise of the *power of accumulating and distributing things* (*potestas procurandi et dispensandi*). This is very close to what the modern economist calls management.

Now, while the actual use of things is personal and individual (I eat my food, you eat yours), there are three possible ways of managing the accumulation and distribution of things to be used: (1) Some individual men may take charge of certain things provided by nature and by the industry of man, and thus manage these things for their own use and that of other men. This is the *private possession* of things for common use. (2) Another possibility is for a group of human beings to take common control over certain useful things, managing the accumulation and distribution on a common, or shared, basis. Here, too, management must be for common use. We have already settled the matter of use; it must be so handled that things are

[13] *S.T.*, II–II, q. 66, a. 1,c.   [14] *Ibid., ad primum.*

available, where there is excess of the needs of the managers, to all who are in need. This is *communal possession* for common use. (3) The third possibility is very simple but hardly practicable for all men. Some men, however, may decide to give up all management of the accumulation and distribution of things, leaving the care of material things to God and to other men. Such men beg for a living and their system is *mendicancy*.

All three of these "systems" of getting things for use were in practice in St. Thomas' day, and are still employed. Private possession was, and is still, most usual. Communal possession was the system of certain religious congregations (and still is), whose members possessed no things privately but which religious groups possessed and managed and distributed things, corporately. There have been, and are, other nonreligious groups practising communal possession. Countries, states, cities, and smaller societies all over the world possess and manage things, such as parks, streets, transportation systems, public utilities, and even factories and businesses, in a communal way. Finally, there are always beggars. The mendicant Orders in the Catholic Church were originally associations of beggars. Possibly, there are still some groups of religious men and women who possess neither private nor communal things. St. Thomas Aquinas was pretty much of a beggar, himself, but his Order (Dominicans) permitted the holding of some common possessions, even in the thirteenth century.

The point is that it is possible for some men to get things to use by following any one of these three systems. So, the natural law does not say that a particular man *must* follow any one of them. That is not to say that each of the three systems is equally reasonable. In the science of ethics, we have to work to conclusions which apply to the general run of men. Our task now is to see which system is best for the ordinary man, under the ordinary circumstances of life, to try to follow. Thus, the conclusion which we reach will be a *positive determination* of moral law, added to the original dictates of man's nature.[15]

¶ *Is Private Possession of Things Permitted by the Natural Moral*

[15] *S.T.*, II–II, q. 66, a. 2, *ad primum;* cf. q. 57, a. 3,c.

Law? The answer to this question is: of course it is! The only reason why the question is asked is because many good people in the Christian Church have not understood what was meant, when Christ told that rich young man to go and sell his goods and give the proceeds to the poor. Some of the early Christians thought that it was wrong to possess things privately. Like some other advice in the New Testament, this was a counsel of perfection, to be followed by some especially good people but not a precept obligatory on all Christians.

It is not only morally permissible for men to possess, or manage the accumulation and distribution of, things privately, this is the most reasonable and best-working method of management. Let us examine the three reasons given by St. Thomas [16] for this conclusion:

(1) A person is usually more careful and conscientious in managing something which is his own. Under communal possession each man has a tendency to let the other fellow do the job, because every man tries to avoid work. (We all know that this is very true. The streets of a city are the common possessions of the citizens; it is in the interests of all to keep these streets clean; very few people would work on them, if not paid, or forced by civil law, to do so.)

(2) It is more orderly for each person to have charge of certain possessions of his own. Confusion results in a situation where there is no division of the things to be managed. (Again, we can see that this is usually true. Let us say that ten men have communal possession of a farm on which there are ten cows. It is not practical to have each man take care of one-tenth of each cow; nor is it practical just to have each man do as much as he can, for they may all decide to milk the same cow at the same time. If each man is given one particular cow to manage all the time, that will be most orderly, but we are then practising private management.)

(3) Finally, private possession and management of things are more peaceful than community management. Where possessions are to be managed by a group, there is far more occasion for quarreling. (The fact that some religious groups practise communal possession suc-

[16] *S.T.*, II–II, q. 66, 2,c.

cessfully is not a contradiction of this argument. Those who are devoted to the perfection of virtue, in the religious life, have special,
supernatural motives and graces which impel them to live peacefully
with their associates. The ordinary man is less fortunate. It is recognized by legal experts that community possessions, such as estates,
should be divided as soon as possible to avoid trouble.)

St. Thomas does not consider private possession natural to man,
in the unqualified sense of natural. The union of male and female is
absolutely a matter of natural right, according to the first manner
in which a right may be called natural. This right to procreate offspring is so natural that it is common to all animals. On the other
hand, the right to private possessions does not pertain to brutes but
only to man who has the rational ability to consider his situation in
relation to the world of material things and to reason to the most
peaceful method of managing these things. By an absolute consideration, there is nothing in the nature of this man and this field to indicate that this field belongs to this man. However, a rational consideration of the fact that this man has the best opportunity to
cultivate this field and to make good use of it leads to the conclusion
that this man should possess and manage this field. Such a right, as
that of private possessions, St. Thomas regards as a determination of
the law of peoples (*jus gentium*). It is not unnatural but natural in
a qualified sense; that is, the right to private possession is not due to
the impulsion of infra-rational "instinct," but to the use of the dictates of reason.[17]

❡ *Is Communal Possession Fundamentally Immoral?* The previous
argument has already indicated that communal possession is not
absolutely opposed to man's nature. That is why this system of
managing things is not immoral. But we have seen that private possession is the more reasonable arrangement for most men living under
the usual circumstances of human life. Hence, our conclusion should
be that, while communal possession is not fundamentally immoral,
private possession is the best working and more peaceful system. The
prudent man will not voluntarily choose to live under a system of
communal possessions, when he knows that such a system is ill-

[17] *S.T.*, II–II, q. 57, a. 3,c.

adapted to rational beings and calculated to foster disorder and quarrels. Under special circumstances, such as are found in a religious community or in the life of a soldier on the field of battle, communal management may be a morally prudent arrangement. The question of involuntary acceptance of a system of communal management is our next problem.

¶ *Why Do Catholic Moral Thinkers Condemn Communism?* The writers who have done most to make communism an important world movement (Marx, Engels, Lenin, and Stalin) are not interested in theoretical definitions and they seem carefully to have avoided defining communism. For that reason it is impossible to quote a short statement of the meaning of this term, from authoritative and sympathetic sources. A writer who is commonly regarded as well acquainted with the literature of communism and who has studied the philosophical background and tendencies of the Soviet Union, while living in Russia, is John Somerville. After describing socialism, in its economic aspects, as: "collective ownership of the means of production, the abolition of private profits, surplus value, exploitation therefrom, economic classes, and involuntary employment"; (which system is "now regarded as attained in the U.S.S.R."), he proceeds to say this. "The second stage is called communism. It presupposes a functioning economy of abundance on the basis of an unhampered utilization of productive potentialities, as a result of which it will be possible to apply the principle, 'From each according to ability, to each according to needs' instead of, as under socialism, 'according to work performed.' " [18]

To make this a little more understandable, let us say that modern communism, in its economic views, grew out of a criticism of the economic system known as capitalism. This latter is: "an economic system in which capital and capitalists play the principal part; specifically, the system of modern countries in which the ownership of land and natural wealth, the production, distribution, and exchange of goods, and the operation of the system itself, are effected

[18] From the essay: "Dialectical Materialism," in *Twentieth Century Philosophy* (New York, 1943), p. 495; the same statement by Dr. Somerville is printed as a definition of communism, in *The Dictionary of Philosophy*, D. Runes, ed. (New York, 1942), p. 59.

by private enterprise and control under competitive conditions." [19] Capitalism encourages private management by allowing the owners of capital to keep all, or some, of the profits from successful business operations. Communism does not like this private enterprise, profit-motivated system of economics.

There are two general reasons why Catholic moralists do not favor communism: (1) Most communists in the modern world are atheists; they do not believe that God exists and they think that people who do believe in God are foolish. Most communists are materialists; they deny the existence of a spiritual soul in man and of an after-life. Most communists are determinists; they do not think that the individual human person is morally free to control his own destiny; they think that the person has no value, apart from his social, economic, and political context. Most communists are irrationalists; they claim that they are not bound by the classical laws of logic and reasoning; they do not accept the principle of noncontradiction; they say one thing today, its contradictory tomorrow, as the expediency of their program demands. These views are not held by all communists, nor are they necessarily connected with the economic position of communism, but present-day communism is identified with them. It is not necessary to demonstrate that these views are unacceptable to Catholic thinkers. Nor can they be accepted by any reasonable and unprejudiced person. (2) The second reason why Catholic moralists oppose communism lies in the nature of its economic program, viewed morally. Whatever else communism stands for, it looks for a coming period in the history of the world, when there will be no private possession and management of things. It has, perhaps, done something of value in criticizing some of the evils and defects in an unregulated capitalist economy. Catholic thinkers and authorities have also criticized these evils. One should not think that because Catholic moralists oppose communism, and because capitalistic thinkers oppose communism, therefore Catholic thought is identical with capitalism.

Now, while St. Thomas Aquinas, who is a leading figure in Catholic moral philosophy, admitted the possibility of communal manage-

[19] *Webster's Collegiate Dictionary*, 5th ed. (Springfield, 1943).

ment of economic goods (though not considering it the most reasonable method of possession for the average man), he did not admit that an *involuntary* community of goods was morally justifiable. That is to say, it is one thing for a small number of men or women *willingly* to give up all concern for economic goods, but it is quite a different matter for a social system, or a world movement, *to force* all men to renounce the exercise of the right to private possessions. "Nothing is more desirable to man than the freedom of his own will. For, through it man is the ruler of others, through it he can use or enjoy other things, through it he even rules his own actions." [20] To force a man to give up his free use and enjoyment of things is to cut out a large part of the exercise of freedom of choice, with a consequent diminution of the importance of the individual person. Thus, as Jacques Maritain has well expressed it,[21] though communism starts with a criticism of the exploitation and abuse of man under capitalism, and it looks to the absolute emancipation of man, it ends with a dehumanization of man because its ideal is the "maximum production of the economic whole," and the interests of the individual person become wholly subordinated and submerged in the struggle for the attainment of collective prosperity. The point at issue now becomes very clear; communism aims to sacrifice everything, man and God, for an "economy of abundance"; Christian ethics is directed primarily to the attainment of the personal happiness of each and every man, in a future life. There is between communism and Christian ethics neither agreement on the end of man, nor on the means to the attainment of that end.

Neither richness nor poverty is a moral fault in itself, but the abuses of them are.[22] Forced poverty gives rise to connected evils, which are quite foreign to voluntary poverty.[23]

[20] St. Thomas, *De Perfectione Vitae Spiritualis*, c. 10; ed. Mandonnet, IV, 213.

[21] *The Person and the Common Good* (New York, 1947), Chap. V, pp. 83–84.

[22] "sicut divitiae non sunt in culpa, sed divitiarum abusus, ita mendicitas sive paupertas non est in culpa, sed paupertatis abusus, quando scilicet aliquis paupertatem invitus et impatienter sustinet; tunc enim desiderio divitiarum in multa peccata quandoque incidit." *Contra Impug. Dei Cult. et Relig.*, c. 6, *ad primum*, p. 85.

[23] "coacta paupertas aliquando pericula habet annexa, quae a voluntaria paupertate sunt procul." *Ibid.*

From the point of view of the principles of thomistic ethics, there is no evident reason why some combination of private possession and communal possession should be called immoral or unjust. Provided the natural rights of persons are respected (and the accumulation of a large fortune is not one of these rights), government regulation of industry, business, and labor is not by any means a moral evil. Nor is there any reason why communities or states should not engage in the management and distribution of utility goods. In fact, it is one of the moral obligations of government so to regulate possessions that the common good is maintained.[24]

Problems in the Possession and Management of Things

Granting that private possession and management are the most reasonable method of providing utility goods for the average man, we may next consider certain basic questions about the exercise of this right. The following problems are chose as typical and are not offered as a complete catalogue of difficulties.

¶ How May the Goods of Nature Be Originally Acquired? We have already noted that the goods of nature are negatively common. That means that before any individual man asserts his right to possess and manage a certain thing, say this field which has never been owned by anyone before, there is no natural fact or mark on the field saying that this field is to be owned by this man.[25] However, it is the work of practical reason to consider a moral situation not only absolutely but also in relation to the circumstances. One of the most important circumstances, in regard to original possession, is the fact that an individual man is the first to take over a certain thing in nature. This fact is called *original occupancy*. Another such circumstance is the opportunity to use a thing. It is a matter of prudence to determine how much land a person may appropriate and use without depriving later arrivals of their just claims to parts of nature. In general, one may say that a first occupant has the right to assert

[24] "regulatio possessionum multum confert ad conservationem civitatis vel gentis." *S.T.*, I–II, q. 105, a. 2, ad 3m.
[25] *S.T.*, II–II, q. 57, a. 3,c.

title, that is, to make a valid claim to the actual ownership, to as much negatively common land as he can actually cultivate, or use.

If we recall that, in granting the first occupant the right to take over as much of the things of nature as he can reasonably manage, we are also limiting his right by requiring him to grant common use of these things, then we can see that no man will be deprived of the means of sustenance by this arrangement. Few men will work too hard to possess large quantities of utility goods, if they know that anyone in need may come along and ask for the surplus goods with perfect justice.[26]

¶ *Is the Laborer Entitled to the Product of His Labor?* If the laborer is also the private possessor of the raw materials, tools, and other means whereby his work is done, then he is reasonably entitled to whatever increase in value is produced by his own work. This is due to the fact that each person is in charge of the use of his own person, and so is entitled to the product of such use. Such a private producer is morally bound to share with others in need the excess of utility goods which he controls. But he may sell the product of his labor at a just price, which is to be determined by a prudent estimate of the value, made with a view to all pertinent circumstances of time and place.[27]

Since the foregoing simple case does not occur frequently in the modern world, it is necessary to consider the more usual case of the worker who is employed by another man to work on materials, and with tools and machines, and in premises owned by someone other than the worker. It becomes very difficult to determine the amount of the product to which the worker is entitled under such complex circumstances, and it is often impossible for the individual worker to be compensated by his taking a portion of the product of his work. Hence, the modern worker most frequently enters into the service-wage contract. This contract presents many moral problems, with which St. Thomas was unfamiliar. The following outline is offered as a basis for discussion and guidance in reasoning about this kind of moral problem.

[26] See *S.T.*, II–II, q. 66, a. 2, ad 2m.
[27] *S.T.*, II–II, q. 78, a. 4, ad 2m.

MORAL CONSIDERATION OF SERVICE-WAGE CONTRACT

In this contract, the worker's services are turned over to the use of the employer who, in turn, pays a regular wage to the employee. It is morally requisite that the services and wages be mutually just.[28] Payment of a just wage is to be considered in relation to both commutative and distributive justice, when we are thinking of the private good of worker and employer; in relation to legal justice, when we have regard, as we must, for the common good.

According to commutative justice the just balance of wage and service is determined by a simple equality; there is no mechanical method of weighing the value of human service in terms of money, of course; the commutative value of services is to be arrived at by a prudent estimate of the economic value of the services of the worker; thus, by commutative justice, if A makes twice as many shoes, in one hour, as B, then A should be paid twice as much as B. Two points are to be noted here: (1) comutative justice cannot by itself provide a reasonable standard for the determination of a minimum living wage; in periods when the supply of labor greatly exceeds the demand for services, the employer could get workers who would work for less than the just wage; moral and legal consideration of justice in the service-wage contract cannot stop at this point; (2) commutative justice offers adequate justification for the paying of larger salaries or wages to good, or more productive workers, than to poor workers; but it cannot tell us what is the lowest wage which may reasonably be paid to the poorest, or least-productive, of workers.

According to distributive justice a just wage is not determined by simple equality of services and wages but by a consideration of the personal needs of the worker. The chief personal circumstance is the need to support a family. The average male worker is, at least potentially, the wage-earner for the family. The family is (as we shall see in Chapter XIV) a natural society contributing to the welfare of the individual and to the common good. Hence, every male worker should be paid enough wages to keep an average sized family

---

[28] "In our work, that is called just which corresponds to something else, according to some sort of equality; for instance, payment of a proper wage for a service rendered. . . ," *S.T.*, II–II, q. 57, a. 1,c.

in reasonable comfort. This includes not only the basic necessities for present existence but also enough money for the education of children, for some recreation, for religious and cultural expenses, for saving for sickness, periods of unemployment, and old age. If the employer provides for some of these employee needs in some other reasonable way, by special insurance or by government taxation for instance, then wages need not be quite so high. Particularly for the unskilled worker, the estimate of a just wage according to distributive justice will usually be higher than that based on commutative justice. The employer is morally required to pay a minimum living wage according to distributive justice and not merely the lowest wage for which he can get labor by bargaining.

According to legal justice both the obligations of commutative and of distributive justice are to be considered in relation to the common good. In a community, such as a state or country, the welfare of all citizens and residents, individually and collectively, is a matter of concern. It is the obligation of the government to use all necessary force and sanction of positive law to bring about a just and equitable distribution and use of economic goods. Not only the strict equality of the commutative contract may be so enforced but also the observation of obligations under distributive justice. We must keep clearly in mind that distributive justice *is justice*, not charity; and its obligations are enforceable at law.

Associations of employees (trade unions, guilds, professional workers' organizations) are just means of promoting the welfare of groups of employees having common aims. These are actually special societies (see Chapter XIV, for the concept of society) and, like any other society, must observe the natural moral law in their corporate actions. The purpose of such employee associations must be morally right; to secure adequate wages, to promote good working and living conditions, reasonable hiring and firing practices, and things of this kind.

If such associations of employees are aimed at attaining control of management, or at making it impossible for an employer to operate economically, at dictation of governmental policies in the sole interest of labor, at the control of international relations to advance the interest of some other country or system of government, then they are no longer employee associations but become political groups and are either not morally justified, or they must be considered as political societies.

It is a question of method, which does not directly concern the ethician, whether these associations are organized within one industry, or one business, or to include all people engaged in one type of work. The larger the association, the greater is its obligation to promote the common good of the whole community. Leaders of such associations must be very just and capable men, for they have it in their power to influence the lives of large numbers of people.

Any reasonable and just means may be used to promote the welfare of labor. Obviously, the individual worker cannot alone do much to influence the behavior of his employer. Arbitration of disputes is by far the most reasonable method of settling difficulties. The strike (cessation of work by numbers of workers who wish to compel an employer to right a grievance) is only morally justifiable in extreme cases. For a strike to be justifiable: (1) the strikers must have a real grievance; (2) the grievance must be such that it is morally possible for the employer to correct it; (3) all less extreme means to improve the situation must first be tried; and (4) the strike must not be of such a nature as seriously to harm the common good.

Employers also have rights under justice. They are entitled to honest and good service, from the workers. Employer associations are morally justifiable, if they have good ends and use just means. Lockouts and wholesale firing of employees are extreme practices, usually deleterious to the common good. But employers and managers take the responsibility for the control of business and industry and they should be permitted the authority to manage their own businesses, within the limits of reason.

In a noncommunistic economy, some margin of profit must be left to the owner and manager of a business. Workers should not expect that all profits from a good year be distributed, for it is necessary to use such profits to main decent wages over a bad period. Bonuses and other plans for the distribution of excess profits should be governed by distributive justice. There should be some reasonable basis for ranking the recipients of such distributions (degree of skill, length of service, value to the business, and other such considerations). Government taxation of excess profits is a reasonable and morally justifiable device.

Professional workers and people who provide services to individual clients (*e.g.*, lawyers, doctors, nurses, architects, barbers, and so on) are governed chiefly by commutative justice in setting their fees. They are justified in expecting greater compensation for their time than the unskilled worker, because of the expense of learning their profession, the higher quality of services required, the added responsibility of their work (thus a doctor works under the continued strain of life and death, while a mailman does not), and the cost of professional equipment. It is not unjust for such skilled workers to adjust their fees to the ability of the client to pay; this is an application of distributive justice to the problem.

Employees of institutions of public welfare (hospitals, social agencies, police agencies, public utilities) are engaged in work which is partly like that of the professional worker, partly like that of the industrial worker. The work of such people is very directly related to the common good. Strikes by such workers will usually be contrary to the common good, and so difficult to justify. Reasoned appeals to public opinion and interest are the best moral means to secure correction of grievances of these workers.

¶ *Is It Wrong to Make a Profit on Buying and Selling?* One of the simplest commutations is barter, the exchange of one useful thing for another useful thing. The owner of a farm wishes a pair of shoes, so he exchanges three bags of potatoes for a pair of shoes made by the village shoemaker. In this commutation, justice is commutative; there should be simple equality between the value of the potatoes and the shoes. This equality is to be determined by mutual agreement, each person making a prudent estimate of the actual worth of his possession. On this simple exchange, neither person should try to make a profit.

For many obvious reasons, barter is usually supplanted by the buying-selling contract. It is difficult to equate one kind of thing with a different kind of thing; it is hard to carry these things around to make the exchange; a man may not be able to use all the things offered in exchange by another, and may wish to divide them with a third person, for some consideration. For these and other reasons, money was brought into use. Money is a kind of common denominator of economic value; it may have some common and rather stable value of its own, as does gold; or, it may have little more than arbitrary, or symbolic value, as in the case of coins made of cheap material or bills made of paper. Money is primarily useful to effect a reasonable exchange of utility goods—so, the primary use of money is to spend it.

Money may be employed in a simple exchange of thing for thing. Thus, the shoemaker may not want all or any of the potatoes. He may take money and one bag of potatoes, or all money, for his shoes. Here again, the value of the shoes should be approximately equal to the value of the money, or money and potatoes. No profit is morally allowable on such an exchange. What is just, is what is simply equal, in this kind of commutation.[29] There is no morally recognizable reason why one person should "get the better" of another person, in such an exchange.

But the man, such as the shoemaker, who takes some raw material and works on it to improve its value, is reasonably entitled to put a higher value on his finished product than that of the original materials. There are other good reasons for increasing the just price of a thing. A reasonable amount may be added to cover the costs of handling, transporting, and storing goods. The owner is also entitled to charge something to cover the danger of loss in transportation, or in manufacturing.[30]

Some persons may engage in the business of buying and selling goods, in order to make their living. These people were called *negotiatores*, by St. Thomas, and we know them as businessmen. There is a danger that the businessman may become too interested in acquiring wealth for its own sake, but it is quite possible for a

[29] *S.T.*, II–II, q. 61, a. 4,c; and q. 78, 4,c, et ad 2m.
[30] *S.T.*, II–II, q. 78, ad 2m.

person to engage in buying and selling with justice. Many businessmen desire to make legitimate profits, in order to support their
homes, to promote the common good, to help the poor. Their
profits, when not excessive, are a justifiable reward for their work
(*stipendium laboris*).

Clerics (priests, monks, bishops) should avoid engaging in the
business of buying and selling, not because it is essentially evil but
because such business tends to make a person too interested in the
affairs of this world and because it presents too many occasions for
acquiring vices of injustice and intemperance. However, it is not
morally wrong for priests to buy and sell things for use, in the
simple commutation described above. The thing may be summed
up by saying that a priest is a minister of God and he should not
try to be a businessman.

¶ *Has One the Right to Dispose of Possessions by Gift or Inheritance?* Gift is taken to mean, here, the transfer of private possession of some economic good by the possessor to some other
person, without compensation. In this, as in all other questions
having to do with detailed problems of property management, it
is best for the ethician to refrain from a too definite system of rules.
It is the work of positive law to determine the exact manner in
which justice may be brought about in the affairs of civil society.
On many questions, there are several possible ways of determining
what is legally right, *i.e.*, the *legale justum*. We have only to read
St. Thomas' discussion of the legal (judicial) precepts of the old
Jewish law [31] to see that this is the attitude of thomistic ethics. If
the law of a society is not opposed to moral law, it should in general be obeyed by all members of that society. In the Jewish law,
there were many rules governing the management and use of
earthly possessions. These were good rules. They were formally of
obligation to the Jewish people. Many of these positive determinations of Jewish law were retained, at least for a time, by the
Christian peoples. So too, were many rules from Roman law.

Now, the right to dispose of possessions by gift is a reasonable
determination of positive law. If a man has charge of certain pos-

[31] *S.T.*, I–II, q. 105, a. 2; in Pegis, *Basic Writings*, II, 932–940.

sessions and he has some reason for wishing to give up this charge, there is no moral reason why he should not do so. If there be some additional circumstance, such as the fact that the recipient will almost certainly put the possessions to bad use, or that the donation will cause injury to some third person, then this changes the problem.

Much the same reasoning applies to inheritance or bequest. Among the Jewish people, the aim of property law was to keep possessions distributed among the various families and tribes. To this end, rules were made requiring property of a deceased person to go to natural heirs (first, to the son; second, to the daughter; third, to the brother; fourth, to the father's brother; and so on); [32] these rules were based on the reasonable conviction that possessions should not be alienated from the family. It is morally approvable for a possessor to determine the distribution of his possessions at death. Much property is such that it can best be managed by members of a family already acquainted with the nature of the property. This is not to say that there is no other way of determining such a problem, according to positive law. If a state rules that some part of an inheritance be collected in taxes, for the common good, this is a reasonable determination. Critics of the right of inheritance usually base their objections on the abuse of inherited property by heirs. This criticism sometimes overlooks the fact that an heir who "runs through a fortune" quickly, is really getting rid of wealth which the heir is not capable of managing. It is a self-righting situation. More reasonable criticism could be directed against the heir who keeps and increases a family fortune, without seeing that it is put to good use. Thriftiness is not a thomistic virtue. To save a reasonable amount for the future is a part of prudence, i.e., foresight (*providentia*); but to save because of a horror of spending is to place a distorted value on wealth.

In a society in which the positive law recognizes gift and inheritance as legitimate titles, it is morally right to abide by these positive laws. Abuses of these titles to possessions do occur; they may be partly restrained by positive laws, but the virtues of moral

[32] *Ibid.*

justice and charity are the best correctives for such disorders. Thus, speaking of good order in society, which is peace, St. Thomas remarks: "peace is the work of justice indirectly; but it is the work of charity directly; for, charity causes peace for an essential reason of its own. . . ." [33]

Offenses Against Private Possessors

We can now examine a few typical problems associated with the possession of things. These will be treated in relation to private possession, but it should be noted that the same, or parallel, offenses could occur under a system of communal possession. Theft, fraud, and robbery are possible in a communistic set-up, but with this difference: to steal, or otherwise misappropriate goods under communism, is to offend the common good directly.

¶ *Is It Unjust to Steal?* Stealing, or theft, is the act (where habitual, the vice) of taking, in a hidden manner, what belongs to another. There are three elements in this definition: (1) theft deals with things *belonging to another person or to other persons;* (2) it is concerned with *the possessions* of others, not with their persons; and (3) it is a usurpation which is *surreptitious, hidden, furtive.*

Theft is unjust because of two of these elements, the first and the third. In regard to the first: theft fails to give to the other person what is his due. In regard to the third element: theft offends justice because of the deception, or furtiveness, by which it is carried out. Hence, there is a double evil in most cases of theft.[34]

Unusual circumstances may change the moral quality of this act. If the goods taken belong to the taker but are taken in a furtive way, there may still be some injustice in the way in which the act is done. Let us say that A has left an automobile on deposit with B; when A asks B for the car, B will not give it up, so A steals the car. This is not an offense against the first element of the definition, but it is an offense against the third element. Such an offense is op-

[33] *S.T.*, II–II, q. 29, a. 3, ad 3m.   [34] *S.T.*, II–II, q. 66, a. 3,c.

posed to the good order of the community (St. Thomas regards
it as against the common good) and restitution or satisfaction may
be required, not to the receiver of the deposit but to the community. This means that it would be morally right for a judge to
assess a fine for such an offense.[35]

Another important circumstance is the *need* of the taker. In a
case of extreme and immediate necessity (say a man is almost dying
from hunger and no one will give him anything to eat), edible
things are to be regarded as available for common use. The hungry
man may, under these precise circumstances, take what he immediately needs from the excess goods of another. This act is not
theft and it is not against justice.[36] One may even take another's
goods to help some third person who is in dire need, if there is no
other reasonable way of helping him.[37]

¶ *May One Justly Keep Anything Found?* There are two typical cases, in regard to finding things: (1) if what is found never
belonged to anyone, or belongs to no living person (*e.g.*, precious
stones at the seaside, or long-hidden treasure), then the finder may
justly keep his findings. He is justified by the principle of original
possession or occupancy. However, if he lives in a society which
regulates such discoveries by positive law, requiring such discoveries to be turned over, in whole or in part to the common
fund, the finder is morally bound to turn over his findings to the
common fund.[38] (2) If the goods found belong to some person,
then: (a) the finder may keep his findings, temporarily, with the
intention of returning them as soon as reasonable opportunity is
afforded; (b) the finder, who cannot identify the owner by using
ordinary means of inquiry, may keep unclaimed goods without
injustice; (c) in all other cases, since the finder can only manage
to keep his findings by concealment, to keep things found, when
they belong to another, is theft.[39]

It may be practical to outline a somewhat similar case under
modern conditions. Suppose A is sent some handkerchiefs with his

[35] *S.T.*, II–II, q. 66, a. 3, ad 2m; and a. 5, ad 3m.
[36] *S.T.*, II–II, q. 66, a. 6, *ad primum*; a. 7,c.
[37] *S.T.*, II–II, q. 66, a. 7, ad 3m.   [38] *S.T.*, II–II, q. 66, a. 5, ad 2m.
[39] *Ibid.*

initials on them, by the Shady Rest Old Peoples' Home. There is an accompanying letter, asking A to send five dollars in return for the handkerchiefs. A has not ordered the things and does not know the Shady Rest people. In this situation, A is not obliged to send the five dollars. He is not obliged to put himself out, or spend any money to return the articles. He is obliged to refrain from using the handkerchiefs for his own use; to keep them for a reasonable period, in case they are sent for. He may, after the passing of some time, say a few months, give the articles to some person who is in need, even to himself, if he needs them as much as anyone else.

¶ *Is It Wrong to Commit Robbery?* Robbery means the taking of another's goods, openly and with violence. The victim is an involuntary loser in this act (as he is in the case of theft). In theft, the astuteness of the thief causes the loser to be ignorant of his loss at the time of taking. In robbery, the victim is not ignorant of his loss but is forced to give up his possessions by actual or threatened violence.[40]

Robbery is immoral and an offense against justice in two ways: (1) it takes away from another what is his due; (2) the force used, or threatened, causes injury to the possessor.[41] However, robbery does not apply to the case of a person in dire need, who openly and with the least violence possible, takes things for his immediate need, or for the immediate need of others.[42] We should also make exceptions of the taking, either furtively or openly, of articles of small value, when the taker may reasonably presume permission of the owner. Thus, it is not necessarily theft or robbery for a policeman to take an apple from a fruit dealer on his beat; this is a public convention and a common hazard of the fruit business.

The open taking of the spoils of war is a special case. A soldier fighting what he believes to be a just war may with justice take some goods from a defeated enemy. This soldier must not be motivated by private concupiscence, however. A soldier fighting an unjust war commits robbery when he despoils the enemy.[43]

¶ *Is It Unjust to Acquire Possessions by Fraud?* Fraud is the

[40] *S.T.*, II–II, q. 66, a. 4,c; et ad 2m.   [41] *S.T.*, II–II, q. 66, a. 5,c.
[42] *S.T.*, II–II, q. 66, a. 7, ad 3m.   [43] *S.T.*, II–II, q. 66, a. 8, *ad primum*.

voluntary use of deception with the intention of causing a loss of possessions of some worth to another person. This act is always immoral and unjust.[44] While fraud may be associated with many commutations, it may be examined best in relation to the buying-selling exchange. We have seen that, in this commutation, both buyer and seller are morally obliged to take care that the things exchanged are approximately of equal value. The principle, *caveat emptor* (let the buyer beware) is not an adequate moral rule, though it has been frequently adopted in legal practice. The seller must also beware lest he engage in a dishonest deal.

Three main possibilities of fraud in the buying-selling commutation, are distinguished by St. Thomas [45] and they form a very reasonable basis for modern discussion of the problem. The thing sold may be defective: (1) in its species or kind (thus one may sell a ring as gold, which is not made of gold but some base metal which looks like gold); (2) in its measure or quantity (thus one may give short weight, or use a smaller unit than is conventional in such dealings); and (3) in its quality (thus one may sell a sick horse, or a boat which will not float). In all these three forms of fraud, the seller is unjust, if he knowingly commits fraud. It is to be noted, too, that the buyer may deal fraudently in all three ways. He may buy a thing too cheaply, because the possessor thinks it less valuable in kind, in quantity, or in quality, than it really is. Of course, the buyer must know that the seller is deceived about the value. Both buyer and seller are morally bound to make restitution to the offended party for an unjust gain made through fraud.[46] This does not mean that the seller is required to make public all the defects of the thing to be sold.[47] If a defect is quite evident to all, for instance, if a horse has but one eye, it need not be mentioned; or, if a one-time saddle-horse which can no longer be used for riding is now being sold at the price of a plough horse, it is not necessary to emphasize the fact that he is not a saddle horse.[48]

Nor is it morally necessary for a businessman to tell his customers to wait till next week, when the prices will be lower, be-

[44] *S.T.*, II–II, q. 77, a. 1,c, *ad init.*   [45] *S.T.*, II–II, q. 77, a. 2,c.
[46] *S.T.*, II–II, q. 77, a. 2,c; et *ad primum* et ad 2m.
[47] *Quaest. Quodl.*, II, a. 10,c.   [48] *S.T.*, II–II, q. 77, a. 3,c.

cause of advance information which he may have of a coming price drop. Things are justly sold at the present just price. However, it is a act of greater virtue to give out such information when possible.[49]

¶ *Is It Unjust to Charge Interest on Loans?*   In mediæval discussions of usury, a loan was regarded as an accommodation to someone, often to a friend, who needed money or things temporarily and who expected to be able to pay back the loan rather promptly. To simplify our reasoning, we will take this case first, and we will deal with the lending of money. A further circumstance to be kept in mind, is that money, in the middle ages, had only one primary use: it could be spent, and with expenditure it was consumed. In such a situation, the use of money is not really distinct from the money. To understand this, let us think of two cases of lending. A lends B his horse, to be used for one day. Here, A may justly charge for one day's use of the horse, because the horse is not greatly changed in value by such use, but A has been deprived of the use for one day. This is really a renting contract. On the other hand, A lends B ten dollars for one day. B spends the ten dollars. This use leaves B without the money. B must return the ten dollars to A the next day; but must B pay for the day's use of the money? It would appear not, because A would not lend the money if he needed it that day. A lends the money because it is of no use to him for the period of the loan. So, A is not entitled to charge for the use of something which is of no use to him at the moment.

In an economic situation where money has only one primary use, namely to be spent, it is unjust to charge for use of the money on loan. This is why the vice, or act, of charging interest on loans of accommodation is called *usury* (from *usus;* use); it constitutes an attempt to charge for being deprived of use, when one is not deprived of use.[50]

In the modern world money seems to have another primary use; that is, *investment*. This is not to be confused with the allied question: has money any productive value? The simple fact of present-

[49] *Ibid.*, ad 4m.

[50] *S.T.*, II–II, q. 78, a. 1–4; *Quodl.* III, q. 7, art. 19; and *De Malo*, q. XIII, a. 4,c, et ad 15m.

day economics is that there is another thing which is normally done with money besides spending it. Money can now be used as capital. Thus, in this modern situation, if A lends a sum of money to B, A gives up the investment use of this money for the period of the loan. Here, A would appear to be justified in charging a reasonable amount of interest as a compensation for the loss of this use. Such a charge is not usury. Excessive interest, of course, should not be charged; the rate of interest will depend on current investment conditions. (St. Thomas did not know modern investment practices and does not deal with this modern problem. However, the student may read of the development of post-thomistic Catholic thinking on this question, in: Bede Jarrett, O.P., *Social Theories of the Middle Ages* [Westminster, Maryland, 1942], pp. 165–172; it is to be noted that the treatise, *De Usuris*, attributed to St. Thomas in the footnotes of this book, is not an authentic work of St. Thomas.)

¶ *Is Gambling or Wagering Unjust?* To win or lose a bet *on some matter of chance* is not an act which is immoral in itself. It is possible to do this, for the sake of amusement or recreation, without doing injustice to anyone. However, gambling may easily become a vice, because of bad circumstances. It is unjust to risk money or things needed by one's family, on a chance wager. It is unjust to induce another man to lose money by gambling, when he needs the money. It is an offense coming under the vice of prodigality, to waste money needed for one's own support, by gambling. It is an offense under avarice, to be too interested in winning money by gambling. It is imprudent to try to earn one's living by gambling. It is an act of superstition to expect the devil to help one's fortune in gambling. It is tempting God to expect God to help in a gamble. It is rather frivolous to risk money on any matter of chance, and so gambling is frequently an act of vanity, *i.e.*, unworthy of a serious-minded person. All in all, there are many forms of immorality connected with gambling.[51]

By the same reasoning, it is not essentially immoral to bet on the

[51] *S.T.*, II–II, q. 95, a. 8,c; q. 32, a. 7, ad 2m; *De Sortibus*, c. 5, ed. Mandonnet, III, 158–162.

outcome of a game of skill. Various circumstances may make such an act immoral, including nearly all those discussed in the preceding paragraph. In addition, cheating is possible in games of skill; the cheater is unjust to those cheated and is required by commutative justice to make restitution to them. If one lives in a state where the positive laws forbid gambling, it is immoral to gamble.[52]

There are other contracts of chance, such as insurance, which are moral in themselves but which become immoral by virtue of bad circumstances, particularly fraud.

Summary of Chapter XII

The right to use material things is basically natural and common to all men; it must be exercised by all men on earth. This right takes moral precedence over the right to possess economic goods. The accumulation and distribution of useful things may be handled by private possession, or by communal possession, or it need not be done at all (mendicancy). Private possession is not opposed to natural moral law and is a reasonable, positive determination of this law. It is the arrangement which St. Thomas considered best adapted to the nature and circumstances of most men, but communal possession is not intrinsically immoral. Mendicancy is not practicable for all men. Modern communism is opposed by Catholic thinkers because: (1) it is usually associated with atheism, materialism, determinism, and irrationalism; (2) it advocates the involuntary loss of exercise of the right to private possessions. Original occupancy and labor are two of the most important titles to private possessions. In the modern service-wage contract, both employer and employee must observe commutative and distributive justice; moreover, both must work for the common good, under legal justice. Reasonable profit-making in business is not an unjust way of making one's living. It is not unjust for a possessor to dispose of things by gift or bequest. Theft is evil in two ways: it is an unjust appropriation of what belongs to another; it is furtively deceptive.

[52] *S.T.*, II–II, q. 32, a. 7, ad 2m.

Robbery is also a double evil, involving misappropriation and the use of open violence. Fraud is evil because it causes an unjust loss to another, particularly in a commutation, by deception. Usury is evil because it charges for a use of money, when there is not use apart from consumption; it is not immoral to take interest on loans of money under modern economic conditions. Gambling and other contracts of chance are not essentially immoral, but are frequently accompanied by vicious circumstances.

Recommended Readings

Thomas Aquinas, St., *Summa Theologiae*, II–II, qq. 66–67; qq. 77–78. (See the references to other works of St. Thomas, throughout Chapter XI.)

Bourke, "Material Possessions and Thomistic Ethics," in *Philosophic Thought in France and the U. S.*, pp. 613–627.

Cronin, Science of Ethics, II, 113–149.

Gilson, *Moral Values and the Moral Life*, pp. 258–261.

Jarrett, *Social Theories of the Middle Ages*, pp. 122–149.

LaFarge, "The Philosophical Basis of Communism," *Proc. Amer. Cath. Philos. Assoc.*, IX (1933) 47–62.

McFadden, *The Metaphysical Foundations of Dialectical Materialism*, (Washington, Cath. U. Dissert., 1938).

Riedl, "The Social Theory of St. Thomas Aquinas," *Proc. Amer. Cath. Philos. Assoc.*, IX (1933) 24–34.

Ryan, "The Economic Philosophy of St. Thomas," in *Essays in Thomism*, pp. 239–260.

———, "The Philosophy of Capitalism," *Proc. Amer. Cath. Philos. Assoc.*, IX (1933) 35–46.

Somerville, "Dialectical Materialism," in *Twentieth Century Philosophy*, pp. 471–502 (not a criticism of communism but may be used for the facts presented).

Topics for Assignment

1. The Difference Between Use and Possession of Things
2. Circumstances to Be Considered in Determining a Just Living Wage
3. How Socialism Differs from Communism
4. Is It Just to Bequeath a Fortune to a Pet Cat?
5. Are Large Lotteries Immoral?

XIII · MAN'S DEBT TO GOD

This chapter is to treat the virtue of religion, its nature, the obligations which it imposes on the moral agent, the problems connected with it. The title of the chapter omits the term, religion, because the modern reader may not think of religion as a part of justice. We are not here to deal with apologetics, that is, the explanation, justification, and defense of a religion, of an established, objective institution, such as the Catholic Church. Apologetics belongs to the theologian, not to the philosopher. Rather, our purpose will be to show that man, in his present condition of existence on earth, must think of his indebtedness to God, must use his will to act in the repayment of this debt, must avoid offending God. This is not the work of justice, in the ordinary sense, for justice works according to an equality, either arithmetic or proportional, and there is no equality between man and a supreme God. However, the obligations of the virtue of religion are something like those of the cardinal virtue of justice, and so religion is classified in ethics as a potential part of justice.

What Does Man Owe to God?

We have just finished considering the duties which the moral agent owes to his fellow man. These include not only the many strict obligations under justice, in its different kinds, but also the obligations associated with the virtues which are potential parts of justice. We have kept to the end of this study of justice, the examination of the problems of one great potential part, *religion*. (This is a conscious reversal of the theological order of presentation used by St. Thomas in his *Summa Theologica*. There, religion is put first among the potential parts of justice, because in theology the highest things come first. But we are to think of it, after all the other species and associated virtues of justice, with the hope that we may now use our acquired knowledge of justice in order to appreciate the nature of man's obligations to God.)

It will be recalled that man owes a great deal to other persons which cannot be repaid in money or things. To our parents, to our benefactors, to our superiors, to our rulers, we owe respect, loyalty, gratitude, an appreciation of their superior excellence. *Honor* is a term which designates pretty well what is owed to superiors of any kind. There are many ways in which we might think of man's indebtedness to God, but we will concentrate on three.

¶ *God Is the Source of All That Man Has and Is.* From the study of the philosophy of being and of man, we know that there is no rational explanation of the coming into being of all finite things, of all the universe and of man in it, unless there be an Infinitely Perfect Being Who is the First Cause of all else. The whole first Part of the *Summa Theologica*, of St. Thomas, is devoted to showing how all things in creation have come from God. No man would exist, no man would be able to think, or love, or act in any way, without God. No man would be able to use and manage external things, unless God had made them. Every man is totally in debt to God for every thing that he has and enjoys; and there is nothing else that man can give back to God to pay this debt, nothing beyond what God has made possible.

¶ *God Is the End, Who Gives Purpose to Human Life and All Morality Is Meaningless Without God.* Much that has been learned in ethical theory, or general ethics, may now have been forgotten, but one great truth should remain with us: the only ultimate end which human life can have is God. It is the purpose of the *Prima Secundae* (I–II) of the *Summa Theologica* of St. Thomas to show us this. The final cause is the principle of all moral acts; the Final Cause of all human action should be God. If there were no God, man would be an agent without a job to do. In a recent lecture on existentialism, Jean Paul Sartre, who is an atheist, showed that he realized this. He said that there is an abyss between theistic existentialism and that of the atheist. The theist, believing in God, has a supreme goal in life; the atheist, wthout God, must continually strive to make his own ideals. Sartre acknowledges that the atheistic philosopher is ever unquiet and in mental anguish, because he has nothing to give meaning and value to his life. All existentialists speak of a disturbing emotion of longing. They do not know the object for which they long. The theist knows that this object is God. Man owes to God the fact that his life may have meaning and purpose.

¶ *God Is Divine Providence, Making It Possible for Man to Act, Seeing to It That Man's Weak Powers Can Effectively Produce Their Natural Effects, Ruling All Mundane Events in Justice and in Charity.* In a modern city, if the sources of power (electricity, gas, coal, and so on) are stopped, nearly all public activities must come to a standstill. Suppose God went on strike. Nothing would work. Man could not think, or talk, or walk, or do anything. No natural force would operate. The whole universe would stop. Man owes it to God that he can do the smallest human act and the greatest. Obviously, man cannot pay this debt to God on the basis of equality. There can be neither equality of things exchanged, nor of the persons to the exchange. This is not a debt of justice. St. Thomas explains it as follows:

The mean in it [the virtue of religion] is taken, not between passions, but according to an equality between the operations which are directed to God. Now, I do not mean equality in the unqualified sense (*non absolute*), for it is not possible to give to God as much as He is owed, but according to a relative consideration of human capacity and divine approval. There can be superfluity in those things which pertain to divine worship, not in regard to the circumstance of how much, but in regard to other circumstances, for instance, if divine worship is shown to that to which it should not, or when it should not, or according to other improper circumstances.[1]

  [1] *S.T.*, II–II, q. 81, a. 5, ad 3m.

Just as we cultivate fields that are subject to us, and just as we are said, in a modified sense, to cultivate certain superior men, so there is a way in which men may cultivate God. A divine *cult* is a way of exhibiting special honor to the supreme Principle of all things.[2]

The Moral Virtue of Religion

Religion is a special virtue of the human will, perfecting the moral agent and his actions, in order that he may give to God the honor, which is owed to Him.[3] It is a virtue distinct from others because of its formal object, which is, "to exhibit reverence to the one God, for one reason, namely insofar as He is the First Principle of creation and of the governance of things." [4]

Religion is not a theological virtue. We shall see in the final chapter that the theological virtues (faith, hope, and charity) have God as their material object. That is to say, "What" a theological virtue is concerned with, is God Himself. Now, the virtue of religion is directed to God *as an End*, but the material object of this virtue is the cult of God. This *cult* is made up of human acts of reverence or special honor. So, the material object of religion is human acts, not God Himself. Religion deals with means to the End and not directly with the End, Himself.[5]

Nor is the virtue of religion identical with the Gift of the Holy Ghost, which is called *Fear*. We shall see the relations of these Gifts to the virtues, in the last chapter [6] but it is enough to notice that there are seven supernaturally infused habits which so perfect man that he is rendered obedient to the instigation of the Holy Spirit. Fear is a Gift, whose act is *to revere God*. Religion, on the hand, deals with the *things which man should do* on account of divine reverence. Thus, Fear is a higher principle than religion; but this Gift is closely related in meaning to the virtue of religion.[7]

[2] *S.T.*, II–II, q. 81, a. 1, ad 4m.   [3] *S.T.*, II–II, q. 81, a. 2,c.
[4] *S.T.*, II–II, q. 81, a. 3,c.   [5] *S.T.*, II–II, q. 81, a. 5,c, et *ad primum*.
[6] Cf. *S.T.*, I–II, q. 68, art. 1–8; in Pegis, *Basic Writings*, II, 527–542.
[7] *S.T.*, II–II, q. 81, a. 2, *ad primum*.

Religion as a virtue, is almost identical with holiness, or sanctity (*sanctitas*). Holiness means a spiritual cleanliness and a firmness of application of one's mind to God. Both aspects are essential to religion, also. There is this distinction of reason, between religion and holiness: religion is chiefly thought of, in relation to acts of divine worship; whereas, holiness suggests not only divine worship but the habit of referring all virtuous acts to God. To speak the precise language of metaphysics: there is no real distinction between religion and sanctity.[8]

Religion is a *natural moral* virtue. This does not mean that it deals with feelings, emotions, passions, that is, with the movements of the sense appetites. It is not necessarily an act of religion to cry in church on Good Friday. Sense feelings, when directed by reason and controlled by will, are of religious value, but it is a mistake to think that religion is a matter of emotional disturbance. Religion centers in the will of man. Like any other part of justice, it deals with one person's *operations* in regard to another person. An operation is a work that is done. In the case of religion, the "other person" is God. So religion is not justice; but the nearest thing to it, among the cardinal virtues, is justice.[9]

All moral virtues deal with human actions which are rationally ordered to the ultimate end. God is this End. But religion is directly concerned with acts of reverence or honor to God. So, religion comes closer to God than does any other moral virtue. In this way, religion holds first place in nobility among the moral virtues.[10] It is below the level of the theological virtues.

While the acts of religion are done to show honor and reverence to God, it must not be thought that God is in need of such actions, or that He is made better thereby. God is an infinitely perfect Being; man cannot add to God's Perfection. Religious activities must be intended for the glory of God, but they result in a perfection of the moral agent. Just as the body which is vivified by a soul is perfected by its subjection to a superior, so man is perfected by subjection to his Superior.[11]

[8] *S.T.*, II–II, q. 81, a. 8,c, et *ad primum*.
[9] *S.T.*, II–II, q. 81, a. 5, ad 3m; and a. 6,c.
[10] *Ibid.*, a. 6,c.   [11] *S.T.*, II–II, q. 81, a. 6, ad 2m; a. 7,c.

The virtue of religion gives rise to two kinds of acts: (1) *Principal and essentially religious acts* are *interior, spiritual* actions of intellect and will, by means of which man's mind (*mens*) is united with, or conjoined to, God. (2) *Secondary acts subordinated to the interior acts* are *exterior* acts of the human body and of internal sensation, done with the purpose of leading the mind up to God; thus, various bodily things and actions are used to induce, or excite, the mind to spiritual action.[12]

The foregoing division and the *interior* and *exterior* acts will be more thoroughly discussed in the next section. This division into interior and exterior acts (or *principal* and *secondary*) applies to those religious acts which are directed to God alone. Of course, the acts of other virtues may be done for a religious motive, that is, under the command of the virtue of religion. In this sense, acts of mercy, of temperance, and so on, become remote acts of religion, when commanded by religion but elicited by another virtue. Thus, a man may habitually dedicate all that he does to the honor of God. The life of a "Religious," that is, of a man or woman who belongs to a religious Order or Congregation, is commanded by the virtue of religion.[13]

Duties Under Religion as a Virtue

We have seen that man owes a great debt to God and that he is morally obliged to do certain things to "pay" this debt. Of course, we realize that the acts of religion do not discharge, or pay off, man's indebtedness. If a rich benefactor pays several thousand dollars for the education of a poor child, the child cannot immediately pay back the money in full, but the child's gratitude is a sort of token payment. Similarly, the acts of religion are very inadequate, token payments of what man owes to God. There is a real, moral obligation to perform these religious acts, however. It is not a matter of choice or personal inclination. One is not justified in saying:

---

[12] *S.T.*, II–II, q. 81, a. 7,c et ad 2m; see also *In Boetii De Trinitate*, q. III, art. 2,c; trans. by Sister Rose Emmanuella (St. Louis, 1946), pp. 83–86.

[13] *Contra Impugnantes Relig.*, Chap. 1; *S.T.*, II–II, q. 81, a. 1, *ad primum*.

"I am not a religious person; I'll leave those duties to others."
Every man is personally indebted to God as to a Supreme Benefactor. Each man's gratitude must be expressed in action.

¶ *What Principal Religious Act Must the Will Do?* The will is
lord and master over the active use of the other powers of man.
It is not superior to the intellect in every way, but the will is first
in the efficient application of the operative potencies of man to
their respective acts. In relation to God, however, the human will
is not a lord but a servant. There is a special act of the will, by
which man *offers himself to the prompt service of God*. This act
is called: *devotion*.[14] Devotion is the first of the principal and interior acts of religion.[15]

Every act of the will stems from some act of intellectual consideration. Intellectual *meditation*, or *contemplation*, on the *Goodness of God* excites a voluntary act of love, which is the proximate
cause of devotion.[16] And meditation on the *deficiencies of man* removes presumption, which could be an impediment to devotion.
Thus, meditation causes devotion in two ways.

The act of devotion causes a *spiritual joy* in the mind. This joy
(which is not a movement of the sense appetite) is the principal
psychological effect of devotion. It springs, of course, from the
appetitive consequence of the intellectual consideration of the
Goodness of God. A similar, secondary effect is *spiritual sorrow*,
resulting from the consideration of man's defects.[17] *Devotion* is the
principal religious act of the will. It is formally defined as: the will-
act of promptly turning oneself over to God, in order to serve
Him.

¶ *What Principal Religious Act Must the Intellect Do?* The
purpose of the speculative intellect is simply to know things. Its
work is purely apprehensive. On the other hand, the function of
the practical intellect is not only apprehensive but also causative.
That is, the practical intellect not only knows, it causes things to
be done by some other potencies or agents. This is done in two
possible ways, either perfectly or imperfectly. The practical in-

---

[14] S.T., II–II, q. 82, a. 1,c et *ad primum*.   [15] *Ibid.*, a. 2,c.
[16] *Ibid.*, 3,c.   [17] *Ibid.*, a. 4,c.

tellect causes action, *perfectly*, by the act of commanding (*imperium*); by this act it imposes a necessity on other powers, members of the body, and on other people. It causes action, *imperfectly*, by inducing or disposing another agent to act. In this imperfect causation, the practical intellect asks, or prays (*petit*) that something be done by some agency which is not under its control, but is equal or superior to the practical intellect.

In both causal actions, command and prayer, the practical intellect deals with an *ordination*, an ordering that something be done by another. Now, to order (*ordinare*) is the work of reason (*ratio*). So, the Latin word, *oratio*, is used as the name of the act of praying [18] and it suggests the connection between prayer and the potency of reason. So, prayer is not an act of the will but of the practical reason or intellect.[19]

If we define prayer as: *an ascent of the practical intellect to God, asking something of God, with some reason that the petition may be granted*,[20] then it is obviously an act showing reverence and honor to God. Thus, prayer is the second of the principal and interior acts of religion.[21]

We may note a few additional points regarding the act of prayer. In the meaning given above, prayer should only be addressed to God, but it is right for a person to ask the angels or saints to pray to God for something which the person wants.[22] Nor is it wrong to pray for temporal benefits, provided these are not the principal object of desire, but are considered as aids to the attainment of future happiness.[23] It is necessary to pray for oneself; it is an act prompted by fraternal charity to pray for other human beings. To pray for one's enemies in general is morally good; not that we thereby approve their faults but rather love their natures as creatures of God; it is not morally necessary to pray for some special enemy but to do this is an act of more perfect virtue.[24] In common with many other authorities on prayer, St. Thomas regarded the

---

[18] Cassiodorus thought *oratio* was formed from "oris ratio," *i.e.*, mouth reason, *Exposit. in Psalmos*, Ps. 38, 13; PL 70, 285; this is probably inaccurate etymology; St. Thomas quotes it without saying it is correct.
[19] *S.T.*, II–II, q. 83, a. 1,c.   [20] *Ibid.*, a. 17,c.   [21] *Ibid.*, a. 3,c.
[22] *Ibid.*, 4,c.   [23] *Ibid.*, 5,c.   [24] *Ibid.*, 8,c.

Lord's Prayer as a most perfect prayer.[25] Because brutes are not possessed of reason, they cannot pray; because God is Superior to all other beings, it is not suitable for Him to pray; therefore, prayer is an exclusive function of rational creatures.[26]

Since it is traditional to pray aloud, we may consider the reasons for *vocal prayer*. In this connection, two kinds of prayer should be distinguished: *common* and *private*.[27] Common prayer is that offered by a priest, speaking for a group of people. It is clear that such prayer should be made known to the people for whom it is offered. Hence, the priest should speak aloud, so that all can hear. Private prayer is said, or offered, by one person for himself or others. This need not be vocal. However, three reasons may be given for saying private prayer aloud: (1) speech is an exterior sign which helps to excite interior elevation of the mind to God, and to encourage personal devotion; (2) as an exterior act of the body, speech enables a man to honor God with his whole being, with his body as well as his soul; and (3) there is a natural tendency to express one's psychic feelings and thoughts in bodily actions; vocal prayer is a kind of overflowing of the vehemence of the soul's actions into bodily acts.[28] However, St. Thomas thought that it is unfitting to attract attention to oneself by praying too loudly, or by beating one's breast furiously.[29]

Prayer is essentially an act of the intellect, so he who prays must attend to what he is doing. There are three things which should be attended to, in a good prayer: (1) the correct words; (2) the meaning of the words; and (3) the End of the prayer, that is, God and the thing which is the object of the petition. The last is the most important; an unlearned person may forget the others, at times, and his prayer will still be good, provided he keeps his mind on God.[30]

The two principal, interior acts of the virtue of religion are, then, *devotion* and *prayer*. These are acts of man's spiritual or immaterial powers, the will and the intellect. But, as we have seen above in connection with vocal prayer, man is not just an im-

[25] "Oratio Dominica perfectissima est, . . ." *Ibid.*, 9,c.   [26] *Ibid.*, a. 10,c.
[27] *Communis et singularis, Ibid.*, a. 12,c.   [28] *S.T.*, II–II, q. 83, a. 12,c.
[29] *Ibid.*, ad 3m.   [30] *Ibid.*, a. 13,c.

material being. He has also a bodily nature and he owes some bodily expression of his reverence to God.

¶ *What Are the Secondary and Exterior Acts of Religion?* The performance of extra-mental acts with the purpose of manifesting interior devotion and prayer to God is an act of religion. To distinguish such worship of God, from the showing of reverence to finite beings, it is called *latria*, or divine worship. It is to be remembered that the following secondary acts of religion are *human acts:* they comprise an external, commanded act, which is secondary to the internal act of will and intellect. Even in these secondary acts, the principal part is the interior devotion and prayer.[31]

Adoration (*adoratio*) is principally the interior act of devotion in the human will, manifested secondarily by an accompanying act of bodily humility (such as genuflection, or any fitting corporeal manifestation of subjection) which is used as a sign of the interior disposition of the mind.[32] The purpose of the bodily portion of the act of adoration is to lead the mind of the adorer to God; so, while it is possible to adore God, with interior devotion, anywhere, the exterior acts are more fittingly performed in some consecrated place, where symbols of holiness lead the mind to consider God, and where a group of adorers are congregated to make their prayer more acceptable to God. In more simple words, St. Thomas thought that it is best to go to church to adore God.[33]

Sacrifice (*sacrificium*) is principally the interior act by which the soul offers itself to God; secondarily, sacrifice includes the exterior act of using corporeal things as an offering to show one's due subjection to, and honor for, God.[34] To offer something to a lord, or superior, as a mark of recognition of his dominion, is so natural to man, that the practice of sacrifice may be considered as coming, in general, under the natural law. The determination of the precise type and manner of sacrifice to be offered to God is a question for the positive law of the Church.[35] Obviously, divine sacrifice should be offered only to God.[36]

Giving to the support of the Church (*oblationes, dare decimas*)

[31] *S.T.*, II–II, q. 84, a. 1,c et *ad primum*.   [32] *Ibid.*, a. 2,c et ad 2m.
[33] *Ibid.*, a. 3,c et ad 2m.   [34] *S.T.*, II–II, q. 85, a. 1,c; a. 2,c.
[35] *Ibid.*, a. 1, *ad primum*.   [36] *Ibid.*, a. 2,c.

is the act of handing over money, or other things of value, to be used in divine worship, or by the ministers of God, or to be distributed by the Church to the needy faithful. If something is consumed, or used up, in being offered to God, it is a sacrifice; if it is not consumed but remains for the use of the priests, for themselves or others, it is not a sacrifice but an oblation.[37] It is a matter of moral obligation to give something to God in His honor. But the determination of the precise nature and amount of the offering is a matter of positive law. The ancient practice of giving the first fruits (*primitiae*) to God, was one such determination for an agricultural people. Similarly, the giving of tithes (*decimas dare*) was a judicial precept of the Old Law of the Jews. Proper moral determination of the obligation to give to the support of the Church and its ministers requires consideration of the customs of one's country and the needs of the priests.[38] It is well to remember that this act of giving is an act of religion and not merely of justice. It should be done primarily for the honor of God. However, this does not mean that a priest has not a just title to the use of such oblations. The point is that it is not enough to pay a "salary" to the priests of one's parish, as a commutation. Even a priest, who has some private possessions, say inherited from his parents, is required to give something to the Church for the honor of God.[39]

Vow (*votum*) is the special religious act of promising God that one will do or omit something.[40] There are three necessary elements to a religious vow: (1) *deliberation*, the act of the practical intellect considering what is to be proposed; (2) *proposition*, the act of the will intending what is to be done; and (3) *promise*, the binding or obliging of oneself to what is proposed. All three elements of a vow may be accomplished in one's inner thinking, but the vow is strengthened by two exterior parts of the complete act of vowing: (4) the *vocal pronouncement* of the promise; and (5) the *presence of others as witnesses*. Vows may be either *simple* or *solemn*. A simple vow is one which derives its efficacy from the

[37] *S.T.*, II–II, q. 86, a. 1,c.   [38] *Ibid.*, a. 4,c *ad fin.*
[39] *S.T.*, II–II, q. 87, a. 4,c.   [40] *S.T.*, II–II, q. 88, a. 1,c.

deliberation of one's own mind, in intending to assume a certain obligation. A solemn vow includes not only this personal assumption of an obligation before God but also a spiritual blessing and consecration by a minister of the Church. It is to be noted that simple vows may be made in public; a public vow is not identical with a solemn vow. The question of dispensation from vows is a matter for determination by ecclesiastical law.[41]

Oath (juramentum) is the act of calling upon God as the witness to the truth of something.[42] The truth so witnessed may be of the past or present (an assertory oath); or, the witness may be to confirm something in the future (a promissory oath). An oath should not be used as a scientific proof; it would be ridiculous to try to demonstrate a conclusion in a scholarly disputation, for instance, by taking an oath.[43] It is a morally good act to take an oath, when God is called to witness something that is true, and when there is a serious reason for this act.[44] The English verb used to name the act of taking an oath is, *to swear;* swearing (*jurare*) under proper circumstances is an act of reverence to God, a special act of the virtue of religion.[45] The act of calling God to witness an untruth is perjury; an act of perjury is morally evil, an offense against the virtue of religion.[46]

There are other acts of religion. *Adjuration* is to use God's name in commanding inferiors, or in asking superiors, to do something. It is not morally good to attempt to bind those who are not under one's charge, or control, by calling upon the name of God. It can be an action of religion for a superior to do this, where there is need, in relation to an inferior.[47] *Invocation* is the use of God's name in prayer or praise of God.[48] The use of God's name in hymns is morally good, if the music is such that it is suited to incite devotion.[49] So also, *reception of the sacraments* is an act of religion.[50]

[41] *Ibid.,* a. 7,c and 11,c.
[42] *S.T.,* II–II, q. 89, a. 1,c.
[43] *Ibid.,* a. 1,c *ad fin.*
[44] *Ibid.,* a. 2,c.
[45] *Ibid.,* 4,c.
[46] *Ibid., ad primum.*
[47] *S.T.,* II–II, q. 90, a. 1,c.
[48] *Ibid.,* q. 91, a. 1,c.
[49] *Ibid.,* a. 2,c.
[50] *S.T.,* II–II, q. 89, prolog.

Problems Connected with the Virtue of Religion

Religion is a moral virtue. Its acts must adhere to the mean of reason between excess and defect. There can be no excess in religious action, in the sense of giving too much honor to God. But excess is possible in giving religious honor to other beings than God. Defects in religious actions are possible in many ways. We shall consider certain typical offenses against religion; first, in regard to excess; second, in regard to defect.

¶ *Is It Wrong to Give Divine Honor to Non-Divine Things?* To set up any finite being and treat it as God, is unreasonable and immoral. This is the chief meaning of the act or vice of *superstition.*[51] Superstition is the general name for several acts of excess against religion.

Idolatry (*idolatria*) is the act or vice of exhibiting *latria*, that is, divine worship, to any beings other than God. God is just One, Supreme Being. To put some other beings in His place, is a grave distortion of man's moral life, for all of man's moral acts are directed to his ultimate end. Since God is the objective, ultimate end the idolator is warping his whole moral life by deliberately taking some other thing as God.[52]

Divination (*divinatio*) is the act or vice of attempting to know something of the future, or to cause something to happen in the future, by giving divine worship (*divinum cultum*) to non-divine beings.[53] The chief way in which men could hope to know or influence contingent events of the future is by an appeal to evil spirits. This is obviously irreligious. It is not divination to use the methods of science to foretell eclipses, to forecast the weather, or to prophesy under divine inspiration. Nor is it divination to use natural causes so as to produce certain generally predictable results, as a farmer tills his fields to produce a future harvest. Divination is unscientific and unreasonable. If there is any pretension to supernatural powers, or use of religious ceremonies, on the part of fortunetellers, horoscope casters, and similar practitioners, then

[51] *S.T.*, II–II, q. 92, a. 1,c.   [52] *S.T.*, II–II, q. 94, a. 1,c.
[53] *S.T.*, II–II, q. 95, a. 1 et 2,c.

their actions and those of their clients are acts of divination. All this sort of thing should be avoided by a reasonable person. (Many types of divination are described and condemned by St. Thomas; see for example his discussion of astrology.)[54]

Magic or *sorcery* (*ars notoria*) is the act or vice of using symbols, or "mystic" ceremonies, or things with supposed supernatural powers, to acquire knowledge, or better health, or beauty, or good fortune, by occult means.[55] St. Thomas is very abrupt in treating all this foolishness. It is immoral and will not work ("ars notoria est et illicita, et inefficax.")[56] He warns Christians about superstition in regard to carrying relics, for instance.[57] It is not wrong to do this out of reverence, but one should watch out that he place no faith in the shape of the container, or in the way they are fastened to his neck.

¶ *Is It Wrong to Act Irreverently toward God and Divine Things?* The generic name for the vice which is opposed to religion by way of defect is irreligion. Acts of irreligion are contemptuous or irreverent in regard to God and sacred things. We shall consider three species of irreligious acts.

Tempting God (*tentatio Dei*) is the act of trying to put God to a test, without any good reason. The tempter of God endeavors to make an experiment of God's knowledge, power, or will.[58] Thus, for a man to stand up and dare God to strike him dead, is to tempt God. There is always some element of ignorance or doubt in this moral offense. Tempting God should not be confused with an act of hope. The tempter thinks that God will not do what He is dared to do; the man who acts in pious hope, firmly expects that God will do some useful and necessary thing. The tempter of God is irreligious because he questions the supreme attributes of God. This is a serious moral offense, but not as great an offense as superstition, because the tempter is in some doubt as to the excellence of God while the superstitious person is in no doubt.[59]

Perjury (*perjurium*) is the act of calling on God to witness the

---

[54] *Ibid.*, a. 5,c.
[56] *Ibid.*
[58] *S.T.*, II–II, q. 97, a. 1 et 2,c.

[55] *S.T.*, II–II, q. 96, a. 1,c.
[57] *S.T.*, II–II, q. 97, a. 4, ad 3m.
[59] *Ibid.*, 4,c.

truth of something which is false.[60] The falsity which is essential
to perjury may be: (1) in the lack of truth in the statement; (2)
in the lack of justice (thus, a criminal who saves himself by perjury evades his just punishment); and (3) in the lack of good
judgment (e.g., swearing where there is not need for it).[61] It is
not only an offense against religion to perjure oneself, but also to
induce another to commit perjury. Of course, a public official, who
compels a man to testify under oath, is not responsible for the
possible perjury of the witness.[62]

Sacrilege (sacrilegium) is the irreverent use of places, things, or
persons especially dedicated to divine service (*ad divinum cultum*)[63] The most serious type of sacrilege is that which is directed
against the person of a man or woman dedicated to God's service.
To strike a priest unjustly is an offense against justice, and also
against religion, for, this act of sacrilege indicates contempt of
God. The second most serious kind of sacrilege involves the misuse
of sacred places, such as churches. Irreverent use of things devoted
to divine worship (the sacraments, sacred vessels) constitutes the
third type of sacrilege.

Simony (simonia) is the act of buying or selling a spiritual
thing.[64] There are three reasons why spiritual things (such as divine grace, forgiveness of sins, happiness in Heaven, and so on)
cannot be bought and sold in a morally approvable way. First,
spiritual things cannot be equated with an earthly price; second,
God is the Owner of spiritual things and ministers of God can
only dispense them, not sell them; and third, the selling commutation is repugnant to the origin of spiritual things, for they come
freely from the Will of God.

Both Catholics and non-Catholics should understand clearly that
the Catholic Church has never countenanced simony. This has
been misunderstood for two reasons: (1) Catholics often give free-
will offerings of money, or other things of value, on the occasion
of receiving the Sacraments, or when a mass is said for their intention; these offerings are not, or should not be, intended as a pay-

[60] *S.T.*, II–II, q. 98, 1,c.   [61] *Ibid., ad primum.*
[62] *Ibid.*, a. 4,c.   [63] *S.T.*, II–II, q. 99, a. 1 et 2,c.
[64] *S.T.*, II–II, q. 100, a. 1,c.

ment for the spiritual benefit but as oblations or contributions to the material support of the Church, its ministers, or the needy who depend on the Church; (2) it need not be denied that some individuals, in the history of the Catholic Church, have practised simony, and thereby given scandal and misinformation about Catholic practices. St. Thomas is quite plain in stating that even the Pope has no right to sell spiritual things.[65] In making a donation at the time of reception of a sacrament, one must take care to do this without the intention of buying a spiritual thing.[66] It is immoral to buy or sell spiritual vessels for their spiritual value; but it is not wrong for a minister of the Church to melt down these vessels and sell them for their material value, when there is need and when they are no longer of spiritual use.[67]

It is to be noted at the conclusion of this chapter that religion is used throughout in a subjective sense. When we speak of religion, here, we mean a habit of the will of the individual person, whereby he is perfected so that he may fulfill his duties of honoring God. In modern languages, religion usually has an objective connotation. That is, religion now suggests primarily a certain Church, or sect, an institution or society to which believers belong as members. Religion, in this objective sense, is not a moral virtue. Nor is it the function of the ethician to discuss the nature and respective merits of the various objective religions now in existence. However, it is the work of the ethician to indicate the nature of reasonable moral conduct. This would seem to include reminding the student that membership in a given objective religion is a most important moral matter. Obviously these religions differ in the mode of their origin, in the nature of their beliefs, in the character of their ceremonies and religious practices, in the picture which they give of man's future reward. The reasonable person, who wishes to live a good life, has a moral obligation to use his reason in choosing his religion. Every human being should make as prudent and thorough a study of the various religions of the world, as is possible to him. He should seek the counsel of other wise and prudent men. He should choose his religion with greatest care,

[65] S.T., II–II, q. 100, a. 1, ad 7m.   [66] Ibid., a. 2 et 3,c.   [67] Ibid., a. 4,c.

remembering that human reason cannot understand all things but that a religion should be able to offer some good reasons for its origin, beliefs, and practices. There should be no attempt to reduce all faith to reason, but there should be a reasonable justification of, and preamble to, one's faith. This is what freedom of religious conscience should mean: that each man be at liberty to deliberate upon his religious obligations, to choose and practise his religion. Religious toleration does not mean thinking that all objective religions are of equal value; such a conclusion is unreasonable because the different religions are at odds on major issues. There should be one, true religion, for there is only One God and one best way of honoring God. (The *Summa contra Gentiles*, particularly in its first three Books, constitutes St. Thomas' reasoned justification of the Catholic Church and its beliefs.)

Summary of Chapter XIII

The virtue of religion is a potential part of the cardinal virtue, justice. Man owes everything to God, in an absolute sense. There is a moral obligation for each man to "pay" this debt by acts of honor and reverence to God. Religion is the habit of the will perfecting man so that he may discharge this natural moral obligation. Unlike theological virtues, whose immediate object is God, religion deals with human acts of reverence to God. The principal acts of religion are devotion in the will, prayer in the practical intellect. The secondary acts are uses of the other human powers, directed by intellect and will. These secondary acts include: adoration, sacrifice, oblation, vow, and oath. Other religious acts are: adjuration, invocation, and reception of the sacraments. Problems associated with religious action arise from excesses or defects. Excess consists, not in too much reverence for God, but in giving divine honor to nondivine things. Superstition includes the following acts opposed to religion: idolatry, divination, and the practice of magic. Defects of religion occur in such irreligious acts as: tempting God, perjury, sacrilege, and simony. Every man is obliged to give prudent consideration to the choice of an objective religion.

Recommended Readings

Thomas Aquinas, St., *Summa Theologiae*, II–II, qq. 81–100 (in English Dominican translation); I–II, 60, 3,c (in *Basic Writings*, II, 461).

——, *Commentary on Boethius' De Trinitate*, q. III, art. 2; trans. by Sr. Rose E. Brennan, pp. 82–86.

——, *Summa contra Gentiles*, III, cc. 118–121; trans. by J. Rickaby, pp. 278–282.

Cronin, *Science of Ethics*, II, 1–31.

Fahey, *Mental Prayer According to the Teaching of St. Thomas Aquinas*, pp. xi–77.

Farrell, *Companion to the Summa*, III, 247–300.

Gilson, *Moral Values and the Moral Life*, pp. 270–274.

Rickaby, *Aquinas Ethicus*, II, 110–195.

ADVANCED READINGS

Amann, "Religion (vertu de)," *Dictionnaire de Théologie Catholique*, XIII, col. 2306–2312.

Gilson, *Le Thomisme*, éd. 5me, pp. 462–487.

Héris, "L'Amour naturel de Dieu," *Mélanges Thomistes*, 289–310.

Lemonnyer, "La vertu de religion," *La Vie Spirituelle*, XLVI (1936) 31–36.

Lottin, "La vertu de religion chez s. Thomas d'Aq. et ses prédécesseurs," *Psychologie et Morale*, III, 313–326.

Rupprecht, "Die Tugend der Religion nach dem hl. Thomas," *Divus Thomas*, IX (Freiburg, 1931) 146–172.

Sertillanges, *La philosophie morale de s. Thomas*, pp. 194–204.

Topics for Assignment

1. The Relation of the Virtue of Religion to Justice
2. The Difference Between Prayer and Devotion
3. Why Must a Person Perform Some External Acts of Religion?
4. Is It Wrong to Use Sacred Images in Divine Worship?
5. Should One Guide His Life by Astrology?

Social and political philosophy are different studies from ethics. It is not the work of ethics to endeavor to determine the best form of government for man, to investigate the various theories of society, or to prescribe a detailed plan for peace on earth. In this course in moral philosophy, we are concerned with what is good and what is bad in the conduct of the individual person. However, man must live in the society of other men, hence he must face certain ethical problems arising from societal membership. Our job in this chapter is to examine these moral problems of the individual member of society.

The Meaning of a Society

Society is a union of men for the purpose of doing one thing in common.[1] Breaking down this definition into its parts, we see that society (we are only considering *human* society) is made up of human beings; its material cause is two or more men. Secondly, we may notice that society is some kind of unity. It is one, not with the unity of an organism or of a substance but with the unity of a group of free and rational agents, *intending one end* and *working together for the attainment of that end*. Its formal cause is this unity of common purpose and action. The purpose of a society can be one of many ends. Different societies have different final causes. The society for the prevention of cruelty to animals has its

[1] "Societas nihil aliud videatur, quam adunatio hominum ad unum aliquid communiter agendum." *Contra Impug. Dei Cult. et Relig.*, c. 3; ed. Mandonnet, IV, 25.

end; the family is a society with a different end. So too, societies may have different efficient causes, the difference depending on what brings them into being.

Man is fitted and impelled by his nature to live in the society of his fellow men. This is a paraphrase of the famous lines of Aristotle's *Politics:* [2] "It is clear that the state (*polis*) is a creation of nature, and that man is by nature a political animal." By taking this in a broader sense, than that intended by Aristotle, we may appreciate the following reasoning of St. Thomas:

It should be noted, then, that because man is naturally a social animal, inasmuch as he needs many things for his life which he cannot in isolation provide for himself, the consequence is that man is naturally a part of some group, through which he is provided with assistance to live well. He needs this assistance for two reasons. Firstly, for those things which are necessary for life, without which the present life cannot be lived, the domestic group of which he is a part is a help to man. For each man is indebted to his parents for his coming into being, for his food, and for his upbringing. Likewise, the individual members of a family in one home are of mutual help to each other, in regard to the necessities of life.

Man is helped, in another way, by the social group of which he is a member, in regard to the complete fullness of life; that is, so that man may not only live but live well, having all things required for a satisfactory life. In this way, the civic group of which he is a member is of assistance to man, not merely in regard to bodily things (of course, there are many products in a state which one household could not supply) but also in regard to moral matters, inasmuch as through public power unruly young people are controlled by the fear of punishment, when paternal correction is not strong enough for them.

It should be noted, too, that this whole, which is a civic group, or a domestic family, possesses only the unity of order, which does not make it one thing, in the simple sense. Therefore, a part of this whole can have an operation which is not an operation of the whole, just as a soldier in an army has an operation which is not that of the whole army. Nevertheless, the whole does have an operation, which is not proper to any one of its parts but to the whole, as an attack pertains to a whole army, and the rowing of a boat is the operation of the group of oarsmen. [3]

There are a good many reasons why social or group life is natural and necessary to man. An adult human being may go off by

---

[2] Book I, c. 2, 1253a2.   [3] *In I Ethic.*, lect. 1; ed. Pirotta, p. 3, nn. 4–5.

himself, or herself, and live alone. If all people did this in any one generation, there would be no next generation. Moreover, solitary living is not possible for young human beings; they need the care of their parents for many years. Besides, the life of a hermit is not a very satisfactory life. Some of the best things are those which are shared with other human beings. An artist is partly rewarded by the appreciation of his work by other men. A scientist desires his knowledge to be communicated to others and even to be useful to them. Men do better work and achieve a better development of moral personality, or character, in the company of others. The ability to use speech to communicate ideas is of no use outside society. It is not necessary to go over these reasons in detail. They reduce to the following two propositions: (1) in his early years, the human being is so dependent on adults that he just could not live at all, without care from other human beings; (2) in his maturity, man cannot live well, live a full, well-rounded life, without human society.[4]

We have noticed that society is a unity, one group ordered to a *common* end. This aspect of society is expressed by the term: *community* (*communitas*). To understand this, we must examine the concept of a *common good*.

A common good is a perfection of a whole, such that the parts of the whole share individually and collectively in the perfection. The common good of human society is not simply the sum of the private goods of all its constituent persons; nor is it simply the good of the group as distinguished from its members. The common good of human society is at the same time a good of the whole group and of each and every person within that group. The meaning of common good seems nowhere to have been stated in definitive form by St. Thomas. He uses it in all his great works, as something generally understood and accepted, *i.e.*, a *dictum authenticum*.[5]

---

[4] *De Regimine Principum*, which is also called, *De Regno*, I, c. 1; ed. Mandonnet, I, 312–316; see the translation of this first chapter, by G. B. Phelan, revised by I. Th. Eschmann, *On Kingship*, pp. 3–10.

[5] See: In III Sent., d. 33, q. 1, a. 1, sol. 3, ad 3m; *Summa contra Gentiles*, III, cc. 112–117; *S.T.*, II–II, q. 58, a. 5,c; a. 9, ad 3m; q. 152, a. 4, ad 3m. The best

The common good of human *civil* society is a natural good. The person who is a citizen of such a society has a private good which is, *on the natural level,* less important than the common good. Positive laws of organized society, and legal justice, place the common good above the good of the person. "Law is instituted for the common good." (*C.G.*, III, c. 123.) That is why civil society has the right to punish malefactors by depriving them of natural goods. So, the *natural* common good of human society is more important than the *natural* private good of the individual person.

However, the good of the human person is more than natural; it is also *supernatural.* Our whole study of ethics is founded on the view that man's moral actions are for the sake of a supernatural end, the Beatific Vision. This attainment is a perfection of the human person. This supernatural perfection is superior to the common good of human society.[6] The union of the saintly man with God, in the Beatific Vision, is not a human but a divine Society. Nor need it confuse the issue to note that St. Thomas identifies God with the Common Good.[7] God, as the Common Good of all things, is not identical with the natural common good of human society; the use of the expression, *common good*, in these two distinct cases, is an analogy.

The importance of this point is evident today. Certain states, or civil societies, have claimed that the person who is a citizen has no rights which take precedence over the good of the state. This is wrong, because man is not merely a citizen, he is a person with a right to pursue his personal and supernatural good. Other political theorists have claimed that the individual is all-important, that the state or civil society has no right to interfere in any way with his pursuit of his private good. This is wrong, because society is

---

brief study is in French: O. Lottin, *Principes de Morale* (Louvain, 1947), II, 55–72; the most useful studies in English: Maritain, J., *The Person and the Common Good* (New York, 1947), pp. 37–79; and Eschmann, I. Th., "In Defense of Jacques Maritain," *The Modern Schoolman*, XXII (1945) 183–208.

[6] *S.T.*, II–II, q. 39, a. 2, ad 2m; q. 152, a. 4, ad 3m.

[7] See the beautiful explanation of this point: that all created goods, including the common good of society, are participations in the Common Good, Who is God, *In Dionysium, De divinis nominibus*, c. 11; ed. Mandonnet, II, 602–605.

needed by man and society must be granted the right to coerce
and punish bad citizens. To find the middle way between totalitarianism on the one side and excessive individualism on the other,
it is hardly enough to emphasize the natural dignity of each human
being. We must also remember the supernatural destiny of each
human person. Peace and good order in human society demand the
subordination of the natural private good of man to the common
good of human society. Christian ethics demands the exaltation of
the supernatural perfection of the human person above the natural
common good of human society. Conflicts between the apparent
rights of society and the apparent rights of the individual person
may occur at any time. We cannot make rules to settle these conflicts in advance; the moral agent requires prudence to deal with
them in the concrete.

Several divisions of society are useful to further study. Human
societies may be either *public* or *private*. A public society results
when a number of men unite in a community to found a republic,
a city, a state. A private society is the result of a number of human
beings joining together (it may be just two or three people) to
accomplish some business (*negotium*) which is their own and not
common.[8]

Another division of society is into *perpetual* and *temporal*. A
perpetual society has no time limit; a temporal society has. It is
possible to have any of the four combinations of these divisions:
(1) a *public and perpetual* society, *e.g.*, a state; (2) a *private and
perpetual* society, *e.g.*, union of husband and wife; (3) a *public and
temporal* society, *e.g.*, a temporary union of businessmen; (4) a
private and temporal society, *e.g.*, the association of two men who
rent a room together.[9]

Finally, there is the division of societies into *perfect* and *imperfect*. A perfect society is a union of a sufficient number of people
to provide for the satisfaction of all the needs of a human being;
thus, a city, or better, a state, is a perfect society. On the other

[8] *Contra Impug. Dei Cult.*, c. 3; Mandonnet p. 25.
[9] These divisions and examples are to be found, *Ibid.*, pp. 25–26.

hand, an imperfect society supplies some of the needs of human life but not all; a family is an imperfect society.[10]

Domestic Society and Its Problems

Under this heading, we are to consider certain moral problems connected with marriage and family life. It is clear than man and woman are fitted by their biological natures to unite for the procreation of offspring. The division into male and female is found throughout the genus of animals, including man. The act of reproduction in itself, without the addition of other moral circumstances, is natural and not immoral.[11]

¶ *What Is the Purpose of Matrimony?* Matrimony is the name of a private society of man and woman. Legally, it is a commutative contract, because it is an agreement mutually to exchange certain rights. Like other contracts, it may justly be regulated by the positive law of state or Church. Some of the rules governing matrimony are even part of the natural moral law, for this society is ordered to the common good of the whole human species, as well as to the private good of the members of a given family.[12]

The primary end or purpose of marital society, or matrimony, is the procreation and upbringing of children.[13] This point needs emphasis, for many people do not seem to know that marriage is not primarily for the good of husband and wife, but for the good of the children. There is a *secondary* end for matrimony. This is the mutual love and assistance of husband and wife.[14]

For the complete attainment of the good, which is the continuance of the race, it is necessary that offspring be cared for,

---

[10] *De Regno*, I, c. 1; Mandonnet, I, 315; *On Kingship*, pp. 9–10.

[11] *C.G.*, III, c. 126.   [12] *S.T.*, II–II, q. 154, 2,c.

[13] "Finis autem matrimonii est proles generanda et educanda. . . ." *S.T.*, III, q. 29, 2,c.

[14] *In IV Sent.*, d. 26, q. 1, a. 1, resp.; cf. *S.T.*, Supplementum, q. 41, a. 1,c. The treatise on marriage is found in the *Supplement* of the *Summa Theologica*, compiled in the fourteenth century to complete the work which St. Thomas' death left unfinished. That is why most references in this section of this chapter are to the *Summa contra Gentiles*.

fed, trained for life. Parents, even among brutes, especially in the case of men, are best suited to care for their own children until they are ready for adult living. This is due to the force of natural instincts, the impulsion of love based on ties of blood and close relationship. Brutes are impelled to care for their young, by the necessity of natural inclinations. Among many types of higher animals, both male and female cooperate in the feeding and training of offspring, sometimes over rather long periods. In the human species, the young are very dependent, requiring long care of soul as well as body. Because of the passions of children, they need correction, too. The father is best fitted to punish them and correct them. Hence, both father and mother must live with their children over quite a long period, in order to do their duty as parents.[15]

¶ *Why Is Marital Society Indivisible?*   Matrimony was given above as an example of a *perpetual* society. This means that the union of husband and wife should not be broken until the death of one or the other. Five serious reasons are given by St. Thomas for the indivisibility of the marriage union:

(1) The father lives on in his son; both parents have a natural interest in seeing that the family possessions, which are for the preservation of life on earth, should be handed on to the children of the family. So, the natural order of things requires that father and mother remain together until death.

(2) There is a special equality between husband and wife. They exchange mutual rights over their bodies. After the mother has ceased to bear children, it would be an offense against this equality of the commutation for the husband to leave his wife, when she has probably lost her attractiveness to other men. On the other hand, the father is the natural head of the family (because of the greater size and strength of the male, because he is the protector and representative of the family in relation to larger social groups, because every society works best under unified direction) and it would be an act of insubordination for the wife to put aside her husband.

(3) It is natural for human beings to be solicitous about their

[15] *C.G.*, III, c. 122.

own children. If marriage could be broken by either husband or wife, it would be difficult or impossible to know whose children belong to whom, and so to satisfy this natural concern about one's own children.

(4) The most intimate friendship between human beings is possible in the married state. This applies not only to the procreative act but to all the love, helpfulness, and mutual associations of domestic life. Such close friendship is not possible between more than two people.

(5) The act of procreation is the only biological function of man which is for the common good of the race, rather than the private good of the individual. The exercise of this act should not be left to personal whim but should be regulated by moral law. Both state and Church law reinforce the natural tendency of most human beings to indivisible marriage. Divine law adds a supernatural reason, drawn from the analogy of one Christ united with one Church. Good moral and social conditions depend, to a large extent, on the indivisibility of marriage. Change of wives or husbands makes for many breaches of morality: quarrels over property, unhappiness of children, occasions for adultery.[16]

Let us now note the precise meaning of three terms bearing on this discussion. *Annulment* means the legal act of declaration, under civil or ecclesiastical law, that a supposed marriage never was valid. Marriages are declared invalid because of some essential impediment. Full consideration of the reasons for invalidation of a marriage contract is a matter for legal experts. However, the student of ethics should know that there may be impediments on the part of the persons (personal incapacity for the marital act, taking of a solemn vow of chastity, previous valid marriage to a living spouse, close relationship, and so on), or from the point of view of the nature of the contract (use of force, presence of essential error). The effect of an annulment is that the persons involved are in the same position toward marriage that they had before the supposed marital contract. *Divorce* means the breaking of a valid matrimonial contract, leaving the parties free to remarry.

[16] C.G., III, c. 123.

In this sense of perfect divorce, there can be no morally justifiable divorce, because of the property of indivisibility in marital society. In marrying, a man and a woman voluntarily enter into perpetual society; if this agreement is valid, neither the contracting parties, nor any other legal body, can dissolve the contract. "The form of matrimony consists in an indivisible joining of minds, through which one spouse is bound indivisibly to be faithful to the other." [17] It is also the teaching of the Catholic Church today, as it always has been, that there are no reasons for divorce, as defined above.[18] The third term to be defined is *separation*. Where there are *serious reasons* why husband and wife should not continue to live together, it is morally possible for them to obtain ecclesiastical and legal permission to live separately, without the right to remarry. This is the condition called separation.[19]

To sum it up: there are no ethical reasons for divorce; there may be morally good reasons for annulment or separation. These conclusions are based on the perpetual character of marital society, which is the same as the indivisibility of matrimony.

¶ *Why Should Marital Society Be Monogamous?* A marital society is *monogamous*, when it is made up of but *one husband* and *one wife*. The contrary of monogamy is *bigamy:* plurality of husbands or wives. More specifically, *polygyny* means plurality of wives; *polyandry*, plurality of husbands. Marriage should be monogamous for the following reasons: (1) Among all animals, plurality of males or females, in association with the act of reproduction, causes fights. This is true, even among rational animals, and especially so, since such plurality may make it difficult to determine ancestry. (2) In higher animals, where the young require a period of care from both parents after birth, there is an instinctive inclination to at least relative monogamy. The natural interest of

[17] *S.T.*, III, q. 29, 2,c; this is not in the *Supplement*.
[18] For a brief treatment in English, with reference to Canons 1128–1132, see: Massimo Card. Massimi, *Catholic Morality*, trans. by J. I. Schade (1943), pp. 206–208.
[19] Sometimes called *imperfect divorce*, cf. Cronin, M., *Science of Ethics*, II, 429; and Massimi, *loc. cit.*

both human parents in their own offspring requires that they know and live with their own children, without intrusion on the part of a third person. (3) Marital society is founded on a special friendship of equality. Plurality of wives or husbands destroys this equality, for it is impossible that several husbands or several wives should be held in absolutely equal estimation by the other spouse. Thus, plurality of wives is almost bound to result in one wife becoming the boss and the others slaves, or concubines. (4) The more wives or husbands there are, the more trouble there is in the family.[20]

Of all these arguments, some of which exclude polyandry more definitely than polygyny, the most important seems to be that which stresses the special equality of friendship in the married state. Husband and wife are free moral agents who deliberately choose to spend their lives in the closest human association. They thus form a society which is imperfect in comparison with civil society, but which is more natural than the state; for, it is possible to live as a member of an isolated family, without the state, though such a life could not be as complete as that of the citizen. The family is the natural small unit of society. Good families help to make good states. Families have the best chance of being good, if they are monogamous. So, monogamy promotes good order in society as a whole.

¶ *Why Should Close Relatives Not Marry?* It is a reasonable conclusion from the experience of mankind that marriage should be contracted with persons outside the family circle. It belongs to positive law, of state and Church, to determine the degree of affinity which is an impediment to matrimony. The same positive law agencies may dispense individuals from the application of these impediments, if there is sufficient reason. Parents should not marry their own children; brothers should not marry their own sisters.[21] State and Church laws usually prohibit marriage of other close relatives, and, in the case of ecclesiastical law, there are prohibi-

[20] *C.G.*, III, c. 124.
[21] *S.T.*, II–II, q. 154, 9,c; in the *Suppl.*, q. 54, a. 3,c, such marriages are said to be opposed to the natural moral law; *C.G.*, III, c. 125, stresses the positive law prohibitions.

tions based on spiritual relationships (for instance, between god-parent and god-child).

The reasons given by St. Thomas for the moral prohibition of marriage between close relatives are: (1) To admit the possibility of sexual acts between relatives in the same home (e.g., brother and sister) would be to open the home to licentiousness; (2) It is good for members of a family to marry people outside the family, and so form new friendships, thus cementing the larger bonds of civil society; (3) Children should be subject to their parents, honoring them as their natural superiors; such could not be the case, if parents married their children; (4) The love among members of a family is based on common origin, their intermarriage should be prohibited, so that there will not be an excessive and unnaturally strong attachment between any two such persons; (5) In un-usual cases, dispensation is possible to those who are not too closely related; so this teaching works no hardship on the individual per-son.[22]

¶ *What Are the Obligations Between Husband and Wife?* In conjugal society (the union of husband and wife) certain rights are exchanged. These rights have chiefly to do with the marital act by which offspring come into being. Both husband and wife should inform themselves as to the nature of this act by consulting com-petent medical doctors and their pastors. It should be clearly un-derstood that sexual intercourse within the bonds of matrimony is not immoral; to use the precise language of religion, it is not a sin.[23] Like any other naturally good action, it may be made morally bad by improper circumstances. One such circumstance is the use of some artificial means of preventing conception. This is called *artificial contraception;* it is always immoral because artificial con-traception works in direct contrariety to the primary end of mat-rimony, which we have seen to be the procreation and care of children. Arguments for the use of artificial contraception, based on so-called social, eugenic, or economic reasons, are not valid. It is not justifiable to use a morally bad means, even for a good end.

[22] C.G., III, c. 125; S.T., II–II, q. 154, a. 9,c.   [23] C.G., III, c. 126.

Mutual continence in regard to the marital act is sometimes necessary and is always morally permissible, provided it is mutual. Both husband and wife must freely agree to abstain.[24]

Adultery is a serious moral offense against the good of conjugal society. It is a breaking of the mutual trust on which the matrimonial bond is based.[25]

In addition, there are the many obligations associated with the expression "mutual love and assistance." Though this has been mentioned as a secondary end of matrimony, it is by no means unimportant. Family life is not always easy. In most cases, sickness, discouragement, death and financial troubles may arise. Each spouse owes the other all that is reasonably possible in the way of understanding, forebearance, encouragement, personal sacrifice, honesty and the fulfillment of family duties. A very large number of family problems are of economic or financial origin. The husband is normally the money-earner. It is his obvious duty to provide for his family as well as he can; to give his wife money when it is needed, without expecting miracles in economy; to make prudent savings for future needs and emergencies; to provide some recreation for his wife and family; to give his wife the opportunity of fulfilling her religious obligations; and to show his appreciation of the efforts of his wife.

The obligations of a wife to her husband are of a reciprocal character. She will need to adjust the family standard of living so that it is not too expensive in relation to income; to expend household funds prudently; to make a home in which her husband may be reasonably happy; to take over a good part of the immediate care of the younger children; to understand and encourage her husband in his work.

Young people contemplating marriage should try to prepare themselves so as to be fitted to fulfill these obligations and they should choose partners, not simply on the basis of personal beauty or social graces, but on the foundation of a prudent consideration

[24] *In IV Sent.*, d. 32, art. 1–5 *in toto*; *S.T., Suppl.*, q. 64, art. 1–7.
[25] *S.T.*, II–II, q. 154, a. 8, ad 2m.

of physical, mental, and moral endowment. Marriage is a lifetime association. It should not be entered hastily but should be prudently considered, as much as any serious choice in life.

¶ *What Are the Obligations of Parents to Their Children?* Parents are morally required to take good care of their children, physically, mentally, and morally. In the physical order, the first duty is to see to it that the child is born with as good organic health as is possible. It is morally wrong to endanger or take the life of an unborn child. (Writing in the February, 1948, issue of the *Homiletic and Pastoral Review*, J. L. McGoldrick, M.D., indicates that therapeutic abortion occurs so infrequently in obstetrical practice that it need no longer be considered a moral problem. In his twenty-year experience in a large New York hospital, with over 3,000 deliveries per year, no occasion arose for the choice between saving the life of a mother and that of her unborn child. In another large hospital, staffed by doctors of various religious faiths, two therapeutic abortions were performed in a total of 5,328 deliveries.) *Abortion*, the direct killing of an unborn child, is not morally justifiable. Parents are obliged to give their children as good food, clothing, health care, and opportunities for physical development, as are permitted by family circumstances.

The obligations of parents in the area of the mental growth of their children come under the heading of education, chiefly. Parents should see to it that the minds of their children are well trained, so that the children may live good adult lives. Neither state nor Church is in immediate charge of the education of children. This is a responsibility of parents. Schools and special teachers may be delegated by parents to teach their children, but the parents must not absolve themselves of all educative responsibility. A good home environment and good example from the parents are major factors in the nonacademic education of children. Parents should recognize the right of state and Church to establish and enforce common standards of education, because it is a matter of concern to civil and ecclesiastical society to train the young properly. Parents should endeavor to discover the qualifications and capacities of their children for special kinds of work, but they should not try to force children into careers for which they are unfitted. Healthy sports and recreations are part of the education of children. Parents should see that these recreations are morally good and are moderately enjoyed.

Morally, parents owe a great deal to their children. If we include, as we should, the spiritual training of children under this head, it is by far the most important division. Very young children are not complete moral agents; it is difficult to determine the exact time at which a given individual reaches the capacity to perform a voluntary act. All during early childhood, children should be encouraged and even forced to do acts which are materially good in the moral order. The reason for this is that moral character is beginning to form, even in the pre-voluntary period. Good moral habits must be acquired in childhood, or they are very difficult to acquire. Moral and religious instruction should be provided by parents for children. The Church is in charge of religious teaching but parents must see that their children learn and profit by such teaching. Books, movies, radio programs, and playmates should be carefully observed by conscientious parents, so that their children will grow up to be morally and spiritually good.

¶ *Have Children Moral Obligations to Their Parents?* As members of a domestic society, children are not, in all ways, complete moral agents. Nor are they full citizens of civil society. They exercise certain moral rights and not others. They are not *sui juris*, that is, in complete charge of themselves morally and legally. Hence, both parents and children should realize this subordinate position of children. Parents are the natural superiors of children. So, children owe honor and obedience to their parents. There may be unusual cases, where parents are unreasonable and morally bad, when a child will have to decide not to follow the immoral directions or commands of a parent. In such a situation the child should seek the advice of some prudent adult, preferably of his pastor.[26]

Filial piety, which has already been discussed as a potential part of justice, is a virtue covering many of the obligations of children. It helps one to be loyal to one's family and respectful to relatives.[27]

[26] *S.T.*, II–II, q. 104, a. 5,c.   [27] *S.T.*, II–II, q. 101, a. 1,c.

Children do not have a general obligation to repay their parents for all that parents do for them, or to pay back the money which has been spent on them. However, if parents are sick, children are obliged (even when they are adult) to visit and see to the healing of their parents; if parents become destitute, children should do their best to provide for them. This is an obligation of filial piety rather than of justice.[28]

Civil Society and Its Problems

We have seen that the family is a natural society and that the moral agent cannot live without the care of parents, during childhood. But life within one family is necessarily restricted. Social relations with persons from other families are necessary to a more complete life. Civil society is that union of human beings, who are already members of families, whose purpose is *to live well*.[29] The state is a somewhat more precise concept than is human society. It is possible to have a society of men (such as the early settlers in the western United States) lacking unity of leadership, formal civil laws, and organized government. This somewhat amorphous group is not a state, though it may be regarded as civil society in a loose sense. We will take civil society as being usually identical with the state, however, and define it as *a perfect human community*.[30] Expanding this definition, we can say that it means that the state is (1) a society of men, (2) united under one rule and law, (3) actually organized for the pursuit of the natural common good, (4) of such a size that the citizen may find within this society all opportunities reasonably needed for the attainment of temporal perfection of life.

¶ *Under What Sort of Civil Rule May a Man Live Best?* It is customary in books on ethics to discuss theories of the origin of civil society, of the source of authority in the state, of the various types of government, of the nature of sovereignty, and so on.

---

[28] *Ibid.*, a. 2,c.
[29] *De Regno*, I, c. 14; Mandonnet, I, 342; *On Kingship*, p. 60.
[30] *S.T.*, I–II, q. 90, a. 2,c; a. 3, ad 3m.

These are questions of political philosophy; they do not fall formally within the field of individual ethics, which we are studying, except inasmuch as the moral agent is variously related to different types of government, law, and societal organizations.

The first point to be emphasized is that political theory is not a division of theology; *there is no official "Catholic" theology of the state*.[31] There is a tradition of political thinking in Catholic circles, but this varies considerably in different centuries and under different political climates. This is not to say that Catholic theology has nothing to offer the political scientist. It just means what it says: there is no theology of politics imposed on Catholics as a matter of dogma. As far back as St. Augustine of Hippo, A.D. 354–430, this negative attitude of leaders of the Catholic Church toward politics was already well defined.[32] The Catholic Church is not planning to take over the world, or any country, to force it into a specific political mold.

Nor is there a thomistic *theology* of the state. St. Thomas drew attention to certain principles and conclusions in political philosophy (chiefly in his commentaries on the *Politics* and *Ethics* of Aristotle, and in his opusculum, *De Regno*) but it is noteworthy that his *Summa Theologica* contains no treatise on the state.

The first proposition to be considered in answering this question, then, is that it is morally possible for a man to attain his ultimate end, living under almost any kind of state. It is even possible for a slave, that is, one who enjoys no political rights, to live a subjectively good moral life. This does not mean that a moral agent can live *equally well* under all forms of government, or in all types of state.

Next, we should note that man may live best in that political situation in which he may live virtuously. It is not the work of the state to force its citizens to be virtuous, except in regard to the regulation of external acts by legal justice. But the good state should provide its citizens with every naturally possible opportu-

---

[31] This point is amply discussed in: Rommen, H. A., *The State in Catholic Thought* (St. Louis, Herder, 1945), pp. 91–122.

[32] See: Bourke, V. J., "The Political Philosophy of St. Augustine," in *Proc. Amer. Cath. Philos. Assoc.*, VII (1931) 45–55.

nity to grow in moral virtue. "It appears that the end of an assem-
bled group is to live according to virtue. This is the reason why
men gather together; that they may live well together; and this
cannot be done by each person living alone. The good life is in
accord with virtue. So, virtuous life is the end of a human as-
sembly."[33]

The best kind of political order is achieved under one ruler.
Peace and good order require that the political group work in
unity for one end. This is best accomplished under one ruler. In
the various members of the human body and in the potencies of
the soul, there must be one ruling principle. In reality as a whole,
God is the One Ruler. All plurality is derived from unity. Even
human experience tells us that a state which is not ruled by one
person is open to dissension, maintains internal peace with difficulty. On the other hand, a state under one ruler may enjoy peace,
justice and affluence.[34]

St. Thomas accepts and repeats the classification of states made
in the third book of Aristotle's *Politics*. These are: (1) *monarchy*,
one-man rule; (2) *aristocracy*, rule by a small select group of citizens; and (3) *polity*, an orderly rule by all citizens. Political order
is possible under all three of these constitutional types. St. Thomas
considered monarchy the best, in theory, but he regarded a mixed
form as more practical.[35] All may degenerate into disorderly types
of government: monarchy into (4) *tyranny*, one-man rule but
not for the common good; aristocracy into (5) *oligarchy*, rule for
the sake of the private good of a few men; and polity into (6) *mob
rule*, which is the most tolerable of these unjust forms because it is
weakest in working toward injustice.[36]

---

[33] *De Regno*, I, c. 14; Mandonnet, I, 342; *On Kingship*, p. 60, gives a slightly
different English version.

[34] *De Regno*, I, c. 2; Mandonnet, I, 316-317; *On Kingship*, pp. 11-13.

[35] *S.T.*, I-II, 95, 4,c; 105, 1,c.

[36] *De Regno*, I, c. 3; Mandonnet, I, 317-318. It should be noticed that *mob rule*
is used above to translate *democratia*. This term has not the same meaning as
democracy, in the modern sense. Democracy comes closest to the classic *polity*,
but is by no means identical. It is quite possible that St. Thomas would have
regarded the U. S. government system as a *monarchy*, certainly not as mob
rule. Adler maintains that the present meaning of democracy does not antedate

We may conclude, then, that man can live best under a form of government which is sufficiently unified to direct and regulate the public actions of its citizens toward their common good and to maintain peaceful order within the state. This is an ideal. No political order will be perfectly good in practice. That is why a state in which the individual citizen has a good deal of freedom to inform himself about the processes of government, to criticize and make effective complaint against injustice, to change government officials by orderly methods, to exercise his natural moral rights without unjust restraint, is the best practical type of state. This approximates what many people call democracy today. But it is not a rigidly fixed form of government. Any state must adjust itself to contemporary circumstances. Positive laws and patterns of political order are not immutable, as are the primary rules of the moral order.[37]

¶ *Are the Positive Laws of One's Country Morally Binding?* In general, a moral agent is morally obliged to obey all laws of his country which apply to him. All such laws should be rules of legal justice, directed to the promotion of the common good. Civil laws are either restatements or determinations of the moral law. If the law of one's country is just, it is obvious that disobedience to it is a moral offense. If the law is unjust, in the sense that it deprives the moral agent of some private good which is not of serious importance, the good citizen will obey it *for the sake of good public order*. Open disobedience, even to a bad law, is disruptive of the common good. However, it is morally good and reasonable for the citizen actively to work for the changing of a law which is bad in this way. (The prohibition laws in the U. S. may have been of this character. Flaunting these laws led to many kinds of legal disorder. It would seem to have been the duty of the good citizen to obey them but to work for their speedy repeal. However, a man who, in his prudently formed conscience, considered such laws unjust and contrary to the common good, would not be morally bound to obey them.) Finally, if a state law is unjust, in the sense that obedi-

J. S. Mill, see: "The Future of Democracy," in *Proc. Amer. Cath. Philos. Assoc.*, XX, (1945) 4.

[37] *S.T.*, I–II, q. 91, a. 3,c, et ad 3m.

ence to it requires one to disobey the natural moral law, such a positive law carries no moral obligation.[38]

¶ *May a Man Be Compelled by the State to Give up the Exercise of His Rights?* We have already seen that a man has certain moral rights deriving from the moral law and certain other positive rights deriving from the law of the state.[39] We have also seen that the moral law is superior to the positive law of the state.[40] It follows that no moral agent can be deprived by the state of the use of his moral rights to attain his ultimate end. The criminal who has been found guilty of breaking the law of the state may be punished by being deprived of various bodily goods: his possessions, repose of the senses (by whipping), local movement and use of bodily members (by being locked up), integrity of body (by mutilation), and life itself (by capital punishment).[41] It is immoral for a private citizen to judge another private citizen to have offended against the common good and as a consequence to inflict state punishments. This must be done by officials having public authority.[42]

The moral individual should recognize the power of the state to regulate his use of his moral rights, *if this regulation be in the common interest*. (Thus, premarital blood tests are morally justifiable as a positive means of improving public health.) But the innocent moral agent need not recognize the power of the state perpetually to deprive him of the exercise of any of his moral rights. (Thus, eugenic sterilization is not morally justifiable.)

It is always difficult to make universal rules indicating the extent of liberty to which the individual citizen is morally entitled and the exact point at which societal authority may justly begin to operate. That is the reason why St. Thomas leaves these matters to prudence, which enables one to reason rightly about such contingent matters. This is the area of *political prudence*, needed in one way in the rulers and officials of the state, in another way by all citizens.[43]

[38] *S.T.*, II–II, q. 104, a. 6,c, et ad 3m; I–II, q. 96, a. 4,c; this should be read in its entirety, in Pegis, *Basic Writings*, II, 794–795.

[39] *S.T.*, II–II, q. 57, a. 2,c.   [40] *S.T.*, I–II, q. 95, a. 2,c.

[41] *S.T.*, II–II, q. 65, a. 3,c.   [42] *S.T.*, II–II, q. 64, a. 3,c. et ad 3m; 65,1,c.

[43] An excellent study of this question is: Yves Simon, *Nature and Functions of Authority* (Milwaukee, Marquette U. Press, 1940), pp. 1–48.

¶ *Is There a Moral Obligation to Perform the Duties of a Citizen?* The duties of a citizen will vary somewhat in different types of state organization but we may think of such things as voting for government officials, engaging in government service, serving on juries and giving court testimony, and paying taxes. This is not an exhaustive list. It is intended to suggest the type of function which is for the common good but which the average citizen neglects or dislikes to perform, because it does not directly pertain to his private good. From the point of view of three virtues, the agent is morally obliged to do whatever he reasonably can to promote the common good of his state:

Prudence requires a man to place the natural common good of the community above his own natural good, in reasoning about practical matters. So each citizen has a moral obligation to give some thought to the common problems of his state. "Because it pertains to prudence to deliberate, judge and command rightly, in regard to those things which lead to the proper end, it is evident that prudence is not only related to the private good of one man but also to the common good of the group." [44]

Legal justice requires a man to do all those external actions which are reasonably demanded of him for the common good of his state. Any type of human action comes under the matter of legal justice, when there is question of the public good. "Every moral virtue when related to the common good is called legal justice." [45]

Charity (to be examined in the final chapter, XVI) requires a man to seek not only his own private good but the good of other men, because of supernatural love of God. "Some people have claimed that prudence does not extend to the common good but only to private good. . . . But this view is opposed to charity, which 'does not seek one's own,' as is said, Corinth. I: 13:5." [46]

It should be evident that, in a democracy in the modern sense, every citizen should make as much of a contribution as he can to the political and social life of his country. If this is not done, such a state organization cannot function well. As a result of such failure

[44] *S.T.*, II–II, q. 47, a. 10,c.
[45] *Ibid., ad primum,* et ad 3m; and q. 58, a. 5–6,c.
[46] *S.T.*, II–II, q. 47, a. 10,c.

of the citizen to do his political duties, evils and injustices occur, which are not inherent in the system but in the poor way in which it is used.

¶ *Is a Man Morally Obliged to Fight for His State?* We have not yet considered war as a moral problem. For the present question, let us presuppose what is commonly accepted: that a state is sometimes justified in making war against another state. The citizen of a state engaged in a just war is morally obliged to fight for his country, if he is personally fit to be a soldier, if he is not an ordained minister of the Church, and if there is need for his participation to promote the common good. This conclusion is based on the principle that the natural common good is superior to the natural private good. We have seen, under fortitude, that the use of physical force is not intrinsically evil. The priest is not required to kill, even the enemies of his country, because he is specially dedicated to the ministry of Christ, in imitation of Whom the priest should not shed blood.[47] The question as to whether there may be a religious sect, in which all members are ordained ministers of the Gospel, is morally difficult. If all the citizens of a state belonged to such a sect, then the state would not be able to protect its autonomy, and it could not endure as a society. This would seem to indicate that such sectarians are enjoying the privileges of citizenship but are not willing to do all the duties of citizens. At any rate, it may be concluded that neither thomistic ethics nor the Catholic religion offers justification to those who profess to be conscientious objectors to military service.

Under a system of military conscription, there is no question that the ordinary citizen who is called up for armed service should accept this call as morally obliging. Under a system of voluntary enlistment, no individual is morally obliged to enlist for military service, unless the situation is such that his services are essential to the good of his country.

If a citizen has good and serious reasons to think that his state is fighting an unjust war, he is not morally obliged to participate;

[47] *S.T.*, II–II, q. 40, a. 2,c.

moreover, he is obliged to do what he reasonably can to stop the war.

¶ *Is the Moral Agent Morally Obliged to Put His Duty to Church Above That to His State?* In dealing with this question, we cannot come to a conclusion unless we make definite our concept of what a church is. To do this, we will limit the discussion to the meaning of the Catholic Church, which will simply be called the Church in what follows.

The Church is a religious society instituted by Christ, composed of all baptized men, united in the mystical Body of Christ, professing the same Faith and sacraments, under the Pope as its head on earth, working together for a supernatural end which is the Beatific Vision.[48]

The end of the state is temporal peace and happiness; that of the Church is supernatural happiness. The first is imperfect happiness and the second is perfect. There is no question that the Church is the higher type of society. If all men were Catholics, then there would be an identity of membership between these two societies, and the secular power would be closely integrated with and subordinated to the spiritual authority of the Church. St. Thomas speaks of the secular power being related to the spiritual, as the body is to the soul.[49] But not all men are Catholics. In states where there are men of various religious convictions, the Church differs from the state in its membership. In such a situation, the moral agent is under the spiritual power of one society and under the political power of another society. He has moral obligations in regard to both authorities. The best working arrangement, under these circumstances, appears to be the separation of Church from state, each authority leaving the other supreme and without interference in its respective sphere.[50]

[48] St. Thomas does not offer a single treatise on the Church; the above definition is based on: *S.T.*, III, q. 8, 3, *in toto;* II–II, q. 1, a. 10,c; *De Regno*, I, c. 14, p. 342; see: Garrigou-Lagrange, R., *La synthèse thomiste* (Paris, 1946), pp. 417–419, for added references.

[49] *S.T.*, II–II, q. 60, a. 6, ad 3m.

[50] *In II Sent.*, d. 44, q. 2, a. 2,c; *S.T.*, II–II, q. 104, a. 6,c, et ad 3m; q. 10, a. 10,c.

The fact that the Pope is the political head of a small state, today, does not mean that the Catholic Church is seeking to dominate politics in other states. The Vatican City state frees the Pope from political subordination and makes the Church impartial in its relations with all other states.[51]

International Society and Its Problems

In our brief consideration of the moral problems arising from the relations of one state, or nation, with others, we must again stress the point that our primary concern is not to work out a theory of international organization, or even of state morality. Our purpose is still to investigate the ethical problems of the individual man in relation to this field of international society.

We have examined the chief obligations of the moral agent to another private individual, to his family as a small natural society and to his state. The state is the largest actually organized civil society. Historically, a state or nation has always been the ultimate in civil authority. That is to say, there has been a tradition in political theory and in historical practice that every autonomous state is a *sovereign society*. Sovereignty is that attribute of a society whereby it is in complete charge of its internal affairs (without interference from foreign powers) and of its external relations with other states. On reflection, we can see that to say that a state is sovereign is much the same as to say that it is a *perfect* society.[52]

In the ancient and mediæval world, sovereign states were often rather small political units, much like modern cities with some farming land around them. At times large empires were organized, however, and these little states were forced to cede their sovereignty. About the only method of settling differences between sovereign states was war. The right to fight a war for a just cause was commonly recognized as pertaining to a sovereign state. War, of course, is not a wholly satisfactory means of achieving justice in

[51] See the very thorough discussion of the relation of Church and state, in: Rommen, H., *The State in Catholic Thought*, pp. 507–612; also see: Maritain, J. *Ransoming the Time* (New York, 1941), pp. 196–216.
[52] Cf. Rommen, H., *The State in Catholic Thought*, pp. 389–390.

interstate relations. Usually the most powerful state, or group of allied states, win a war, irrespective of the justice of the situation.

In modern times, roughly from the sixteenth century on, states became larger and came to be called nations. With this development, cities gave up their sovereignty and stopped making war against each other. Of course, nations continued to make war and their wars have grown more destructive, because bigger and more bloody. Up to the twentieth century, however, war meant a fight between armies of more or less professional soldiers. In our century, wars have developed into total conflicts between large groups of nations, in which it has become difficult to distinguish combatants from noncombatants. Wars have always caused great evils, physical and moral, but modern war is much worse than anything in ancient or mediæval history.

As a result of this, two efforts have already been made to provide some method of settling international disputes, short of war. These have been the League of Nations, following the War of 1914–1918, and the United Nations, consequent upon the Second World War. The theory behind these movements is that nations might be brought to settle their differences by peaceful negotiation, if there were some world-wide organization superior to national states. In practice, the difficulty has been that sovereign nations will not give up their sovereignty to a world-state; instead they agree to form a loose association of nations, without the power to enforce decisions reached in international assemblies.

The situation reduces to this: either modern nations must give up some of their sovereign rights to a world-state, or they must face the probability of increasingly destructive wars between sovereign nations. But it is debatable whether a super-state would actually prevent war. It is true that a world-state would have no rival; but it is also true that civil war would still be possible. Geographic, ethnic, linguistic, historical and religious divisions of men would still continue in a world-state. Strife between such divisions of men would still be possible. We need not further investigate proposals to set up a world court and a world policing agency. Nations of the present hesitate to grant too much power to a world organization, for fear that they will lose their ability to protect the common good of their present citizens.

It is in relation to this actual situation that we must now consider the moral obligations of the moral agent.

❡ *Could a Man Be a Citizen of His Own Nation and of a Super-State?* To make this question precise, we could put it in concrete terms: Is it morally possible for a man to be a loyal citizen of his own country, say Ireland, and of a world-state? If both Ireland and the world-state maintain their claim to sovereignty, that is, to be regarded as perfect societies, the answer would seem to be in the negative. It would not be possible to be loyal to two political societies, since their respective common interests as societies might conflict at any time.

If we take the question to mean: Is it morally permissible for a man to advocate and work for the establishment of a world-state, with the knowledge that his own country will have to accept some limitations of its sovereignty within a larger state?—then, it would seem to become an open question, morally. No citizen should work for the destruction of his own state. But a citizen may work toward a common good which is more universal than that of his state, particularly if he is sincerely convinced that the greater common good will ameliorate conditions in his own state. It is not necessary to regard the nation, as presently constituted, as the ultimate type of political society. There is a world society of all men directed and ruled by God in relation to the supernatural common end, at present. This is not organized as a functioning political group, at present. It might be, however. There would seem to be nothing in thomistic ethics to prevent a man working for this ideal. In fact, St. Thomas says: "the more universal a government (*regimen*) is, the more perfect it is, extending to a greater number and attaining a more ultimate end." [53]

Two points should be noticed however. St. Thomas did not advocate the formation of a world-state. He did think that justice alone is not an adequate basis for world peace; charity is the real basis for peace, and it is not acquired merely by organizing a super-

[53] *S.T.,* II–II, q. 50, a. 1,c.

government. "Peace is the work of justice, indirectly, insofar as it removes an impediment. But it is the work of charity, directly, for charity causes peace by virtue of its own essence." [54] We shall leave the consideration of peace and war to the last chapter, where charity is discussed.[55]

¶ *May One Regard the Jus Gentium as an Adequate Law of International Relations?* The *jus gentium*, or Law of Peoples, is one part of positive law, according to St. Thomas. The other part is civil law (*jus civile*). The law of peoples is made up of rational conclusions from the principles of natural moral law. These conclusions are concerning the various operations, such as buying and selling and such like, which enable men to live together.[56] Thus, the law of peoples is natural to man, *as a social animal.*

The common principles of the natural moral low are known to all peoples, and usually certain obvious conclusions from these principles are accepted by all men. However, there is not a universal acceptance of the conclusions from the principles. The law of nations is widespread but not invariably accepted. St. Thomas gives the example of Caesar's report that the Germans did not regard stealing as wrong, yet it is expressly contrary to the law of nature.[57]

Today, the situation is the same. Theoretically, all men should accept certain reasonable conclusions from the natural moral law. But they do not. If the law of nations were universally recognized, a world court could be set up to judge according to this law. It appears to be the only possible foundation for justice in the international realm. But this does not mean that the world is ready to be ruled by the *jus gentium.*[58]

¶ *What Should One Think About the Punishment of a Whole Nation, Which Has Done Wrong?* This is an important moral question, especially when peace treaties are being made after a war.

[54] *S.T.*, II–II, q. 29, a. 3, ad 3m.
[55] Rommen, *The State in Catholic Thought*, gives arguments for and against a world-state, but leaves the question unsettled, pp. 728–735.
[56] *S.T.*, I–II, q. 95, 4,c.   [57] *S.T.*, I–II, q. 94, a. 4,c.
[58] See the report of a discussion of this question, led by R. P. McKeon and V. J. Bourke, recorded by E. G. Salmon under the title: "Philosophers on World Cooperation," *New Scholasticism*, XXI (1947) 284–302.

It is hardly practical to enslave a whole nation, which has unjustly waged war and lost it. But, if nothing is done to the loser, there is little point in winning a war. This happens to be a question which St. Thomas has treated formally, though not with reference to the concrete circumstances of our day. We offer his answer as a basis for discussion:

When a whole group has done wrong, then it is to be punished, either as a whole group (as the Egyptians were drowned in the Red Sea . . .), or in the large part of the group, as was the case in the punishment of those who adored the calf, according to Exodus, 32:27. Sometimes, if the correction of the group is hoped for, the severity of vindication should be applied to a few leaders, so that the rest may be frightened when they are punished. . . . However, if the whole group has not done wrong, but only a part, then, if the evil ones can be distinguished from the good, they should be punished; provided this can be done without harm to the others. Otherwise, the group should be spared and not severely treated. And the same reasoning applies to the leader whom the group follows. His offense is to be tolerated, if the group cannot be punished without harming others (*sine scandalo*); unless, by chance, the wrongdoing of the leader was such that it harmed the group more, either spiritually or temporally, than the original wrongdoing from which it took its origin.[59]

Summary of Chapter XIV

Taking society as a union of men for the purpose of doing one thing in common, we have seen that the moral agent is inclined by nature to live in the association of other men, so as to be able to live a good and perfect life. The end of a society is a common good, a perfection of the whole group and of each member of the group. While the natural private good of the person is inferior to the natural common good of society, the supernatural good of the person is superior to the natural common good. The family is the most natural of societies but it is not a perfect society, since it does not provide for a complete human life. Domestic society is for the sake of one primary end: the procreation and upbringing of children; mutual love and assistance between spouses is a secondary end. The conjugal union should be indivisible and monogamous.

[59] *S.T.*, II–II, q. 108, a. 1, ad 5m.

Civil society, or state, is a natural and perfect society whose end, or common good, is the happiness of men on earth. The citizen is obliged to respect the laws of his country and to work for its common good. The Church is a religious society whose end is the eternal happiness of its members. The moral individual should give some thought to the problems of international relations but these problems are contingent upon present circumstances which make it difficult to know whether a world-wide political organization can succeed at the present time.

Recommended Readings

Thomas Aquinas, St., *On God and His Creatures* (*Summa contra Gentiles*) trans. by J. Rickaby, pp. 283–298.

——, *On Kingship to the King of Cyprus* (*De Regno*) trans. by G. B. Phelan, revised by I. Th. Eschmann (Toronto, 1949) pp. xxxix–119.

——, *Summa Theologiae*, I–II, 90, 2–3 (in *Basic Writings*, II, 744–746); q. 94, 4–5 (*B W*, II, 777–780); q. 95, 1–4 (*B W*, II, 782–789).

Adler and Farrell, "The Theory of Democracy," *The Thomist*, III, 397–449, 588–652; IV, 121–181, 286–354, 446–522, 692–761; VI, 49–118, 251–277, 367–407; VII, 80–131.

Eschmann, "In Defense of J. Maritain," *The Modern Schoolman*, XXII (1945) 183–208. (On the common good and the good of the person.)

Gilson, *Moral Values and the Moral Life*, pp. 309–328.

Maritain, *The Person and the Common Good*, (New York, 1947) 98 pp.

O'Rahilly, "The Democracy of St. Thomas," *Studies* (March, 1920); reprinted in Leibell, *Readings in Ethics*, pp. 913–925.

Riedl, "The Social Theory of St. Thomas Aquinas," *Proc. Amer. Cath. Philos. Assoc.*, IX (1933) 11–34.

Rommen, *The State in Catholic Thought* (St. Louis, 1945) 745 pp.

Salmon, "Philosophers on World Cooperation," *New Scholasticism*, XXI (1947) 284–302.

Simon, *Nature and Functions of Authority* (Milwaukee, 1940) 78 pp.

Topics for Assignment

1. "Man Is a Political Animal"
2. The Dignity of the Human Person
3. The Arguments Against Divorce
4. Civil Authority and Moral Obligation
5. Does the Moral Law Apply to Nations?

Thus far, we have considered some of the special moral problems which any and all men might have to face, in the course of human life. These difficulties are common to mankind as a whole. It is appropriate to think, also, of certain ethical questions which are not common to all men, but which differ with the various kinds of lives which men may live. This is the subject matter of the present chapter. It does not pretend to offer a complete treatment of the ethics of the various professions. There are books and courses which deal with the various fields of professional ethics. These are for the people who are to work in these professions. Our aim is to show why different kinds of lives and work give rise to specific problems, so that the student of ethics may appreciate the moral difficulties and advantages of some of the careers open to men.

The Active and the Contemplative Life

Man's life is distinguished from that of other animals by the fact that the human being possesses understanding, or intellect. The human intellect may be used practically or speculatively. Those men who use their intellects to think chiefly about *exterior actions*, use the practical intellect and are devoted to the *life of action*. Those men who use their intellects to contemplate truth, chiefly, use the speculative intellect and are devotees of the *life of contemplation*. These two kinds of lives represent the primary division; there is no more general or ultimate division.[1] A life, in which contempla-

[1] *S.T.*, II–II, q. 179, a. 1, c, et 2,c.

tion and action are combined, (the mixed life) is possible but it does not constitute an entirely new division.[2]

The contemplative life is not a life of inaction. In its essence, contemplation is an action which goes on within the intellect. Nor is it exclusively intellectual; the will intends the end of contemplation, *to know the truth*. The will also climaxes the achievement of contemplation by an affection of joy and love for the truth which is discovered.[3] The moral virtues, which we have been studying, are not essential principles of the act of contemplation, but they prepare the way for this act. The passions and the difficulties of external dealings with other men are reasonably controlled by the use of the moral virtues; hence, these virtues *dispose* one toward contemplation.[4] Contemplation of already attained truth is but one simple act. However, the intellect must perform many acts, in proceeding toward contemplation, acts of accepting principles, and acts of deducing the truth from principles. Man is aided by others in moving toward truth; by God, and thus *prayer* is necessary to contemplation; by other men, and thus *listening* and *reading* are necessary acts of the contemplative. Finally, the contemplative must study the truth, by himself; this is *meditation*.[5]

The object of contemplation is ultimately God, insofar as He can be known by man on earth. The reason for this is that God is the highest Truth. This does not mean that the contemplative sees the Divine Essence with his bodily senses. The immediate vision of God's Essence is reserved for the Beatific Vision, in the future life. The supreme grade of contemplation possible in this life is like that of St. Paul, when he was enraptured in a state midway between the condition of the soul animating the body in this life, and the condition of the soul in a future life. This state of rapture, to which specially favored contemplatives, or mystics, may attain, is a supernatural experience.[6]

Thus, in the analysis made by St. Thomas, four steps are found in the order of the contemplative life: (1) the practice of the moral virtues: to dispose one for the best use of the intellect; (2)

---

[2] *Ibid.*, a. 2, ad 2m. [3] *S.T.*, II–II, q. 180, a. 1,c. [4] *Ibid.*, 2,c.
[5] *Ibid.*, 3,c, et ad 4m. [6] *Ibid.*, a. 5,c.

other acts than contemplation: the use of the senses and the will; (3) the contemplation of the divine effects: which leads man to the final stage; (4) the contemplation of divine Truth.[7] It is, of course, impossible to describe the final experience of contemplation; no second-hand description is identical with personal experience. It is accompanied by a joyful love of God,[8] but contemplation is a simple cognitive act, not of long duration at its peak but enduring indefinitely in its lower stages, both because of the lasting nature of its Object and because it does not involve bodily labor.[9]

The active life, on the other hand, is that to which most human beings must devote themselves, at least in great part. It is distinguished by its ordination to exterior activity. Exterior, here, means outside the intellect. Such activity is not without use of the intellect. All human acts require the use of the intellect but not in the same way. The person who devotes himself to practical action intends a different proximate end from that of the contemplative. The active life is ordered to the essentially good use of the moral virtues. It is chiefly a life of justice, because it brings one into communication with other persons, but it includes the acts of prudence, temperance, and fortitude.[10]

To explain how these lives may be combined, St. Thomas took as his example his own work, teaching. This work has two objects. We may say that what the teacher deals with is *knowledge of truth*. When he considers this for its own sake, he is performing an act of contemplation. When he regards it as capable of directing external action, he is using his practical intellect and is living the active life. It may also be said that the object of the teacher is the student who is to learn. In relation to the student, the teacher's life is indeed an active one.[11]

Comparing the active with the contemplative life, we must conclude that the latter is the better kind of life, from the point of view of an absolute, or unqualified, consideration (*i.e.*, *simpliciter*). Contemplation is superior to external action, because it is the best use of man's best power, and because it is directed to the best object of

---

[7] *Ibid.*, a. 4,c, *ad fin.*   [8] *Ibid.*, a. 7,c.   [9] *Ibid.*, a. 8,c, et ad 2m.
[10] *S.T.*, II–II, q. 181, 1,c, et *ad primum*; a. 2,c.   [11] *Ibid.*, a. 3,c.

the human intellect.[12] St. Thomas gives a long list of additional reasons for this judgment: contemplation is less open to interruption, more enjoyable, more self-sufficient, more of an end in itself, more restful and quiet, more like the divine Life, more human because the active life requires the use of powers which brutes have as well as intellect, and better because it will not stop with this life. However, this does not mean that all men should choose the contemplative life. The needs of the present life often make it better to choose the active life. More supernatural merit may be gained in the life of contemplation, but this is not to say that every contemplative is more meritorious in his actions than every active person. Generically, it is better to know and love God immediately, than to work for one's neighbor.[13]

In one sense, external activity is a hindrance to contemplation. It is impossible to be very busy about the concerns of external life and also to concentrate upon the vision of truth. But some activity of morally virtuous living is a help to contemplation, in that moral virtue quiets the passions and easily settles the ordinary problems of life, which are present even to the contemplative.[14]

We may conclude that the contemplative life is superior in nature to the active. In a way contemplation rules action, for it is necessary first to know, before there can be any question of applying knowledge to action. However, in the development of the life of the individual person, the active life is prior to the contemplative. The disposition to moral virtue must be acquired by one's own actions, before one can be freed from the concerns of the body, of the passions, and of right dealings with others.[15]

This may seem like a rather idealistic, abstract, or impractical discussion to go into before considering the actual careers open to men. It is necessary, however. It will enable us to understand why some very intelligent people choose careers that are inwardly and spiritually rewarding but which attract little worldly honor and make little or no money. If we take a long view, the successful people in this world are not necessarily the people who make the

[12] S.T., II–II, q. 182, a. 1,c. [13] Ibid., a. 2,c.
[14] Ibid., 3,c. [15] Ibid., a. 4,c.

most money, or who are more honored by their fellows. Some
rather dirty old man who has no money in the bank and no apparent job may turn out to be the greatest moral success.

States, Offices, and Grades

The meaning of a *state of life* (*status*) is a very precise one in
the language of St. Thomas. State is derived from the verb, *stare*, to
stand. The man who is standing is in an upright position, head up-
permost and feet straight underneath. Moreover, the standing man
is not moving. His status is a position of his body, arranged in a
certain order, with a certain immobility.

Transferred to the field of human actions, state comes to mean
*an order or proper disposition in human affairs, accompanied by
some immobility*. Thus, conditions of life which are easily changed,
such as wealth or poverty, high or low social or political position,
are not called states of life. Rather, a state of life is an obligation of
the person of man, such as the condition of being permanently in
charge of one's own person (*sui juris*) or permanently under the
direction of another person (*alieni*). The condition of a freeman
is one state of life; that of a slave is another state. Since one can be
free or in bondage, both in civil and in spiritual life, there are four
chief states of human life: (1) civil freedom; (2) civil servitude
(slavery); (3) spiritual freedom; and (4) spiritual servitude.[16]

In civil life, the freeman is in charge of, and responsible for, himself (*sui causa est*); the slave belongs economically and politically
to another man (*alterius est*). This means that only the freeman
can be a citizen of the state and can participate fully in the political
common good.[17] A slave is not only not in a position to make legal
contracts and to perform political duties, he is subject to the personal control of his master in some external acts of religion. Thus, a
mediæval slave could not take religious vows.[18] However, the slave

[16] *S.T.*, II–II, q. 183, a. 1,c.

[17] *De Regno*, I, c. 1; Mandonnet, I, 314; cf. Jarrett, *Social Theories of the
Middle Ages*, pp. 100–102.

[18] *S.T.*, II–II, q. 88, a. 8, ad 2m.

could get married without the consent of his master.[19] The slave was regarded as morally free in regard to his internal actions and also in regard to the performance of the natural bodily actions necessary to the maintenance of his own life and the continuance of the race, but his other external actions were all under the control of his master. Slavery was considered by St. Thomas to be a state prescribed for certain persons by the *jus gentium*.[20] He seems neither to approve, nor disapprove of the institution of slavery. It was sanctioned by the laws of his day. It did not prevent a man from attaining his ultimate end. The slave had somewhat the same position in the family society which the children had. (It should be noted, however, that childhood is not a status of life, for it is not immobile.)

The life of a free person in civil society is a state which has the various social and political rights which slaves are denied. Our reason for describing the mediæval view on slavery is to show by contrast the freedoms which a free citizen now enjoys. Formal slavery has disappeared from most modern civil societies. The so-called wage-slave is not in the restricted status of a mediæval slave. Most people today have the status of freemen. The *jus gentium* may change, in some of its rules at least, and the modern condemnation of slavery is probably indicative of changed circumstances and better ethical practice.

Turning to the distinction between the state of freedom and that of servitude in spiritual, or ecclesiastical, life, we find that the state of spiritual servitude is entered by the taking of solemn vows. A monk, or member of a religious Order, freely promises God to give up control of his own life, to renounce worldly things, and to devote himself completely to the service of God. Thus, he freely chooses the life of religious servitude. He becomes a slave of God.[21] Such a person is said to embrace the *state* of religious perfection, which does not mean that he is religiously perfect in his person but

---

[19] *S.T.*, II–II, q. 104, a. 5,c; *Suppl.*, q. 52, 2,c.

[20] *S.T.*, I–II, q. 94, a. 5, ad 3m.

[21] *S.T.*, II–II, q. 183, a. 4,c; see the much more thorough discussion, *De Perfectione Vitae Spiritualis*, c. 15–26, ed. Mandonnet, IV, 229–264.

that he is in a condition of life which is *permanent* and which *offers the opportunity* for personal perfection.

Similarly, a bishop enters the state of religious perfection by his solemn consecration. His life is less contemplative and more active than that of most monks, but the bishop is totally dedicated to the service of God and his diocese.[22] The function of the bishop in the Church is active; he is a *perfecter* of his flock. The monk, or religious, is contemplative in function; he is *perfected* in himself. Therefore, the office of bishop is superior in the Church hierarchy to that of a monk.[23]

The ordinary members of the Church are in the state of spiritual freedom. So too, are the secular clergy. This is the state of a man who retains charge of himself in spiritual matters, keeping his liberty, not vowing special obedience, beyond what is required by the precepts of the Church. Every cleric has a higher *grade* in the Church than any lay person. But it is possible for a lay person to have a higher *status* (this is the case with a monk who is not ordained a priest but who has taken on the state of perfection).[24] We will look at the meaning of *grades* and *offices*, in a minute. Of course, a lay person, even one who is married, may live a saintly life, and may achieve the personal perfection of charity. Men are not technically in the state of perfection, however, unless they are vowed to this permanent condition.[25]

The distinction of *offices* (*officia*) is based on the different species of actions, or types of work. The office of a bishop is different from that of a monk, because they do different work. The work of the monk is to save his own soul and to achieve personal religious perfection. The work of a bishop is to save the souls of other people and, of course in the process, to save his own.[26] This distinction of offices also applies to the lay life. The office of a judge is one kind of work; that of a teacher is another kind.[27]

The distinction of *grades* (*gradus*) is one of rank or dignity in a

[22] *S.T.*, II–II, q. 184, a. 5–6,c; *De Perf. Vitae Spir.*, c. 16, p. 231.
[23] *S.T.*, *loc. cit.*, a. 7,c.   [24] *De Perf. Vit. Spir.*, c. 20, p. 244.
[25] *Ibid.*, c. 23, p. 254.   [26] *S.T.*, II–II, q. 184, a. 5,c; q. 185, a. 4, *ad primum*.
[27] *S.T.*, II–II, q. 183, a. 3, ad 2m.

certain order.[28] Where one man is set above another, in civil or ecclesiastical society, there is a difference of grade. Rank in an army is a distinction of grade. If difference in rank also implies difference in work, then there is a distinction of office.

These distinctions of status, offices, and grades are found in the spiritual life and in civil life. We will not discuss the moral problems arising from such distinctions in ecclesiastical life, though they are treated at some length by St. Thomas in the *Summa Theologica*.[29] These include such questions as whether it is permitted to desire to be a bishop, whether a bishop may own private possessions, whether a monk may live on alms, whether it is permitted to leave one religious Order to enter another, whether young boys may take religious vows, and whether a bishop may retire to a monastery. These and similar questions are frequently matters of canon law. They are not problems which face the ordinary moral agent, for whom this course is designed.

Moral Consideration of Various Offices or Careers

The principle of the division of labor (which is often regarded as the discovery of the Industrial Revolution, or of the political economy of Adam Smith) was well known to St. Thomas. "It is necessary that different men be assigned to diverse tasks, so that all things may be accomplished more expeditiously and without confusion." [30] This is said with reference to the different work to be done in ecclesiastical society, but the same rule is true of civil society. The diversification of offices in the state, "has an immediate relation to the common good of the city." [31] It is because no man can do everything for himself that society is natural.

Obviously, the choice of one's life work is an important moral decision. It is possible to live a good life in the practice of any trade or profession, provided it is not specifically a type of work which

[28] *De Perf. Vit. Spir.*, c. 23, p. 251; *S.T.*, II–II, q. 183, a. 2,c, et ad 2m.
[29] II–II, qq. 183–189. [30] *S.T.*, II–II, q. 183, 2,c.
[31] *S.T.*, II–II, q. 57, a. 4, ad 3m.

is immoral in kind. No one, of course, should select a career that requires one to do immoral work. Nor should one take a job when it provides frequent occasions for immorality.

A young person should try to bring as much prudence as is possible to this decision. He should consider his own capacities, the opportunities for training, the possible demand for a special kind of work, the end of the work itself, the need to support self and family, the relation of his work to the common good, and other serious circumstances. In other words, this is an occasion for the use of parts of prudence, such as foresight, circumspection, and the ability to take good counsel. It is not reasonable to choose a career because of some minor advantage, without thinking of the whole problem.

As far as professional, or career, ethics is concerned, nearly everyone can understand that he should not engage in directly immoral work. A more practical rule is the following: "It is immoral for anyone to cooperate in doing wrong, either by counselling, by helping, or by giving consent in any way." [32] This means that a physician, for instance, is not justified in giving advice to another to do something which he knows to be immoral. It means that one assumes some moral responsibility for the probable use of one's products; thus, a locksmith should not make special keys for known thieves. It means that a lawyer is morally obliged to use no illegal means of defending his client. With this rule in mind, we will proceed to examine certain typical careers.

¶ *Moral Aspects of the Practice of Law.* This profession is taken first because, apart from the ecclesiastical life of a cleric, it is the office or career which has been most thoroughly studied by St. Thomas. His discussion of the problems of legal practice could serve as a model for the development of a thomistic ethics of any other profession.

The central act of court procedure is that of *legal judgment*. No one should judge another, legally, unless he is in authority over him.[33] This rules out lynching and "trials" by unauthorized groups. The judge should follow the recognized rules of procedure in hear-

[32] *S.T.,* II–II, q. 71, 3,c.   [33] *S.T.,* II–II, q. 67, a. 1,c.

ing testimony, allowing arguments and giving his sentence. His judgment is not to be based on private information which he has, or thinks he has, but on what is brought out in court.[34] A judge should not judge himself.[35] For the judge to give less than the proper punishment is unjust to the plaintiff, or to the common good of the state.[36]

From the side of the *accuser or plaintiff*, he is morally obliged to denounce a criminal who has offended against the common good; he is not obliged to accuse a man who has offended the accuser's private good only. He must be able to back up his accusation with proof in court.[37] False accusation is a moral offense in two ways: it is against the private good of the accused; it is against the common good of the state.[38]

The *accused* must answer truthfully in court the questions which the judge, or other officials, ask. He is not morally obliged to answer questions which are not according to the law; he cannot lie to such questions but he can evade them.[39] The right of appeal should be used only when there is good reason for questioning the justice of a judgment, not to delay sentence or for any other bad reason. Many evasions permitted by the letter of positive law are immoral.[40] A condemned man cannot justly resist punishment, if he has been justly condemned. If unjustly condemned to death, the victim may defend himself from this punishment, provided he can and provided he does not make too much disturbance. The case of a man condemned to die of hunger, but who has a chance to get food secretly, is much like the long-discussed example of the man who is commanded to execute himself. The condemned man is not required to execute himself; he can eat food, if it is available. No man should be required to be his own executioner.[41]

The *witness* is required to give true testimony when asked by court officials. A person is also morally bound to volunteer information to the court, if this information is such that it materially affects the prospectively unjust execution or punishment of another

[34] *Ibid.*, a. 2,c.   [35] *Ibid.*, a. 3, ad 3m.
[36] *Ibid.*, a. 4,c.   [37] *S.T.*, II–II, q. 68, a. 1,c.
[38] *Ibid.*, a. 3,c.   [39] *S.T.*, II–II, q. 69, a. 1,c.
[40] *Ibid.*, a. 2–3,c.   [41] *Ibid.*, a. 4,c, et ad 2m.

person.[42] The testimony of two or three witnesses against a criminal, who denies wrongdoing, should ordinarily be accepted by the
court.[43] It is not unusual, or necessarily immoral, for witnesses to
disagree about things like whether it was a fine day or not, or
whether a house was painted or not, and so on (these are St.
Thomas' examples and they seem to indicate that he had some experience in court!); they are to be considered trustworthy if they
agree on essentials.[44] There are various good reasons for refusing
the testimony of certain persons; they may be associated in guilt;
they may be relatives of the accused; they may be defective in intelligence, and so on.[45] Deliberate false testimony in court is a serious offense, morally; religiously, a mortal sin. It is quite right for
the court to require a witness to give testimony under oath.[46]

The *lawyer* is practising a profession in which all the foregoing
matters of court procedure and morality are important. He has a
general obligation to see that he works in a manner which is not
opposed to the formal end of his profession: which is to achieve
legal justice. In addition, there are many problems peculiar to his
work. This is the way that St. Thomas handles four of these professional problems:

Must a lawyer defend a pauper? The general answer to this is
that a lawyer (like any other worker) is not morally required to
work for nothing. He may do so, as a work of mercy. In certain
cases, when a poor person asks for immediately needed assistance,
the lawyer is obliged to give what help he can at that time. He is
not obliged to drop his whole remunerative practice and devote all
his time to uncompensated work.[47]

*Is there any moral reason for barring a person from serving as
an advocate in court?* A person may be barred from such work
because of incapacity, or because of some unbecoming feature
(*propter indecentiam*). Incapacity may consist of lack of experience, physical handicap (inability to talk plainly, or to hear, for
instance). It is unbecoming for a cleric to serve as advocate in civil
court; so also, for a notorious criminal, or a person under sentence.

[42] *S.T.*, II–II, q. 70, 1,c.   [43] *Ibid.*, 2,c.   [44] *Ibid.*, ad 2m.
[45] *Ibid.*, 3,c.   [46] *Ibid.*, ad 3m.   [47] *S.T.*, II–II, q. 71, a. 1,c.

However, in case of necessity, unbecomingness gives way. A priest may plead for his parish, if necessary.[48]

May a lawyer defend an unjust cause? If a lawyer is sure that his client is criminally guilty, he should not try to get him set free, without punishment. He may participate in the court process, to the extent of seeing that his client is not unduly punished. If the lawyer participates in a civil case, in which damages are unjustly collected, he is morally obliged to make restitution, for he has profited by the injustice. If he is in ignorance of the injustice of his case, the lawyer is excused from wrongdoing, provided his ignorance is not voluntary. If the lawyer discovers that his case is unjust, but only after some part of the trial has elapsed, he can and should abandon the case; or, he may induce his client to yield to just punishment, or to modify his case. The lawyer is not to give secretly acquired information to the opposing party in a civil case. It is not immoral, in pleading a just case, to conceal prudently some information prejudicial to one's case; it is immoral to use any falsity.[49]

May a lawyer charge fees for his services? No man needs to work for another for nothing. It is just for a lawyer to charge reasonable fees for his work. In setting his fee, he should consider the circumstances of the persons with whom he is dealing, the nature of his work and its amount, and the customs of his country. To extort immoderately large fees is unjust. (The judge, of course, should be paid from the public treasury. Witnesses are not paid for their services but their expenses may be paid.)[50]

¶ *Moral Aspects of Medical and Nursing Practice.* This is a technical field of ethics and it is not to be expected that St. Thomas would know the problems which arise in modern medical practice. The following questions are selected from examples and chance references in the *Summa Theologica.*[51]

Health is the end of the work of medical practice. The doctor and nurse work with God in keeping people healthy and in endeavoring to restore health to those who are sick and infirm. Health

[48] *Ibid.*, a. 2,c.   [49] *Ibid.*, 3,c, et ad 3m.   [50] *Ibid.*, 4,c, et ad 3m.
[51] Nurses will find many of their moral problems treated in: McFadden, C. J., *Medical Ethics for Nurses* (Philadelphia, 1946), pp. xiii–356.

includes soundness and proper functioning of body and of mind. Since the thomistic philosophy of man stresses the intimate association of soul and prime matter in the human being, it would seem to grant that many "mental" disturbances have an organic basis and may legitimately be treated by physical means. The use of psychological and psychoanalytical treatment is not at all immoral. However, to reduce all the causes of mental disturbance to sex frustration (as in the popular conception of psychoanalysis) is unreasonable.

Is a doctor ever justified in killing people? For the surgeon or doctor to kill a human being voluntarily, is to work in contradiction to the end of the work of medical practice. This is always immoral. Neither abortion nor mercy-killing (*euthanasia*) can be justified morally.[52] Of course, a doctor is not morally responsible for the death or sickness of a patient to whom he has given reasonably good care. Negligence, failure of the doctor to acquaint himself with improved techniques, culpable ignorance, precipitation in diagnosis or imprudence in treatment, failure to keep himself in good mental and bodily condition (through use of excessive amounts of liquor or drugs), are conditions which may make the medical practitioner morally guilty, at least in part, for the death or serious suffering of an improperly treated patient. If a person cannot do the work of a physician properly, he should abandon practice.

May a doctor or surgeon treat a hopeless case? "The doctor who takes over the care of a desperate illness does injury to no one."[53] Diagnosis does not have metaphysical certitude; new techniques of treatment are constantly being discovered; the hopeless case of yesterday is being cured today. To alleviate pain and make even a dying person comfortable is a good work. Experimentation with dangerous new treatments should not be done without the patient's consent and full understanding. It is morally justifiable for a sick person to volunteer to be treated with a new and untried remedy or technique of surgery, provided the patient intends to risk his life for the common good.

May a doctor induce a minor illness to cure a greater one? It is

[52] See *supra*, Chap. XI.   [53] *S.T.*, II–II, q. 71, a. 3, *ad primum*.

morally justifiable to do so. "The wise physician suffers the patient to incur a lesser illness, in order to cure a greater." [54] The reason is obvious: of two physical evils, the smaller should be chosen.

Is surgery morally permissible? As we have seen in the discussion of mutilation,[55] it is right to sacrifice a part of the body for the good of the whole. There is no ethical reason why a surgical operation, with some chance of success, should not be performed.

May force be used to treat a person in a frenzy? A person who resists treatment because he is temporarily "out of his mind," may be forced to take reasonable treatment for his own good.[56] Relatives and guardians should be consulted, in the case of children or permanently insane people.

May a doctor or a nurse tell a professional lie? The general prohibition of falsehood applies to all human beings; however, the professional person may make use of prudent dissimulation, when a blunt disclosure of the full truth would seem unreasonable under the given circumstances.

May a doctor charge fees for his professional work? Of course he may. The same reasoning applies as in the case of a lawyer.[57] It is a praiseworthy work of mercy for a doctor to treat poor people for nothing. He has an obligation to give treatment in an emergency, without first requiring payment. In general, a man with a special talent should use it where there is need.[58]

¶ *The Ethics of Other Kinds of Work.* The foregoing discussions of law and medicine indicate the manner in which special moral problems arise which are peculiar to distinct types of work. Those who are interested may find the bases of other forms of professional ethics, in the works of St. Thomas. Business morality is largely a matter of commutative and legal justice. This has been treated in Chapter XII. The question of usury is important in this field. The reasons why priests should not engage in business for profit are instructive.[59]

Of course, St. Thomas has much to say about teaching and the life of scholarship; that was his own *office*, though his *state in life*

[54] *S.T.*, II–II, q. 162, 6, ad 3m.
[55] *Supra*, Chap. XI.
[56] *S.T.*, II–II, q. 33, a. 6, *ad primum*.
[57] *Supra*, p. 453.
[58] *S.T.*, II–II, q. 71, a. 1,c, et ad 2m.
[59] *S.T.*, II–II, q. 187, a. 2,c.

was that of religious perfection; that is, he was a monk in the Order of Friars Preachers. The learning process is analyzed in the *Disputed Questions on Truth*, qq. IX–X. Advice for the student is given in a short work: *De modo studendi.*[60] The whole question of the organization of a school as a society of scholars is well treated.[61]

The work of a priest and religious has been mentioned earlier in this chapter and there is a full treatise on this profession in the *Summa Theologica.*[62] We have mentioned several *opuscula* dealing with the religious life.

Some indications of the dignity and utility of manual labor are given, in the discussion of whether a monk must do this kind of work.[63] Many remarks are to be found regarding the military life.[64] It is worth noting that St. Thomas thought it was bad for a soldier to engage in trade and business.[65] Both military and government service are treated from the point of view of the prudence which they demand.[66]

We can see now, at the end of this chapter, that there is quite a difference between the morality of the active and that of the contemplative life. Justice is very important in the life of the practical man. To the contemplative, the moral virtues are but preliminaries to the use of the intellectual virtues and especially the theological virtues. These latter we are to examine in the final chapter. It is not possible to evaluate and understand the goodness and importance of the life of contemplation, unless we know something about the supernatural virtues and habits of the soul. The state of life which is most proper to the life of contemplation is that of religious perfection.

On the other hand, the active life can be lived by one in any state of life. It is subdivided into a large number of specifically different offices, or types of work. Each kind of work has its particular moral problems. We have not been able to examine all in detail but we

---

[60] *Opuscula Omnia*, ed. Mandonnet, IV, 535; see also: *S.T.*, II–II, q. 188, a. 5,c; q. 181, a. 3,c.

[61] *Contra Impugnantes Dei Cult.*, c. 3; Mandonnet, IV, 21–30. Cf. Mayer, M. H., *The Philosophy of Teaching of St. Thomas* (Milwaukee, Bruce, 1929).

[62] II–II, qq. 183–189.   [63] *S.T.*, q. 187, a. 3,c.

[64] *S.T.*, I–II, q. 100, a. 6,c; II–II, q. 23, a. 4, ad 2m; III, q. 63, a. 3,c.

[65] *S.T.*, II–II, q. 40, a. 2,c.   [66] *S.T.*, II–II, q. 50, a. 1–4 inclus.

have done enough to show the ordinary student of ethics that the taking up of a profession is an important matter in morality. A doctor would not have to know much about legal ethics, and so on, but everyone should be aware that each kind of work has its moral duties and privileges.

Different grades, or levels of dignity, do not cause many moral problems. A person of higher rank is worthy of honor and respect on the part of those inferior. We have discussed this under the heading of: *Respect for Persons.* (*Supra*, Chap. X.) We need only add that the distinctions of state, office, and grade, in thomistic ethics, are not class distinctions. With the exception of slavery, which is not a practical problem in present-day ethics, all states and offices are freely chosen or awarded for merit. Social classes form no proper division for ethical problems.

Summary of Chapter XV

The active life is that of men who devote themselves mostly to exterior actions, *i.e.*, to the field of the practical intellect. The contemplative life is devoted to the knowing of truth, in particular, of God as the Source of all truth. A state of life is a permanent condition of human life. The four chief states are: civil freedom or servitude, spiritual freedom or servitude. An office is a specific kind of work, a trade, or profession. Diverse offices present diverse special problems of ethics. A grade is a rank in dignity.

Recommended Readings

Thomas Aquinas, St., *Summa Theologiae*, II–II, qq. 179–189 (see English Dominican translation).

———, *De perfectione vitae spiritualis* (ed. Parmae, XV, 76–102). An unpublished English translation by Schmitt, Kloster, and Guenther is available in St. Louis University Library.

Farrell, *Companion to the Summa*, III, 493–521.

Gilson, *Moral Values and the Moral Life*, pp. 323–328.

Holaind, *Natural Law and Legal Practice* (New York, 1899).

Jarrett, *Social Theories of the Middle Ages* (Chap. I: Law; II: Education;
    IV: Slavery; VI: Money-Making; VII: War; and IX: Art).

Lull, Ramon, *Blanquerna: A Thirteenth-Century Romance*, trans. from
    the Catalan by E. A. Peers (London, 1925). (Not a technical ethical
    work but illustrative of the theory of states of life in actual mediaeval
    life.)

Mayer, *The Philosophy of Teaching of St. Thomas* (Milwaukee, 1929).

McFadden, *Medical Ethics for Nurses* (Philadelphia, 1946).

Moore, T. V., *Principles of Ethics* (New York, 1925).

Topics for Assignment

1. The Value of the Contemplative Life
2. Moral Problems Connected with Studying
3. Is the Hippocratic Oath Morally Sound?
4. Why the Choice of a Life Work Is Ethically Important
5. Professional Secrets

The examination of the supernatural life is arranged here according to the three theological virtues: faith, hope, and charity. There are various principles of supernatural action in man but, as St. Thomas has pointed out,[1] the matter of these virtues includes other related topics, such as the Gifts of the Holy Ghost and the vices.

The Theological Virtues and Moral Life

Naturally acquired moral virtues perfect man so that he may attain that *imperfect happiness* which is possible on earth. This is not the ultimate end of man. *Perfect happiness* in the Beatific Vision is his ultimate end. We have seen in ethical theory that no man exists in a state of pure nature. Each human agent is actually directed by God to an end which exceeds the natural capacities of man. So, God gives to man supernatural help, or grace, to enable him to reach this ultimate end.

The natural potencies and acquired habits of the moral agent require to be supplemented by certain supernatural principles of action. The theological virtues are instances of such principles. By means of them, man is said to participate, or share, in the Power and Nature of God. Man does not cease to be a member of the human species, but he retains his natural perfections as he is elevated to a higher level of existence and activity. There are three reasons why these virtues are called *theological* (which means "pertaining

[1] *S.T.*, II–II, Prolog., cited *supra, Introduction to Part Two.*

to the study of God"): (1) their *object* is God; unlike the moral virtues which are concerned with means to the end, these virtues order man's life directly to God; (2) their *sole Cause* is God; they are not acquired by our own efforts but are infused into us by the divine Power; and (3) they are known to us only *through God's special revelation;* we would not know these principles by using unaided reason.[2]

We may, then, define a theological virtue as: *a supernatural habit of the human soul, ordering man directly to God as an End, infused by God and known only through divine revelation.* Strictly speaking, the specific difference of a theological virtue is the fact that it *orders man directly to God.* This is enough to mark it off from all other virtues.[3]

Just as the human intellect needs to be able to know certain first principles in order to be able to reason to natural conclusions, so does the intellect need a supernatural habit to enable it to believe the supernatural principles of knowledge beyond the natural power of his intellect. This supernatural, cognitive habit is *faith.* So too, the will needs a supernatural habit to enable it to intend its supernatural end directly. This habit is *hope.* Finally, the will requires a supernatural habit to perfect it for union with God in love. This third theological virtue is *charity.*[4]

While all three habits, faith, hope, and charity, are infused together into the human soul, the act of faith comes first in the spiritual life of the individual man. Next comes the act of hope, and finally the love of God, which is the act of charity.[5] These theological virtues, when considered in relation to their proper object (God), do not follow a mean between excess and defect. It is impossible to believe, hope, or love, *excessively,* in regard to God. However, the doctrine of the mean applies to the secondary objects of these virtues. The things which are believed about God may be in excess or defect. In relation to himself, the moral agent may hope too much or too little, because he does not properly measure his own subjective condition. The act of charity includes

[2] *S.T.,* I–II, q. 62, a. 1,c; read all four articles in: Pegis, *Basic Writings,* II, 475–480.

[3] *Ibid.,* a. 2,c.   [4] *S.T.,* I–II, q. 62, a, 3,c.   [5] *Ibid.,* 4,c.

not only the direct love of God but also the love of creatures for the sake of God; it may be excessive in regard to this latter object. Still, it should be stressed that the theological virtues, in their essence, have no extreme of excess.[6]

¶ *Faith as a Theological Virtue.* Belief is the act of faith. Even in the natural course of life, it is necessary to accept some things on the authority of another person or institution. No man can know everything by personal experience or prove all his convictions by logical demonstration. Many things may be taken as true because they are vouched for by some good authority. The cognitive act of faith is one in which the reasons for the truth of a proposition are not clearly understood. In this way belief resembles opinion, doubt, or suspicion. However, belief includes the fact that the thinker gives *firm assent* to what he is thinking. In this way, belief resembles knowledge or understanding.[7] While belief is essentially a cognitive act of the intellect, the intellect assents to what is believed because it is *determined by the will* to accept one alternative rather than another.

Supernatural faith is distinguished from natural belief by its direct relationship to God. The *material* and *formal object* of the intellectual habit of faith is God; the *end* of the will determining the intellect to supernatural belief is God.[8] The reason why man needs this supernatural faith in this life is found in the fact that man's ultimate end is above nature. "The perfection of the rational creature consists not only in that which pertains to him according to his nature but also in what is attributed to him from the supernatural perfection of divine Goodness. Hence, it has been said above that the ultimate happiness of man consists in a supernatural vision of God. Man cannot reach this vision unless he learn as a student from God as a Teacher . . ."[9] So, just as every student must have some faith in his teacher, so must every man place his faith in God, as a Divine Teacher.

From the point of view of the human intellect, what is believed about God (the material object of supernatural faith) is in the form

[6] *S.T.*, I–II, q. 64, a. 4,c; in Pegis, *Basic Writings*, II, 492–494; see also: II–II, q. 17, a. 5, ad 2m.

[7] *S.T.*, II–II, q. 2, a. 1,c.   [8] *Ibid.*, a. 2,c.   [9] *Ibid.*, 3,c.

of certain judgments. These expressed judgments of faith are
enunciated in the form of articles of faith, that is, the propositions
of a religious Creed. These articles of faith are the first principles
of man's knowledge of God. They remain always the same in their
substance (nothing entirely new is believed in the twentieth-cen-
tury Catholic Church as compared with the same Church in Apos-
tolic times); however, the number of articles of faith may be increased in the course of time, by making explicit, or by explaining
what was formerly believed implicitly.[10] In the Catholic Church,
only the Pope has the authority to add to the number of articles
in the Creed.[11] Such additions are not novelties but determinations
of what has always been believed. By means of theological reasoning many reasonable conclusions may be reached concerning the
meaning of the articles of faith.[12] However, the most highly trained
Catholic theologian accepts just the same articles of faith as the
least educated member of the Church.

The exterior act of supernatural faith is called *confession*. One
is required to confess, or exhibit externally, his acceptance of the
articles of faith, when the failure to do this would detract from the
honor which is due to God.[13] This external act is what is frequently
called the *profession of faith*, in modern terms. The confession of
sins is not the same act; it pertains to the sacrament of penance;
the confession of the action of God's grace (as in St. Augustine's
famous *Confessions*) is an act of divine worship, that is, of *latria*.[14]

St. Thomas defines faith formally as: *a habit of the mind
(mentis) by means of which eternal life is begun in us, making the
intellect assent to things which are not apparent.*[15]

The effects produced in man by his faith are twofold: *fear of
God* and *purification of the heart*. One may have a holy fear of
divine punishment (servile fear), or a fear of being separated from
God (filial fear). Both types of fear are related to faith. Purification of heart is a condition of freedom from unworthy love of

---

[10] *S.T.*, II–II, q. 1, a. 7,c.   [11] *Ibid.*, a. 10,c.   [12] *S.T.*, II–II, q. 2, a. 10,c.
[13] *S.T.*, II–II, q. 3, a. 1–2,c.   [14] *Ibid.*, a. 1, *ad primum*.
[15] *S.T.*, II–II, q. 4, a. 1,c; Pegis, *Basic Writings*, II, 1096.

earthly things. By faith, one's interests are turned away from temporal things and up to God.[16]

Two Gifts of the Holy Spirit are intimately associated with faith. These Gifts are habits of the soul whereby man is perfected in such a way as to obey readily the prompting of the Holy Spirit, the Third Person of the divine Trinity.[17] The *Gift of understanding* is connected with faith, because this Gift is a supernatural light (remember that the intellect of man is a natural "light") enabling man to penetrate to the knowledge of things which exceed the natural power of the intellect.[18] The *Gift of knowledge* is a habit of the soul, perfecting man so that he may have certain and right judgment concerning the things which are to be believed as distinguished from those which are not to be believed.[19]

The reason why special Gifts are needed, besides the virtues, may be explained as follows. The human reason is perfected so as to be able to perform certain natural operations well, *by the natural virtues*. The same reason, elevated by divine Grace, is perfected for supernatural operations *by the supernatural virtues*. However, even the theological virtues do not make man capable of knowing or doing everything in the supernatural sphere of existence. God's help is needed to avoid folly, ignorance, dullness of mind and so on. The Gifts of the Holy Spirit *render man amenable to divine instigation*, and so, are special remedies to these spiritual defects.[20] The moral problems associated with faith will be treated later in this chapter.

¶ *Hope as a Theological Virtue.* The supernatural act of hope is not a passion of the irascible appetite but an action of the rational part of the soul.[21] Like the passion, supernatural hope looks forward to a future good, which is difficult, with confidence in the possibility of its attainment. However, by natural hope we expect to overcome the difficulty by relying on our natural powers; with

---

[16] *S.T.*, II–II, q. 7, a. 1–2,c.

[17] *S.T.*, I–II, q. 68, 3,c; on the Gifts in general: understanding, counsel, wisdom, knowledge, piety, fortitude, and fear of God, read: Pegis, *Basic Writings*, II, 527–542.

[18] *S.T.*, II–II, q. 8, a. 1–2,c.

[19] *Ibid.*, q. 9, 1,c.

[20] *S.T.*, I–II, q. 68, a. 2, ad 2m et ad 3m.

[21] *S.T.*, II–II, q. 17, 1, *ad primum*.

supernatural hope man intends eternal happiness, relying on the help of God to attain this most difficult end.[22]

Eternal life is the proper and principal object of the infused habit of hope. Because hope is a will-act, this principal object is a final cause. The purpose of hoping is: *to attain eternal happiness.* But there is a secondary final cause of hope; that is, one hopes *for the means* to obtain ultimate happiness. The formal object of hope is the help of the divine Power, with which one expects to attain the highest Good. This means that an act of hoping to attain the supernatural end, without the help of God, is not an act of the theological virtue; in fact, it would be an act of presumption.[23] Of course, the divine help is God, so the principal object of hope, as of each of the other theological virtues, is God Himself.[24]

Faith precedes hope, in the order of the performance of their acts by the individual man. Similarly, the act of hope is prior in performance to the act of charity.[25] Charity is prior, or superior to, both faith and hope, in the order of nobility. Neither the act of faith nor that of hope will be needed by one who has attained the ultimate end; but charity will endure eternally.

Since hope is a movement toward a good to be attained, it belongs to the appetitive powers of the soul. This object is not a sensible good but an immaterial, spiritual good. So, supernatural hope belongs to the intellectual appetite, to the will. The subject of this theological virtue is the human will.[26] Moreover, it is a habit of the will of a human being living in this present life and not in the future life.[27]

We may define the theological virtue of hope as: *the infused, supernatural virtue of the human will, by which man intends the attainment of eternal beatitude, through the help of God.*[28]

The *Fear of God* is a Gift of the Holy Spirit which is associated with hope. Obviously, the man who is hopeful in the proper way does not fear that God will fail him. But he will have a pious fear

---

[22] *Ibid.*, 1,c; *Quaest. Disp. De Spe*, q. unic., a. 1,c.
[23] *S.T.*, II–II, q. 17, a. 2 et 4,c.   [24] *Ibid.*, a. 5,c.   [25] *Ibid.*, a. 7–8,c.
[26] *S.T.*, II–II, q. 18, a. 1,c.   [27] *Ibid.*, a. 2,c.
[28] A formal definition does not seem to be offered in the text of St. Thomas; this definition is gathered from: *Q.D. De Spe*, a. 1,c; and *S.T.*, II–II, q. 17, a. 5,c.

of the punishment of God which would arise from trying to get along without the help of God. This is not the fear of physical evil (*timor mundanus*) which arises from a love of earthly things, but the fear of the loss of the greatest spiritual good.[29]

Supernatural Wisdom is another Gift which takes its origin in a holy fear. This is not the wisdom of the philosophers, that is, metaphysics. It is the knowledge of divine things in their divine principles.[30] Thus, supernatural wisdom is indirectly related to the virtue of hope.

¶ *Charity as a Theological Virtue.* Charity is the greatest of all the virtues. Literally, charity (*caritas*) means love. By it man is united to God in a most intimate union. To describe this union of love, St. Thomas uses the concept of friendship (*amicitia*). The love which pertains to friendship is not an ordinary love. Usually, things are loved, or liked, not for their own good but for the good which they may afford man. Things like wine, or a good horse, are loved with the love of concupiscence. This is for the good of the lover, not of the thing loved. It would be ridiculous to speak of a friendly love between a man and his wine. But between human beings there may be the love of friendship, in which one person loves another with benevolence. In such love, the first person loves the second for the good of the second. This might be illustrated by the love of a good mother for her child.

Nor is benevolence enough to define friendship essentially; there must be a mutual, or reciprocal, willing of the good between friends. The second person must want the good for his friend. There is a kind of communion (*communicatio*), a mutual sharing of love between friends. This is found in its highest form in the communication of supernatural goodness between God and man, united in the act of charity.[31] That is why charity may be described as a "friendship of man with God." [32] Love arising from charity is a sort of conversation, and interchange, between man and God. This is not in the area of sensible operations but in the inner, men-

---

[29] *S.T.*, II–II, q. 19, a. 3,c.   [30] *Ibid.*, a. 7,c.
[31] *S.T.*, II–II, q. 23, a. 1,c; *Quaest. Disp. De Caritate*, a. 1,c.
[32] "Caritas amicitia quaedam est hominis ad Deum," *Ibid.*

tal, spiritual life of man. Such a mutual exchange is possible imperfectly in this life, perfectly in a future life.[33]

Even in the case of friendship between human beings, there is a kind of extension of the circle of friendship to include the friends of our friends. That is to say, other persons may be loved with mutual benevolence, because they are associated with one's friend. So, in the friendship of divine charity, man may love other creatures, *because of their connection with God.* Even our enemies may be included in the circle of divine charity, not because they are enemies, nor because they have been good to us, but because they are related to God as His creatures.[34]

Because of the lofty character of this act of charity, some theologians in the Middle Ages (Peter Lombard is the best known example) thought that charity is really the Holy Spirit dwelling in the human soul. Of course, it is true that the soul infused with divine charity is in intimate possession of God, and in particular of that divine Person Who is the Principle of divine Love, the Holy Spirit. The question arises, metaphysically, whether any supernatural quality is needed by the human soul to render it fit for the act of divine Love. This is precisely what a habit does, and in this case, a supernatural habit. Were the soul not elevated by a created habit of charity, the act of charity would be performed by God in man but not by man in God. So, St. Thomas insisted that charity is a theological virtue, that is, *an infused habit of the soul.*[35] Charity may be defined as: *an infused, supernatural habit of the will, elevating man to love God for Himself in a divine friendship, and to love his neighbor for the sake of God.*[36]

The formal act of charity is, then, the love of the Object of eternal beatitude, of God. This can only be loved perfectly when eternal beatitude has been attained. Previous to this, it can be believed in, hoped for, and loved imperfectly. It should be clear that charity, in this exalted sense, is the *form and end* of all the acts of all the virtues. Man's end is God. If he does not love God, there is no point in loving other things, and in doing naturally good acts.

[33] *S.T., loc. cit., ad primum.*   [34] *Ibid.,* ad 2m.
[35] *S.T.,* II–II, q. 23, a. 2,c; *Q.D. De Caritate,* a. 1,c.
[36] *S.T., loc. cit.,* a. 3–5,c.

Without charity, man lacks the bond with God, which gives super-natural meaning and merit to the whole moral life.[37]

It is evident that the habit of charity is infused into *the will*, not any other power. The act of love is an appetitive function. Charity is not the principle of the beatific vision (which belongs to the in-tellect) but of the love which accompanies this vision.[38] All the Gifts of the Holy Spirit are connected with charity. In addition to understanding, wisdom, science, and fear, which we have seen in association with faith and hope, these Gifts are: counsel, piety, and fortitude.[39] *Counsel* is a supernatural habit of the practical reason, enabling it to apprehend truths beyond the capacity of the in-tellectual and theological virtues. *Piety* is a supernatural habit of the will, perfecting man in his relations to other persons. *Fortitude* is the Gift which perfects the will so that man may be able to face spiritual dangers.[40]

We have already noted that the proper object of the act of charity is God, but that the love of charity also extends to other creatures who are loved in the friendship of God. There are certain problems in regard to the extent of this love of charity, which we shall consider now briefly.

Does the object of charity include all human beings? Since all men are creatures of God, and *rational* animals, they are included in the friendship of all men under God. One must love his neighbor, under charity, for the sake of that supernatural common Good, Who is God.[41]

Must irrational creatures be loved in charity? Brutes, plants, and inanimate things have not the capacity to enter into a relation of friendship with man. Thus, they cannot be loved in such a way as to desire that they attain their proper goods. These irrational crea-tures have no goods which they can attain by free choice. How-ever, they are indirectly included in the love of charity, inasmuch as man may love them to be preserved for the honor of God and the utility of other men.[42] They are not directly loved in charity.

Should a man love himself with the love of charity? Of course,

---

[37] *S.T.*, II–II, q. 23, a. 7,c.
[38] *Ibid.*, q. 24, a. 1–2,c.
[39] *S.T.*, I–II, q. 68, 5,c.
[40] *Ibid.*, a. 4,c.
[41] *S.T.*, II–II, q. 25, a. 1,c.
[42] *Ibid.*, a. 3,c.

friendship in the strict sense is only possible between *two persons*. However, the root of friendship is that unity of union, which makes two to be one. Moreover, each man is a creature beloved by God. So, one must love himself because God loves him. This is to love oneself in charity.[43]

Should a man love sinners in charity? Sinners are *men* who are *guilty* of having offended God. Their *guilt* should be detested. Yet they are still men, capable of achieving eternal happiness. So, they should be loved charitably, *as men*.[44]

Should a man love his enemies? Their *enmity* is evil and should be detested. They should be loved *as men who are creatures of God*, not as enemies.[45]

Must a man show his love for his enemies by external signs? The general answer is, No. It is necessary to perform the interior act of loving them as men, but it is not necessary to do anything special for them as enemies. There are external manifestations of charity for all men, such as praying for their happiness; enemies should be included in these. It is a work of more perfect charity to do good works for enemies, as such, but this is not absolutely required by precept.[46]

Should a man love angels in charity? The angels are intelligent creatures capable of the love of friendship. They should be loved in charity. Even bad angels (demons) should be loved, not for their evil, but as creatures of God.[47]

Should a man love God more than he loves himself? Yes, because God is the greatest Good. Moreover, God is the common supernatural Good of all men, so we owe Him more love than to any one created being.[48]

Should a man love himself more than his neighbor? The simple answer to this question is: Yes, he should love himself more than his neighbor. We are not speaking here of the love of bodily but of spiritual nature. God should be loved most, because He is the Principle of the love of charity. Each man loves himself as participating in the goodness of this divine Love. He loves his neigh-

[43] *Ibid.*, 4,c.   [44] *Ibid.*, a. 6,c.   [45] *Ibid.*, a. 8,c.
[46] *Ibid.*, a. 9,c.   [47] *Ibid.*, a. 10–11,c.   [48] *Ibid.*, q. 26, a. 3,c.

bor as an associate in the society of men united by divine Love. This society is a *union* of men under God, but its unity is not as great as the unity of one person united with God in charity. Therefore, in charity, each man should love himself more than his neighbor. The verification of this is found in the fact that no man should undergo the evil of sin, which is contrary to the participation in beatitude, in order to free his neighbor from sin.[49]

Should a man love his relatives more than other persons? The natural bond of family unity and origin adds a special reason for loving relatives more than others, in the love of charity. There is an order of intensity of charitable love based on the kind of social association which obtains: the members of one's family should be loved most, next the fellow citizens in one's state, next one's co-belligerents in war.[50]

Problems Associated with Faith

The following is an outline of certain moral difficulties which fall in the field, or within the material object, of the theological virtue of faith. The references which are given for the thomistic solution of these problems all refer to the treatise on faith, at the beginning of the *Summa Theologica*, IIa IIae. Other noted treatments of faith may be found in the *Compendium Theologiae*, Prima Pars, c. 1–245 (Chapters 185–245 are translated by Ross J. Dunn, Toronto, 1934); in *Q.D. De Veritate*, q. XIV; and in extended form, in the four books of the *Summa contra Gentiles*, the subtitle of which is: *On the Truth of the Catholic Faith* (available in condensed translation by J. Rickaby, S.J., and in the complete English version by the English Dominican Fathers).

Is it wrong to be without faith? Infidelity is the name of the vice opposed to faith in God. Now, infidelity may mean two conditions: (1) the pure negation of faith, and (2) belief in things contrary to faith. With regard to (1), those who lack faith are not guilty of a personal offense because of their infidelity, if they have

[49] *Ibid.*, a. 4,c.   [50] *Ibid.*, a. 11,c.

never had an opportunity to hear of the true faith. Their infidelity is a result of original sin. Concerning (2), the person who rejects faith, or who holds it in contempt, has had an opportunity to learn of it; his offense stems from his own free choice and his moral offense is due to his own failure to cooperate with the inner impulse of faith and with the external preaching of truth.[51]

Can there be more than one true faith? If we consider faith as the habit infused in the soul of the believer, then there are as many habits of faith as there are believers. If we consider faith from the point of view of the truths which are to be believed about God, then there can be only one faith. The reason for this is that there is but one God, Who is a Perfect and Immutable Being. It is not possible that contrary or contradictory propositions concerning such a Being should be true. Catholics believe that the faith of the Jewish people before the coming of Christ was true but incomplete; it was perfected in the revelation of the New Testament. Thus, the Christian faith as expressed in the articles of the Catholic Creed is the one, true faith.[52]

Are the rites of nonbelievers in the true faith to be tolerated? Generally speaking, civil authorities in a state should tolerate the rites of those who are not of the Catholic faith. The reason for this is that state regulations and prohibitions of the practice of various beliefs might do more harm than good. The Jewish religion, in particular, is a prefiguring of the Christian and has a special claim to the toleration of its rites. Even heretical and pagan rites should usually be tolerated, in order to avoid scandal and quarreling.[53] Catholics, of course, may not participate in rites, or church services, of other beliefs. It is not wrong to attend a wedding in a non-Catholic church, *as a social function*.

What is heresy? Heresy is a species of infidelity found in those who profess the faith of Christ but who choose (literally, *heresy* comes from the Greek word for choice) to assent to beliefs which their own minds suggest, rather than to the essential beliefs of

[51] *S.T.*, II–II, q. 10, a. 1,c.

[52] *In Boetii De Trinitate,* q. III, a. 3,c; see the translation by Sister Rose Emmanuella Brennan, pp. 87–89; cf. *S.T.*, II–II, q. 1, a. 1,c; et a. 10,c.

[53] *S.T.*, II–II, q. 10, a. 11,c.

Christian tradition. Thus, heretics are like Christians, in that they believe in Christ, but they differ from Christians in the articles of faith which they accept or reject. Heresy is a moral offense arising from pride in one's own opinions or from cupidity.[54] Since heretics profess to be Christians but do not assent to the articles of the Christian faith, they may be punished by Church authority, or by civil authority. They are to be shown mercy and given opportunity to change their beliefs.[55]

What is apostasy? Apostasy is a species of infidelity found in those who have possessed the true faith and have left it. This involves a deliberate rejection of God's Truth. This is called apostasy from faith. A man who leaves a religious Order without ecclesiastical permission, or one who abandons Holy Orders is also called an apostate, but in a secondary sense.[56]

What is blasphemy? Blasphemy means a derogation, or denial, of the Goodness of God. This may be done internally, in the intellect, or also in the will. If expressed externally, blasphemous thoughts or desires are offenses against the confession of faith. If done with full knowledge of the meaning of what one expresses, blasphemy is a very serious moral offense.[57] It is also an offense against the virtue of religion.

Problems Associated with Hope

The moral difficulties connected with hope are few in number but of paramount importance. In this life, man must maintain his confidence in the Power of God to help him overcome any obstacle to the attainment of the Beatific Vision and he must never feel that he can do this without the help of God. Besides the references given below, to the *Summa Theologica*, there is a very complete discussion of this theological virtue in the *Quaestio Disputata De Spe*, and in the unfinished second part of the *Compendium Theologiae*.[58]

[54] *Ibid.*, q. 11, a. 1,c, et ad 3m. [55] *Ibid.*, a. 3,c.
[56] *Ibid.*, q. 12, a. 1,c. [57] *Ibid.*, q. 13, a. 1–2,c.
[58] Part II, c. 1–10; on presumption, see also: *De Malo*, q. IX, a. 3,c.

Is it wrong to lose the hope of eternal happiness? Despair is the
name of the defect of hope in the Power of God to help one to
attain eternal happiness. It is false for the intellect to judge that
God cannot help one; the corresponding movement of the will is
to turn away from the assistance of God. This is contrary to the
good movement of hope. So, despair is a moral evil. It is to be noted
that despair of attaining any other end than eternal happiness (a
doctor may give up hope of curing his patient; one may despair of
making a fortune) is not necessarily a moral evil.[59] It is also important not to confuse despair with infidelity. The man who despairs
of eternal happiness may believe all the truths of faith (these are
universals), yet he may despair of his own salvation (this is a particular end and he may be defective in his estimation of the particular facts).[60]

Is it wrong to be immoderate in one's hope? One cannot hope
for too much in regard to the object of hope. That is to say, what
one hopes for is the greatest possible good for man: eternal happiness. But one can have an excess of hope by expecting to attain this
ultimate end *by the use of one's own powers only*. This immoderation of hope is called *presumption*. It is particularly presumptuous
to hope to attain something, by the help of God, when this thing
is not suitable or fitting. Thus, to hope to get to Heaven without
merit, to expect forgiveness of sin without penance, is presumptuous.[61]

Is it wrong to expect spiritual help from other men? Provided
one keep in mind that God is the Principal Source of spiritual help,
it is not wrong to hope that other men, or creatures, will aid one to
achieve eternal happiness by lending secondary, instrumental assistance. This is the way in which the saints may help man spiritually; even other men in this life may help a person spiritually by
praying to God for him.[62]

Should one fear God? Since God is the most powerful Being,
He certainly should be feared. One should not be afraid that God
will injure one unjustly, but a man should fear doing anything

---

[59] *S.T.*, II–II, q. 20, a. 1,c.   [60] *Ibid.*, a. 2,c.
[61] *Ibid.*, q. 21, a. 1–4,c.   [62] *Ibid.*, q. 17, 4,c.

which would call down God's punishment, and he should fear being separated from the greatest Good, that is, from God.[63]

Problems Associated with Charity

Charity covers many problems. It is the greatest virtue. No man can possess the other virtues perfectly without charity. We shall only be able to discuss some of the most typical moral difficulties which arise in connection with this virtue. Those who would like to understand more about it can read St. Thomas, *Quaestiones Disputatae De Caritate; De 'Correctione Fraterna;* and for certain offenses against charity: *De Malo,* q. VIII, a. 2, c; q. XI, a. 2,c.[64]

What are the effects of charity within the soul? Much is written by contemporary psychiatrists and psychologists on how to attain peace of mind. Internal contentment and serenity are great goods of the soul. They result from the theological virtue of charity. If one does one's best to love God in a supernatural friendship, and if one includes all men in the ambit of this love of charity, there is little reason for mental dissatisfaction and disturbance. Joy in spiritual things and peace of the soul are two major effects of charity within the possessor.[65] A third effect, within the soul, is the virtue of mercy. To be merciful is to feel compassion for others who are suffering. Mercy is a habit of the will and it is obviously connected with the love of our fellow men.[66]

What are the external effects of charity? Charity is a quality of the soul but, like justice, it should be expressed in external operations which relate one to other men. There are three chief external effects of charity: (1) *Beneficence* is not a separate virtue but simply any act of charity by which one does good to others;[67] (2) *Almsgiving* is directly an act of mercy, thus it is indirectly related to charity. Unfortunately, charity is frequently identified almost wholly with corporeal almsgiving. This is an important

[63] *S.T.,* II–II, q. 19, arts. 1, 4 and 5,c.
[64] An easily understood, and yet profound, explanation of charity may be read in: Sheen, F. J., *Preface to Religion* (New York, 1946), pp. 217–228.
[65] *S.T.,* II–II, qq. 28–29.   [66] *Ibid.,* q. 30, a. 1 et 3,c.   [67] *Ibid.,* q. 31, a. 1,c.

work of mercy but not the only one and not by any means identical with charity. Almsgiving consists in helping others who are in need of food, drink, clothing, housing, or those who are infirm, or in prison, or those who are dead and need to be buried fittingly. The foregoing are bodily works of mercy. Almsgiving also includes many spiritual works of mercy: praying for others, giving them good counsel, consolation in sorrow, correcting sinners, forgiving those who have offended us, and suffering peacefully the societal results of the bad deeds of others.[68] (3) *Fraternal correction* is the act of charity whereby one endeavors to punish an offender for *his own moral and spiritual good*. Correction under justice (vindication) is for the common good of civil society; fraternal correction is immediately for the good of the offender, ultimately for the love of God.[69]

Is it wrong to hate other men? Obviously, it is wrong to hate God, for there is no reason for such an action. God is wholly Good; the good is what should be loved. But, in regard to other men, it is not wrong to hate the evil which they do. It is wrong to hate them, as men.[70]

Are envy and jealousy morally wrong? To be sorry that others have achieved some spiritual good is opposed to the love of our fellow men. Even unexpressed envy is morally bad; it is not an offense against justice but against charity. These acts also cause moral disturbance within one's own soul.[71]

What are the effects of a lack of charity? The results of the lack of charity are five: (1) *Internal discord* is the condition of the will which is the opposite of concord. By concord, the hearts or wills of many men are united in peace for the sake of the divine Good, and secondarily, for the good of one's neighbor. Discord is a lack of agreement of the will with the rule of divine charity.[72] (2) *Contention* is the oral expression of disagreement or discord with others. It is an offense against charity, when it is immoderate and inordinate. It is not wrong to disagree with others when there is reason, but to disagree with what is true and good is conten-

[68] *Ibid.*, q. 32, a. 1–2,c.
[69] *Ibid.*, q. 33, a. 1,c, et a. 8, *ad primum.* Cf. *Q.D. De Correctione Fraterna.*
[70] *Ibid.*, q. 34, a. 2,c.   [71] *Ibid.*, qq. 35–36.   [72] *Ibid.*, q. 37, a. 1–2,c.

tious.[73] (3) *Schism* is the act of destroying the unity of the members of the Church, by denying the authority of the Head of the Church. The result of this is a disruption of the unity of the members with each other, that is of ecclesiastical communion. This causes a lack of peace among Christians.[74] Schismatics believe all the articles of faith; heretics do not. (4) *Private fighting* is simply the expression of discord between individual persons by mutually injurious deeds. It is not morally wrong to defend oneself against attack, provided one has a good intention. Even in self-defense, it is wrong to use more force than is necessary. Private fighting is an offense against justice and also against charity.[75] Duelling is a serious example of such an offense, as is also feuding. (5) *War* is armed conflict between states. Charity demands that one love all men, not just one's fellow citizens. War is an offense against charity, unless it satisfies certain conditions of justification: first, a just war must be waged under the authority of the ruler of the state; second, there must be a just cause or reason (the defense of the common good of the state against external attack is one such reason, but St. Thomas would admit other reasons; what is necessary is that the enemy should be guilty of some fault which deserves to be fought against); finally, there must be a good intention on the part of the belligerents (to accomplish some good or combat some evil).[76]

Is peace among nations possible without charity? While one state may be justified in waging a certain war, it is difficult to understand how the enemy could be justified in the same war. If all men were possessed of charity, there would be little or no occasion for war. Since this is an imperfect world and men cannot be expected to achieve moral perfection in it, there might be occasions in which differences of state interest would arise. However, such differences would not lead to wars, if the leaders and citizens of each and every nation were possessed of some degree of charity. Justice, implemented by a world court, by an international policing agency, and by reasonable determinations of international law, would provide the external framework in which world peace

[73] *Ibid.*, q. 38, a. 1,c.　　[74] *Ibid.*, q. 39, a. 1,c.
[75] *Ibid.*, q. 42, a. 1,c.　　[76] *Ibid.*, q. 40, a. 1,c.

might be achieved. But justice is not enough to remove discord and suspicion from the hearts of men. The difficulties arising in international relations would require a superhuman motivation for their peaceful settlement. This is precisely what charity could supply. What we now call peace among nations, St. Thomas called concord (*concordia*). This is a union of hearts, that is, of human wills, in which there is peace. What is first necessary is to promote peace within each man. Then, peace among men would follow. It is charity, rather than world organization, which is needed to avoid the awful evils of warfare.[77]

Is sedition opposed to charity? Sedition is the act of one man, or of a group of private individuals, in exciting discontent and strife within a state. It is an offense against the concord of a state. It is opposed to charity, and also to legal justice.[78]

Is it always wrong to give scandal? Scandal is a situation in the process of the spiritual life, in which the words or deeds of one person dispose another person to spiritual ruin.[79] It is not always immoral to be the occasion of scandal to another man. A word or deed may be the occasion of another's wrongdoing, either essentially (*per se*) or accidentally (*per accidens*). It is so essentially, when the word or deed is intended to lead another to do wrong, or when something which has the appearance of immorality is done publicly. The man who does such things is causing *active* scandal. On the other hand, *passive* scandal attaches to an act which is the occasion of wrongdoing in another person, but which act is not intended to give scandal and is not the kind of act which would ordinarily lead another to do evil. An example would be the possession of goods, which might cause envy in another person who is badly disposed.

Active scandal is always wrong on the part of the person who gives it. On the part of him who takes scandal, active scandal is sometimes the source of actual sin, sometimes not. It is the source of actual sin in the taker of scandal, if he consents to the materially sinful result. Passive scandal is always indicative of wrongdoing in

[77] *S.T.*, II–II, q. 29, a. 1,c.   [78] *Ibid.*, q. 42, a. 1–2,c.
[79] *Ibid.*, q. 43, a. 1,c.

the taker of the scandal. The giver of passive scandal is not necessarily performing an immoral act.

To be guilty of giving scandal, or to take scandal when one should not, are offenses against the good act of fraternal correction, indirectly against charity, and against whatever other virtue is involved. Thus, if I openly steal candy from a store, and if a child observes me and does the same thing, my act is an offense against commutative justice. It also gives scandal to the child, and is thereby an offense against charity.[80]

Summary of Chapter XVI

A theological virtue is a supernatural habit of the human soul, ordering man directly to God as an End, infused by God, and known only through divine revelation. Faith is a habit of the mind by means of which eternal life is begun in us, making the intellect assent to things which are not apparent. Hope is the infused, supernatural habit of the human will, by which man intends the attainment of eternal beatitude, through the help of God. Charity is an infused, supernatural habit of the will, elevating man to love God for Himself in a divine friendship, and to love his neighbor for the sake of God. The problems connected with the practice of these virtues are treated in summary fashion in the chapter. It is sufficient to say here that the practice of the four cardinal virtues is not enough to bring man to his ultimate end; he must also have faith, hope, and charity.

Recommended Readings

Thomas Aquinas, St., *Summa Theologiae,* I–II, q. 62 (in *Basic Writings,* II, 475–480); II–II, qq. 1–7 (in *Basic Writings,* II, 1055–1121).
———, *Compendium Theologiae,* trans. by R. J. Dunn (Toronto, 1934); also trans. by C. Vollert (St. Louis, 1947) pp. xx–366.
Farrell, *Companion to the Summa,* III, 1–114.
Gilson, *Moral Values and the Moral Life,* pp. 215–232.

[80] *S.T.,* II–II, q. 43, a. 1,c, et 3,c.

Jarrett, *Social Theories of the Middle Ages*, pp. 181–212.

Osbourn, "The Theological Ingredients of Peace," *Essays in Thomism*, pp. 23–54.

Philbin, "The Scholastic Teaching on the Nature of Charity," *Irish Eccles. Record*, LXIX (1933) 20–46.

Ryan, *Modern War and Basic Ethics* (Milwaukee, 1940) pp. 5–22.

Sheen, *Preface to Religion*, pp. 173–228.

Topics for Assignment

1. Why the Moral Virtues Are Not Sufficient for a Good Life
2. Is It Unreasonable to Believe Things We Cannot Understand?
3. The Difference Between Presumption and Ambition
4. Am I My Brother's Keeper?
5. Justice and Charity as Foundations for World Peace

GENERAL BIBLIOGRAPHY

Adler, M., "A Question About Law," in *Essays in Thomism*, ed. R. E. Brennan (New York: Sheed and Ward, 1942), pp. 205–236, 388–410.

—— and Farrell, W., "The Theory of Democracy" (a series of articles), *The Thomist*, III (1941) to VII (1945).

Amann, E., "Religion (vertu de)," *Dictionnaire de Théologie Catholique*, XIII, col. 2306–2312.

Aristotle, *Nicomachean Ethics*, trans. by W. D. Ross, in *The Basic Works of Aristotle*, ed. R. P. McKeon (New York: Random House, 1941), pp. 935–1112.

Baker, R. R., *The Thomistic Theory of the Passions and Their Influence Upon the Will* (Notre Dame, Ind., Univ. Dissert., 1941).

Bernard, R., "Renseignements Techniques (La Vertu)," in S. Thomas d'Aquin, *Somme Théologique*, I–II, qq. 49–60; qq. 61–70 (Paris, Revue des Jeunes, 1933), tome I: 381–460; tome II: 397–486.

Bésiade, Th., "La justice générale d'après s. Thomas d'Aquin," in *Mélanges Thomistes* (Paris, Vrin, 1935), pp. 327–340.

Bourke, V. J., "Habitus in the Thomistic Metaphysics of Potency and Act," in *Essays in Thomism*, pp. 101–109.

——, "Material Possessions and Thomistic Ethics," in *Philosophic Thought in France and the U. S.* (Buffalo: U. of Buffalo Press, 1950), pp. 613–627.

——, *St. Thomas and the Greek Moralists* (Milwaukee, Marquette U. Press, 1947).

Brennan, Sr. Rose Emannuella, *The Intellectual Virtues According to the Philosophy of St. Thomas* (Washington: Catholic U. Dissert., 1941).

Brosnahan, T. J., *Prolegomena to Ethics* (New York: Fordham U. Press, 1941).

Browne, M., "De intellectu et voluntate in electione," in *Acta Pont. Acad. Rom. S. Thomae* (Romae: Angelicum, 1936), pp. 32–45.

Bruyne, E. de, "Réflexions sur les méthodes en morale," *Revue Néoscolastique de Philos.*, XXXVIII (1935) 194–212.

Cathrein, V., "The Norm of Moral Rectitude," in Leibell, *Readings in Ethics* (Chicago: Loyola U. Press, 1926), pp. 156–162.

Chenu, M. D., "La surnaturalisation des vertus," *Bulletin Thomiste*, IX (1932) 93*–96*.

Childress, M., "The Prudential Judgment," *Proc. Amer. Cath. Philos. Assoc.* (Washington, D. C.) XXII (1947) 141–151.

Cronin, M., *The Science of Ethics*, rev. ed. (Dublin: Gill and Son, 1939), 2 vol.

Deman, Th., "Sur l'organisation du savoir moral," *Revue des Sciences Philos. et Théol.*, XXIII (1934) 270–280.

Deploige, S., *The Conflict Between Ethics and Sociology*, trans. by C. C. Miltner (St. Louis–London: Herder, 1938).

Dittrich, O., *Geschichte der Ethik. Die Systeme der Moral Altertum bis zur Gegenwart* (Leipzig: Meiner, 1926), 3 Bd.

Eschmann, I.Th., "In Defense of J. Maritain," *The Modern Schoolman*, XXII (1945) 183–208.

Fahey, D., *Mental Prayer According to the Teaching of St. Thomas Aquinas* (Dublin: Gill and Son, 1927).

Farrell, W., *A Companion to the Summa* (New York: Sheed and Ward, 1939–1942), 4 vol.

Garrigou-Lagrange, R., *Christian Perfection and Contemplation*, trans. by Sr. M. T. Doyle (St. Louis: Herder, 1937).

———, "La prudence. Sa place dans l'organisme des vertus," *Revue Thomiste*, n.s. IX (1926) 411–426.

Gemmel, J., "Die Justitia in der Lehre des hl. Thomas," *Scholastik*, XII (1937) 204–228.

Gilson, E., *La philosophie au moyen âge*. 5me éd. (Paris: Vrin, 1927).

———, *Saint Thomas d'Aquin*. (*Les moralistes chrétiens*.) (Paris: Gabalda, 1930.) Translated as: *Moral Values and the Moral Life*, by L. R. Ward (St. Louis: Herder, 1941).

———, *Le Thomisme*. 5me éd. (Paris: Vrin, 1944). Third edition is translated as: *The Philosophy of St. Thomas*, by E. Bullough (St. Louis: Herder, 1929; Cambridge: Heffer, 1930).

Glenn, P. J., *The History of Philosophy* (St. Louis: Herder, 1932).

Grabmann, M., "Das Naturrecht der Scholastik von Gratian bis Thomas von Aquin," in *Mittelalterliches Geistesleben* (Münster: Aschendorff, 1926), pp. 65–103.

Gundlach, G., "Klugheit als Prinzip des Handels," *Gregorianum*, XXIII (1942) 238–254.

Hart, C. A. (ed.), *The Natural Law and International Relations*, *Proc. Amer. Cath. Philos. Assoc.*, XXIV (1950); papers by a number of authors.

Hering, H. M., "De genuina notione justitiae generalis seu legalis juxta S. Thomam," *Angelicum*, XIV (1937) 464–487.

Héris, C. V., "L'Amour naturel de Dieu," in *Mélanges Thomistes*, pp. 289–310.

Holaind, R., *Natural Law and Legal Practice* (New York: Benziger, 1899).

Hugon, E., "De Epikeia seu Aequitate (II–II, q. 120)," *Angelicum*, V (1928) 359–367.

Jarrett, B., *Social Theories of the Middle Ages: 1200–1500* (London: Benn, 1926); reprinted Westminster, Md., Newman Press, 1942.

Kendzierski, L., "Object and Intention in the Moral Act," *Proc. Amer. Cath. Philos. Assoc.*, XXIV (1950) 102–110.

Klubertanz, G. P., "Ethics and Theology," *The Modern Schoolman*, XXVII (1949) 29–39.

———, *Notes on the Philosophy of Human Nature* (St. Louis: St. Louis U. Press, 1949).

———, "The Unity of Human Activity," *The Modern Schoolman*, XXVIII (1950) 75–103.

Lachance, L., *Le concept de droit selon Aristote et saint Thomas* (Montréal: Levesque; Paris: Sirey, 1933).

Lafarge, J., "The Philosophical Basis of Communism," *Proc. Amer. Cath. Philos. Assoc.*, IX (1933) 47–62.

Lehu, L., "La 'recta ratio' de s. Thomas signifie-t-elle la conscience?" *Revue Thomiste*, n.s. VIII (1925) 159–166.

Leibell, J. F., *Readings in Ethics* (Chicago: Loyola U. Press, 1926).

Lemonnyer, A., "La vertu de religion," *La Vie Spirituelle*, XLVI (1936) 31–36.

Le Senne, R., *Traité de morale générale* (Paris: Presses Universitaires, 1942).

Lottin, O., *Principes de morale* (Louvain: Editions de l'Abbaye du Mont-César, 1947), 2 vol.

———, *Psychologie et Morale aux XIIe et XIIIe siècles* (Louvain-Gembloux: Duculot, 1942–1949), 3 vol.

Lull, Ramon, *Blanquerna: A Thirteenth-Century Romance*, trans. from the Catalan by E. A. Peers (London: Jarrold, 1925).

Maritain, J., *Les degrés du savoir* (Paris: Desclée, 1932). Trans. as: *The Degrees of Knowledge*, by B. Wall and M. Adamson (New York: Scribners, 1938).

———, *Education at the Crossroads* (New York: Scribners, 1943).

———, *The Person and the Common Good* (New York: Scribners, 1947).

———, *Man and the State* (Chicago: University of Chicago Press, 1951).

———, *De la philosophie chrétienne* (Paris: Desclée, 1933).

————, *The Rights of Man and the Natural Law* (New York: Scribners, 1943).

————, *Science and Wisdom*, trans. by B. Wall (New York: Scribners, 1940).

Martinez, Mother M. L., "Distributive Justice According to St. Thomas," *The Modern Schoolman*, XXIV (1947) 208–223.

McFadden, C., *Medical Ethics for Nurses* (Philadelphia: Peter Reilly, 1946).

————, *The Metaphysical Foundations of Dialectical Materialism* (Washington: Catholic U. Dissert., 1938).

McWilliams, J. A., *Philosophy for the Millions* (New York: Macmillan, 1942).

Meier, M., *Die Lehre des Thomas von Aquin 'de passionibus animae,'* BGPM XI.2 (Münster: Aschendorff, 1912).

Meyer, M. H., *The Philosophy of Teaching of St. Thomas* (Milwaukee: Marquette U. Press, 1929).

Moore, T. V., *Principles of Ethics* (New York: Lippincott, 1925).

Murray, T. B., "Reason and Morality according to St. Thomas," *Month*, CLI (1928) 417–423.

Noble, H. D., "L'Action volontaire," in *Mélanges Mandonnet* (Paris: Vrin, 1930), I, 275–288.

————, *Les passions dans la vie morale* (Paris: Lethielleux, 1932), 2 vol.

O'Brien, Sr. M. Consilia, "Recta Ratio in Relation to Moral Truth," *Proc. Amer. Cath. Philos. Assoc.*, XVIII (1942) 120–126.

O'Connor, W. R., *The Eternal Quest* (New York: Longmans, Green, 1947).

————, "The Natural Desire for God in St. Thomas," *New Scholasticism*, XIV (1940) 213–265.

————, "Some Historical Factors in the Development of the Concept of Human Finality," *Proc. Amer. Cath. Philos. Assoc.*, XXIII (1949) 15–35.

O'Neil, C. J., "Prudence, the Incommunicable Wisdom," in *Essays in Thomism*, pp. 187–204.

O'Rahilly, A., "The Democracy of St. Thomas," *Studies*, IX (1930); reprinted in Leibell, *Readings in Ethics*, pp. 913–925.

Osbourn, J. C., "The Theological Ingredients of Peace," in *Essays in Thomism*, pp. 23–54.

Pegis, A. C., "Matter, Beatitude and Liberty," in *Maritain Volume of the Thomist* (New York: Sheed and Ward, 1943), pp. 265–280.

————, "Nature and Spirit: Some Reflections on the Problem of the End of Man," *Proc. Amer. Cath. Philos. Assoc.*, XXIII (1949) 62–79.

————, "Necessity and Liberty," *New Scholasticism*, XV (1941) 18–45.

Phelan, G. B., "Justice and Friendship," in *Maritain Volume of the Thomist*, pp. 153-170.

———, "Person and Liberty," *New Scholasticism*, XV (1941) 53-68.

———, "Theology in the Curriculum of Catholic Colleges and Universities," in *Man and Secularism* (New York: Nat. Cath. Alumni Assoc., 1940), pp. 128-140.

Philbin, W. J., "The Scholastic Teaching on the Nature of Charity," *Irish Eccl. Record*, LXIX (1933) 20-46.

Pieper, J., *Traktat über die Klugheit* (Leipzig: Meiner, 1937).

Ramirez, J. M., "De philosophia morali Christiana," *Divus Thomas* (Fribourg) XIV (1936) 87-122, 181-204.

———, "La science morale pratique," *Bulletin Thomiste*, XI-XIII (1934-1936) 424-427.

Renz, O., *Die Synteresis nach dem hl. Thomas von Aquin*, BGPM X, 1-2 (Münster: Aschendorff, 1911).

Rickaby, J., *Aquinas Ethicus* (London: Burns, Oates, 1892).

Riedl, C., "The Social Theory of St. Thomas," *Proc. Amer. Cath. Philos. Assoc.*, IX (1933) 24-34.

Rommen, H., *The State in Catholic Thought* (St. Louis: Herder, 1945).

Rupprecht, P., "Die Tugend der Religion nach dem hl. Thomas," *Divus Thomas* (Fribourg) IX (1931) 146-172.

Ryan, J. A., "The Economic Philosophy of St. Thomas," in *Essays in Thomism*, pp. 239-260.

———, "The Philosophy of Capitalism," *Proc. Amer. Cath. Philos. Assoc.*, IX (1933) 35-46.

Ryan, J. K., *Modern War and Basic Ethics* (Milwaukee: Bruce, 1940).

Salmon, E., "Philosophers on World Cooperation," *New Scholasticism*, XXI (1947) 284-302.

Sertillanges, A. D., *La philosophie morale de saint Thomas d'Aquin*, nouvelle édition (Paris: Aubier, 1946).

———, *Saint Thomas d'Aquin* (Paris: Aubier, 1922).

Sheen, Fulton, *Preface to Religion* (New York: Kenedy and Sons, 1946).

Sidgwick, H., *History of Ethics* (London: Macmillan, 1931).

Simon, Y., *Critique de la connaissance morale* (Paris: Desclée, 1934).

———, *The Nature and Functions of Authority* (Milwaukee: Marquette U. Press, 1940).

Smith, G., "Intelligence and Liberty," *New Scholasticism*, XV (1941) 1-17.

———, "The Natural End of Man," *Proc. Amer. Cath. Philos. Assoc.*, XXIII (1949) 47-61.

Somerville, J., "Dialectical Materialism," in *Twentieth Century Philosophy*, ed. D. Runes (New York: Philosophical Library, 1943), pp. 471–502.

Thomae Aquinatis, S., *Opera Omnia jussu impensaque Leonis XIII, P.M., edita* (Romae: Typis R. Garroni, 1882———.) 16 vol.

———, *Opera Omnia* (Parmae: 1852–1873); reprinted New York, Musurgia, 1949–1950, 25 vol.

———, *Opuscula Omnia*, cura P. Mandonnet (Paris: Lethielleux, 1927), 5 vol.

———, *In X Libros Ethicorum Aristotelis ad Nicomachum*, ed. A. Pirotta (Turin: Marietti, 1934).

———, *Basic Writings*, ed. A. C. Pegis (New York: Random House, 1945), 2 vol.

———, *The Commandments of God*, trans. by L. Shapcote (London: Burns, Oates, 1937).

———, *Compendium of Theology*. Part I, Tr. 2, trans. by R. J. Dunn, Toronto, St. Michael's Coll., 1934; complete trans. by C. Vollert (St. Louis: Herder, 1947).

———, *On Kingship to the King of Cyprus*, trans. by G. B. Phelan, rev. by I.Th. Eschmann (Toronto: Pontifical Institute of Med. Stud., 1949).

———, *The Summa Theologica*, trans. by the Fathers of the English Dominican Province, 2d rev. ed. (London: Burns, Oates, 1912–1936), 22 vol.

———, *The Trinity and the Unicity of the Intellect*, trans. by Sr. R. E. Brennan (St. Louis: Herder, 1946).

Wittmann, M., *Die Ethik des hl. Thomas von Aquin* (München: Hueber, 1933).

INDEX

Abelard, Peter, 57
Abortion, 355, 426, 454
Abstinence, and temperance, 307
Abuse of material things, 370–371
Accumulation and distribution of things, 372. *See also Potestas procurandi*, etc.
Accusation, unjust, 363, 451
Act, human, 6, 18; interior as root of moral quality, 144–145; exterior may modify whole action, 145–147; some good, some evil in themselves, 154; receives species from object, 154; morality of interior and exterior, 158–160; principles of, 279–282. *See also* Actions; Human actions; Moral act
Act of man, 6, 18
Actions, determined by nature or by reason, 47; moral because voluntary, 54; immoral if opposed to right reason, 126–136; species of, 138; material classification by virtues, 138–139; formally considered, 140; never morally neutral in concrete, 141–142, 157; influenced by consequences, 146–147; right or wrong, 147; praiseworthy or culpable, 147–148; meritorious or demeritorious, 148–149, 160; bad, cannot be done rightly, 156; differentiation of immoral, 157–158; causes of immoral, 273–278; right, in relation to other persons, 325–349
Actiones sunt suppositorum, 45
Activity, better than inactivity, 36
Adjuration, act of religion, 407
Adler, M., 166, 196, 441
Adoration, act of religion, 405
Adulation, vice, 344
Adultery, 312, 425
Affability, and temperance, 310. *See also* Friendship
Agent, is the whole man, 45, 98; a member of some group, 148–149; interior and exterior principles of, 162
Alienation of friends, 363
Almsgiving, effect of charity, 473–474

Amann, E., 413
Ambrose, St., 127
Anger, vice, 312, 316
Annulment, and marriage, 421
Apathy, Stoic theory of, 86
Apologetics, and religion, 396; reasoned justification of beliefs, 412
Apostasy, 471
Appetites, sensory, participate in reason, 257. *See also* Passions
Appetition, natural or free, 106–114; rightness of, 135; sensitive and intellective, 325–326
Apprehension of end, first step in moral act, 58
Apprehension of suitability, eleventh step in moral act, 63–64
Aristocracy, 430
Aristotle, 4, 5, 20, 22, 25, 32, 36, 38, 41, 55, 95, 101, 106, 127, 128, 186, 251, 253, 254, 263, 323, 335, 341, 415, 429; cited as The Philosopher, 48, 102, 103, 110, 112, 214, 247, 280, 282, 283
Art, defined, 7; not same as ethics, 7; mechanical, 23; habit of practical intellect, 262
Astrology, 409
Astuteness, a vice, 303
Attainment of ultimate end, 35–43
Augustine of Hippo, St., 33, 86, 127, 210, 247, 259, 281, 288, 429 ⸻
Authority of the state, 432–433
Autonomy of practical reason, Kantian, 167, 201
Avarice. *See* Miserliness
Averroes, 281; cited as The Commentator, 109, 281

Baker, R. D., 94, 304, 314, 323
Beatific vision, 39–43, 52, 82, 92, 165, 180, 417, 443
Beatitude, act of intellect, 49. *See also* Happiness
Beneficence, effect of charity, 473
Bergson, H., 41
Bernard, R., 289
Bésiade, Th., 350
Bigamy, 422

485

4501